Winning in Asia, Japanese Style

Winning in Asia, Japanese Style

Market and Nonmarket Strategies for Success

Edited by
Vinod K. Aggarwal and Shujiro Urata

WINNING IN ASIA, JAPANESE STYLE
© Vinod K. Aggarwal and Shujiro Urata, 2002

All rights reserved. No part of this book may be used or reproduced in any manner whatsoever without written permission except in the case of brief quotations embodied in critical articles or reviews.

First published 2002 by
PALGRAVE MACMILLAN™
175 Fifth Avenue, New York, N.Y. 10010 and
Houndmills, Basingstoke, Hampshire, England RG21 6XS
Companies and representatives throughout the world

PALGRAVE MACMILLAN is the global academic imprint of the Palgrave Macmillan division of St. Martin's Press, LLC and of Palgrave Macmillan Ltd. Macmillan® is a registered trademark in the United States, United Kingdom and other countries. Palgrave is a registered trademark in the European Union and other countries.

ISBN 0–312–23910–6

Library of Congress Cataloging-in-Publication Data

Winning in Asia, Japanese style: market and nonmarket strategies for success/co-edited by Vinod K. Aggarwal and Shujiro Urata.

p. cm.
Includes bibliographical references and index.
ISBN 0–312–23911–4
  1. Japan—Foreign economic relations—Asia. 2. Asia—Foreign economic relations—Japan. 3. Marketing—Japan. 4. Marketing—Japan—Case studies. 5. Marketing—Asia—Case studies. 6. Investments, Japanese—Asia. 7. Investments, Foreign—Asia. I. Aggarwal, Vinod K. II. Urata Shujiro, 1950–

HF 1602.15.A74 W56 2002
658.8'0095—dc21   2002068417

A catalogue record for this book is available from the British Library.

Design by Newgen Imaging Systems (P) Ltd., Chennai, India.

First edition: October, 2002
10 9 8 7 6 5 4 3 2 1

Printed in the United States of America.

CONTENTS

Preface		vii
Contributors		ix
List of Abbreviations		xi
Part One	**Theoretical Framework**	**1**
Chapter One	Analyzing Japanese Firms' Market and Nonmarket Strategies in Asia *Vinod K. Aggarwal*	3
Chapter Two	Japan's Foreign Direct Investment and Trade in Asia *Shujiro Urata*	27
Part Two	**Case Studies**	**59**
Chapter Three	Banking on East Asia: Expansion and Retrenchment of Japanese Firms *Masahiro Kawai, Yuzuru Ozeki, and Hiroshi Tokumaru*	61
Chapter Four	Cartels, Competition, and Consolidation in the Japanese Chemical Industry *Tametsugu Taketomi*	98
Chapter Five	On the Road to Asia: Japanese Automakers in ASEAN *Gregory W. Noble*	123

Chapter Six	Ringing off the Hook! Japanese Telecommunications Responds to the Call of Asian Markets *Yumiko Okamoto*	157
Chapter Seven	Cracking the Code: Japanese Software Strategies in Asia *Trevor H. Nakagawa*	184
Chapter Eight	Short Circuiting Keiretsu: Japanese Electronic Firms in Asia *Hidetaka Yoshimatsu*	220
Part Three	**Conclusion**	**241**
Chapter Nine	Lessons from Japanese Firms' Strategies in Asia *Vinod K. Aggarwal*	243
Index		273

PREFACE

The unbounded enthusiasm of European, American, and Japanese firms for Asian markets was tarred by the Asian crises of 1997–1998. As currencies plunged and fear grew that the crises would continue to spread, many firms began to reassess their commitment to Asian markets. Yet the rapid descent of these economies was followed almost uniformly by rapid recovery. Faced with opportunities to secure assets at bargain basement prices and anticipating greater liberalization of Asian markets, many firms once again rushed into the breach.

This book analyzes how Japanese firms have attempted to succeed in Asian markets, both before and after the Asian crises. A central focus of this volume is the formulation and implementation of market, nonmarket, and organizational strategies. Market strategies have been the topic of many works. Yet as the case studies in the book demonstrate, the most successful firms have succeeded in Asia by integrating market strategies with nonmarket and organizational strategies that help firms respond to and benefit from shifts in the political, economic, and social environment. Firms that have been able to leverage their capabilities to secure assistance from their home governments, and that have pursued and developed strategic relationships with Asian governments and firms, have repeatedly emerged as winners. By examining integrated market, nonmarket, and organizational strategies, both from an analytical and empirical perspective, we hope that this book will enhance or understanding of firm strategies in Asia that will be of benefit to both analysts and practitioners.

This project has been generously supported by the Center for Global Partnership of the Japan Foundation. Over a three-year period, their financial assistance has allowed us to examine Japanese, American, and European firm strategies in a changing Asian market. In particular, we would like to thank Takashi Ishida, the current director, and

Junichi Chano, the previous director, Junichi Chano, as well as staff members Susan Hubbard, Mary McCarthy, Sandhya Rao, and Lisa Weiss. The earlier work on Europe was supported by a grant from the Institute of European Studies of the University of California. We are greatly indebted to the Institute's director, Gerald Feldman, and its associate director, Beverly Crawford, for their help.

Two workshops were convened to discuss the papers in this volume, one at Berkeley and another in Tokyo at Waseda University. A wrap-up conference brought together participants from the European, American, and Japanese subprojects, and allowed participants to share ideas, compare notes, and better understand different sectors from a comparative perspective. The contributions of other readers are acknowledged by the authors of each of the chapters.

We are especially indebted to the staff of the Berkeley APEC Study Center (BASC). At BASC, Ed Fogarty, Ralph Espach, Elaine Kwei, Trevor Nakagawa, Kun-Chin Lin, Min Gyo Koo, Zachary Zwald, and Chris Tucker have provided valuable research assistance, comments, and help in organizing the Berkeley workshops. A number of undergraduates also assisted in preparing the manuscript and in editing papers. For their help, we are particularly grateful to Joel Burgos, Justin Kolbeck, Matt Odette, Mytoan Nguyen, Jennifer Rho, and Dan Xu, all of whom have worked or currently work at BASC as part of the Berkeley Undergraduate Research Apprenticeship program.

Toby Wahl of Palgrave has ably taken over from Karen Wolny who originally signed the "Winning in Asia Series." Gabriella Pearce, who works with Toby, has been of immense help in managing the publication process.

Vinod K. Aggarwal
Berkeley, California
and
Shujiro Urata
Tokyo, Japan

CONTRIBUTORS

VINOD K. AGGARWAL is Professor in the Department of Political Science, Affiliated Professor in the Haas School of Business, and Director of the Berkeley APEC Study Center (BASC) at the University of California, Berkeley

MASAHIRO KAWAI is Professor of Economics in the Institute of Social Science, University of Tokyo and Deputy Vice Minister of Finance for International Affairs at the Ministry of Finance, Japan

TREVOR H. NAKAGAWA is a Ph.D. candidate in the Department of Political Science at the University of California, Berkeley

GREGORY W. NOBLE is Associate Professor of Political Science at the Institute of Social Science, University of Tokyo

YUMIKO OKAMOTO is Associate Professor of Economics at the Graduate School of International Development, Nagoya University

YUZURU OZEKI is Professor in the Asian Public Policy Program, Graduate School of International Corporate Strategy, Hitotsubashi University

TAMETSUGU TAKETOMI is Director of Monday (formerly PwC Consulting), Japan

HIROSHI TOKUMARU is Manager, Bank Supervision Department, Bank of Japan

SHUJIRO URATA is Professor of Economics at Waseda University

HIDETAKA YOSHIMATSU is Associate Professor of Economics, Graduate School of East Asian Studies, Yamaguchi University

LIST OF ABBREVIATIONS

AAF	ASEAN Automotive Federation
ADB	Asian Development Bank
AEM–MITI	ASEAN Economic Ministers and the Minister of International Trade and Industry (Japan)
AFTA	ASEAN Free Trade Area
AIC	ASEAN Industrial Complementation
AICO	ASEAN Industrial Cooperation
ANIEs	Asian Newly Industrialized Economies
APEC	Asia-Pacific Economic Cooperation
ASEAN	Association of Southeast Asian Nations: Brunei Darussalam, Cambodia, Indonesia, Laos, Malaysia, Myanmar, Philippines, Singapore, Thailand, Vietnam
ASEAN4	Four members of ASEAN: Thailand, Malaysia, Indonesia, and the Philippines
ASP	Average Selling Prices
ATM	asynchronous transfer mode
B2B	business-to-business
B2C	business-to-consumer
BBC	brand-to-brand complementation
BCC	business cooperation contracts
BIS	Bank for International Settlements
BOI	Board of Investors (Philippines)
BTO	build-transfer-operate
CAGR	compound annual growth rate
CAT	Communication Authority of Thailand
CCITT	Comite Consultatif International Telephonique et Telegraphique

CEPT	Common Effective Preferential Tariff
CER	Closer Economic Relations
CLM-WG	Working Group on Economic Cooperation in Cambodia, Laos, and Myanmar
CMS	cash management services
CNC	China Net Communications
DRAMs	Dynamic Random Access Memories
DSPs	Digital Signal Processors
EDI	Electronic Data Interchange
EIAJ	Electric Industries Association of Japan
EMS	Electronics Manufacturing Services
FDI	Foreign Direct Investment
FNC	Fujitsu Network Communications
FSC	Fujitsu Software Corporation
FY	Fiscal Year
GATT	General Agreement on Tariffs and Trade
GDP	Gross Domestic Product
GUI	graphical user interfaces
IC	Integrated Circuit
ICI	Imperial Chemical Industries
IDC	International Data Corporation
IFIs	international financial institutions
IJPC	Iran–Japan Petrochemical Company
IMF	International Monetary Fund
INDRA	Indonesian Debt Restructuring Agency
IPO	International Procurement Offices
IPR	intellectual property rights
ISV	Independent Software Vendors
IT	Information Technology
ITAs	Information Technology Agreement
ITU	International Telecommunications Union
JAMA	Japan Automobile Manufactures Association
JAPIA	the Japan Auto Parts Industries Association
JEMA	Japan Electrical Manufacturers' Association
JETRO	Japan External Trade Organization
JPO	Japan Polyolefins
JSR	Japan Synthetic Rubber
JV	Joint Venture
LCD	Liquid Crystal Display
M&A	Mergers and Acquisitions
MEPCO	Matsushita Electric Philippines

List of Abbreviations

MHFG	Mizuho Financial Group
MIS	Management Information Systems
MITI/METI	Ministry of International Trade and Industry/Ministry of Economy, Trade, and Industry (Japan)
MJC	Montell-JPO Company
MMC	Mitsubishi Motor Company
MNCs	Multinational Corporations
MPT	Ministry of Posts and Transportation
MPUs	Microprocessor Units
NAFTA	North American Free Trade Agreement
NCCs	new common carriers
NICs	Newly Industrializing Countries
NIE3	Newly Industrialized Economies: Singapore, South Korea, and Taiwan
NIE4	Newly Industrialized Economies: Hong Kong, Singapore, South Korea, and Taiwan
NPLs	non-performing loans
NRCCs	nonresident controlled companies
OECD	Organization for Economic Cooperation and Development
OEM	Original Equipment Manufacturing
OS	operating systems
PC	Personal Computer
PVC	Polyvinyl Chloride
R&D	Research and Development
ROA	Return on Assets
ROEs	Return on Equity
ROI	Return on Investment
SISIT	Specific Industry Structure Improvement Treatment
SMBC	Sumitomo Mitsui Banking Corporation
SME	small and medium enterprise
SMEs	Small and Medium-scale Enterprises
SWOT	Strengths, Weaknesses, Opportunities, and Threats
TOT	Telephone Organization of Thailand
TRIMs	Trade Related Investment Measures
TT&T	Thai Telephone and Telecommunication company
UFJ	United Financial of Japan
WTO	World Trade Organization

PART ONE

Theoretical Framework

CHAPTER ONE

Analyzing Japanese Firms' Market and Nonmarket Strategies in Asia

VINOD K. AGGARWAL[1]

I. Introduction

Despite the lingering effects of the regional currency crises in the late 1990s, and Japan's stubborn economic affliction, the Asia-Pacific economies continue to be among the most attractive markets in the world. The track record of these newly industrialized countries, both before and after the crises, China's phenomenal growth rates, and the widespread regional trend of economic liberalization speak for themselves. But the ups and downs of East Asian markets have forced Japanese, American, and European firms to rethink their strategies. Some firms responded by increasing investments in the region, hoping to snatch up distressed assets that will strengthen their position to profit from renewed growth. Other firms are concerned that excessive reliance on Asia has made them vulnerable. As a result, they have sought to diversify their operations to position themselves in newly emerging markets in Latin America, Eastern Europe, and elsewhere.

The principal aim of this book is to analyze the strategic interplay between governments and firms in Asia. By systematically examining the nature of Japanese investment and trade strategies in developing Asian markets across a variety of sectors, and by comparing Japanese firms with American and European firms (in two companion volumes), we hope to understand the factors that affect competitive success.[2]

An important element of firm strategies in Asia is their nonmarket component. Whereas firms must pursue market strategies to position themselves in the global and regional economies, they also interact with governments to secure favorable policies. Firms seek to obtain access to closed or restricted markets for exports and investment, are concerned about regulations on their subsidiaries, and are wary of changing tax policies, among other issues. They often work with both their home and host governments to implement policy changes. At the same time, home and host governments have objectives of their own vis-à-vis both their own and foreign firms, which require firms to negotiate with governments.

From a case selection perspective, our focus on Asia is driven by four key factors: First, East Asian countries provide examples of both extremely high growth rates and markets that have recently suffered severe recession, accompanied by the International Monetary Fund (IMF) and U.S. pressures for liberalization. Thus, a focus on Asia provides an excellent laboratory to analyze shifting firm strategies in times of good and bad economic prospects. Second, developing Asian firms pose a significant competitive challenge to foreign firms in some sectors. Not only do they often have dominant positions in their home markets, but they also have been successful in European and American markets. Third, many Asian firms have close ties to governments. Indeed, the nature of government-business relations is particularly intricate in the Asian context. Most of the newly industrializing countries, both the so-called first and second tier, have actively used industrial policy measures in an effort to bolster their firms' competitiveness. Restrictions on investments, technology transfer, export performance requirements, preferential financing, and a host of other instruments have been commonplace in most of these countries. Fourth, the Asia-Pacific has been one of the most interesting arenas in the world to understand the interplay of different types of institutional arrangements. The mix of different regime forms in terms of regionalism, sectoralism, and globalism is illustrated by the evolution of the recent Information Technology Agreement (ITA). Although this agreement to liberalize trade in a host of information technology products was initially vetted in the Quad group (United States, Canada, European Union, and Japan), it was promoted actively on a sectoral basis in the regional grouping known as Asia-Pacific Economic Cooperation (APEC). It was then globalized in 1996 at the Singapore World Trade Organization (WTO) ministerial meeting and has been accepted by most countries in the world.

This chapter presents the analytical framework and theoretical approach that forms the foundation for the empirical analysis in this volume.

My analysis is divided as follows. Section II discusses what I term *positional analysis*—how market forces, the nonmarket environment, and firm competencies influence firms' choices of trade and investment at the national, regional, or global level. In Section III, we turn to *strategic analysis,* an examination of the choices firms make in response to their market environments, a distributive politics analysis of nonmarket issues, and a transaction cost analysis of organizational forms for market penetration. These elements combine to influence the firm's integrated strategic choice. Once these strategies are formulated, firms can choose from a range of options for implementation. These means of implementation are the subject of the *tactical analysis* presented in Section IV. Tactical analysis considers the market, nonmarket, and organizational tactics that firms pursue to succeed with their chosen strategies. Figure 1.1 provides a roadmap of the analysis that follows in Sections II through IV.

As Figure 1.1 indicates, a firm's choice of trade or investment, integrated strategic choice, and implementation efforts can be conceptualized using an analytical model of three "triangles": positional, strategic, and tactical analysis. Each triangle, representing a phase or component of a firm's integrated strategy, includes factors that must be accounted for in its analysis. Moreover, the policy or policies that a firm pursues, along with those with which its competitors respond, can create a cycle of feedback and continued analysis.

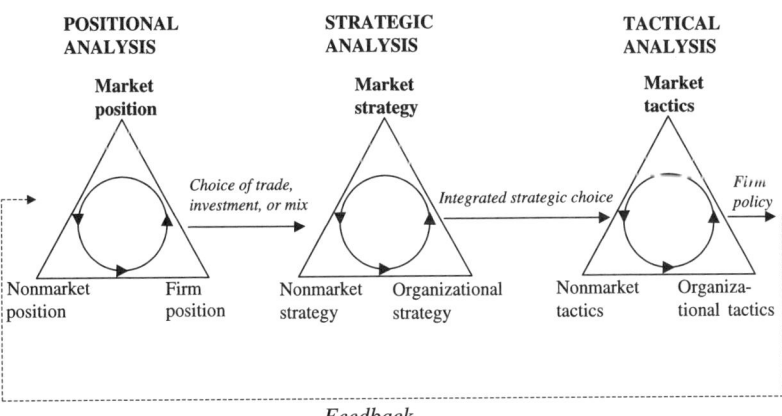

Figure 1.1 An overview of integrated strategy: triangulating strategic responses to market and nonmarket forces

II. Positional Analysis: Market Factors, the Nonmarket Environment in Diverse Geographical Arenas, and Core Competencies

Firms operate in both a market and nonmarket environment. Corporate strategists have traditionally focused on the market environment within which firms operate, and on the organization of firms. Traditional market analysis focuses on elements such as an industry's technological profile, the number of major players, the barriers to entry, and so forth. Market analysis of corporate strategy and organization often also covers the internal structures of firms and their implications for competitiveness, the effects of different types of firm organization, the design of incentive systems, and so on.

In addition to these two critical factors—the market environment and a firm's organization—a firm's performance also depends on the social, political, and legal context within which it operates: that is, its nonmarket environment.[3] This includes analyses of key issues, relevant interests, availability of information, and existing institutions, and how they relate to a firm's positioning at the national, regional, or global level. For instance, as Japanese firms decide whether or not to enter developing Asian markets, to increase their investments, or to alter their trading patterns, they must consider the nonmarket characteristics of specific country markets. Their strategies must also be sensitive to the broader regional and global international environment, and especially to the roles played by various relevant international institutions.

These elements provide the basis for the positional analysis of the "triangle" of factors depicted in Figure 1.2.

As illustrated in Figure 1.2, positional analysis helps firms define their initial choices of proceeding with a strategy of trade, direct investment, partnership with a local firm, or some mix of strategies in Asia. Before we consider the various elements of this analysis in more detail, we consider the importance of the geographical arena.

Geographical Orientation

Before undertaking market and nonmarket firm strategies, managers must consider the appropriate geographic area for their operations. First of all, firms must focus on the market and nonmarket characteristics of the particular country or countries they plan to enter. This "multidomestic" focus suggests that a firm's analysis must be sensitive to the individual characteristics of different target countries.[4] Regarding a country's

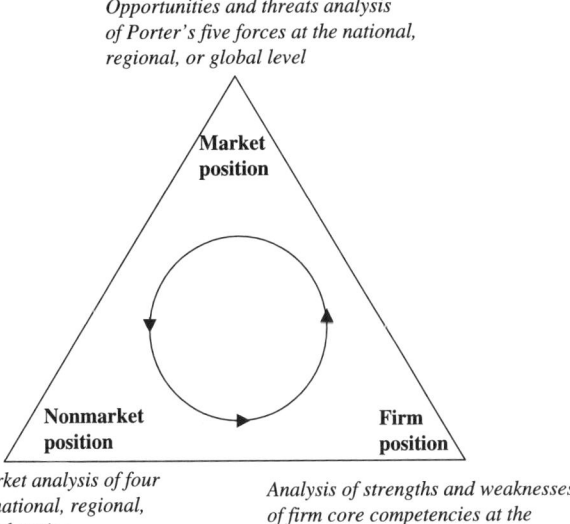

Figure 1.2 Positional analysis

market, this involves a consideration of existing and potential competitors, suppliers, and the like. An assessment of a country's nonmarket environment focuses on the types of its existing or potential policies regarding investment, including joint venture requirements, export performance demands, local content rules, technology transfer agreements, and multilateral investment initiatives. In addition, both market and nonmarket environments are shaped by previous political bargains or coalitions, historical precedents, and cultural values.

Increasingly, however, firms must look beyond factors at the country level to those of the regional and global environments as well. Theoretical work on global corporate positioning is quite advanced. However, analyses of regional strategies, both from a market and nonmarket perspective, have been given short shrift. From a nonmarket perspective, the proliferation of regional accords such as the Association of Southeast Asia Nations (ASEAN), APEC, and the European Union (EU) is often accompanied by increasingly tight political or institutional ties. In the most advanced integration project, the movement toward a single European market radically altered market calculations and forced many European firms into mergers or alliances. Firms also began to develop a lobbying apparatus as many aspects of policymaking, at both the European and broader international levels, shifted to the European Commission in Brussels.[5] In the Asia-Pacific Asia, APEC, ASEAN, and the Closer Economic Relations (CER) accord have become important arenas for firm influence, while the institutional policies of these accords affect corporate strategies.[6] The development of these regional institutions means that firms cannot focus only on the policymaking in specific countries but must also be aware of and engaged in policymaking at the regional level.

In particular, two areas of policymaking at the regional level can influence the trade and investment strategies of firms: widening and deepening. The process of widening refers to the accession of new members into existing arrangements. The process of deepening regional institutions entails the enhanced coordination of monetary, fiscal, social, labor, foreign, and other policies. These can include trade policies such as regional content requirements, regional patent protection, regional lobbies, and so on. Obviously, efforts to widen and deepen regional institutions can significantly alter regional market and nonmarket conditions.

Firms can, of course, concentrate on becoming globally oriented and competitive. From a global nonmarket perspective, the arrangements reached in the General Agreements on Tariffs and Trade (GATT) and its successor, the WTO, have greatly influenced firm strategies. For example, the liberalization of specific sectors through the GATT—including tariff reductions and the removal of nontariff barriers—has considerably increased global competition. In the aircraft industry, agriculture, steel, electronics, financial services, and other sectors, firms must take into account the new regulations of the WTO. The Uruguay Round introduced a host of new issues that affect firms, including changes in intellectual property protection, and the linkage between trade and investment through the TRIMs (Trade Related Investment Measures) Agreement. Firms have, of course, been a key driving force in setting the agenda of the GATT and WTO, and have lobbied their governments with specific concerns. For example, financial service firms in the United States were instrumental in putting the issue of financial sector liberalization on the GATT Uruguay Round agenda in 1986, and many information technology firms, the entertainment industry, and pharmaceutical companies actively pushed for the institutionalized protection of intellectual property.[7]

At the global sectoral level, arrangements such as the Multifiber Arrangement in textiles and apparel or steel voluntary export restraints have long influenced sourcing and production decisions. These arrangements have coexisted uneasily with the GATT and now the WTO, and pressure has built to eliminate such sectoral arrangements.[8] The latest trend at the global sectoral level, however, is the *opening* of markets.[9]

		TARGET MARKET FOR SALES		
		National	Regional	Global
TRADE OR INVESTMENT LOCATION	National	(1) Domestic	(2)	(3)
	Regional	(4)	(5)	(6)
	Global	(7)	(8)	(9) Pure global

Figure 1.3 Geographical arenas: location and target markets

Following the creation of the ITA in 1996, APEC ministers in 1997 agreed to consider nine additional sectors for fast-track trade barrier reduction: chemicals, energy-related equipment and services, environmental goods and services, forest products, medical equipment, telecommunications equipment, fish and fish products, toys, and gems and jewelry. Although firms actively lobbied on all sides of this issue to advance their interests, the 1998 APEC meeting in Kuala Lumpur saw a failure to advance this agenda because of Japanese resistance to liberalizing forestry and fishery products. At this point, the whole package of nine sectors has been shifted to the WTO for negotiations.[10]

When assessing geographically-based strategies, it is useful to distinguish production from marketing orientations, both on a market and nonmarket basis. To graphically illustrate the possibilities, we can briefly consider the nine cells in Figure 1.3, with two extreme points labeled to provide some bearings on strategies.

Thus, for example, one could invest in China (national), and simply sell domestically. Or, one could sell throughout Asia (regional), or globally. Or, alternatively, one could invest or set up on a regional basis in several countries in Asia through a trading company or production hub, and then sell only in a single country, to the whole region, or worldwide. Finally, globally-based firms could focus on single countries, a region, or on the global market. Firms must make such choices about their location strategy based on consideration of market forces, their core competencies, and the nonmarket environment. I now turn to a discussion of each of these elements individually.

Market Forces

The most popular analytical approach to market-based decisionmaking is that developed by Michael Porter, based on the vast literature in industrial organization.[11] Porter proposed five specific factors, or the "five forces model." These forces are: (1) rivalry among established firms; (2) risk of entry by potential competitors; (3) threat of substitutes; (4) bargaining power of suppliers; and (5) bargaining power of buyers. These forces also provide a basis for the analysis of what firms face in terms of strategy formulation. Reflecting the second half of the well-known SWOT acronym (Strengths, Weaknesses, Opportunities, and Threats), market analysis examines the opportunities and threats posed by the five forces.[12]

The notion of rivalry among firms refers to the classic issue of market structure, that is, whether the market is atomistic, oligopolistic, duopolistic, or monopolistic. The implications of structure come from the ability of firms to pursue strategy autonomously or from the interdependence that arises in a market with few players. The other two elements of the rivalry concept are demand conditions and barriers to exit. The first of these refers to the growth potential of the industry, and the second concerns the impediments firms face in leaving the industry. In a market with high growth potential, rivalry will be less intense since the game is not zero-sum. Competitive firm strategies can coexist with each yielding success. Attention to exit barriers can improve understanding of why firms might resist exiting a relatively poor market, because of the high costs such a move may entail. Exit barriers can also explain why firms might be more willing to take political action to block the entry of foreign competitors.[13]

The analysis of potential competitors is based on barriers to entry. These barriers include such factors as existing brand loyalty, the cost advantages of various production techniques, and economies of scale that arise from large-scale production.[14] Other factors include the need for extensive capital investments, the cost of switching to another product, and access to distribution channels. Each of these barriers poses an obstacle to entry. Over time, however, these barriers tend to erode, as in the example of the effect of the entry of minimills on the steel industry. Governments may also help their own firms overcome barriers by subsidizing their initial efforts at entry.

The third factor—the threat of substitutes—is straightforward. With few substitutes, firms in an industry will face little competition from outsiders. Finally, the fourth and fifth factors—the bargaining power of buyers and suppliers—are part of the downstream and upstream game of market power. If buyers or suppliers are few in number, their oligopolistic position will allow them to secure better prices when interacting with firms in a particular industry.

Each of these five forces can be analyzed in terms of the opportunities and threats it poses. Put most simply, the stronger the market forces in a particular industry (a highly competitive market structure, low barriers to entry, many substitutes, and buyers and supplies with market power), the greater the challenges facing its firms.

Nonmarket Environment

Just as firms must consider the prevailing market forces, so too must they be concerned about their nonmarket environments. As David Baron has argued, they must understand certain key nonmarket issues: the interests of major groups, the institutional setting within which policies are formulated, and the information available to actors.[15]

Issues can include market-related questions as well as nonmarket problems that may have an impact on market activity. In an international context, and particularly in Asia, issues such as the environmental and labor standards immediately raise potential nonmarket problems that can affect a firm's market strategy. Actors respond strategically to these issues in various institutional settings through negotiation, sometimes using tactics of "issue-packaging" or issue linkage. The strategic linking of issues may be based on knowledge (substantive links) or power (tactical linkages). Understanding the basis of a proposed issue linkage is crucial to analysis of its future stability and hence affects the formulation of strategy.[16]

Many analysts take a pluralist view of government-business relations, seeing nonstate actors as competing for government attention. More sophisticated approaches to the relationship between state and societal actors focus on the formulation of the interests of state actors. According to this analysis, institutions are not simply arenas for the political activity of governments, firms, and other nonstate actors; the norms, rules, and practices of institutions also influence the interests of major actors. That is, the motivations and capabilities of state actors both by themselves and within international institutions form an essential part of nonmarket analysis and strategy.

The last factor, information, refers to the commonly accepted bank of knowledge about particular issues. The word "information" as used by Baron is potentially misleading. The key component of the issue packaging and negotiation process is more aptly characterized as "knowledge," implying a certain type of theoretical and causal understanding rather than just an accumulation of facts. In this context, knowledge provides a conceptual framework for the formulation of policy and affects the evolution of institutions. From a strategic perspective, the creation of new knowledge may provide a basis for cognitive agreement among different groups, allowing them to supercede zero-sum competition and enter into a mutually beneficial bargaining situation.

Firm Core Competencies

Much has been written about the factors that contribute to a firm's competitive ability. Our focus in this book is primarily on the external factors of markets and nonmarket environments, rather than on corporate organization or management. Regarding a firm's ability to respond strategically to changing market and nonmarket conditions, most analysts focus on the division between a firm's resources and its capabilities.[17] The term "resources" refers to both tangible and intangible factors, ranging from buildings, plants, and so on, to less tangible items such as a firm's reputation, know-how, patents, and the like. "Capabilities" refers to a firm's ability to use resources in a systematic way to advance its interests, based on its structure and control system.

In terms of analysis, the focus is on considering a firm's strengths and weaknesses. Yet there is considerable debate as to which resources and capabilities constitute strengths—and under what conditions—and which constitute weaknesses. Thus, consultants and business school analysts have attempted to direct attention away from the actual products that firms produce to focus on their capabilities and competencies. The most popular work on core competencies, developed by C. K. Prahalad and Gary Hamel, examines firms in terms of their basic sets of competencies, ones that might be transferred to other areas and products. Rather than focusing on specific resources, core competencies focus on a vaguer sense of capabilities including "communication, involvement, and a deep commitment to working across organizational boundaries."[18] Starting from these core competencies, Hamel and Prahalad argue that firms must then go on to develop core products and organize their business accordingly. This view contrasts with the focus on products made by single business units within an organization that operate in a semi-autonomous manner.

There is much debate in this literature on firm-level abilities, but the basic view is that of the firm as one that is capable of managing structural constraints systematically, rather than being at the mercy of Porter's five forces. Indeed, the literature on corporate strategy has evolved from a rather static picture of firms attempting to fit into the environment within which they are operating to a more dynamic perspective in which firms generate and create market opportunities for themselves.

Hamel and Pralahad, for example, speak of strategic "intent" as opposed to strategic fit.[19] In their view, firms draw on their resources and capabilities to affect their market environments and to position themselves dynamically to enhance their profit potential. To complete the picture, we must also add to these market strategies the manipulation by firms of their nonmarket environments.

Positional Analysis and the Choice of Trade and/or Investment in Asia

Our analysis to this point provides a basis for exploring the decision of firms to enter or increase their presence in developing Asia through either a trade or investment strategy, or some combination of the two. This choice of strategy cannot be interpreted or predicted without a specific analysis of the market and nonmarket environment of the industry in question and the position of the firm in that industry. During the crisis period in the late 1990s, however, in several East Asian markets—but by no means all—weakened domestic firms provided obvious opportunity for rapid market entry. This environment favored a strategy of investment, instead of increasing trade. Favorable exchange rates also encouraged foreign investors to increase their presence in Asia. IMF demands on East Asian countries to reduce their barriers to both trade and investment were an additional stimulus for investment and, to a lesser extent, to increased trade (although exports to East Asia obviously suffered from severely low regional demand).

By contrast, both before and after the crisis period, the determinants of a trade or investment strategy were not so clearly in favor of investment, although some barriers have been reduced after the crisis. Under more normal conditions, the choice of strategy involves a more detailed analysis of the firm's core competencies, as well as the market and nonmarket environment for specific industries. The case studies in this volume provide some insights on these types of decisions on the part of Japanese firms from a range of sectors.

III. Strategic Analysis: Markets, Nonmarket, and Organizational Elements

The choice to focus primarily on trade or investment, based on an integrated consideration of market forces, the nonmarket environment, and firm core competencies, provides a first cut at assessing a firm's overall strategy toward the Asian market. However, firms must face several other issues: (1) What is a firm's market strategy with respect to product cost and quality, the transfer of technology, and which specific market segments to

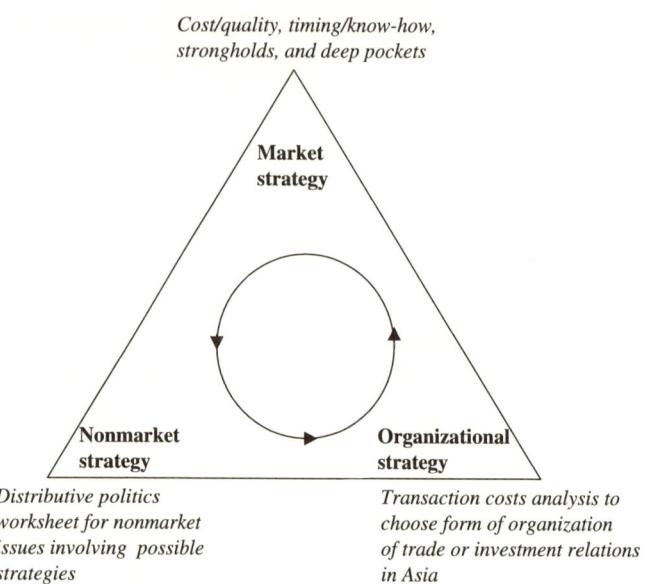

Figure 1.4 Strategic analysis

enter? (2) What types of opposition or support is the strategy likely to receive from various nonmarket actors, and how should the firm position itself advantageously? and (3) How does a firm organize its regional or country-level trade or investment operations? Figure 1.4 depicts the components that make up the "strategic analysis" triangle.

The following conceptual tools can be applied in analyzing these various strategic dimensions.

Market Strategy and Hypercompetition

Richard D'Aveni's work regarding the transformation of markets into states of hypercompetition can help us understand strategic choices in markets.[20] According to his analysis, firms compete in four different *arenas*: (1) cost and quality, (2) timing and know-how, (3) strongholds, and (4) deep pockets. Traditional analysis suggests that firms position themselves in one of these arenas, in cost and quality, for instance, and attempt to secure for themselves a high-cost/high-quality position. As D'Aveni argues, however, these static positioning efforts are ultimately futile—and with improved technology and global competition, this futility is reached with increasing speed. Thus, as markets evolve, firms must not only reposition themselves continually *within* arenas, but also must be prepared to move vigorously into *different* arenas as opportunities (or threats) present themselves.

In the first arena of competition, firms compete on the basis of cost and quality. In an "ideal typical characterization," firms initially begin with a homogeneous product and compete primarily on the basis of price. As price wars escalate, however, firms begin seeking other means of competition. Eventually, each differentiates itself from its competitors using new dimensions of quality and service. Although some firms try to cover the entire market by offering high-priced and high-quality products as well as low-priced and low-quality products, new competitors still have room to enter at either end by using niche or outflanking strategies.

In order to escape the unending cycle of price-quality competition present in the first arena of competition, firms focus on a second arena of competition, timing, and know-how. First movers who undertake a large investment may seize control of the market. Often, however, their products are easily imitable. To prevent imitation and maintain its control of the market, the first mover often creates barriers to market entry and develops its product in such a way as to make imitation difficult. Eventually, however, competitors do succeed in entering the market and learn to imitate the first mover's product. In response, the first mover may use a strategy of leapfrogging innovations in which new products are developed from large technological advances, entirely new resources, and know-how. While this again impedes the efforts of imitators, eventually they will again catch up to the leader. Again, the first mover will likely attempt a new leapfrog move, and the cycle begins again. According to D'Aveni, it continues until the "next generation leapfrog strategy" is too costly and the cycle becomes unsustainable.[21]

In the third arena of competition, firms seek an advantage on a playing field already leveled by price-quality competition and rapid innovation. They do this by creating strongholds to exclude competitors from their regional, industrial, or product market segments. As discussed by industrial organization theorists generally and Michael Porter in his analysis of five forces, entry barriers that firms create serve to insulate them from the price-quality and innovation-imitation cycles. Yet, in contrast to this somewhat static view of barriers, in hypercompetition, such barriers provide only short-term relief, and are rarely sustainable in the long run. Competitors are likely to build war chests in their own strongholds and then fund their entry into the strongholds of others. Usually, the attacked firm will respond by defending itself and then counterattacking in the initiating firm's stronghold. In the long run, these attacks and counterattacks weaken the stronghold of both firms until no stronghold remains.

In the fourth arena of competition, firms use their "deep pockets" to their advantage. Essentially, firms with the greatest financial resources try to gain an advantage by bullying smaller competitors. Such bullying often includes wearing down and undercutting smaller competitors, who have fewer financial resources and therefore cannot endure in the market as long as the deep-pocketed firm. In response, smaller competitors may develop formal or informal alliances, turn to the government for help, or seek to avoid competition with their powerful competitor. Eventually, after a series of moves and countermoves, the deep-pocketed firm exhausts its resources and its advantage is either substantially diminished or neutralized.

Nonmarket Strategy

When firms pursue a market strategy, they often must deal with nonmarket actors such as labor or environmental groups, or governmental regulatory or deregulatory policies. The "distributive politics spreadsheet" presented in Figure 1.5 provides a schematic breakdown of the supporting and opposing interests involved in a particular nonmarket issue. The figure describes the costs and benefits that accrue to each party

Supporting interests	Demand side			Supply side				Prediction
	Benefits from supporting			Ability to generate political action				Amount of effective political action
Interests	Substitutes	Magnitude	Per capita	Numbers	Coverage	Resources	Cost of organizing	
Opposing interests	Demand side			Supply side				Prediction
	Benefits from supporting			Ability to generate political action				Amount of effective political action
Interests	Substitutes	Magnitude	Per capita	Numbers	Coverage	Resources	Cost of organizing	

Figure 1.5 A distributive politics spreadsheet
Source: Adapted from Baron (2000).

from supporting or opposing a particular course of action on an issue that may have consequences for a firm.[22]

This figure, based on the well-known literature on interest group politics, provides a means of assessing the likely effectiveness of political actions of groups on each side of an issue. Turning first to the demand side, we can observe the incentives of varying interest groups based on three factors: (1) substitutes, which refers to alternatives available to a particular interest group to engaging in action on the issue at hand; (2) overall magnitude of benefits, which refers to the total benefits that would result from success on an issue; and (3) the per capita benefits, which represents the motivation of a particular interest group based on the direct benefits that its members will receive.

The supply side column presents the power capabilities of the actors in question, focusing on their numbers (how many groups or individuals can be involved), the coverage in terms of relevant political jurisdictions, and the resources that can be brought to bear on the issues. The last element, the cost of organizing, reflects the problems of overcoming collective action in view of the possibility of free riding and information dissemination.

This analysis can be conducted for both the supporting and opposing side on any issue. The definition of the issue-area(s) involved, as well as which groups or individuals should be considered relevant political actors, depends on the problem that is being addressed and the geographical arena in which the interaction occurs. Once defined, this analysis of distributive politics offers a window on a firm's calculations regarding which markets to enter and which integrated market and non-market strategies to apply.

Organizational Strategy

The well-developed literature on transaction costs helps to illuminate the organization by firms of their investment or trading activities.[23] In examining contracts and organizational forms, Oliver Williamson emphasizes the importance of bounded rationality, opportunistic behavior by actors, and the problem of highly specific assets to construct predictions about governance structures. According to Williamson, the fundamental problem of contracts is that, given the nature of bounded rationality and opportunism, one cannot be sure that one's counterpart will perform as promised. In such cases, a firm that undertakes investments in highly specific assets is highly vulnerable to exploitation because these assets cannot be transferred to other economic activities without substantial loss.

Witold Henisz has recently applied concepts of both economic and political transaction cost dilemmas to examine how firms might organize their foreign investment activities.[24] Henisz explores how the interaction of contractual and political hazards affects firms' choices. Specifically, he argues that where contractual hazards exist, firms are likely to choose majority controlled plants. These contractual hazards include a high need to invest in specific assets, a concern that technology might be inappropriately used or exploited by a joint venture partner, and free-riding on brand name or reputation.[25] By contrast, in the face of political hazards—which include, for instance, a fear of take-over by a host government—firms are likely to prefer minority investment stakes in which they might be able to use the skills and political standing of their venture partners to mitigate such hazards. The interaction effect of contractual and political hazards turns out to be empirically interesting. Henisz argues convincingly that when both contractual and political hazards are high, firms prefer majority-owned subsidiaries because their joint venture partners might well use the power of the state against them. Henisz's work combines market, firm, and nonmarket analysis in an interesting way.

For our purposes, focusing on contractual hazards provides insight on how firms might organize both their trade and investment activities. Figure 1.6 presents an array of possible organizational forms that vary according to asset specificity concerns and nonmarket factors and hazards.

Regarding trade, organizational forms will vary according to the level of concern regarding contractual hazards. Where hazards are perceived to be few, parties are likely to transact at arm's length. Where concern about such hazards is high, firms may choose to organize different operations internally, to ensure compliance. Similarly, for investment, contractual hazards could be mitigated by higher levels of ownership, albeit with the

ASSET SPECIFICITY (BASED ON INDUSTRY CHARACTERISTICS)			
← Low ———————— Medium ———————————— Higher →			
TRADE ORGANIZATIONAL FORMS			
Arms length	Sales organization	Trading company	Intrafirm trade
INVESTMENT ORGANIZATIONAL FORMS			
Minority owned	50/50 venture	Majority owned	Wholly owned

Figure 1.6 Choosing organizational forms based on transaction cost analysis

negative costs involved with maintaining a bureaucratically organized firm. Although our primary focus in this book is not on firm organization and structuring, this model provides some insights into firms' organizational responses to market and nonmarket factors.

Integrated Strategic Choice

Firms must make strategic decisions about their positioning with respect to arenas, as well as their positioning within a specific arena. For example, a firm must decide whether or not to concern itself with cost/quality at the national or regional level. From a market perspective, the success of its strategy will depend largely on whether or not there are other entrants, perhaps at the global level. This factor could be controlled through market actions and organizational strategies, thus moving the firm to cost/quality competitiveness in preparation for any competition, even potentially from global competitors. Alternatively, firms may try to insulate the national or regional arena through nonmarket protectionist actions. The decision between investing in market competitiveness versus investing in political activity is one that firms must make on an ongoing basis. To take a concrete example, firms in the telecommunications industry, faced with deregulation and new competition, have tried to position themselves globally both in respect to setting standards (through the CCITT in the ITU) as well as engaging in buy-outs in other countries, alliances, and the like. This has involved positioning themselves for timing (standard setting) as well as in the cost/quality and strongholds arenas.

IV. Tactical Analysis: Implementing Strategy

In order to implement a dynamic strategy successfully, firms must focus on three different tasks. The first is to implement their market strategies through the development and use of their capabilities. The second involves executing nonmarket strategies, both as an adjunct to their market strategies and to create competitive space for a longer-term market strategy. Finally, firms must utilize and restructure their organizations to fit their dynamic market and nonmarket strategies and to position themselves for new opportunities. These tasks are depicted in Figure 1.7.

Market Tactics

There are three basic firm tasks in implementing market strategies: research and development (R&D), production, and marketing.

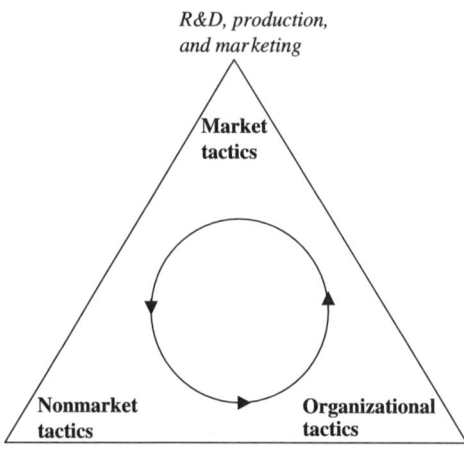

Figure 1.7 Tactical analysis

When positioning themselves in various arenas (for example, in cost/quality and timing and know-how), firms must decide how best to compete. Thus, if the strategy chosen is to compete with other multinationals using know-how, it is self-evident that emphasis is placed on R&D and therefore a critical question is where such activities might best be pursued. Japanese firms, for instance, have located their design centers for automobiles in the Los Angeles area to take advantage of that region's superior resources and to market autos for the U.S. market more effectively. Or, in choosing to use production networks across a number of Asian countries, European firms must decide where to conduct R&D, and must choose an appropriate market for production to lower their costs without excessively sacrificing quality.

Nonmarket Tasks

Nonmarket problems require a carefully formulated, strategic response. Elements of such a strategy can include lobbying, grassroots activity, coalition building, testimony, political entrepreneurship, electoral support, communication and public advocacy, and judicial strategies. For the most part these are self-explanatory. Grassroots activities refer to efforts to generate broad public support in order to influence office holders. Political entrepreneurship means an active effort to shape a political agenda to benefit the interests of the firm. Examples of this tactic include negotiations for more open market policies in Japan, putting intellectual property issues on the GATT agenda in the Uruguay Round, and the promotion of liberalized trade arrangements such as NAFTA. In most cases, entrepreneurship of this type will involve the building of coalitions with like-minded firms as well as various other tactical efforts to affect the agenda setting process.

Organizational Tactics

Having chosen an appropriate form of trade or investment in light of transaction costs considerations, firms must structure their organization and management to succeed in their chosen market arena. Wholly-owned subsidiaries require knowledge of sourcing partners and personnel who understand local markets and who can deal with host governments. In the case of a firm that enters with a local partner in a joint venture, some of these tasks could be shifted to the local level, to take advantage of its local network and expertise. In such cases, however, skill in organizing and managing joint ventures with respect to contracting, financing, and control are essential.

Similarly, with respect to trade strategies, firms must organize themselves to maximize their competitiveness. Sears' failed effort to compete with Japanese trading companies illustrates the challenges of operating in highly competitive markets, and the need for organizational skill and learning.

With respect to nonmarket strategies and tactics, firms must develop their abilities to interact with governments, nongovernmental organizations, and other interest groups. Firms that concentrate only on market issues and attempt to outsource nonmarket tasks often suffer as a result of their neglect of this aspect of their integrated strategy.

V. The Layout of the Book

Japanese firms, for the most part, have been highly successful in competing in developing Asian markets. The contributors to this volume provide us with insightful analyses of a host of examples of successful strategies—both of the market and nonmarket variety, along with organizational strategies and tactics.

In Chapter 2, Shujiro Urata provides an analysis of recent trends in trade and foreign direct investment in Asia to sketch the context for the case studies that follow. Urata finds that after years of active investment, many firms are rapidly retrenching in the wake of the Asian crisis—although recent surveys indicate that they are likely to resume regional investment in the near future. Urata also demonstrates that FDI and trade strategies can be complementary and, at least over the last decade, Japanese exports to Asia have been more significant than FDI in the region.

The ensuing case studies provide a systematic positional, strategic, and tactical analysis of Japanese firms' activities in the banking, chemicals, automobile, telecommunications, software, and electronics industries. In Chapter 3, Masahiro Kawai, Yuzuru Ozeki, and Hiroshi Tokumaru show how Japanese banks successfully used domestic protection to engage in traditional deposit-taking and lending activities, which they then expanded in East Asian markets as they followed Japanese firms into the region. The Asian crisis, however, forced Japanese banks to retrench and turn back to the Japanese domestic market. Meanwhile, the Japanese banks' aggressive, but ultimately unsuccessful push for government intervention has led to a steep decline in the market value of their debt. In the wake of the Asian crisis then, Japanese banks have dramatically shifted their strategies, making deep cuts to bolster their financial position, undertaking strategic alliances and mergers, and seeking to develop new sources of revenue.

In Chapter 4, Tametsugu Taketomi analyzes how Japanese chemical companies have operated in an industry marked by a high degree of government intervention. Until the Japanese financial bubble burst in the early 1990s, Japanese companies had focused primarily on their protected domestic market. By contrast, highly competitive foreign firms made inroads into developing Asian markets. Domestic deregulation forced the relatively smaller Japanese firms to compete, but they were able to find ready customers in Japanese multinationals relocating to Southeast Asia. Still, intense competition and eroding *keiretsu* relationships forced Japanese chemical companies to begin a process of restructuring, led both by managers and by the Ministry of International Trade and Industry (MITI). It remains to be seen if these measures, together with internal management changes, will lead to significantly enhanced competitiveness.

Chapter 5, by Gregory Noble, shows how Japanese firms successfully penetrated and achieved a dominant position in Southeast Asian markets. This achievement is now being challenged by a number of factors, including increases in the power of major international suppliers, the ability of Southeast Asian countries to bargain with firms in a highly competitive market, and the successful incursions of foreign auto assemblers. To respond, Japanese auto firms have engaged in deep cost cutting, alternative sourcing patterns, new offerings, and strategic investment in research and development. They are also becoming more aggressive in their lobbying efforts with their home government and with host governments, calling for aid and new trade arrangements. These strategies have been matched by significant organizational changes, including, in some cases, the takeover of Japanese firms by foreign companies.

In Chapter 6, Yumiko Okamoto shows how deregulation, privatization, crumbling barriers to entry, and new technologies have altered the competitive dynamics of the Asian telecommunications market. Japanese firms have responded by offering new products and services, and by allowing foreigners to invest. Still, Japanese telecom firms continue to enjoy close links to Japanese MNCs operating in East Asian markets, thus giving them a competitive edge versus foreign firms. To better compete, Japanese telecom firms have also developed partnerships and alliances with foreign firms to offer more value-added services. From a nonmarket perspective, their successful efforts to secure concessions from the Japanese government has given them greater leeway in their domestic operations.

In Chapter 7, Trevor Nakagawa analyzes the Japanese software industry. Although U.S. firms remain dominant in East Asia through their alliances with hardware firms, larger Japanese firms like Fujitsu, NEC, and Hitachi have focused on the enterprise software market to leverage their knowledge of the Japanese corporate environment. Still, intense competition from American software firms has forced Japanese software firms to conform to U.S. global standards to survive, and often to collaborate with their potential rivals to provide total enterprise solutions. Companies like Fujitsu have been successful primarily because they have been effective at implementing an integrated strategy at multiple platform levels and adopting an "Everything on the Internet" business strategy. Fujitsu has also complemented this market strategy by establishing closer ties with local government authorities to promote their large-scale enterprise solutions throughout the economy and among the governments themselves. Furthermore, it has been able to take advantage of a wide array of favorable trade, tax, and R&D policies as well as to use Asian countries as both an export base to third party markets and as localization centers.

Chapter 8, by Hidetaka Yoshimatsu, focuses on the Japanese electronics industry. Until recently, major Japanese firms have used their production networks with subcontracting parts suppliers to improve quality and reduce costs. These networks were replicated more broadly as these suppliers worked with Japanese firms as the latter moved into North America, Europe, and Southeast Asia in the late 1980s. Since the mid-1990s, however, the Japanese firms have faced more difficult times, as South Korean firms have challenged their dominant position in the Asian electronics markets and technological innovation has catalyzed a new wave of competitors. Yoshimatsu argues that the failure of Japanese firms to develop locally-oriented price competitive products or to draw on expertise from the emerging Asian supply base, and the devaluation of local currencies after the Asian financial crisis—which increased the import price of intermediate goods from Japan—has made firms less competitive. Japanese firms are now responding with nonmarket strategies of working with East Asian-based associations, implementing more efficient procurement plans, and transferring management positions and R&D to East Asian branches.

The concluding chapter assesses the variety of market, nonmarket, and organizational strategies that Japanese firms have pursued. Based on the theoretical framework, it also draws more general lessons about the combination of strategies that have allowed firms to successfully penetrate Asian markets in the face of changing market and nonmarket conditions.

Notes

1. For comments on earlier versions of this chapter, I would like to thank David Baron, Cédric Dupont, Ralph Espach, Ed Fogarty, Kun-Chin Lin, Trevor Nakagawa, and John Ravenhill.
2. *Winning in Asia, European Style: Market and Nonmarket Strategies for Success, Winning in Asia, American Style: Market and Nonmarket Strategies for Success*, both edited by Vinod K. Aggarwal, and *Winning in Asia, Japanese Style: Market and Nonmarket Strategies for Success*, edited by Vinod K. Aggarwal and Shujiro Urata. All three books are being published by Palgrave (New York). The case studies include an examination of software, financial services, aircraft, autos, chemicals, telecommunications, and electronics.
3. See Baron (2000) for a good overview of nonmarket strategies.
4. Bartlett and Ghoshal (1989).
5. Dupont (2001).
6. For discussion of such influence efforts, see Ravenhill (2001). For background on APEC, see Aggarwal and Morrison (1998).
7. Aggarwal (1992).
8. See Aggarwal, Keohane, and Yoffie (1987).
9. For a discussion of the dangers of this approach, see Aggarwal and Ravenhill (2001).
10. Aggarwal (2000).
11. Porter (1980).
12. It is worth noting that other analysts have criticized Porter's approach for being excessively structural and unresponsive to firm strategies. This debate, similar to the "Great Man" versus "Forces of History" argument in both political science and history, concerns the plasticity of structural forces as opposed to the initiative that firms might take to mold the factors themselves.
13. See Aggarwal, Keohane, and Yoffie (1987).
14. See Bain (1956).
15. Baron (2000) The four is noted here provide a useful but limited first cut to understand the nonmarket environment, as I discuss in the following paragraphs.
16. See among others, Haas (1980), Stein (1980), Oye (1979) and Aggarwal (1998).

17. Hill and Jones (1995).
18. Prahalad and Hamel (1990), p. 82.
19. Hamel and Prahalad (1989).
20. D'Aveni (1994).
21. D'Aveni (1994), p. 22.
22. See the discussion in Baron (2000).
23. See Coase (1960), Williamson (1985) and (1996), among others.
24. See the excellent work by Henisz (2000), who draws on Oliver Williamson's work on economic transaction costs and work by Douglass North (1981) and (1999) on political transaction costs to examine organizational form choices for direct foreign investment in the context of possible expropriation.
25. Klein and Leffler (1981) and Henisz (2000).

References

Aggarwal, Vinod K. (1992). "The Political Economy of Service Sector Negotiations in the Uruguay Round," *The Fletcher Forum of World Affairs,* vol. 16, no. 1 (Winter), pp. 35–54.

——— ed. (1998). *Institutional Designs for a Complex World: Bargaining, Linkages, and Nesting* (Ithaca, N.Y.: Cornell University Press).

——— (2000). "The Wobbly Triangle: Europe, Asia and the U.S. after the Asian Crisis."
In *After the Asian Crises: Perspectives on Global Politics and Economics,* ed. Maria Weber (London: Macmillan), pp. 173–198.

Aggarwal, Vinod K., Robert Keohane, and David Yoffie (1987). "The Dynamics of Negotiated Protectionism," *American Political Science Review,* vol. 81, no. 2 (June), pp. 345–366.

Aggarwal, Vinod K. and Charles Morrison, eds. (1998). *Asia-Pacific Crossroads: Regime Creation and the Future of APEC* (New York: St. Martin's Press).

Aggarwal, Vinod K. and John Ravenhill (2001). "Undermining the WTO: The Case Against 'Open Sectoralism,'" *Asia Pacific Issues,* no. 50 (February).

Bain, J. E. (1956). *Barriers to New Competition* (Cambridge: Harvard University Press).

Baron, David (1999). "Integrated Market and Nonmarket Strategies in Client and Interest Group Politics," *Business and Politics* 1 (1) (April).

Baron, David (2000). *Business and Its Environment,* 3rd edition (Upper Saddle River, NJ: Prentice Hall).

Bartlett, C. and S. Ghoshal (1989). *Managing Across Borders: The Transnational Solution* (Boston: Harvard University Press).

Coase, Ronald (1960). "The Problem of Social Cost," *Journal of Law and Economics* (October), p. 186.

D'Aveni, R. (1994). *Hypercompetition: Managing the Dynamics of Strategic Maneuvering* (New York: The Free Press).

Dupont, Cedric (2001). "Euro-Pressure: Avenues and Strategies for Lobbying the European Union." In *Winning in Asia, European Style: Market and Nonmarket Strategies for Success,* ed. Vinod K. Aggarwal (New York: Palgrave).

Haas, Ernst (1980). "Why Collaborate? Issue-linkage and International Regimes," *World Politics,* vol. 32, no. 3, pp. 357–405.

Hamel, Gary and C. K. Prahalad (1989). "Strategic Intent," *Harvard Business Review* (May–June), pp. 63–76.

Hill, Charles and Gareth Jones (1995). *Strategic Management Theory: An Integrated Approach* (Boston: Houghton Mifflin).

Henisz, Witold Jerzy (2000). "The Institutional Environment for Multinational Investment," *Journal of Law, Economics and Organization,* 16(2): pp. 334–364.

Klein, Benjamin and Keith B. Leffler (1981). "The Role of Market Forces in Assuring Contractual Performance," *Journal of Political Economy* 89, pp. 615–641.

North, Douglass C. (1981). *Understanding the Process of Economic Change* (London: Institute of Economic Affairs).

North, Douglass C. (1999). *Structure and Change in Economic History,* 1st edition (New York: Norton).

Oye, Kenneth (1979). "The Domain of Choice." In *Eagle Entangled: U.S. Foreign Policy in a Complex World,* eds. Kenneth Oye, Robert Lieber, and Donald Rothschild (New York: Longman), pp. 3–33.

Prahalad, C. K. and Gary Hamel (1990). "The Core Competence of the Corporation," *Harvard Business Review* (May–June), pp. 79–91.

Porter, M. E. (1980). *Competitive Strategy* (New York: The Free Press).

Ravenhill, John (2001). "Nonmarket Strategies in Asia: The Regional Level." In *Winning in Asia, European Style: Market and Nonmarket Strategies for Success,* ed. Vinod K. Aggarwal (New York: Palgrave).

Stein, Art (1980). "The Politics of Linkage," *World Politics,* vol. 33, no. 1, October.

Williamson, Oliver E. (1985). *The Economic Institutions of Capitalism: Firms, Markets and Relational Contracting* (New York: The Free Press).

Williamson, Oliver E. (1996). *The Mechanisms of Governance* (New York: Oxford University Press).

CHAPTER TWO

Japan's Foreign Direct Investment and Trade in Asia

SHUJIRO URATA[1]

I. Introduction

Developing Asia has successfully attracted foreign direct investment (FDI) since the mid-1980s. FDI inflows to Asia increased sharply from $7 billion in 1986 to $94 billion in 1997.[2] Although the recent financial crisis in Asia resulted in a drastic reduction in bank loans and portfolio investment, FDI inflows remained relatively strong, declining by only 7 percent from 1997 to 1998.[3] Between 1997 and 1998, FDI inflows to five crisis-hit countries, Indonesia, South Korea, Malaysia, the Philippines, and Thailand, declined by only 2 percent. Compared to other forms of investment, FDI inflows remained relatively stable during that turbulent period. Indeed, FDI inflows to Asia rebounded to register a 10 percent increase in 1999.

Between the mid-1980s and the 1997 financial crisis, FDI contributed significantly to the rapid economic growth of the Asian economies. Furthermore, FDI kept the crisis-hit countries from slipping away. FDI not only provided financial resources for fixed investment but also technology and managerial know-how, which are both critical in promoting economic growth. In addition, FDI enabled the recipient economies to utilize various networks of foreign firms in areas such as sales, procurement, and information resources, through which the recipients could access efficient production and marketing. Indeed, after a long period of restrictive policies, many Asian governments liberalized their FDI policies in order to reap these manifold benefits.

Among foreign investors in Asia, Japanese firms have assumed an especially important position. In terms of total FDI value, Japan has been the leading investor in many Asian economies. Japanese investors have been active in the region for various reasons, of which geographical proximity is only one. Other regional attractions include promising economic prospects and abundant, cheap, and well-disciplined labor. Furthermore, the Japanese government has had a strong strategic interest in promoting the region's economic growth and has provided assistance to Japanese investors. From a Japanese perspective, economic growth in Asia not only leads to economic, political, and social stability in the region but also creates and expands important markets for Japanese exports.

During the 1990s, however, Japanese FDI fell into an uneven decline, mainly as a result of the nation's prolonged recession. Japanese FDI to developed countries experienced the greatest reduction, but FDI to Asia also diminished significantly. As a result of increasing FDI inflows to Asia from the United States and Europe and the decline in Japanese FDI, the total share of Japanese FDI in Asia fell. Despite this decline, Asian affiliates of Japanese firms actively expanded their operations. In particular, those engaged in exports increased their production and competitiveness after the crisis by taking advantage of substantial depreciation of the Asian currencies.

This chapter analyzes the motivations and trends of Japanese FDI in Asia, with a focus on the strategies implemented by Japanese firms. In Section II, I assess various patterns in Japanese FDI by splitting my analysis into pre- and postcrisis periods. In Sections III and IV, I examine the motives of Japanese FDI in Asia and the problems Japanese firms face in Asia, respectively. Section V covers the impact of the crisis on the business strategies of Japanese firms, while Section VI focuses on their future FDI plans. Section VII examines Japan's trade with Asia, and, finally, Section VIII presents some concluding remarks.

II. Japanese FDI in Asia

This section reviews Japanese FDI in Asia in recent years by dividing the phenomenon into its precrisis and postcrisis phases.[4] In my analysis, I attempt to capture not only continuing trends, but also the factors behind decisions on whether or not to invest in East Asian markets.

Before the Crisis

Japanese foreign direct investment in Asia rose steadily between 1990 and 1997 (see Table 2.1). After a downturn in 1993 to ¥4.2 trillion,

Table 2.1 Japanese FDI in Asia (billion yen)

	1989	1990	1991	1992	1993	1994	1995	1996	1997	1998	1999
Asia	1100.3	1034.3	810.7	831.6	767.2	1008.4	1192.1	1308.3	1494.8	835.7	798.8
South Korea	79.9	41.9	35.7	29.1	28.9	42.0	43.3	46.8	54.3	38.7	109.3
Taiwan	66.2	65.3	55.4	37.6	34.3	29.2	43.9	58.7	55.2	28.7	31.8
Hong Kong	250.2	261.0	126.0	96.6	144.7	117.9	110.6	167.5	85.3	77.0	108.5
Singapore	257.3	123.2	83.7	87.5	73.5	110.1	114.3	125.6	223.8	81.5	107.3
Indonesia	84.0	161.5	162.8	214.2	95.2	180.8	154.8	272.0	308.5	137.8	102.4
Thailand	170.3	169.6	110.7	84.9	68.0	74.9	119.6	158.1	229.1	175.5	91.0
Philippines	26.9	38.3	27.7	21.0	23.6	68.3	69.2	63.0	64.2	48.5	68.8
Malaysia	90.2	106.7	120.2	91.9	89.2	77.2	55.5	64.4	97.1	65.8	58.6
Vietnam	0.0	0.1	0.0	1.3	5.2	17.7	19.2	35.9	38.1	6.5	11.0
China	58.7	51.1	78.7	138.1	195.4	268.3	431.9	282.8	243.8	136.3	83.8

Note: Reported value.
Source: Ministry of Finance.

Japanese FDI increased to ¥6.6 trillion in 1997. This steady increase was largely attributed to the appreciation of the yen and buoyant economic growth in the U.S. and European markets. The appreciation of the yen reduced the price competitiveness of Japanese goods, providing Japanese firms with incentive to shift their production from Japan to less expensive foreign countries. Japanese FDI, aimed at producing goods for regional markets that were underpriced relative to Japan's, was "pulled" toward moving production overseas. Furthermore, during this period a number of East Asian governments sought to attract this FDI by liberalizing their policies regarding foreign investment, making the region increasingly attractive for Japanese firms.[5]

The geographical and sectoral composition of Japanese FDI changed notably over the course of the 1990s. Asia's share of total global Japanese FDI increased from 12.2 percent in 1989 to 24.2 percent in 1996 before declining in 1997. In contrast, over the same period, Europe's share fell from 21.9 percent to 15.4 percent, while North America's share remained more or less constant at around 50 percent. Several factors contributed to this expansion of Japanese FDI in Asia. First, Japanese firms were lured by impressive growth in the region's local markets. Second, firms that produced export goods found Asian economies with their currencies pegged to the U.S. dollar attractive sites for production. Third, Asian governments cognizant of the financial support, technology transfer, worker training, managerial skills, and other benefits that FDI brings, introduced various measures to attract outside investment. In addition to liberalizing their FDI policies, a number of countries offered potential investors incentives such as tax relief and infrastructure development. It is important to note that these three factors noted above were closely related. FDI attracted by a favorable export environment, rapid economic growth, and liberalization in FDI policies in turn reinforced economic growth, export growth, and trade and FDI liberalization among FDI recipients in East Asia.[6]

Since the latter half of the 1980s, the geographical distribution of Japanese FDI within Asia has changed notably. After a substantial decline from the 1980s to the early 1990s, Japanese FDI in the four newly industrialized economies of South Korea, Hong Kong, Taiwan, and Singapore (NIE4) registered a steady increase through 1997. A major increase came from FDI in Singapore, as Singapore's share of Japanese FDI in Asia increased from 9.6 percent in 1993 to 15 percent in 1997, due largely to several large investments in the chemicals and semiconductor sectors. Four of the members of the Association of Southeast Asian Nations, Thailand, Malaysia, Indonesia, and the Philippines (ASEAN4), also saw a substantial increase in Japanese FDI from 1993 to 1997. As a consequence, the share of ASEAN4 in Japanese FDI in Asia increased from 36 percent in 1993 to 46.8 percent in 1997. Among the ASEAN4 countries, Japanese FDI in Indonesia and Thailand increased sharply from the early 1990s to 1997, from ¥95.2 and ¥68.0 trillion in 1993 to ¥308.5 and ¥229.1 trillion in 1997, respectively (see Table 2.1), representing an increase in their respective shares of Japanese FDI in Asia from 12.4 and 8.9 percent in 1993 to 20.6 and 15.3 percent in 1997. Indeed, Indonesia regained its position as the most attractive country in Asia for Japanese FDI in 1997 after losing that position to China four years earlier.

Japanese FDI in China increased notably from the early 1990s, as the Chinese government restored political stability after the Tiananmen Square incident and started to pursue outward-oriented trade and FDI policies rigorously. Although Japanese FDI in China increased remarkably in the first half of the 1990s, it started to decline in 1996, two years before Japanese investment in the NIE4 and ASEAN4 began to fall. Beijing's reduction of preferential treatment accorded to foreign firms negatively affected FDI inflows. Specifically, the reduction in the amount of drawback given to exports and the end of tariff exemptions on imports used for export production diminished China's appeal as a host to FDI. More generally, China has been a relatively less important FDI destination for Japanese firms than other countries: China's share of Japanese FDI in Asia has been about 20 percent, which is significantly smaller than its share of overall investment inflows in Asia (about 50 percent). In contrast, the Japanese presence in the ASEAN4 has been much more prominent.

An examination of the sectoral distribution of Japanese FDI reveals that a large portion of Japanese FDI has been in nonmanufacturing sectors (see Tables 2.2 and 2.3). Although the share of manufacturing increased

Table 2.2 Japanese global FDI by sector (billion yen)

	1989	1990	1991	1992	1993	1994	1995	1996	1997	1998	1999
Total	9033.9	8352.7	5686.2	4431.3	4151.4	4280.8	4956.8	5409.4	6622.9	5216.9	7439.0
Manufacturing total	2177.3	2271.8	1691.9	1303.8	1276.6	1442.6	1823.6	2282.1	2373.1	1568.6	4719.3
Food	177.8	121.1	87.2	67.1	97.3	133.4	81.1	82.2	70.2	162.6	1662.8
Textiles	71.2	116.2	84.5	55.7	57.7	67.4	100.8	68.2	117.6	43.7	29.0
Wood products	72.4	45.4	43.0	55.9	40.6	14.8	35.1	69.8	43.1	86.7	12.9
Chemicals	280.4	336.3	220.2	258.4	204.2	271.5	207.9	232.0	369.8	287.6	188.9
Metal products	209.8	153.3	123.9	107.2	88.5	107.1	149.8	275.6	173.4	156.6	162.6
General machinery	235.9	213.7	175.3	142.8	136.3	169.7	181.0	162.0	157.5	101.8	111.0
Electric machinery	600.1	835.8	314.7	235.7	313.3	273.4	519.0	733.7	820.8	437.7	1823.7
Transport machinery	273.8	274.1	271.3	155.8	109.8	213.6	193.9	436.3	356.9	205.7	533.3
Other manufacturing	255.8	175.9	371.8	225.2	228.9	191.6	354.9	222.4	263.9	86.2	195.1
Nonmanufacturing	6756.5	5964.2	3930.7	3081.0	2844.9	2797.8	3039.5	3012.4	4179.3	3602.5	2696.8
Agriculture	20.0	22.4	38.3	18.3	8.5	15.8	13.4	15.7	6.9	4.2	9.0
Fishery	6.2	8.7	9.9	11.7	6.5	21.4	5.4	11.0	13.4	2.5	2.9
Mining	168.3	195.8	136.5	162.5	109.3	49.3	103.4	176.8	329.6	111.9	102.8
Construction	84.8	43.7	58.7	69.9	31.6	36.7	38.5	36.1	56.0	37.6	20.3
Commerce	684.6	903.5	715.0	478.8	593.4	458.0	514.9	538.7	536.8	483.5	432.4
Finance	2042.4	1180.2	681.3	596.2	726.5	687.2	527.2	876.0	1468.8	2096.4	1102.6
Services	1441.9	1671.6	737.0	853.5	410.8	718.1	1035.0	455.8	795.0	262.8	481.2
Transport services	389.2	316.2	338.9	222.5	251.6	272.2	220.6	202.7	287.3	243.0	309.1
Real estate	1894.2	1621.0	1213.7	667.0	705.5	539.3	581.3	699.6	679.0	359.7	235.8
Other nonmanufacturing	24.9	1.1	1.4	0.0	1.2	0.0	0.0	0.0	6.6	0.9	0.9
Branch offices	100.1	116.7	63.6	46.5	29.9	40.4	93.8	114.9	70.5	45.7	22.9

Note: Reported value.
Source: Ministry of Finance.

Table 2.3 Japanese FDI in Asia by sector (billion yen)

	1989	1990	1991	1992	1993	1994	1995	1996	1997	1998	1999
Total	1100.3	1034.3	810.7	831.6	767.2	1008.4	1192.1	1308.3	1494.8	835.7	798.8
Manufacturing total	434.4	449.6	400.9	399.5	417.8	539.6	781.4	746.6	897.8	473.2	489.2
Food	75.2	17.3	21.6	9.1	16.0	25.7	27.0	31.4	21.5	16.1	32.3
Textiles	26.0	43.3	29.7	29.3	34.7	51.9	72.8	40.3	52.0	28.5	25.1
Wood products	8.1	10.9	4.8	6.6	9.5	6.5	10.1	25.8	16.2	17.1	4.8
Chemicals	39.0	81.7	79.2	134.5	46.4	96.3	61.5	100.4	161.9	75.9	74.3
Metal products	41.3	33.2	33.5	34.3	39.4	51.0	91.8	106.8	96.5	70.4	77.5
General machinery	46.8	38.7	34.8	27.9	50.3	41.0	77.1	62.5	64.7	36.3	36.7
Electric machinery	124.3	121.9	119.7	70.2	101.8	143.9	238.8	205.9	222.6	85.2	104.7
Transport machinery	19.0	55.1	26.0	22.1	30.4	41.6	82.2	89.7	104.7	102.1	67.9
Other manufacturing	54.8	47.5	51.6	65.6	89.2	81.7	120.1	83.9	157.7	41.5	65.9
Nonmanufacturing	652.1	570.8	393.8	410.1	335.7	439.0	357.4	475.5	564.0	348.4	298.3
Agriculture	2.6	5.0	3.7	1.9	2.3	1.9	4.7	0.9	0.6	0.4	0.5
Fishery	3.0	2.8	3.1	8.7	2.6	16.8	3.0	9.3	11.7	0.5	1.4
Mining	28.5	34.1	35.4	47.5	30.8	18.7	25.7	52.2	127.0	37.5	13.5
Construction	38.1	14.1	13.0	21.4	4.9	17.6	16.0	17.4	26.7	17.0	5.6
Commerce	87.9	178.2	97.0	99.4	82.3	63.0	78.7	89.4	95.7	145.2	100.8
Finance	142.1	94.3	108.8	88.7	79.6	121.1	73.8	89.1	70.6	54.8	86.3
Services	147.9	130.4	70.7	65.7	58.4	113.2	58.5	86.2	67.6	48.7	28.8
Transport services	52.1	16.6	13.2	43.2	32.9	34.0	31.4	30.2	48.6	26.7	47.6
Real estate	148.6	94.4	48.8	33.8	41.8	52.6	65.6	100.7	108.9	16.9	12.8
Other nonmanufacturing	1.1	0.9	0.0	0.0	0.0	0.0	0.0	0.0	6.5	0.9	0.9
Branch offices	13.7	13.9	16.0	22.0	13.7	29.8	53.3	86.2	33.0	14.1	11.3

Note: Reported value.
Source: Ministry of Finance.

until 1996, its share (42.2 percent) in that year was still lower than that of nonmanufacturing (55.7 percent). The share of manufacturing was higher for Japanese FDI in Asia, increasing from 39.5 percent in 1989 to 65.5 percent in 1995, before starting to decline. Japanese firms' share of manufacturing investment in Asia as compared to in other parts of the world implies that they see Asian affiliates as their production and export bases. I will come back to the strategies of Japanese firms in Asia later.

Among manufacturing subsectors, electric machinery firms have invested the most, with their share of Japanese FDI in Asia fluctuating between 10 to 15 percent throughout the 1990s. The chemicals, transport machinery, and metal products sectors follow. Since chemicals and metal products are used as parts for the production of electric and transport machinery, Japanese FDI in these sectors appear to be closely related. Indeed, there have been many cases where parts and components suppliers set up their affiliates in Asia at the request of electric or transport machinery assemblers who relied on these chemicals and metal products producers for parts and components in Japan.

It is important to observe two very different motives behind FDI by two groups of Japanese firms. One group, represented by transport machinery, was motivated by protectionist policies in Asia. In protected markets, FDI is the only way that Japanese automobile firms could sell their products. The other group, consisting of several sectors such as electric machinery and precision machinery, was motivated by a freer production and trade environment that enabled Japanese firms to take advantage of abundant low-wage labor. One could characterize the former type as market-seeking and the latter as efficiency-seeking FDI. It is noteworthy that Japanese firms in the latter category have established production networks throughout Asia, through which they have been able to exploit locational advantages in different economies in Asia. I will come back to these two different types of FDI when I discuss the motives of Japanese FDI and the reaction of Japanese firms to the Asian crisis.

As for Japanese FDI in nonmanufacturing sectors in Asia, one observes the prominence of commercial, financial, real estate, and other services. Japanese real estate investors had speculative motives, while those in commerce and finance were largely driven to serve the demand for such services by the Asian affiliates of Japanese firms. However, with the rise in income levels resulting from rapid economic growth in East Asia, an increasing number of Japanese firms in the nonmanufacturing sector, most notably in the commerce sector, have begun to undertake FDI to serve local demand.

After the Crisis

The East Asian financial and economic crisis changed the FDI environment drastically. On one hand, the substantial devaluation of Asian currencies increased the attractiveness of their economies as a host for FDI. For foreign firms interested in export production, devaluation improved the price competitiveness of products produced in stricken economies. Furthermore, devaluation reduced the amount of foreign currencies required for investments in devaluating economies. Coupled with the collapse in local stock prices, sharp currency depreciation enabled foreign firms to purchase equity in existing Asian firms at very low prices.

On the other hand, the crisis also had a discouraging impact on FDI. For foreign firms interested in local sales, a substantial decline in local economic activities reduced the attractiveness of the crisis-stricken economies as a destination for FDI. In addition, an increased uncertainty in macroeconomic performance had a discouraging impact on FDI, as foreign firms regard certainty or low risk as an important factor for making investment decisions.[7]

The postcrisis investment data reflect these trends. Annual flows of Japanese FDI into Asia in 1997 showed continued growth because of active FDI in the early part of 1997 (see Table 2.1). Indeed, based on optimistic expectations of future economic developments, a number of large FDI projects were carried out in early 1997. For example, in Indonesia in April in 1997 a Japanese petroleum company invested a large sum to purchase oil drilling rights as part of its long-term strategy for expanding and strengthening its operations.

Japanese FDI in the latter half of 1997 declined in many Asian economies (see Table 2.4). The rate of decline was large for Hong Kong, Taiwan, Indonesia, the Philippines, and China, while Japanese FDI in South Korea and Malaysia increased significantly. In 1998, Japanese FDI declined in all East Asian economies, most substantially in Singapore, Taiwan, Hong Kong, Indonesia, Thailand, and China. These observations indicate that Japanese FDI cannot be explained wholly by the severity of the impact of the economic crisis in the host economies. Specifically, Taiwan and China, which performed more favorably than other economies during the crisis, saw a huge decline in Japanese investment after the crisis, while Thailand, where the crisis began, saw a relatively small decline in the second half of 1997. In 1998, Japanese FDI in Asia continued to decline, but the patterns of these changes were different among the Asian countries (Table 2.1). Japanese FDI in the NIE4 increased, while Japanese FDI in many ASEAN4 countries and China continued to decline.

Table 2.4 Japanese FDI and the Asian crisis (percent change from the previous period)

	1997		1998
	1st half	2nd half	
NIE4	−21.5	15.9	−64.7
South Korea	−53.8	116.8	−29.1
Taiwan	−0.0	−28.2	−58.6
Hong Kong	−51.2	−55.6	−47.7
Singapore	27.6	96.4	−83.4
ASEAN4	62.4	−17.7	−36.4
Indonesia	58.1	−35.7	−49.8
Thailand	80.6	−3.1	−40.6
Philippines	18.4	−24.8	−8.4
Malaysia	86.5	20.3	−12.9
China	−19.1	−23.1	−44.7

Note: Reported value.
Source: Ministry of Finance.

The impact of the economic crisis affected Japanese FDI differently among sectors. Compared to nonmanufacturing sectors, Japanese FDI in manufacturing sectors dropped precipitously. Specifically, from 1997 to 1998 Japanese manufacturing FDI in Asia declined by 47.3 percent, while the corresponding rate for nonmanufacturing sectors was 38.2 percent. Among manufacturing subsectors, electric machinery saw a huge decline of 61.8 percent. This may be explained by overinvestment in the previous period, which was attributable to optimistic future prospects on the part of Japanese electric firms for the demand for electric products.

Among nonmanufacturing sectors, the rate of decline of Japanese FDI was substantial in real estate. A huge decline in Japanese FDI in real estate in 1998 is attributable to the collapse of real estate market resulting from the economic crisis. Commerce was the only nonmanufacturing sector that saw an increase in FDI in 1998. A decline in Japanese FDI in finance is worth noting, as many European and American financial institutions invested heavily by taking advantage of good opportunities in Asia. One of the most important factors behind the Asian economic crisis was the weakness of the financial sector in Asia. Crisis-stricken countries undertook financial reforms that gave foreign financial firms an opportunity to purchase local financial companies. Despite a good business opportunity, Japanese financial institutions reduced their FDI. This somewhat unexpected behavior may be explained by their relations with other Japanese firms.

One of the major reasons for Japanese financial companies to invest in Asia was to serve the demand of other Japanese firms. In response to the reduction in the amount of business of other Japanese firms during the crisis, Japanese financial institutions correspondingly cut their FDI in Asia.

There also are many cases in which Japanese firms stepped up their FDI in the wake of the economic crisis. For example, while it was noted above that Japanese transport machinery firms reduced FDI in Asia as a whole, some specific firms actually expanded investment. A case in point is Mitsubishi Motor Company (MMC), which increased capital subscription in Thailand Mitsubishi Motor Company through FDI in August 1997, ostensibly to strengthen managerial capabilities in its subsidiary.[8]

More generally, FDI that increased capital subscription is classified as one type of mergers and acquisitions (M&As), where the equity holding of Japanese firms rose over 50 percent as a result of the increase in capital subscription. This type of M&A by Japanese firms, different from another type of M&A used as a means of new entry, has increased since the economic crisis. According to an investigation conducted by Daiwa Securities, the number of M&As in Asia by Japanese firms from January to September 1998 was sixty, higher than the fifty-seven for the entire year of 1997.[9] The study also showed that M&As by Japanese firms were particularly active in South Korea and in Thailand.

There are at least two reasons why the number of M&As increased after the crisis. First, Japanese parent firms provided financial support to their Asian affiliates, which were faced with a credit crunch and stagnating sales by increasing the equity share of the affiliates. Second, in realizing that FDI could contribute to recovery and sustainable economic growth, Asian economies liberalized FDI policies. Among various measures to attract FDI, the relaxation of restrictions on equity participation was particularly successful. Previously, due to fear of the possible dominance of local market and industry by foreign firms, East Asian governments had strong restrictions on the level of equity participation by foreign firms. In many industries that these governments regarded as important, only minority equity participation was allowed. However, with the relaxation of these restrictions, in many cases majority ownership, and even 100 percent ownership, became possible.

III. Motives behind Japanese FDI in Asia

This section examines closely the motives behind Japanese FDI in Asia by using the results of a questionnaire survey conducted by the Ministry of Economy, Trade and Industry (METI, formerly MITI) of the Japanese government, because these motives influence the patterns of geographical distribution of Japanese FDI.[10] Table 2.5 summarizes the results of the 1998 MITI survey conducted on the motives for Japanese FDI in Asia and the world as a whole.

Expansion of local sales is an important motive for FDI by Japanese firms, regardless of the location of FDI. In particular, this is the most important motive for Japanese FDI in developed countries such as North America. For the Asian affiliates, local sales were an important motive particularly for sectors producing materials used for further processing, such as chemical products, iron and steel, and nonferrous metals. This observation indicates that local suppliers of materials have not been developed and thus Japanese firms have invested in order to meet the demand from material users such as firms in machinery sectors. This also may reflect a close relationship between Japanese material suppliers and users. A sizeable proportion of respondents identified the use of local labor as a motive for FDI in Asia.[11] This observation suggests that Japanese firms have shifted their production base to Asia in order to produce labor-intensive products for exports. Japan has long lost its comparative advantage in labor-intensive products, so Japanese firms are taking advantage of abundant labor in the Asian host countries. Japanese FDI in textiles may be a typical case reflecting such an FDI strategy. Indeed, as many as 29 percent of respondents in textiles, a labor-intensive industry, noted the use of local labor as their motive for FDI in Asia.

Despite the fact that machinery products are capital- and technology-intensive, a substantial proportion of the respondents in the machinery sectors undertook FDI in Asia to take advantage of local labor. This seemingly inconsistent behavior of Japanese firms may be explained by their strategy of breaking up the entire production process into several sub-processes and locating labor-intensive subprocesses in labor-abundant Asian countries.

The use of local labor appears to reflect rational behavior of Japanese firms from the point of view of comparative advantage in Asia. Richly endowed with labor, Asian countries have a comparative advantage in production that requires labor-intensive techniques. This observation points to the differences between the expectation of host countries, on the one hand, and the actual behavior of foreign firms, on the other hand, regarding the types of technologies utilized in the host countries. Host countries would like foreign firms to bring in advanced technologies in hopes of gaining a comparative advantage in high value-added production. Unsurprisingly, foreign firms are generally more interested in exploiting host countries' comparative advantage in labor.

Table 2.5 Motives behind Japanese foreign direct investment in Asia and the World: 1998 (percent)

	World			Asia			North America		
	Local sales	Use of local labor	FDI promotion policies by hosts	Local sales	Use of local labor	FDI promotion policies by hosts	Local sales	Use of local labor	FDI promotion policies by hosts
Total industry	24.2	14.6	7.5	21.4	20.2	9.5	29.3	6.7	3.1
Manufacturing	22.8	18.5	8.9	20.2	23.3	10.5	30.1	8.7	3.7
Food	24.4	17.8	7.3	22.6	26.7	9.9	30.2	6.3	4.8
Textiles	13.4	27.8	8.9	12.5	29.2	8.9	34.5	17.2	6.9
Wood and pulp	14.5	16.3	8.4	19.2	17.7	8.5	13.0	14.8	5.6
Chemical products	26.8	13.1	6.9	25.3	18.0	7.9	32.1	5.7	3.3
Iron and steel	26.3	19.0	8.8	26.4	20.3	10.8	29.0	14.5	0.0
Non-ferrous metals	27.1	18.5	8.2	26.3	22.3	8.0	34.0	5.7	3.8
General machinery	25.4	14.3	6.6	20.9	22.4	8.9	31.1	5.7	2.8
Electric machinery	20.4	20.7	10.4	16.9	25.6	12.2	31.8	6.5	3.7
Transport machinery	25.2	18.2	10.0	25.5	21.8	11.5	25.2	13.2	6.0
Precision instruments	20.2	18.9	8.2	13.0	25.5	11.4	32.3	9.7	1.6
Petro and coal products	25.0	11.4	9.1	21.4	14.3	10.7	28.6	0.0	14.3
Other manufacturing	23.1	18.1	9.2	19.8	22.0	11.4	33.0	10.2	2.2

Note: The figures indicate the percentage share of the firms indicating the motive in total number of surveyed firms. Other motives reported include exports to third countries, exports to Japan, acquisition of raw materials, information collection, and so on.
Source: MITI, *Kaigai Toshi Tōkei Sōran* [Comprehensive Statistics on Japanese Foreign Direct Investment], no. 7, 2001.

FDI promotion policies by host governments appear to have played an important role in attracting Japanese FDI in Asia, since 10 percent of the respondents in manufacturing undertook FDI in response to incentives given to FDI. However, there are some sectoral variations on this issue. For example, the relatively high response rate observed for Japanese machinery firms in Asia reflects the fact that these sectors have been the targets of industrial promotion policies in a number of countries in Asia.

IV. The Problems Encountered by Japanese Firms in Asia

Overseas affiliates of Japanese firms face various problems in conducting their business in the world and in Asia. These problems must be dealt with appropriately by host countries, in particular by host governments, to successfully attract Japanese FDI.

Table 2.6 shows the responses given by Japanese firms as to some of the problems in their overseas operations. Among the problems, tough competition was regarded as the most serious problem by overseas affiliates of Japanese firms regardless of their location. Approximately one out of five affiliates indicated the problem. The problem of tough competition was felt more by the affiliates in North America than those in Asia. Although competition is regarded as a problem by the affiliates, it is not the kind of problem that should be corrected from the point of view of host economies. This is because tough competition brings various benefits to the host economies such as lower product prices and greater productive efficiency.

A comparison of the responses from the affiliates in Asia and those in North America reveals some serious problems that should be taken care of in Asia in order to attract more FDI. Underdevelopment of infrastructure, political instability, a dearth of supporting industries, and high inflation were each regarded as a hindrance by the Asian affiliates. It is important to point out that among manufacturing subsectors, machinery firms in particular (which use a number of parts and components) suffer from a lack of supporting industries (figures are not shown in the table). Approximately one out of twelve affiliates in Asia indicated that shortage of labor was a problem. Indeed, this problem received the largest number of responses, reflecting the severity of the problem. Relatively speaking, however, the affiliates in Asia did not consider this as a serious problem when compared to those in other regions such as North America.

Table 2.6 The problems faced by Japanese firms in Asia and the World: 1998 (percent)

	World								Asia								North America							
	Competition	Political instability	High inflation	Under-developed infra-structure	Under-developed support industries	Shortage of labor			Competition	Political instability	High inflation	Under-developed infra-structure	Under-developed support industries	Shortage of labor			Competition	Political instability	High inflation	Under-developed infra-structure	Under-developed support industries	Shortage of labor		
Total industry	18.0	5.0	4.6	5.8	4.9	8.8			14.4	6.2	5.1	7.4	5.8	8.1			25.9	0.4	1.8	1.3	2.9	11.9		
Manufacturing	15.9	4.9	4.9	6.3	6.0	9.2			13.0	6.1	5.2	7.6	6.6	8.2			24.9	0.4	1.9	1.4	4.0	14.1		
Food	17.0	3.8	4.8	7.0	1.6	11.2			14.1	5.4	6.1	10.4	2.0	8.1			16.2	0.0	1.5	0.7	0.7	16.2		
Textiles	10.7	5.8	6.4	6.7	4.1	7.4			9.3	5.9	6.3	6.8	4.3	7.7			38.9	0.0	0.0	0.0	5.6	22.2		
Wood and pulp	13.2	5.7	5.3	4.5	7.5	7.9			12.2	7.1	5.1	5.6	9.1	7.1			16.2	0.0	0.0	0.0	5.4	10.8		
Chemical products	19.7	4.4	4.8	6.0	3.9	9.1			17.7	6.4	5.9	7.4	4.0	8.3			25.2	0.0	1.7	2.0	2.7	12.1		
Iron and steel	16.8	5.5	4.8	6.3	4.2	9.0			16.0	6.2	4.9	7.4	4.2	7.9			22.1	0.0	1.5	0.0	5.9	16.2		
Non-ferrous metals	19.5	4.2	3.0	6.5	6.2	8.7			16.8	4.9	3.2	7.2	6.4	8.1			50.0	0.0	0.0	0.0	3.1	15.6		
General machinery	17.0	4.2	5.4	7.2	6.3	9.4			12.3	6.0	4.9	8.4	8.5	8.9			30.5	0.9	3.3	1.9	3.8	11.3		
Electric machinery	15.6	4.8	4.5	6.4	6.2	9.7			12.7	5.8	4.6	7.8	7.0	8.6			27.2	0.5	1.9	1.7	3.2	15.0		
Transport machinery	13.3	4.4	4.6	6.1	8.7	9.1			10.5	5.7	5.0	8.1	9.6	7.5			19.4	0.2	1.2	0.5	6.3	16.4		
Precision instruments	16.7	4.6	3.4	5.6	9.3	10.2			11.8	6.3	2.5	6.8	8.9	10.5			32.0	0.0	4.0	0.0	8.0	16.0		
Petro and coal products	32.7	5.5	1.8	7.3	5.5	3.6			18.2	9.1	3.0	9.1	9.1	3.0			75.0	0.0	0.0	0.0	0.0	0.0		
Other manufacturing	17.4	5.8	5.4	6.0	5.6	8.9			14.3	6.9	5.9	7.1	6.0	8.3			26.5	0.7	2.6	2.3	6.0	12.1		

Note: The figures indicate the percentage share of the firms indicating the problem in total number of surveyed firms. Other problems listed include regulations, labor relations, and so on.

Source: MITI, Kaigai Toshi Tokei Soran [Comprehensive Statistics on Japanese Foreign Direct Investment], no. 7, 2001.

V. Responses to the Crisis by Asian Affiliates of Japanese Firms

The Asian economic crisis had a serious impact on Asian affiliates of Japanese firms. A survey by the Export and Import Bank of Japan (1998) shows that more than 80 percent of Asian affiliates experienced an unfavorable impact, and 36.2 percent experienced a very serious impact.[12] There are substantial variations among different industries regarding the seriousness of the impact of the crisis. Because of sharp reduction in domestic demand in Asian countries, domestic market-oriented industries such as automobiles and iron and steel were seriously hurt, while the impact on export-oriented industries such as electrical machinery and textiles was relatively limited. Differences in procurement patterns also affected the postcrisis performance of Asian affiliates of Japanese firms, as those with high local procurement ratios fared better than those with high import procurement ratios. However, these procurement effects were relatively small compared to those coming from sales. This section examines how Asian affiliates of Japanese firms fared in the crisis by focusing on their sales, exports, and employment practices.

The figures in Table 2.7 reveal a substantial decline in the level of sales by Asian affiliates of Japanese manufacturing firms in 1998 and 1999, before recovering in 2000. Aggregate sales declined notably from 100 in 1997, the year of the crisis, to 87.3 in 1998, and further down to 84.1 in 1999, recovering to 95.1 in 2000, which was still five percentage points lower than the level achieved in 1997.

The impact of the crisis on the Asian affiliates of Japanese firms varied widely depending on their locations and sectors. In terms of sales in Japanese yen, manufacturing affiliates in the NIES3 (South Korea, Taiwan, and Singapore) saw their sales declined by 27 percent in 1999 from the 1997 level, while the impacts were less severe for the affiliates in ASEAN4, with a 16 percent decline in sales. In contrast to affiliates in the NIES3 and ASEAN4, the affiliates in China and other Asian countries did not suffer a decline in annual sales.[13]

An examination of the impact across sectors reveals significant variation in sales among the different sectors. For the Asian affiliates as a whole, the affiliates in transport machinery and metal products suffered most seriously as their sales levels declined by more than 30 percent in 1998 from 1997 levels. Their sales levels recovered steadily afterward to 85 percent of 1997 levels in 2000. The experiences of most other manufacturing sectors were less severe, as the declines in their sales levels were around 10 percent, with the exceptions of food and tobacco, ceramics,

Table 2.7 Changes in sales of Asian affiliates of Japanese firms (1997=100)

	1997	1998	1999	2000	1997	1998	1999	2000
	Asia				*NIES3*			
Manufacturing	100	87.3	84.1	95.1	100	83.0	73.4	80.3
Food and tobacco	100	100.2	90.5	91.1	100	89.1	81.3	80.7
Textiles	100	91.0	85.3	86.0	100	93.2	91.0	111.3
Chemicals	100	89.0	82.2	91.4	100	89.1	78.8	84.0
Ceramics, soil, and stone	100	100.1	98.5	123.9	100	92.9	87.0	86.7
Non-ferrous metals	100	85.7	74.6	80.3	100	95.1	81.9	80.2
Metal products	100	67.1	82.8	88.7	100	63.1	81.2	77.3
General Machinery	100	97.2	92.7	108.0	100	85.9	73.8	78.1
Electrical machinery	100	88.9	85.8	98.2	100	78.3	69.0	78.1
Transport machinery	100	66.9	74.8	85.0	100	94.6	90.1	97.7
Precision machinery	100	104.1	77.0	85.8	100	94.6	73.2	77.2
	ASEAN4				*China and other Asia*			
Manufacturing	100	82.7	84.4	97.4	100	105.9	104.1	118.2
Food and tobacco	100	96.6	75.8	71.0	100	139.8	136.9	147.7
Textiles	100	87.2	80.6	81.1	100	100.6	96.2	91.4
Chemicals	100	91.1	88.8	102.3	100	84.5	78.0	89.3
Ceramics, soil, and stone	100	93.6	95.1	141.5	100	130.7	131.9	169.8
Non-ferrous metals	100	68.3	55.6	57.1	100	177.1	197.9	301.0
Metal products	100	56.1	74.6	81.1	100	117.0	118.1	133.9
General Machinery	100	109.5	117.6	154.7	100	99.1	93.5	105.6
Electrical machinery	100	92.0	90.5	103.6	100	106.4	114.4	132.3
Transport machinery	100	52.8	68.4	80.9	100	89.8	75.8	75.3
Precision machinery	100	100.8	82.2	96.1	100	108.6	76.8	85.9

Notes: ASEAN4 are Indonesia, Malaysia, Philippines, and Thailand. NIES3 are South Korea, Singapore, and Taiwan.
Source: MITI (METI since year 2001), *Kigyo Doko Chosa* [Report on Activities of Japanese Firms], various issues.

and precision machinery, which recorded a slight gain in 1998 before recording a decline afterwards.

One observes large variations in the impacts on industries among the different groups of economies. In the ASEAN4 the metal products, non-ferrous metals, and transport machinery sectors experienced a dramatic decline in sales in 1998. In contrast, the general machinery sector was largely unaffected. Indeed, sales value increased notably after the crisis. To a somewhat lesser degree, electrical machinery and chemicals also fared well.

These divergent outcomes across sectors can be explained by their sales orientation. General machinery and electrical machinery, which have high export–sales ratios, performed more favorably than transport machinery, which has a low export-sales ratio (see Table 2.8). One would expect to see these contrasting patterns as a result of devaluation and the economic downturn in Asian economies, as discussed above.

Unlike their experience in the ASEAN4 countries, Japanese transport machinery affiliates performed favorably compared to other sectors in the NIE3. Sales of transport machinery in the NIE3 declined less than 10 percent from the 1997 level after the crisis. Equally favorable sales performance was observed for the textile affiliates, whose sales declined in 1998 and 1999 before registering a sharp increase in 2000. Noting relatively low export–sales ratio for textiles, the rise in sales of textile affiliates in the NIE3 was mainly attributable to the economic recovery in these countries.

Compared to the performance of affiliates in the ASEAN4 or the NIES3, affiliates in China and other Asian countries fared well. However, among the manufacturing subsectors, textiles, chemicals, general machinery, transport machinery, and precision machinery each experienced a decline in their sales at one time or another after the crisis, although the impacts were not so serious as those in the crisis-hit countries. Experiences in other sectors were quite favorable, as their levels of sales increased notably.

Faced with depressed demand and currency depreciation in local markets, one would expect firms to shift their sales from the domestic to the export market. However, the experiences of Asian affiliates of Japanese firms are mixed in this regard. The overall export–sales ratio for these affiliates remained more or less the same throughout the crisis and its aftermath, at around 60 percent. One observes different patterns for the affiliates in different groups of countries. For the affiliates in the ASEAN4, the export–sales ratio increased from 59.5 percent in 1997 to 68.2 percent in 1998 before declining to 61.4 percent in 2000. In contrast, export–sales

Table 2.8 Changes in export–sales ratios for Asian affiliates of Japanese firms (percent)

	1997	1998	1999	2000	1997	1998	1999	2000
	Asia				*NIES3*			
Manufacturing	59.5	61.7	60.2	59.1	57.2	55.9	53.9	53.5
Food and tobacco	45.2	35.6	31.1	30.6	46.5	44.2	40.8	41.2
Textiles	52.3	52.8	51.8	50.6	19.1	21.1	32.9	30.4
Chemicals	45.0	48.9	49.1	49.2	49.9	49.3	51.8	54.1
Ceramics, soil, and stone	43.7	43.2	40.6	42.1	36.9	35.5	36.2	34.2
Non-ferrous metals	40.2	41.4	43.7	40.0	51.5	47.8	50.7	43.6
Metal products	50.6	43.9	36.8	35.9	21.6	19.7	16.6	7.6
General Machinery	73.0	73.2	69.6	67.0	56.5	58.2	54.1	53.5
Electrical machinery	68.1	68.6	68.0	67.5	58.6	56.8	54.9	54.8
Transport machinery	25.2	33.7	30.1	26.2	49.5	49.6	46.6	47.3
Precision machinery	71.3	68.1	73.4	74.7	94.3	92.4	87.8	85.5
	ASEAN4				*China and other Asia*			
Manufacturing	59.5	68.2	64.1	61.4	64.0	59.2	61.6	62.3
Food and tobacco	74.7	49.8	40.1	34.7	6.1	6.7	7.0	10.2
Textiles	55.2	57.5	56.4	55.3	54.9	51.1	47.0	47.0
Chemicals	41.4	49.3	46.7	43.8	39.0	46.5	47.0	49.6
Ceramics, soil, and stone	46.5	52.1	50.4	58.6	52.9	41.7	32.0	21.7
Non-ferrous metals	29.9	39.7	41.4	40.8	49.5	21.4	27.6	30.9
Metal products	58.8	52.3	42.2	41.1	53.3	43.8	40.4	43.6
General Machinery	79.1	77.7	71.6	65.2	81.9	80.1	77.1	75.6
Electrical machinery	76.5	80.8	78.2	76.6	70.9	63.9	67.4	68.2
Transport machinery	14.3	22.7	21.3	14.9	32.7	30.6	29.1	33.9
Precision machinery	80.6	78.5	80.7	79.6	60.1	57.6	66.1	69.5

Notes: ASEAN4 are Indonesia, Malaysia, Philippines, and Thailand. NIES3 are South Korea, Singapore, and Taiwan.
Source: MITI (METI since year 2001), *Kigyo Doko Chosa* [Report on Activities of Japanese Firms], various issues.

ratios declined for affiliates in the NIE3, China, and others. Despite differing changes in the direction of export–sales ratios for the affiliates across country groups, some sectors seem to have similar patterns of change. Specifically, the export–sales ratios for metal products and general machinery declined in all three groups. This observation may reflect a rising local demand for basic materials as a result of economic recovery. For other sectors, the changes in export-sales ratios were quite different among the groups. For example, the export–sales ratio for the nonferrous affiliates in the ASEAN4 rose, while the corresponding ratios for the NIE3, and China and other Asia declined. These contrasting patterns for the affiliates in the different groups may be attributable to the strategies of Japanese firms, under which they attempt to maintain stable levels of sales in Asia by adjusting their export levels.

VI. FDI Strategies of Japanese Firms in Asia in the Coming Years

This section examines the future prospects of Japanese foreign direct investment in Asia. The analysis mainly utilizes the results of three surveys conducted on Japanese firms, two by the Export and Import Bank of Japan (1998 and 1999) and the other by JETRO (1999b).[14] We first examine FDI plans by Japanese firms and then turn to their business strategies in Asia.

FDI Plans

Concerning the future investment plans of Japanese firms, one observes a negative trend over time. According to the survey by the Export and Import Bank of Japan (1999), the share of Japanese firms indicating "expansion" in FDI in the medium-term future declined sharply from 54.0 percent in 1994 to 28.0 percent in 1998, while the corresponding shares indicating "maintaining the same level" and "reduction" increased from 9.9 and 3.1 percent in 1994 to 31.3 and 14.1 percent in 1998, respectively (see Table 2.9). Particularly noticeable is the drastic change from 1997 to 1998, when the future prospects of FDI by Japanese firms deteriorated. The declining trend of future FDI plans by Japanese firms appears to reflect the deterioration of their financial situation, which in turn is due to the prolonged recession in Japan. In addition, financial turmoil and economic recession in Asia and other parts of the world triggered by the Asian economic crisis reduced the attractiveness of FDI in these economies to Japanese firms. One also notes that the existing excess production

Table 2.9 Medium-term prospects of Japanese FDI (percent)

	1994	1995	1996	1997	1998
Expansion	54.0	51.7	49.6	41.3	28.0
Same level	9.9	15.9	13.4	16.6	31.3
Reduction	3.1	6.2	6.7	6.0	14.1
No FDI plans	33.0	26.2	30.4	36.1	26.5
Total	100	100	100	100	100

Note: The firms were asked to give the FDI level in three years in comparison with level of the previous three years.
Source: Export and Import Bank of Japan (1999).

Table 2.10 Medium-term prospects of Japanese FDI by sector (percent)

	1994	1995	1996	1997	1998
Electric/electronic products	22.0	26.0	21.6	20.7	16.8
Chemicals	17.3	15.9	19.2	19.6	17.6
Automobiles	17.3	13.1	12.5	15.6	20.0
General machinery	7.9	11.1	10.1	10.1	11.2
Textiles	4.7	4.3	4.3	5.6	2.4
Others	30.9	29.6	32.3	28.4	32.0
Total	100	100	100	100	100

Note: Medium-term means next three years.
Source: Export and Import Bank of Japan (1999).

capacity in Asia resulting from previously extraordinarily active FDI, fixed investment, and the drastic decline in demand has made Japanese firms hesitant to undertake additional FDI.

Sectoral patterns of the firms with FDI expansion plans did not change much over time, as electric and electronic machinery, chemicals, and automobiles maintained a combined dominant share around 55 percent (see Table 2.10). However, even in these three sectors, the shares of firms indicating future expansion declined over time.

It is important to observe that geographical allocation of planned Japanese FDI did change dramatically over time (see Table 2.11). Asia's share in future Japanese FDI plans declined steadily from 72.4 percent in 1994 to 49.6 percent in 1998, while the shares of the United States/Canada and the European Union increased from 11.4 and 8.6 percent to 18.5 and 15.1 over the same period, respectively. Among the Asian economies, the attractiveness of China and the ASEAN4 to Japanese investors declined substantially. Several reasons may be noted for this decline. First, a number of Japanese firms appear to be of the opinion that they have more or less

Table 2.11 Medium-term prospects of Japanese FDI by region (%)

	1994	1995	1996	1997	1998
Asia	72.4	69.2	65.1	59.3	49.6
China	29.5	24.0	21.1	18.5	17.4
ASEAN4	24.7	23.9	24.0	21.3	16.4
NIE4	10.3	11.2	9.4	9.5	8.1
Other Asia	7.9	10.1	10.6	10.0	7.7
U.S./Canada	11.4	13.4	13.8	14.2	18.5
EU	8.6	9.3	9.9	10.9	15.1
Latin America	4.4	4.7	6.3	8.7	7.3
Others	3.3	3.4	4.9	7.0	9.5
Total	100	100	100	100	100

Note: The geographical distribution of FDI by Japanese firms that indicated an FDI expansion in the next three years.
Source: Export and Import Bank of Japan (1999).

carried out their planned FDI in Asia and that they now need to reformulate their strategies in Asia. Second, as noted above, the current recession in Asia does not provide for good business opportunities. Third, uncertainty in exchange rates for Asian currencies has made it difficult for Japanese firms to commit investment. Still, Japanese companies considered many Asian countries—primarily China—as providing promising investment opportunities (see Table 2.12).

The JETRO survey (see Table 2.13) brings out a more encouraging picture of Japanese FDI in Asia than the survey by the Export–Import Bank of Japan (Table 2.14). According to the JETRO survey, approximately 50 percent of the affiliates of Japanese firms in ASEAN5, Vietnam, South Korea, and China plan to expand their operations, while only 5 percent are considering reduction. There are some variations among the affiliates in different countries, however. A large share of Japanese subsidiaries in China, Vietnam, and the Philippines have expansion plans, while the corresponding share is smaller for those in Singapore, Malaysia, and South Korea (Table 2.13). China remained the most promising economy for future Japanese investment in 1998, although the percentage of Japanese firms that shared this opinion has declined over time. In addition to China, other Asian economies including ASEAN economies ranked high on the list. These cross-country findings more or less agree with those from the survey by the Export and Import Bank of Japan—although in the JETRO survey relatively fewer firms indicated plans to expand investment in Malaysia.

Table 2.12 Ten most promising economies to Japanese FDI

	2000	%	1999	%	1998	%	1997	%	1996	%	1995	%	1994	%
Medium-term (next three years)														
1	China	65	China	55	China	55	China	64	China	68	China	74	China	71
2	U.S.	41	U.S.	39	U.S.	41	U.S.	36	Thailand	36	Thailand	36	Thailand	32
3	Thailand	88	Thailand	27	Thailand	23	Indonesia	28	Indonesia	34	Indonesia	33	U.S.	30
4	Indonesia	15	India	15	Indonesia	16	Thailand	25	U.S.	32	U.S.	32	Indonesia	24
5	Malaysia	12	Indonesia	15	India	15	India	23	Vietnam	27	Vietnam	28	Malaysia	24
6	Taiwan	11	Vietnam	11	Philippines	14	Vietnam	19	Malaysia	20	Malaysia	22	Vietnam	14
7	India	10	Malaysia	9	Malaysia	14	Philippines	14	India	18	India	17	Singapore	14
8	Vietnam	9	Philippines	9	Vietnam	14	Malaysia	13	Philippines	13	Philippines	15	Taiwan	10
9	South Korea	9	U.K.	9	Brazil	11	Brazil	8	Singapore	10	Singapore	10	U.K.	8
10	Philippines	8	Brazil	8	U.K.	8	Taiwan	8	U.K.	7	U.K.	7	Philippines	6
									Taiwan	7			India	6
Long-term (next ten years)														
1	China	70	China	66	China	64	China	73	China	74	China	78	China	93
2	U.S.	38	U.S.	30	U.S.	34	India	36	India	39	Vietnam	41	Vietnam	40
3	India	22	India	27	India	25	U.S.	31	Vietnam	33	India	36	Thailand	32
4	Thailand	21	Thailand	24	Indonesia	20	Vietnam	24	U.S.	31	U.S.	30	U.S. N22	30
5	Indonesia	14	Vietnam	18	Thailand	19	Indonesia	21	Indonesia	24	Indonesia	24	Indonesia	29
6	Vietnam	14	Indonesia	18	Vietnam	18	Thailand	16	Thailand	24	Thailand	24	Malaysia	15
7	Malaysia	10	Brazil	14	Brazil	14	Brazil	11	Malaysia	12	Myanmar	15	India	13
8	Brazil	9	Malaysia	9	Philippines	13	Philippines	11	Myanmar	11	Malaysia	13	Mexico	9
9	U.K.	9	Philippines	9	Malaysia	8	Malaysia	9	Philippines	11	Philippines	11	Singapore	8
10	Taiwan	8	Mexico	7	U.K.	7	Myanmar	6	Mexico	6	U.K.	6	Taiwan	7
													Philippines	7

Source: Japan Bank for International Cooperation (2001).

Table 2.13 Prospects of future operations in Asia by Japanese firms

	Number of responses	Percentage shares				
		Total	Expansion	Remain the same	Reduction	Withdrawal
Total	1758	100	51.7	42.4	5.0	0.9
ASEAN5	1053	100	45.8	47.4	5.7	1.1
Thailand	264	100	49.6	44.3	5.7	0.4
Malaysia	310	100	42.3	50.3	6.1	1.3
Singapore	109	100	31.2	52.3	10.1	6.4
Indonesia	264	100	47.3	47.3	5.3	0.0
Philippines	106	100	57.5	41.5	0.9	0.0
Vietnam	79	100	58.2	38.0	2.5	1.3
South Korea	61	100	42.6	49.2	8.2	0.0
China	493	100	61.1	34.3	4.1	0.6

Source: JETRO (1999b).

Table 2.14 Export and local procurements of Asian affiliates of Japanese firms: 1998 (percent)

	Export–sales ratios			Local procurement rratios		
	Present	Future plans		Present	Future plans	
		1–3 years	3–5 years		1–3 years	3–5 years
Chemicals	42.5	41.4	38.3	44.8	46.7	50.9
Electronic products	42.5	47.7	51.5	44.4	50.0	56.3
Electronic parts	50.7	57.4	58.4	41.8	34.1	34.0
Automobiles	12.7	16.6	18.5	55.6	55.6	56.6
Auto parts	17.2	23.9	27.0	49.1	57.8	60.4

Source: Export and Import Bank of Japan (1998).

Although comparing the results of two different surveys is tricky because their coverage is different, one gets the impression that future prospects of FDI by Japanese firms in Asia improved with passage of time since the crisis. The results of the survey by Export and Import Bank of Japan (1998) show that it would take about ten years for most Japanese firms to recover to their precrisis FDI levels in 1997. These views appear quite pessimistic, compared to the results of the JETRO survey, which was conducted about seven months later. These changes in attitude toward more optimistic future FDI plans appear to result from the speedy recovery taking place in Asia. By recognizing the importance of future economic prospects for making FDI plans, one may find that Japanese firms, along with firms from other countries, will invest aggressively once Asian economies get back on a rapid growth path.

FDI Motives, Business Strategies, and Problems

As we saw earlier, motives for investing in China and other Asian economies include local market sales and export to Japan and other countries. There are differences in the importance of these motives among Asian economies. As one would expect from the size of the domestic market, the local sales motive is stronger for FDI in China while export expansion is relatively more important in Thailand, Malaysia, and the Philippines. As trade liberalization is likely to proceed in the future in various guises, the export motive is likely to increase in importance.

The Asian economic crisis clearly affected the business strategies of Japanese firms in Asia. As discussed in Section V, the Asian economic crisis generally brought serious hardships to firms oriented toward local markets and dependent on imports for the procurement of parts and components. To protect themselves in the event of future financial crises, many Japanese firms have developed plans to increase export-orientation in their sales and local procurement of parts and components. According to Table 2.14, Japanese firms in the electronics and automobile sectors plan to increase the share of exports in their sales in their subsidiaries in Asia. Japanese electronics firms, which already exhibit a high export–sales ratio of approximately 40 to 50 percent, plan to increase these ratios to 50 to 60 percent in the next few years. The firms in the automobile sector with lower export–sales ratios around 15 percent plan to increase these ratios to 20 to 30 percent over the next few years. The business strategy of increasing export–sales ratios by the Japanese firms in the electronics and automobiles sectors in Asia indicates extension and intensification of an intrafirm, interprocess division of labor.[15] Under this system, an entire production process is divided into subprocesses that are located in an economy in which that particular process can be performed most efficiently. For example, an electronics firm may set up a semiconductor plant in Taiwan, a Braun tube factory in Thailand, and a TV assembly plant in Malaysia. To produce TVs, semiconductors and Braun tubes are exported to an assembly plant in Malaysia in the form of intrafirm trade.

In addition to pursuing intrafirm division of labor in Asia, Japanese firms are keen on reducing the cost of production in Asia to improve the price competitiveness of their products. At the same time, in their longer-term plans a number of Japanese firms would like to improve the quality of their products and to diversify their product lines in Asia. To achieve these somewhat contradictory goals, some Japanese firms have set up R&D facilities in Asia to develop new products that are well suited to local demand.

To avoid an increase in the cost of imported components as a result of currency devaluation, Japanese firms in Asia plan to increase local procurement. The results of the survey shown in Table 2.14 show that all the sectors surveyed except electronic parts plan to increase the share of local procurement to the 50 to 60 percent level in the next few years from 40 to 50 percent level at present. Electronic parts producers, by contrast, plan to reduce the local procurement ratio from 41.8 percent at present to 34 percent over the same period. Two factors may explain this somewhat unexpected result. First, the technical capability of local suppliers in the electronic parts sector is very low and Asian affiliates of Japanese firms in that sector do not expect their capabilities to improve in the near future. Indeed, in the face of rapid technological progress in that sector, they may expect local procurement ratios to decline. Second, Japanese firms in electronic parts production may see freer trade in electronic components in the future, possibly as a result of the WTO agreement on information technology trade, and thus they plan to increase procurement from foreign countries.

The discussion of local procurement elucidates the shortage of local technical capability as one of the major problems encountered by Japanese and other foreign firms operating in Asia. There are other problems as well. According to the survey by Export and Import Bank of Japan (1999), more than 50 percent of Japanese firms operating in China point out the "legal system," "infrastructure," and "tax system" as problematic. In addition, a lack of transparency in its FDI policies is said to cause problems for doing business in China. For Japanese firms doing business in Thailand, the Philippines, and Malaysia, wide fluctuations in currency values are the most serious problem. A lack of political stability has made Japanese firms' operation difficult in Indonesia. Underdeveloped infrastructure is a serious obstacle for Japanese firms in many Asian economies, particularly in Vietnam and India.

VII. Japan's Trade with Asia

So far, we have examined Japan's foreign direct investment in Asia. Besides FDI, foreign trade has been an important means of utilizing firms' competitiveness overseas. For example, a multinational firm has a choice between exports and FDI to serve a foreign market. As it is well known in the FDI literature, FDI is likely to be chosen when the locational advantage of overseas production is substantially large. Although this argument treats export and FDI as substitutes, it is often the case that they are complements rather than substitutes. One such example is when an overseas affiliate set up by FDI imports equipment for production from its parent company. In such a case FDI results in an expansion of imports in the host country from the home country. If an overseas affiliate exports its products to its parent company, an expansion in exports from the host country to home country takes place. In both cases FDI and foreign trade are complements.[16] Keeping these close relationships between FDI and trade in mind, we examine the changes in Japan's foreign trade with Asia.

Table 2.15 shows Japan's exports and imports with Asian economies. Japan's trade with Asia increased substantially from 1990 to 1999. Specifically, Japan's exports and imports with Asia increased approximately 1.8-fold during the period, respectively. Since these rates of growth were greater than those for its trade with the world, which increased approximately 1.5-fold over the same period, the share of Asia for Japan's overall exports and imports increased from 29.8 and 29.1 percent in 1990 to 35.8 and 37.6 percent in 1999. The increase in the share

Table 2.15 Japan's trade with Asia

$million	Value ($million)				Share (%)			
	Exports		Imports		Exports		Imports	
	1990	1999	1990	1999	1990	1999	1990	1999
World	287,664	417,442	207,609	309,745	100.0	100.0	100.0	100.0
East Asia	85,728	149,433	60,502	116,532	29.8	35.8	29.1	37.6
NIE4	57,342	90,088	30,272	36,055	19.9	21.6	14.6	11.6
South Korea	17,499	22,957	12,638	16,084	6.1	5.5	6.1	5.2
Taiwan	15,998	28,831	8,338	12,771	5.6	6.9	4.0	4.1
Hong Kong	13,106	22,034	4,680	1,780	4.6	5.3	2.3	0.6
Singapore	10,739	16,265	4,616	5,420	3.7	3.9	2.2	1.7
ASEAN4	22,241	36,009	21,020	37,596	7.7	8.6	10.1	12.1
Malaysia	5,529	11,099	4,506	10,899	1.9	2.7	2.2	3.5
Thailand	9,150	11,292	3,969	8,838	3.2	2.7	1.9	2.9
Philippines	2,510	8,742	1,622	5,299	0.9	2.1	0.8	1.7
Indonesia	5,052	4,877	10,923	12,560	1.8	1.2	5.3	4.1
China	6,145	23,336	9,210	42,881	2.1	5.6	4.4	13.8
U.S.	91,121	128,089	48,585	66,942	31.7	30.7	23.4	21.6
EU	58,701	74,281	30,911	42,634	20.4	17.8	14.9	13.8

Source: JETRO.

of Asia for Japan's trade contrasts with the decline in the shares of NAFTA and the EU over the same period.

The preceding findings indicate an increasing importance of Asia for Japan's trade in the 1990s. It is remarkable once one realizes that many Asian economies suffered seriously from the impact of the economic crisis in the late 1990s. Among different groups of countries in Asia, the NIE4 maintained a large share in Japan's exports of around 20 percent through the 1990s. The shares of ASEAN4 and China increased from 7.7 and 2.1 percent in 1990 to 8.6 and 5.6 percent in 1999, respectively. The changing patterns on the shares of these groups in Japan's imports were significantly different. The share of the NIE4 in Japan's total imports declined from 14.6 percent in 1990 to 11.6 percent in 1999, while the corresponding shares for the ASEAN4 and China increased from 10.1 and 4.4 percent to 12.1 and 13.8 percent during the same period, respectively. As a result of these changes, the shares of the NIE4, ASEAN4, and China in Japan's total imports became similar in 1999.

A comparison of the importance of Asia in Japanese FDI and Japanese trade reveals an interesting finding. Although not shown in the table, Asia and its subgroups have significantly larger shares in Japanese trade than in Japanese FDI. The shares of Asia, the NIE4, ASEAN4, and China in Japanese total (manufacturing) FDI were 10.2 (9.7), 4.8 (3.9), 4.3 (4.5), and 1.1 (1.3) percent, respectively in 1999, which were significantly smaller when compared to the case for Japanese exports. The contrasting patterns can be identified for Japanese trade and FDI relationships with the United States and the EU. That is, their shares in Japanese FDI are significantly larger than their corresponding shares in Japanese exports.

Several reasons may be identified to explain the lower importance of Asia in Japanese FDI than in Japanese exports. First, geographical proximity is a factor that promotes trade with Asian countries, as the cost of transportation plays an important role in foreign trade but not in FDI. Second, restrictions on FDI in Asia in comparison with those in developed countries discouraged Japanese FDI in Asia. Although substantial FDI liberalization has taken place, the FDI regime is still more restrictive in Asia than in developed countries. Third, risks involved with FDI in Asia are significantly higher when compared to those in developed countries. Since FDI entails significant risks, firms hesitate to undertake FDI in risky countries, in terms of political as well as commercial risks. These findings indicate that there is potential for Asian countries to increase FDI inflows from Japan, but at the same time these findings point out the need on the part of Asian countries to remove obstacles to FDI in order to attract it.

VIII. Conclusion

Faced with the Asian economic crisis and its aftermath, Japanese firms generally reduced their foreign direct investment in Asia. The precarious financial positions of Japanese firms and tight borrowing conditions in Japan have contributed to a decline in FDI by Japanese firms. Still, a large number of Japanese firms consider Asia as a very promising destination of their FDI in the future, as they see bright economic prospects for the region. Accordingly, many observers expect Japanese FDI in Asia to recover and to increase, perhaps not at the rapid rate of the latter half of the 1980s but at a rate similar to that in the mid-1990s. Two surveys conducted by the Export and Import Bank and by JETRO appear to support such a view.

Although not captured in the surveys noted above, it appears that Japanese FDI in Asia is going to change both qualitatively and quantitatively. To begin with the quantitative change, one should note that the prodigious Japanese FDI in the second half of the 1980s resulted from the emergence of very special circumstances, including the appreciation of the yen and the bubble economy in Japan, and the liberalization of FDI regimes in recipient countries. Since such special circumstances are not likely to reemerge, it seems reasonable to assume that Japanese FDI is not going to easily regain previous heights.

Another reason that Japanese FDI does not appear likely to increase much in the future is that Japanese firms are paying more attention to the quality (i.e., profitability) of their investments. Faced with the unfavorable performance of their operations in Asia because of the economic crisis, many Japanese firms have started to reevaluate and reformulate their past FDI strategies in Asia. Large Japanese firms have undertaken this exercise as a part of the broader reassessment of their global strategies. Based on these reassessments, many Japanese firms are planning to rationalize their FDI in Asia by reducing or in some cases closing their unprofitable operations. These moves have been accelerated by the introduction of a new accounting practice in April 2000, under which consolidated financial statements of large Japanese corporations, including the financial performance of their affiliates, must be prepared.

Actual and expected trade and FDI liberalization in Asia under the framework of APEC and the WTO is also likely to push Japanese firms to rationalize their operations in Asia. Under liberalized trade and FDI regimes firms would benefit from scale economies, which may be realized by rationalizing their FDI operations. This does not mean that all production processes would be consolidated into one location.

More likely a particular subprocess would be centered in one location from which it could be carried out most efficiently. Indeed, this development is already taking place in the electronics sector, and will likely spread to other sectors such as automobiles. Thus, competition in developing Asia to attract FDI is likely to be tougher in the future as a result of the trade and FDI liberalization in the region. Under such circumstances, the gap in economic performance between successful and unsuccessful economies in attracting FDI is likely to widen.

To attract FDI as a means of promoting economic growth, economies must provide a suitable environment. Specifically, previous studies on the determinants of FDI (and economic growth) have shown the importance of a stable macroeconomic environment, educational and training systems for improving the quality of human resources, well-functioning markets with effective legal systems, efficient and reliable transportation and communication systems, and a stable supply of electricity, among others. Finally, it should be emphasized that availability of high-quality human resources—which should be nurtured through Asian countries' own means as well as the wise allocation of foreign assistance—is crucial for the successful acquisition and assimilation of technology that foreign firms bring to the recipient economies.

Notes

1. I would like to thank Vinod K. Aggarwal and Ed Fogarty for their comments on earlier versions of this article.
2. IMF, *Balance of Payments Statistics,* various issues.
3. UNCTAD (1999).
4. This analysis provides the context for the case studies, which are based on the theoretical framework developed in Chapter 1, by Vinod K. Aggarwal, of this volume. Urata (1998) examines the patterns of overall FDI in East Asia in the precrisis period.
5. PECC (1999) reports that many APEC economies liberalized their FDI regimes. It also points out that liberalization mainly came in the form of market access, and not in the form of reduction in performance requirements such as local content requirements.
6. Urata (2001) analyzes the mechanism of economic growth in East Asia during the mid-1980s through the mid-1990s, and he argues that the formation of the trade-FDI nexus is one of the most important factors.
7. In their study of the locational determinants of Japanese firms, Urata and Kawai (2000) found those countries with low macroeconomic risk in terms of variations in exchange rate and inflation are important "pull" factors for Japanese FDI. In addition to the low economic risks, they also found that low wages, well-developed infrastructure, agglomeration, and good governance are important factors for attracting Japanese FDI.
8. JETRO (1999a).
9. Ibid.
10. The METI (formerly MITI) conducts a comprehensive survey of overseas activities of Japanese firms every three years starting 1980. The results of the survey are published under the title of

Kaigai Toshi Tokei Soran [Comprehensive Survey of Overseas Activities of Japanese Firms]. In the 1998 survey, a questionnaire was sent to 3,841 Japanese multinationals, 2,151 of whom responded. The respondents covered the activities of 13,017 overseas affiliates. The METI also conducts an annual survey with the more limited number of questions except for the years of Comprehensive Survey. The results of the survey are published under the title of *Wagakuni Kigyo no Kaigai Jigyo Katsudo* [Overseas Activities of Japanese Firms]. Motives of FDI are asked in the comprehensive surveys but not in the annual surveys.

11. There are some variations regarding the importance of securing inexpensive labor as an FDI motive among the Asian countries. The results of its survey of Japanese multinationals by the Export and Import Bank of Japan (1996) reveal that as many as 60 percent of the affiliates in China, Indonesia, Vietnam, India, and the Philippines noted securing inexpensive labor as one of their motives behind their establishment, while the corresponding figures are much smaller for the affiliates in Thailand, Malaysia, Singapore and others.
12. Japan Export and Import Bank was merged with Overseas Economic Cooperation Fund to become Japan Bank for International Cooperation on October 1, 1999.
13. It should be reminded that the figures in Table 2.7 are on yearly basis. The patterns of sales are different when they are measured on monthly or quarterly basis. For example, based on quarterly data, even the affiliates in China and other Asia suffered a decline in sales after the crisis.
14. One survey by the Export and Import Bank of Japan (1998) was conducted to examine the impact of the Asian economic crisis on Japanese manufacturing firms in May–July 1998. The questionnaire was sent to 259 firms, and responses were received from 157 firms. The other survey by the Export and Import Bank of Japan (1999) of 749 manufacturing firms with more than three overseas affiliates in July–August 1998, and responses from 445 firms were obtained. This is the last survey in a series of annual surveys by the Export and Import Bank of Japan, which started in 1989. The survey has continued after the Export and Import Bank of Japan was merged with the Overseas Economic Cooperation Fund to become Japan Bank for International Cooperation in 1999. However, the questions asked changed substantially so that it is difficult to undertake a time-series comparison. Because of this reason, the results of the more recent 2000 survey are not used in detail. In the survey by JETRO, questionnaires were sent out to 5,518 manufacturing affiliates of Japanese firms in nine Asian countries (five ASEAN countries, South Korea, China, Vietnam, and India) in November–December 1998; 1,794 responses were received.
15. For the discussions on intrafirm division of labor and intrafirm trade, for example, see Urata (1993).
16. In their analysis of Japanese trade and FDI, Kawai and Urata (1998) find that they are complements in many industries.

References

Export and Import Bank of Japan (1996). "EXIM Japan FY 1998 Survey: The Outlook of Japanese Foreign Direct Investment," *Journal of Research Institute for International Investment and Development* 22(1) (January/February).

Export and Import Bank of Japan (1998). "The Effects of Asian Crisis on Japan's Manufacturing FDI: Based on the Research Survey to 259 Japanese Major Manufacturing Firms," *Journal of Research Institute for International Investment and Development* 24(9) (September/October).

Export and Import Bank of Japan (1999). "EXIM Japan FY 1998 Survey: The Outlook of Japanese Foreign Direct Investment: The Asian Crisis and the Prospects of Foreign Direct Investment by Japanese Manufacturers," *Journal of Research Institute for International Investment and Development* 25(1) (January/February).

Japan Bank for International Cooperation (2001). "Japanese Manufacturing Companies Show Intention to Expand Overseas Operations as They Continue Domestic and International Management Reformation at Brisk Pace: The Results of FY 2000 Survey," *Journal of Research Institute for Development and Finance* 5 (January).

JETRO (1999a). JETRO *Toshi Hakusho*. White Paper on Foreign Direct Investment in the World and in Japan, Tokyo.
JETRO (1999b). *Zai Ajia Nikkei Kigyo Katsudo Jittai Chosa*. Report on the Activities of Japanese Firms in Asia, Tokyo.
Kawai, Masahiro and Shujiro Urata (1998). "Are Trade and Direct Investment Substitutes or Complements? An Analysis of the Japanese Manufacturing Industry," *Economic Development and Cooperation in the Pacific Basin: Trade, Investment, and Environmental Issues*. Hiro Lee and David W. Rowland-Holst (Cambridge: Cambridge University Press).
Pacific Economic Cooperation Conference (PECC) (1999). *Assessing APEC Individual Action Plans and Their Contribution to APEC's Goals* (Manila: Pacific Economic Cooperation Conference).
United Nations Conference on Trade and Development (UNCTAD) (1992). *World Investment Report* (New York and Geneva: United Nations Conference on Trade and Development).
United Nations Conference on Trade and Development (UNCTAD) (1999). *World Investment Report* (New York and Geneva: United Nations Conference on Trade and Development).
United Nations Conference on Trade and Development (UNCTAD) (2000). *World Investment Report* (New York and Geneva: United Nations Conference on Trade and Development).
Urata, Shujiro (1993). "Japanese Foreign Direct Investment and Its Effect on Foreign Trade in Asia." Takatoshi Ito and Anne O. Krueger in *Trade and Protectionism* (Chicago: University of Chicago Press for NBER).
Urata, Shujiro (1998). "Foreign Direct Investment and APEC." In *Asia-Pacific Crossroads: Regime Creation and the Future of APEC*. Vinod K. Aggarwal and Charles E. Morrison (New York: St. Martin's Press).
Urata, Shujiro (2001). "Emergence of an FDI-Trade Nexus and Economic Growth in East Asia," *Rethinking the East Asian Miracle*. Joseph Stiglitz and Shahid Yusuf (New York: Oxford University Press).
Urata, Shujiro and Hiroki Kawai (2000). "The Determinants of the Location of Foreign Direct Investment by Japanese Small and Medium-sized Enterprises," *Small Business Economics* 15.

PART TWO

Case Studies

CHAPTER THREE

Banking on East Asia: Expansion and Retrenchment of Japanese Firms

MASAHIRO KAWAI, YUZURU OZEKI, AND
HIROSHI TOKUMARU[1]

I. Introduction

The Japanese banking sector is now going through major consolidation, reorganization, and restructuring on a scale unprecedented in its history, all against a background of an increasingly market-oriented policy environment and more deregulated and globalized financial markets. This process was set in motion and propelled along by the recent domestic and external shocks—that is, the asset disinflation at home that started in the early 1990s and led to the systemic banking crisis in 1997–1998, and the East Asian financial crisis that began in 1997 and deepened in 1998.

The focus of this chapter is Japanese bank operations in developing East Asia. In documenting the behavior and strategy of Japanese banks in East Asia over the two crises, we show that they have been intrinsically linked with financial developments at home and in the region. Namely, they had a major role in East Asia's economic growth and expansion in the 1980s and 1990s until the eruption of the regional financial crisis and the rapid contraction of credit and economic activity during the crisis. When the crisis-affected economies opened their domestic financial markets to foreign strategic investors for private recapitalization and upgrading of skills and management, many non-Asian financial institutions rushed in. Japanese banks, by contrast, have been unable to participate because of serious domestic difficulties and as a result, their relative presence in the region has diminished substantially.

Naturally, the Japanese banking sector, as well as its monetary authorities, had a critical stake in the outcome of the crisis. The banking sector's approach to crisis management, although never fully articulated, was suggestive of the revival of the Japanese traditional administrative policy often called the "convoy" scheme. For example, some major Japanese banks advocated nonmarket solutions such as exchange rate and interest payment guarantees to be provided either by the international financial institutions (IFIs), including the International Monetary Fund (IMF), the World Bank, and the Asian Development Bank (ADB), or by their own government as part of regional crisis management. However, these banks rejected another type of nonmarket solution, partial debt forgiveness on a unilateral and uniform basis, arguing that it would further damage their capital positions and create a moral hazard on the part of the borrowers. These nonmarket solutions were never adopted. Instead, with a massive infusion of public funds and the institutional reform programs supported by the Washington-based IFIs and the ADB, the regional financial markets began to recover (with the exception of Indonesia) from a systemic collapse, when many analysts feared recovery would not happen so soon. Markets also forced creditors to accept reductions of asset values to lower, more realistic levels. In the end, reform-oriented market outcomes prevailed, albeit at the cost of a deep recession. This raises the following questions: Why did the reform-oriented market outcomes prevail over the interventionist nonmarket solutions? In what sense was the latter an expedient but suboptimal outcome in the long run?

We analyze the process of consolidation and restructuring of the Japanese banking sector in the 1990s and its impact on their operations in East Asia. We find that the banks' strategic and operational focus has been shifting to the domestic financial markets where the battle for survival has become very serious. Banks are now completing mergers and integration in search of new core competencies in such areas as investment banking, e-finance, cash management services, asset management, structured finance and securitization, and high-skill, fee-based services (a *sine qua non* for survival in the future) in addition to the traditional commercial banking business based on client relationships. Meanwhile, the banks' East Asian operations are diminishing in a dramatic turnaround from the phenomenal expansion observed up to 1997, although the banks' East Asia focus is said to be intact. We argue that East Asian operations are now left up to each bank's individual strategy, which has in most cases not yet been defined, thus creating considerable uncertainty about their future operations in the region.

The chapter is organized as follows. Section II summarizes the expansion and contraction of Japanese banking activity abroad in the 1980s and 1990s and the evolution of the Japanese banking system crisis at home in the 1990s. Section III examines the strategic response of Japanese banks to the East Asian financial crisis of 1997–1998 and how their nonmarket approaches failed. Section IV discusses the way in which Japanese banks are responding to the new market environment by consolidating their activities in the domestic and foreign (particularly East Asian) markets through mergers, integration, and alliances. Section V provides a brief overview of the business activities, with a focus on East Asian operations, of the big four financial groups that are expected to dominate the Japanese banking industry. Section VI provides a summary of the chapter.

II. Positional Analysis/Market Environment

Market Environment

An Overview of International Operations since the 1980s

The Japanese banking sector expanded overseas operations at a phenomenal pace in the 1980s on the back of a buoyant stock market, abundant liquidity, low interest rates, and active investment by the private sector. Japanese banks conducted international financial intermediation on a large scale through short-term borrowing from offshore markets and long-term lending. By the late 1980s, the world's top ten banks in asset size were Japanese.[2] The expansion occurred *pari passu* with multinational firms' foreign direct investment (FDI) and institutional investors' portfolio investment mainly in the U.S. and European markets. The banking sector's external borrowing exceeded lending, resulting in substantial inflows of capital on net.[3]

However, in a sharp turnaround from the expansion in the previous decade, the 1990s have witnessed a general contraction of Japanese banks' international financial intermediation. They contracted and virtually halted international financial intermediation by reducing both external assets and liabilities—that is, making fewer external loans and paying off loans faster than accumulating external debts, resulting in net outflows for the banking sector. The credit retrenchment was touched off by the collapse in the Japanese asset and property markets that began in the early 1990s, eroding banks' capital base and portfolio quality, raising the cost of funding, and eventually causing a credit crunch at home.

The expansion of Japanese banks' international operations in the 1980s and the early 1990s was reflected in the rising number of overseas branches. The number of Japanese bank branches overseas expanded in the 1980s and continued to expand until the mid-1990s. The total number of bank branches rose to 309 in 1990 and reached its peak of 402 in 1995. However, the number generally began to decline in 1996, mirroring the decline already observed in North America and Europe in 1994. The expansion was most dramatic in Asia, where the upward trend continued until 1997, the year of the outbreak of the East Asian financial crisis. The recent reduction of the number of branches in Asia, although not insignificant, has been relatively modest in comparison to other regions. Beginning in the mid-1980s, Japanese banks adopted an East Asia-oriented overseas operational strategy that reflected the regional expansion of overseas operations in Japanese firms. The expansion of bank operations in East Asia continued well into the 1990s, while banks severely curtailed their exposure in the United States and in Europe.

The BIS data indicates that Japanese banks' exposure in five East Asian countries—Indonesia, South Korea, Malaysia, the Philippines, and Thailand—rose by over 80 percent between 1993 and 1996, of which exposure in Thailand rose the sharpest (130 percent) followed by South Korea (100 percent) (see Figure 3.1). Meanwhile, Japanese banks' exposure in Hong Kong rose relatively modestly by 25 percent between 1993 and its peak in 1995, and declined by mid-1998 by about 40 percent from the level in 1993. Exposure to Singapore followed a similar trend. Thus, one

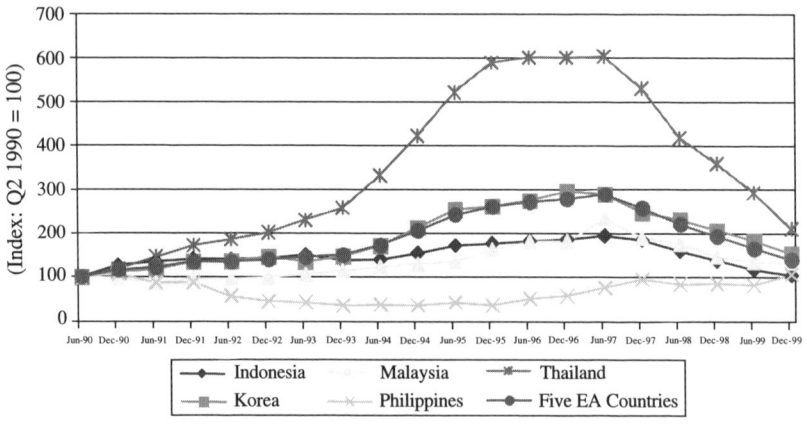

Figure 3.1 Japanese banks' exposure to Asia

Source: BIS, *Consolidated International Banking Statistics*.

can observe two main trends in Japanese overseas banking operations in the 1990s:

a. phenomenal expansion in exposure to East Asia amid the overall retrenchment in overseas lending and borrowing by Japanese banks; and
b. within East Asia, a trend of diversification from the conventional wholesale banking in regional financial centers such as Hong Kong and Singapore to direct lending to other East Asian countries such as China, South Korea, Malaysia, and Thailand.

What drove Japanese bank expansion in East Asia in the precrisis period? And what caused the diversification of East Asian operations from wholesale banking to direct lending to client countries? The yen appreciation that began in the mid-1980s was a driving force behind expanding manufacturing FDI into the region, and the Japanese banks followed their manufacturing clients by expanding their own operations to support them. Japanese FDI fueled regional growth, further enhancing the economic prospects of the region. This process coincided with the liberalization of FDI inflows and banking services in the regional economies.[4] The outward-oriented growth performance of East Asia, accompanied by sound macroeconomic policies, stimulated FDI inflows into the region. In addition, cross-border bank loans expanded sharply in the mid-1990s. With the domestic credit market beginning to stagnate and the U.S. and European markets becoming too saturated, the Japanese banks expanded their East Asian operations in the 1990s in an attempt to seize an opportunity.

The correlation between FDI and the exchange rate movements is well documented in the literature.[5] Indeed, Japanese FDI began to accelerate in the mid-1980s *pari passu* with the value of the yen (Figure 3.2). FDI picked up again beginning in 1994 on the back of an appreciating yen. To some extent, these co-movements reflect exchange rate valuations as Japanese FDI was funded with yen sources. Nevertheless, it is clear that there were volume changes in parallel with exchange rate changes. What is interesting is that the correlation extends to banking sector capital flows as well as banks' overseas lending activities. An appreciating yen had a positive effect on banks' overseas operations through FDI as banks tried to finance investments and support the businesses of Japanese-affiliated firms. Moreover, as the yen appreciated, it increased the capital adequacy ratios, giving banks room for further credit expansion.

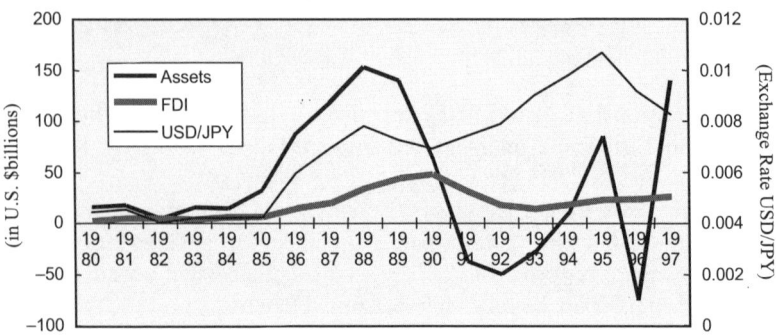

Figure 3.2 Japan: FDI, banking sector flow and exchange rate
Source: IMF, *International Financial Statistics*.

Domestic Banking Sector Crisis in Japan

The Japanese banks' stellar performance in the second half of the 1980s underwent a dramatic turnaround in the early 1990s. During the second half of the 1980s, bank credit expanded against a background of robust growth, a stable price level, and an expansionary monetary policy. The phenomenal expansion of credit during the second half of the 1980s created an asset bubble, as the regulatory framework was underdeveloped and the corporate governance was weak, setting the stage for a financial crisis. An important factor that contributed to the bubble was the deregulation of capital, which raised a substantially larger portion of Japanese banks' funding requirements in the domestic and euro bond markets. This development, along with other deregulation—for example, the lifting of interest rate controls and of restrictions on nonbank lending—intensified competition among banks and depressed interest rate spreads. In response, banks expanded into riskier lending such as consumer loans, real estate loans, and small- and medium-enterprise (SME) lending where the regulatory and supervisory framework proved to be woefully inadequate. The bubble burst as the government abruptly tightened its monetary policy and restricted real estate loans in the early 1990s.[6]

Stock prices peaked at the end of 1989, and began to collapse in the following two years, losing more than half of their value by early 1992. Land values also started to fall soon after, losing close to 20 percent of their value by 1992.[7] The banks' nonperforming loans (NPLs) increased as real estate prices collapsed and their loan portfolios deteriorated, reflecting the nature of traditional collateral-based loans rather than cash-flow based loans. Moreover, the banks' capital base was eroded as their real estate and stock holdings lost a substantial part of their values,

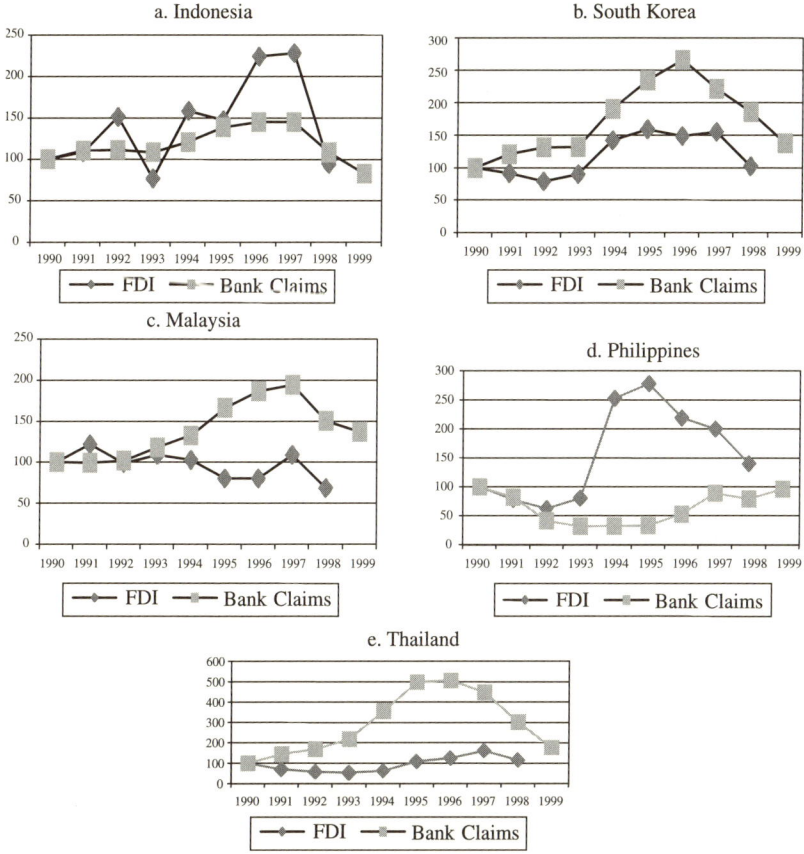

Figure 3.3 Japan: bank claims and FDI into East Asia (index: 1990=100)

Note: FDI represents the accumulated amount since 1951.

Sources: Ministry of Finance, Japan, *Annual Report of International Finance*, BIS, *Consolidated International Banking Statistics*.

prompting banks to call in loans to remain in conformity with the Basil capital adequacy guideline. Coincidentally, the Bank for International Settlements (BIS) announced in 1989 and implemented in 1992 the guideline on risk-weighted capital adequacy that prompted the retrenchment of banks' lending operations globally. The Japanese banks' credit squeeze was observed on the external lending side first, whereas the squeeze on domestic lending was more gradual with the rate of credit growth slowing over the first half of the 1990s, turning negative thereafter. Meanwhile, in order to replenish their capital base, eroded by provisioning and write-offs, banks liquidated their once considerable "hidden reserves" by selling their holdings of real estate, bonds, and stocks.

Impact of the Asian Financial Crisis

The East Asian financial crisis of 1997–1998 dealt the Japanese banking sector another strong external shock just as the sector had begun to adjust to the domestic asset disinflation. Almost simultaneously with the outbreak of the regional crisis in 1997, Japanese banks, along with U.S. and European banks, sharply reduced their exposure in East Asia. They later clamored for public intervention in resolving the crisis, fearing for their solvency as the domestic and regional crises juxtaposed to threaten the soundness of their capital base.

Volatile swings of capital flows characterized the period before and during the financial crisis in East Asia. FDI and portfolio flows were relatively stable while a boom and bust cycle occurred in banking sector flows, in which Japanese banks played a prominent role. The cycle was most pronounced in Thailand, from a net inflow equal to 11 percent of GDP in 1996 to a net outflow of 11 percent and 13 percent of GDP in 1997 and 1998, respectively. South Korea also registered a net inflow of 5 percent of GDP in 1996 to a net outflow of 2 percent in 1997–1998 (see Table 3.1). Indonesia registered a net inflow of 5 percent of GDP in 1996 and a net outflow of 11 percent in 1998. A similar cycle was observed in Malaysia and the Philippines, but was more moderate.

The BIS data indicate that Japanese banks accounted for about half of the banking sector outflows from Indonesia during 1997 and the first half of 1998, one third of outflows from Thailand, and one quarter of outflows from South Korea. Those amounts were significantly less than commensurate with their shares in credit exposure to those countries among foreign banks, suggesting that in the initial stage of the crisis U.S. and European banks withdrew proportionately larger amounts of credit from those three countries. However, Japanese banks continued to withdraw credit well into 1999, particularly sharply in Thailand, when U.S. and European banks' exposure in the region leveled off.

Thus, the timing of withdrawal of credit by Japanese and other banks differed from one another. Japanese bank loans to the region began to decline in the second half of 1997, and the pace of decline was steady thereafter through 1998. However, the reduction continued throughout 1999. U.S. banks began to reduce loans to the five Asian countries prior to the outbreak, subsequently reducing their exposure at a faster pace than Japanese and European banks, but leveling off in 1999. In contrast,

Table 3.1 Capital flows of five East Asian countries (percent of GDP)

	Indonesia			South Korea			Malaysia			Philippines			Thailand		
	96	97	98	96	97	98	96	97	98	96	97	98	96	97	98
Financial account, net	4.8	−0.3	−11.0	4.6	−1.9	−2.4	2.2	0.6	−3.5	13.6	7.9	1.5	10.5	−11.0	−13.0
Direct investment, net	2.5	2.1	−0.4	−0.5	−0.3	0.2	1.2	1.0	3.0	7.7	5.3	−2.9	0.8	2.2	6.1
Portfolio investment, net	2.2	−1.2	−2.1	3.0	4.1	−0.5	−0.1	−0.1	0.4	6.2	0.7	−0.4	1.9	3.1	0.1
Other investment, net	0.1	−1.1	−8.4	2.1	−4.6	−2.1	1.1	−0.2	−7.0	7.7	5.3	−0.2	6.4	−14.4	−15.6
Banks	−0.3	−0.1	−2.6	1.3	−2.4	−1.5	−3.0	−0.8	−3.7	−6.8	−2.0	−0.6	−1.5	−1.6	−10.2
Memorandum items:															
Current account balance	−0.03	−0.02	0.03	−4.4	−1.7	11.8	−4.6	−4.8	13.0	−4.8	−5.3	−2.4	−6.5	−1.4	11.2
GDP (billions of US$)	227	216	160	520	476	345	101	100	72.5	83	82.2	65.2	227.4	216	125

Source: The Annual Report of International Finance, Japanese Ministry of Finance; various issues.

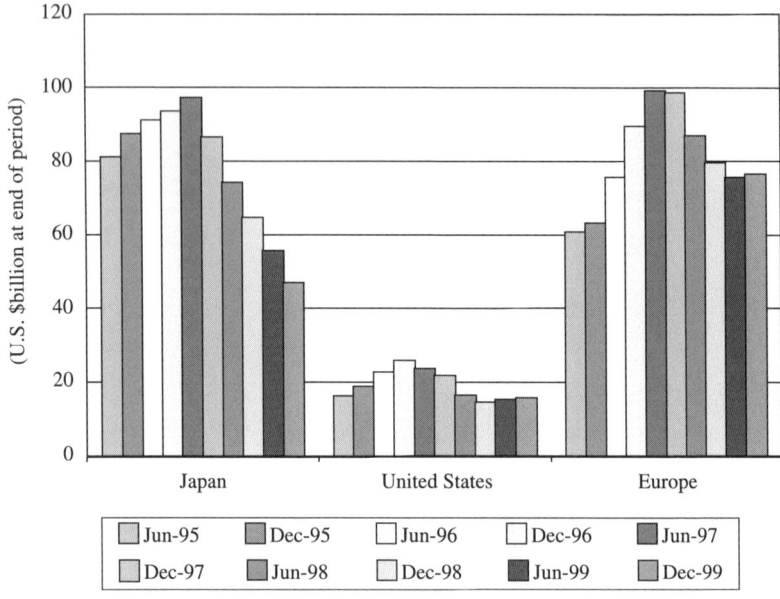

Figure 3.4 Trends in bank claims on five East Asian countries
Source: BIS, *Consolidated International Banking Statistics*.

European bank loans to the region grew rapidly until mid-1997, stayed at about the same level in the second half of the year, and then declined sharply in 1998, leveling off in 1999.

Japanese banks cut back loans to both Japanese and non-Japanese affiliated borrowers in Asia by about 20 and 22 percent, respectively, between late March 1998 and late March 1999. In terms of volume, Japanese banks reduced loans to non-Japanese affiliated borrowers more sharply than to Japanese affiliates in the region (see Figure 3.5).[8] The decline in Japanese bank loans to non-Japanese affiliates accounted for approximately 70 percent of the total decline in Japanese bank loans to the region. The primary reason for this pattern of loan reduction was that customer relations with Japanese affiliates were considered more important for Japanese banks than those with non-Japanese affiliates. Japanese banks needed to use scarce non-yen loanable funds for Japanese-affiliated borrowers from the standpoint of overall customer relations, including consideration toward the parent companies. In addition, the credit risks of non-Japanese-affiliated borrowers were considered generally higher than those of Japanese affiliates whose credit was often enhanced by the Japanese parent

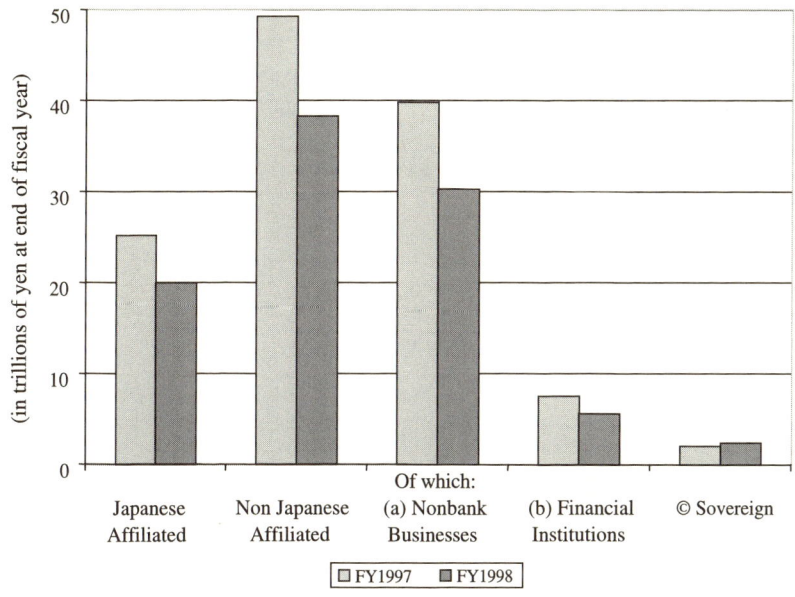

Figure 3.5 Selected Japanese banks: East Asian exposure by borrower

Note: The selected banks are: Asahi Bank, Bank of Tokyo-Mitsubishi, Dai-Ichi Kangyo Bank, Fuji Bank, IBJ, Sakura Bank, Sanwa Bank, Sumitomo Bank, and Tokai Bank. "Selected Banks" noted in subsequent figures of this paper refer to the same group of banks unless otherwise specified.

Source: Banks' annual reports and financial statements.

companies. During the outbreak of the East Asian financial crisis, which increased the risk premia for bank loans to clients operating in the region, Japanese banks tried to improve the credit quality of Japanese-affiliated borrowers by securing new guarantees from their parent companies.

Japanese banks, in the process of resolving NPLs in their domestic portfolio,[9] made significant provisions for loan losses and writeoffs, keeping the banks perilously close to the BIS capital adequacy ratio threshold. The pressure for maintaining capital adequacy provided Japanese banks with a strong incentive to reduce assets, including cross-border loans. Moreover, lending in foreign currency (denominated assets) by Japanese banks was constrained by their deteriorating dollar funding capacity. The capacity of Japanese banks to raise foreign currency funds, in particular U.S. dollars, had declined because of a fall in their creditworthiness(U.S. and European banks reduced credit limits applied to Japanese banks. Japanese banks were forced to raise funds at a large premium ("Japan premium") from U.S. and European counterparts in the interbank markets. From late 1997 into late 1998, the Japan premium rose significantly, coinciding with the severe problems in the Japanese financial market, peaking at 100 basis points in early December 1997 in the aftermath of the failures of Hokkaido Takushoku Bank and Yamaichi Securities.

In the East Asia region, the liberalization of foreign investment in financial services is progressing in the context of the IFI programs and more broadly through the commitments under the WTO. Some U.S. and European banks are aggressively moving into the region, acquiring troubled banks, providing technical advice on bank and corporate restructuring, and serving as intermediaries in the resale markets of nonperforming assets. Moreover, they are competing with Japanese banks in the latter's traditional business involving Japanese and Japanese-affiliated clients, resulting in a significant narrowing of the profit margin. As U.S. and European banks aggressively acquire discounted assets in the aftermath of the financial crisis, Japanese banks' relative presence in the region is diminishing notwithstanding their stated reemphasis on East Asia. The restructuring of the financial sector is progressing in South Korea, Thailand, and Indonesia while the banking sector is being consolidated and restructured in Singapore in the context of its post-crisis strategy. U.S. and European banks play a dominant role in most cases, while Japanese banks retreat to attend to domestic problems.

Nonmarket Environment

Financial and Capital Flow Liberalization in Emerging East Asia

It appears that while Japanese banks initially expanded their operations on the back of rising FDI by Japanese firms, they later began to expand into local lending, reflecting in part a departure from the conventional operations that concentrated on Japanese or Japanese-affiliated firms. As a result, the latest bank-specific data indicates that substantial parts of their exposure are vis-à-vis local firms. What prompted this shift away from the conventional operations with Japanese-affiliated firms where relationship banking prevailed and credit risks were minimal? It is interesting to note that the patterns of Japanese aggregate FDI and bank exposure differ considerably across countries. The five East Asian countries affected by the crisis may be divided into two groups. The first group, including Thailand, South Korea and Malaysia, exhibited a sharp acceleration of bank loans outpacing the growth of FDI during 1993–1996, while the second group, including Indonesia and the Philippines, showed faster growth of FDI than bank loans (Figure 3.3). These differences can be explained in part by the scope and scale of capital and financial liberalization that took place in each country.

South Korea South Korea promoted capital and financial liberalization beginning in the early 1990s. This policy was driven by a desire to stimulate the FDI flows needed to enhance technological progress and to promote industrial restructuring from a labor-intensive to a more capital-intensive economy. It was also to help South Korean firms circumvent chronically high domestic interest rates. The scope of foreign borrowing was broadened gradually for foreign-invested companies first in 1993, then for high-tech firms and small- and medium-sized enterprises in 1995, and finally for all firms in 1996. The capital liberalization translated the strong credit demand for foreign capital into a surge in Japanese banks' lending beginning in the mid-1990s. South Korean firms' creditworthiness increased with its membership in the Organization for Economic Cooperation and Development (OECD) and also contributed to greater exposure of Japanese banks to local retail banking in South Korea.

Malaysia Malaysia also preferred direct and portfolio investment to bank loans, as evidenced by the fact that foreign exchange controls (prior permission requirements) applied only to foreign bank loans. Foreign loans were allowed only for financing productive activities, especially those that generated foreign exchange earnings. In an attempt to foster the development of domestic banks, the government tried to limit the lending opportunities for foreign banks, although the growing need to finance big infrastructure projects proved favorable to foreign banks. By contrast, the domestic borrowing by nonresident-controlled companies (NRCCs) was strictly restricted.

Thailand To sustain high economic growth with a chronic current account deficit, Thailand aggressively implemented capital and financial liberalization in the 1990s. Exchange controls were relaxed (1990–1994) and interest rate ceilings were lifted (1992). The establishment of the Bangkok International Banking Facility in 1993 promoted out-in lending in foreign currency. Moreover, the Provincial International Banking Facility in 1994 promoted baht-denominated out-in lending. Thus, all types of firms enjoyed access to cheap offshore funding. The strong credit demand, high growth prospects, and large interest rate differentials, combined with the lure of "carry trade," resulted in an influx of foreign banking capital. Taking advantage of these favorable conditions, Japanese banks increased their exposure to local companies directly or via local banks.

Indonesia   Indonesia removed all foreign capital controls in the early 1970s. This policy was reversed in 1991 when its economy came under inflationary pressure. To curb the credit expansion, the government imposed a ceiling on offshore loans and subjected all offshore borrowing to prior approval. Since then, the government has continued to control bank loans and export credits while prioritizing FDI and portfolio investment. As a result of this restrictive policy toward foreign bank loans, Japanese banks could not expand their exposure to local retail banking.

Philippines   Given the experiences of a debt moratorium in 1984 and a balance of payment crisis in 1991, the Philippines was very cautious in liberalizing foreign borrowing during the 1990s. The restrictions were only gradually lifted on FDI and portfolio investment, foreign exchange transactions, and foreign bank access to the domestic market. Strict limits on foreign loans curbed the extension of Japanese banking activity to local retail banking.

The onset of the financial crisis in 1997 exposed some of the weaknesses of each of these countries' financial systems and the ever-worsening position of Japanese banks in the region. Beginning in early 1998, IFI's and bilateral donors provided massive balance of payments support to the crisis-hit countries of Thailand, South Korea, Indonesia, the Philippines, and Malaysia on the condition of implementing sweeping reforms. Regional financial markets bottomed out in late 1998 and thereafter began to gradually improve. With the stabilization of short-term capital flows, the crisis was all but over. But structural problems remained in debt and corporate restructuring, hampering the post-crisis recovery. The recovery was relatively swift in some instances where reforms were effectively implemented. However, NPLs still remain, their resolution is far from over, and moral hazard still grips the region's financial markets.

Firm Position

In the mid-1990s, housing loan companies (*Jusen*), credit cooperatives, and regional banks—became insolvent and were liquidated. The government, in a departure from its traditional protectionist policy, did not bail them out. However, traditional regulatory forbearance and weak governance led to the government's inaction on other troubled institutions. In the absence of adequate deposit insurance and a legal framework for dealing with insolvent institutions, there was hesitation in taking decisive measures for fear that it might touch off a banking sector panic.[10] The government continued to supply prime fiscal resources and the Bank of Japan relaxed its monetary policy stance and hoped for an economic recovery that would ease the banks' problems. While there was indeed a short-lived economic recovery in 1996, a second wave of bankruptcies was touched off by a further deterioration of the stock market in 1997. In 1997, one insurance company, two securities companies, and one city bank went into bankruptcy, and banks' share prices tumbled on the stock market in a full-blown systemic crisis. These developments prompted the government to take action to stabilize the system, putting in place the 1997 Prompt Corrective Action, a rule-based framework that mandated corrective actions when capital adequacy ratios deteriorate and injected public funds of ¥1.8 trillion in subordinated debt to help major banks meet the required capital adequacy in March 1998. When the Japanese banking system was in systemic distress, the East Asian regional crisis had already erupted.

Those Japanese banks with a large exposure to the East Asian markets were seriously affected by the regional crisis, which undermined their profits and asset positions to the point where solvency became a major concern. The impact of the regional crisis, real or potential, was particularly threatening as it came on the heels of a protracted period of asset price deflation and recession at home, which had already weakened banks. Their capital positions were particularly in jeopardy because of depressed equity markets.

Although several categories of foreign nonperforming loans were disclosed at aggregated levels in a regular and uniform manner by Japanese banks, major internationally active Japanese banks had disclosed NPLs by geographic area. Those banks' NPL ratio of the Asian portfolio deteriorated to 4.2 percent in March 1999, compared with a mere 0.6 percent for the Americas, 0.8 percent for Europe, and under 7.0 percent at home. In volume terms, however, NPLs to Asia accounted for about 5 percent of total NPLs for the five Japanese banks; the bulk of NPLs were domestic (see Figure 3.6).

The most damaged portfolio in the region were loans to Indonesia, with NPL ratios exceeding 30 percent, while the other Asian NPLs were well below 10 percent (see Figure 3.7). It is noteworthy that the NPL ratio was low at about 2 percent for South Korea. Japanese banks attributed the relatively low NPL ratio in South Korea to the fact that their loans were mainly to the largest *chaebols* and financial institutions, the latter of which were guaranteed by the South Korean government.[11] Loan loss reserves against East Asian NPLs ranged from 25 to 100 percent.

In the aftermath of the crisis, loans to Asia became the least profitable foreign portfolio for Japanese banks (see Figure 3.8).[12] For ten

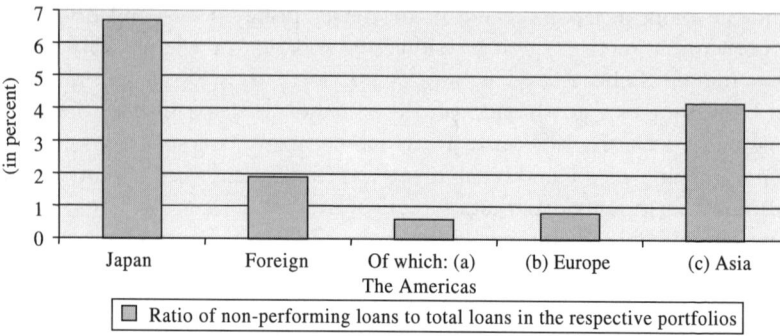

Figure 3.6 Selected Japanese banks: non-performing loan ratios by geographic area

Note: Selected Banks include: *Sanwa,* Sumitomo, Fuji, and Tokyo-Mitsubishi, as of March 1999. "Foreign" is a weighted average of NPL ratios for the Americas, Europe, and Asia.
Sources: Banks' annual reports and financial statements; and staff estimates.

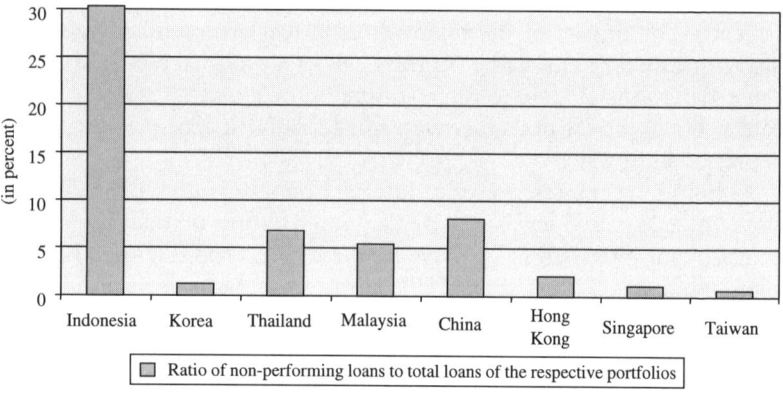

Figure 3.7 Selected Japanese banks: NPL ratios to the East Asian region
Source: Japanese banks' financial statements.

internationally active Japanese banks, segment earnings and returns on assets in the Asian region for fiscal year 1998 were negative ¥244 billion or −0.66 percent, respectively, compared with those in the Americas (positive ¥304 billion, or 0.58 percent) and in Europe (negative ¥27 billion, or −0.11 percent). The impact on Japanese bank earnings of the damaged Asian portfolio, although serious in itself, was smaller in quantitative terms. Losses from operation in the Asian region accounted for only 5 percent of total losses of the ten Japanese banks.

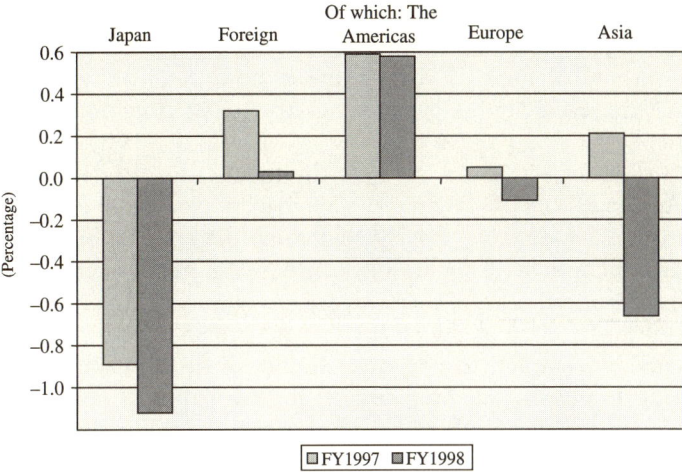

Figure 3.8 Selected Japanese banks: segment return on assets by geographic area
Source: Japanese banks' financial statements.

III. Strategic and Tactical Analysis

Nonmarket Strategies Following the Financial Crisis

In coping with the impact of the regional financial crisis, Japanese banks argued for intervention by public entities, either by international financial institutions or bilateral donor governments, in the form of guarantees and subsidies that would directly facilitate the servicing of external debt. This was a nonmarket strategy facilitated by the fact that Japanese creditors were still by far the most dominant among foreign creditors in East Asia, accounting for roughly one-third of total outstanding bank credit and nearly 40 percent if the Japanese general trading companies were included.[13]

Japanese creditors' planning horizon was considered longer than that of other foreign creditors. Thus, restructuring negotiations progressed on a bilateral basis with a focus on medium-term viability. Partial debt forgiveness was an option only if it assured enhancement of long-term productivity and the debt servicing capacity of the debtor.[14] It was thus considered important to create an enabling environment to support the ongoing voluntary restructuring that was consistent with the market-based approach.

In the wake of a regional financial crisis of systemic proportions, Japanese banks thought that a nonmarket interventionist approach would be justified. They feared that extensive corporate bankruptcies in the region would further erode their own capital base and drive some of them into insolvency. In this context, consideration was given to schemes that facilitated ongoing voluntary negotiations, including:

- *Exchange rate guarantee.* Under the Indonesian Debt Restructuring Agency (INDRA) scheme, the approach was to avoid currency mismatch and currency risk by converting the external debt into local currency debt. The Indonesian Government would bear the exchange rate risk, but not any other commercial risks. The perception of Japanese creditors was that the scheme as designed was not attractive enough to corporate Indonesia or to Japanese creditors. Hence, Japanese creditors argued for the potential need for public assistance, either in the form of an exchange stabilization fund or an interest guarantee scheme.[15]
- *Japanese yen debt conversion.* Some Japanese creditors, as part of the debt restructuring, refinanced U.S. dollar-denominated loans by converting them into Japanese yen-denominated loans to take advantage of the greater availability of yen funds. Consideration was given to the wider use of Japanese yen debt conversion as a way to facilitate debt restructuring by Japanese creditors.

However, this nonmarket approach advocated by Japanese banks did not materialize. Instead, massive official resources, in the face of looming private capital outflows, were channeled into the crisis-hit countries mainly through commercial banks. Regional financial market stabilization began to be restored in the second half of 1998 as a result of the return of confidence among foreign investors that was based on the provision of financial resources and the implementation of restructuring and reform programs. Indeed, debt restructuring began in a market-based "London Rules" framework where overdue individual loans were renegotiated and repackaged in exchange for corporate restructuring. It is of interest that Japanese banks were inclined to rely on public intervention in times of difficulty, as in the past, but that their approach was not adopted in the reform programs under the aegis of the Washington-based IFIs.

At the height of the crisis, there were also serious discussions on partial debt forgiveness, possibly on a unilateral and uniform basis. Japanese banks were adamantly opposed to this type of nonmarket strategy, arguing that it would create a moral hazard, punishing those who were making good faith efforts to service the debt and rewarding those that were lagging in their efforts. Although no consensus developed for partial debt forgiveness and debt was never forgiven in any systematic way, markets are now forcing closure on the pending debt restructuring by reducing the asset values to negligible levels. In other words, a market outcome prevailed over a nonmarket strategy.

In the meantime, some of the constraints on the international banking of Japanese banks eased. The Japan premium substantially narrowed in April 1999 when the market reacted favorably to the Bank of Japan's downward guidance of the overnight interbank market rate to virtually zero percent. Additionally, the pressure on capital adequacy had been alleviated to some degree by bank recapitalization through public resources. In March 1998, ¥1.82 trillion of public funds were injected to recapitalize twenty-one Japanese banks, and in March 1999, an additional ¥7.45 trillion were injected into fifteen major banks. Some increased capital by issuing common and preferred stocks. Consequently, despite the negative impact on bank capital of sizable loan writeoffs and loan loss provisions, the risk-based capital ratios of Japanese banks were raised by 1 to 2 percentage points by 1999.[16]

It is noteworthy that major internationally active Japanese banks continue to regard Asia as the most important market because of the fact that a large number of Japanese-affiliated clients operate in the region and that the long-term growth potential of the region is considerable. Thus, it can be reasonably expected that, despite the recent reduction in Asian exposure and the current cautious credit stance toward the region, internationally active Japanese banks will redirect their resources to East Asia when the regional economy recovers on a sustained basis and regional corporate debt and businesses are adequately restructured.

In the aftermath of the domestic and regional financial crises, Japanese banks began to adjust under the guidance of the Banking Sector Revitalization Commission and the Financial Supervisory Agency. The restructuring of the banking sector took the form of closure of non-viable banks, recapitalization, greater provisioning and writeoffs, and a cutback on cross-border operations in order to conform to Basle capital adequacy guidelines. As a result of the restructuring undertaken so far, banks' capital adequacy ratios improved and NPLs are almost fully dealt with from an accounting point of view. However, bank portfolios still include assets that are not generating income. Insofar as no potential exists for future profits on these assets, the situation is tantamount to *de facto* debt forgiveness. They can, in fact, be disposed of in a bulk fire sale to market intermediaries for a fraction of their face values. In this respect, it might have been a tactical error on the part of Japanese banks to insist on absolutely no debt forgiveness, as it might have been more advantageous to negotiate a *quid pro quo* for partial debt forgiveness. Now Japanese banks not only suffer from a *de facto* debt forgiveness but also are saddled with the moral hazard that would impede future lending operations in the region.

IV. Market and Organizational Strategies

Under the government's protection, the banking sector had for a long time enjoyed exclusive access to the captive domestic financial markets characterized by abundant financial savings and investment activities of a large economy. The traditional protectionist policy, while contributing to large-scale financial intermediation in the past, had created various inefficiencies such as overstaffing, high costs, low ROEs, and general overbanking. These inefficiencies, which were tolerated in the past when the banking sector was protected, will have to be eliminated if banks are to survive during the policy shift from the traditional convoy system to one of market-based principles as the financial markets become more competitive and integrated.[17] In the past, Japanese banks' core competency used to be the deposit-taking and loan business segmented by borrower types and regions. The paradigm shift is forcing banks to develop a new core competency, as the traditional core competency in a niche either in a certain region or with respect to certain borrowers is no longer sufficient to assure business viability. Among other things, banks will have to reduce the number of redundant executive officers and personnel while maintaining the core part of business activity, quickly catch up on cost-saving techniques, develop new skills in investment banking, cash management services, and the emerging ebusiness, and improve ROEs. This strategy is obviously easier said than done, given a corporate culture nurtured by a long history of protection under the "convoy" system. However, there appears to be no alternative if banks are to survive.

Japanese banks are now restructuring and repositioning on the heels of the prolonged financial crisis. The challenge is formidable. The restructuring and repositioning are pursued against the background of the Japanese Big Bang,[18] the IT revolution,[19] and a policy shift from protection to a more market-oriented environment. Moreover, the general overbanking situation is made worse by the shrinking banking business because of the recession and a structural change in the Japanese financial intermediation toward direct finance and capital markets.[20]

Evolving Restructuring—Domestic Focus

The foremost challenge for the major Japanese banks now is to survive in the domestic market. Overseas operations appear to be subordinated to the near-term objective of survival in the domestic market. In strategic moves, banks are forming new alliances in pursuit of new skills and economies of scale. The banking sector is now in the final stage for mergers, vertical integration, and alliances to be completed in the near future.

As a result of their weakened financial and capital positions, Japanese banks reduced international banking as part of their restructuring. Seven major Japanese banks (one city bank, five trust banks, and two nationalized long-term credit banks) announced they will cease operations in foreign countries altogether. Other major Japanese banks that remain internationally active have reduced their presence overseas. The largest reduction in segment assets of ten internationally active Japanese banks during the fiscal year of 1998 was observed in Asia where substantial risks materialized because of the regional financial crisis and associated political/social instability. Moreover, those banks are planning to restructure international operations, shifting their operational focus toward core banking businesses with Japanese firms and their affiliates. Japanese banks will continue to use scarce non-yen loanable funds for Japanese affiliates to protect their customer relations. In the midst of overall retrenchment, however, Asia is still considered the last best hope for Japanese banks. Their Asia focus is still largely intact, despite their relatively reduced presence in the region.

Overall indicators of city banks' positions show that their loan portfolio composition is predominantly domestic, that NPLs still constitute significant proportions of total assets (averaging over 3 percent), and that operating profits are still low (see Table 3.2). The banks' exposure to Asia typically halved in relation to total assets, from 5.4 percent in 1998 to 2.6 percent in 2000. A shifting emphasis in overseas operations by Japanese banks can be seen in changes in the numbers of overseas branches. As seen in Table 3.3, the overall number of bank branches overseas began to decline in 1996 and the decline has been most dramatic in North America, followed by Europe. The reduction of the number of branches in Asia began only after the East Asian crisis, and has been relatively modest in comparison to other regions. By mid-1999, more than half of Japanese banks' overseas branches were in Asia.

Future Strategic Focus and Core Competency

The banks' behavior and strategy have been, and will be in the near term, driven by the official guidance of the Financial Revitalization

Table 3.2 Selected indicators of city banks, March (in billions of yen)

	Assets			NPL			Profits			Foreign currency operations (US$ billion)			No. of branches	
	Domestic	Foreign	Total	Domestic	Foreign	Total	Domestic	Foreign	Total	Assets	Liabilities	Domestic	Foreign	Total
Daiichi Kangyo Bank	45,033	6,966	51,999	1,623	103	1,726	636	106	742	58	60	334	39	373
Sumitomo Bank	45,323	8,445	53,768	1,801	83	1,884	565	157	723	64	64	284	58	342
Sakura Bank	42,045	6,451	48,496	1,660	12	1,672	665	46	712	40	40	469	45	514
Tokai Bank	25,873	4,677	30,550	633	19	652	358	36	394	21	19	231	41	272
Asahi Bank	26,147	2,641	28,788	842	16	857	384	24	408	10	10	328	9	337
Fuji Bank	45,216	13,031	58,247	1,207	89	1,296	472	129	601	43	43	284	64	348
Sanwa Bank	35,004	11,898	46,902	1,169	83	1,252	523	119	642	57	57	335	54	389
Bank of Tokyo-Mitsubishi	49,082	25,714	74,796			1,722			862				75	75
Daiwa Bank			15,494			1,140			287	5	5	442	11	453

Source: Various financial reports of banks.

Table 3.3 Japanese banks' overseas branches, 1990–2000

	90/12	92/12	95/12	96/7	97/7	98/7	99/7
North America	126	137	132	120	108	78	48
Europe	71	83	82	76	74	66	42
Asia	83	99	161	155	164	154	133
Others	29	30	27	27	27	27	23
Total	309	349	402	378	373	325	246

Source: The Oriental Economist and Kinyu Journal; various issues.

Committee under the Financial Supervisory Agency mandated by the Law Concerning Emergency Measures for Early Consolidation of the Financial Sector. As a *quid pro quo,* each bank receiving official fund is required by law to submit a bank restructuring plan (*Kenzenka Keikaku*). The main elements of the plan are: (a) an organizational restructuring plan including mergers, subsidiaries, alliances with partners both in and outside the banking industry; (b) an operational restructuring plan mandating a clear plan for improving ROEs and also a plan to discontinue or retrench overseas operations through regional banks; (c) a cost-reduction plan for personnel, materials, and the number of executive officers; (d) a clear plan to liquidate nonperforming loans; and (e) a plan to reduce the wage cost and dividends. Thus, an overall framework of bank restructuring in the near term, until such time that the public funds would be fully repaid, was set by the restructuring plans submitted in March 1999.

Banks are now restructuring in alliance with other banks and nonbanks. Mergers and alliances are resulting in four major financial groups, or the Big Four, three of whom have more than ¥100 trillion in assets and a fourth with assets just under ¥100 trillion, placing them among the ranks of top world banks in terms of asset size. The largest group will be Mizuho Financial Group (consisting of Daiichi Kangyo, Fuji, and the Industrial Bank of Japan) with a consolidated asset portfolio of ¥152 trillion as of March 2000, accounting for about one-third of the total asset portfolio of all the city banks. Sumitomo Mitsui Banking Corporation will come in second, followed by the Mitsubishi Tokyo Financial Group, with consolidated asset portfolios of ¥106 and ¥102 trillion respectively (see Table 3.4).

The strategic objectives common to most of the alliances are to gain maximum market power in a region or a niche market, attain economies of scale and drastically reduce operational costs, generate enough profits to invest in IT development, and build a critical mass capacity in strategic areas (for example, investment banking, asset management, and high-skill fee-based businesses). All those objectives are pursued to substantially

Table 3.4 Future banking corporations and consolidated assets (in trillions of yen)

New groups	Former banks	Consolidated assets end March 2000
1. Mizuho Financial Group (MHFG) (A holding company; fully integrated in April 2002)	Daiichi Kangho Bank, Fuji Bank, Industrial Bank of Japan, Yasuda Trust Bank	152.7
2. Sumitomo Mitsui Banking Corporation (SMBC) (Merger effective in April 2001)	Sumitomo Bank, Sakura Bank	102.2
3. Mitsubishi Tokyo Financial Group (A holding company; fully integrated in April 2001)	Bank of Tokyo-Mitsubishi, Mitsubishi Trust and Banking, Nippon Trust Bank	91.42
4. UFJ Group (A holding company; fully integrated in April 2002)	Sanwa Bank, Tokai Bank, Toyo Trust Bank	85.7
5. Asahi Bank	Asahi Bank	28.8
6. Daiwa Bank	Daiwa Bank	15.4

Source: Kinyuu Zaisei Jijo, June 19, 2000.

improve their ROEs, which now woefully lag behind those of competitive foreign banks.

Banks are trying to strengthen their stakes in domestic retail and wholesale markets for both individuals and corporations, which is the core business that yields a large portion of operational profits for all banks. By customizing services and further strengthening client relations, banks are trying to position themselves in a more competitive and shrinking domestic market. The core competency of banks, according to their own statements, is in most cases their business or client base in traditional domestic banking.[21] Their client relationship is solid and based on long-term considerations, constituting the so-called "relationship banking." Their strategic objective in the near term is survival, and only after their survival and improvement of their ROEs and other financial indicators can they invest the profits in developing new skills and capacities. The extent of this client base stability after the full impact of the Japanese financial big bang, however, is uncertain.

All in all, the strategic focus on the core domestic business appears to be the right one. Major money center banks can learn from the experience of U.S. banks during the 1980s when they created economies of scale and circumvented competitive pressure in the domestic retail and wholesale markets through mergers in order to compensate for the Latin American debt problems and real estate price disinflation at home. Examples include the Bank of America's acquisition of Security Pacific and the merger of Chemical Bank, Manufacturers and Hanover, and Chase Bank.

The consolidation of the banking sector will presumably result in economies of scale. Whether or not the forthcoming banking sector integration, mergers, or alliances that are about to be completed will yield the desired results remains to be seen. For instance, there is an expectation that increased size will reduce operational costs per unit of asset, given the inverse relationship between the asset size and cost per unit of asset. However, reductions in operational costs and gains in efficiency will result from increases in asset size if and only if all the redundancies created by the alliance are eliminated and the opportunities for synergy are fully exploited.[22]

Overseas operations, meanwhile, are to be cut back—including those in East Asia, which most of the major Japanese banks still consider their best overseas strategic market. The retreat is now driven by the mandate of the Financial Supervisory Board as a *quid pro quo* for the use of public funds for recapitalization. For some banks, the retreat now is a tactical one, and an adjustment to that policy is expected later on. The adjustment, however, will have to come after the borrowed public funds are repaid and the domestic order is restored.

V. Case Studies

This section provides a brief overview of the domestic and international (particularly East Asian) activities of the Big Four financial groups and a city bank that has recently decided to retreat from its international operations.[23]

Mizuho Financial Group (MHFG)

Background Mizuho Holdings opened for business on September 29, 2000. As a holding company established jointly by Daiichi Kangyo Bank, Fuji Bank, and Industrial Bank of Japan, Mizuho Holdings manages the business strategies of the three banks through its nine business units with the possibility of a full merger in April 2002 under the new company name of the Mizuho Financial Group. The merger created a mega-bank with a total asset portfolio exceeding ¥150 trillion, the largest in the world. It also provided an impetus to sector-wide restructuring involving other mergers and heightened the level of competition in the Japanese banking sector.

Overseas Operations The Mizuho Financial Group had the largest exposure to Asia among the Big Four financial groups at ¥2.1 trillion or a 32.1 percent share as of September 2000. The Asian NPL ratio (the ratio of risk-monitored loans to total loans in Asia) was the highest among the Big Four at 7.5 percent. A geographical breakdown of the three banks' operating profit in the fiscal year of 1999 shows that the contribution from Asia and Oceania was ¥54 billion or 9.1 percent of total operating profit, following those from Japan at ¥409 billion and North America at ¥120 billion.

Mizuho purports to be the premier financial group in Asia, capable of providing top-level, full-line services for Japanese and non-Japanese (European and North American) global enterprises through the use of the integrated global networks of the three banks. These services include local currency transactions, trade finance and settlements, project finance, cross-border mergers and acquisitions (M&As), management advisory services relating to business strategies and financial risk management, and other investment banking services. Mizuho has a wide regional network in Asia consisting of their existing close relations with the Industrial Bank of Japan in Hong Kong and China, Daiichi Kangyo Bank in Taiwan and Thailand, and Fuji Bank in the Philippines, Thailand, Vietnam, and Singapore.

Restructuring Mizuho intends to solidify their present hold on the largest domestic client base, including over 30 percent of major corporations in Japan and seeks to create synergy in the merger. It purports to eventually become a major player in the global markets, ranking as one of the world's top five banks. Mizuho's role model is Chase Manhattan Bank, which became the dominant leader in the industry by creating new services and developing new markets in addition to cutting the operational costs of the bank after the merger among Chemical Bank, Manufacturers and Hanover Bank, and Chase Manhattan Bank during the first half of the 1990s. Although Mizuho's asset size is the world's largest, its ROE is much lower, presently estimated at 3.8 percent, than those of major U.S. and European banks, which exceed 20 percent. The major reason for the low ROE is that approximately 80 percent of Mizuho's profits are generated by interest earnings on loans; investment banking services that command higher rates of return are relatively underdeveloped. Moreover, NPLs amounting to 3.5 percent of total assets have been a factor behind the low ROE because of the need for provisioning and writeoffs. Also, the main lending operations are with large enterprises, where the spreads are thin.

Mizuho's strategy includes the expansion of lending operations with SMEs and individuals as well as fee-based services such as mergers and acquisitions, securitization, the development of security-based investment banking, the expansion of syndicated loans, and increased fees instead of interest earnings. Mizuho already commands 50 percent of the syndicated loan market and stands to dominate such areas as commitment lines and securitization.

Sumitomo Mitsui Banking Corporations (SMBC)
Background In October 1999, Sumitomo Bank and Sakura Bank announced their decision to merge with each other in April 2002, creating a group called the Sumitomo Mitsui Banking Corporation (SMBC) with the combined asset size exceeding ¥100 trillion (see Table 3.4). The date for the establishment of the new bank was subsequently brought forward one year to April 2001. The merger decision closely followed the announcement of the creation of the Mizuho Financial Group, which is expected to be the largest bank in the world in asset size.

The merger between the two banks link two traditional *keiretsu* groups. Sumitomo Bank is the core city bank of the Sumitomo *keiretsu* group, while Sakura Bank, a product of the merger between Mitsui Bank and Taiyo-Kobe Bank in 1990, is a major city bank of the Mitsui *keiretsu* group. Sumitomo Bank and Sakura Bank rank second and fifth, respectively, among the nine city banks in asset size, with the former having a well balanced operational mix of corporate and consumer lending and capital market services, and with the latter having a strong consumer loan portfolio, especially housing loans, and a strong client base in the Tokyo Metropolitan area and in Kobe.

Overseas Operations The Sumitomo Mitsui Banking Corporation's balance of loans to Asian countries as of September 2000 was the third largest among the Big Four financial groups at ¥1.5 trillion, which represented a 23.2 percent share. Its NPL ratio was 6.2 percent of total loans to Asia. A geographical breakdown of the aggregate operating profit for the two banks in the fiscal year of 1999 indicates that they earned ¥23 billion from Asia-Oceania (or 6.2 percent of total domestic and overseas operating profits), ¥244 billion from Japan, and ¥94 billion from North America.

While both Sumitomo Bank and Sakura Bank consider the long-term potential of East Asia to be positive, they remain very cautious in investing in the region in the near term, concentrating now on capacity building and information gathering. The two partner banks are restructuring their operations with a focus on domestic markets and retrenching overseas operations. The stated policy in overseas operations is that non-Japanese or non-Japanese-affiliated companies are not its targeted clients, and they will withdraw from business with such clients with the exception of selected local overseas Chinese businesses. As of March 1998, the two partner banks had sixty overseas branches. By March 2000 this had been reduced to thirty-six, and a further reduction to twenty-two is expected by March 2004. Nonetheless, the Sumitomo Mitsui Banking Corporation will have a network covering the whole of Asia. In particular, the merger will create an extensive network of offices in China and other parts of Asia.

One of the SMBC's major business targets for the next few years is the restructuring and expansion of its overseas business based on a clearly defined strategy. Several specific strategic directions have been identified. First, the new bank needs to boost its business in Asia by leveraging both its geographic advantages over European and American banks, and by strengthening and integrating the combined customer base and branch network of the two partner banks. Second, it needs to improve its capacity to develop new financial services so as to compete with leading banks in North America and Europe and to provide Japanese and non-Japanese corporations with advanced services. Third, it needs to form new alliances with foreign partners. Finally, it needs to strategically allocate management resources freed by the elimination of duplicated businesses and branches.

Restructuring   Sumitomo Bank has been clarifying its strategic areas and prioritizing resource allocation. It has identified domestic consumer banking services, domestic corporate banking services for small and medium-sized enterprises, and capital markets as its three priority areas and will allocate human and management resources to those areas. To focus on the target customers and markets, it has been restructuring the operational organization. It has also been trying to improve the efficiency of its assets and capital.

Sakura intends to become a premier retail bank with its resources strategically allocated to retail businesses with SMEs and individuals. With respect to corporate clients, Sakura will shift to commitment lines of credit and other types of new services with the expectation that more corporate clients will shift to capital markets for fundraising. With the express purpose of improving overall ROE, Sakura will create inhouse companies under independent management whose performance will be assessed by their own ROEs. Sakura will expand its business in investment trust funds, financial advisory services, and private banking. Sakura will install ATMs in convenience stores.

The two partner banks' own restructuring will set the stage for the merger scheduled for April 2001. The merger is considered unique in that it is cross-*keiretsu*. The merger brings together different segments of regional markets and types of services in a complementary way, paving the way for cost saving and synergy creation. Moreover, the new bank will have under its umbrella securities and insurance companies in the same *keiretsu* groups that are forging alliances in their own right.

Mitsubishi Tokyo Financial Group

Background The Bank of Tokyo-Mitsubishi reached a basic agreement in April 2000 on the integration of its operations with those of Mitsubishi Trust and Banking Corporation and the Nippon Trust Bank. The major objectives of the integration are (a) to create an open and growth-oriented organization with the flexibility to respond to opportunities for further partnerships and linkages, and (b) to maximize the benefits of rationalization, groupwide efficiency improvement, and cost reduction by economizing on management resources. In September 2000, it was announced that the Mitsubishi Tokyo Financial Group, Inc. would be established in April 2001 as the holding company for the group.

The Bank of Tokyo-Mitsubishi was a product of the merger in 1996 between the Bank of Tokyo, a specialized bank for foreign exchange transactions that provide international financial services for a broad-based clientele, and Mitsubishi Bank, the main bank for the Mitsubishi *keiretsu* group. The Bank of Tokyo had numerous offices throughout the world, including Asia, and enjoyed an excellent reputation in the field of international business, while Mitsubishi Bank focused mainly on domestic markets. The Bank of Tokyo-Mitsubishi, with the largest asset portfolio and a generally better operational performance among Japanese banks, was the only city bank that did not receive an infusion of public funds for recapitalization in March 1999.

Overseas Operations The Bank of Tokyo-Mitsubishi has had a particular emphasis on business in Asia, providing universal banking services that include leasing, derivatives, and securities in the region. It does business with more than 80 percent of major Japanese corporations operating in Asia and its customer base is among the broadest of any Japanese bank. It has the highest proportional exposure in Asia among Japanese banks with about 10 percent of total outstanding loans in the region at the end of March 1998. The Mitsubishi Tokyo Financial Group as a whole had ¥1.7 trillion as a balance of loans to Asia in September 2000, a 40 percent reduction from ¥2.9 trillion in March 1999. Its NPL ratio was, however, low at 5.9 percent. A geographical analysis of the group's operating profits indicates that in the fiscal year of 1999 the Asia-Oceania region contributed ¥42 billion (or 8.5 percent of the group's total operating profits), while Japan contributed ¥333 billion and North America ¥99 billion. The group will have the most extensive global network among the big four, not only in Asia but also in many parts of the world, thanks to the excellent network developed by the former Bank of Tokyo.

Restructuring The integration of the Bank of Tokyo-Mitsubishi, the Mitsubishi Trust and Banking Corporation, and the Nippon Trust Bank is expected to enhance the group's competitiveness through the acquisition of specialized skills, improve the efficiency of its overseas networks, and share operational systems to reduce costs. The incorporation of Mitsubishi Trust and Banking strengthens the group because of an advantage over other competitors in the asset management business. In the area of international operations, it will broaden and strengthen the global network by consolidating it in a hub and spoke formation for more efficient cash management services (CMS) and other services for large enterprises. It will also expand cross-border securities transactions, M&As, derivatives, structured finance, and securitization. The group is said to have allocated ¥80 billion of its IT investment to upgrade its overseas CMS system, which will make it the only Japanese bank able to offer global real-time netting and pooling.

United Financial of Japan (UFJ) Group

Background Asahi Bank and Tokai Bank agreed to integrate their operations because they would complement each other well regionally (Asahi in the Kanto area and Tokai in the Nagoya-Tokai area), especially in the retail market. The inclusion of Sanwa Bank, strong in the Kansai area, in March 2000 brought the number of banks to be integrated to three, widening the regional coverage. However, Asahi Bank withdrew in June, and the remaining two banks agreed to integrate with Tokyo Trust Bank to form a three-bank partnership in July. The three banks announced in October that they would establish UFJ Holdings, Inc. as a holding company in April 2001. It was also announced that Sanwa Bank and Tokai Bank would merge in April 2002.

Overseas Operations The three banks' balance of loans to Asia as of September 2000 was the smallest among the Big Four financial groups at ¥1.2 trillion, or 17.9 percent of the Big Four loans in the region. They also had the lowest NPL ratio at 5.7 percent in Asia. A geographical analysis of the three banks' operating profit shows that Asia-Oceania contributed ¥52 billion or 13.3 percent of the total, much bigger than operating profits from North America.

Although the Asia strategy was not mentioned in the basic integration agreement or the document announcing the establishment of the holding company, the UFJ Group is expected to maintain a network covering major Asian countries. The key behind this strategy is Sanwa Bank's investment in local banks, especially in ASEAN countries since the 1970s. In May 1997, immediately prior to the outbreak of the financial crisis, Sanwa launched the Sanwa Asian Bankers Forum for closely aligned local banks with the aim of facilitating information sharing and communication at the banks' presidential level. In June 1998, Sanwa Bank was reported to have linked its global CMS with two local banks. It injected additional capital into the Siam Commercial Bank (Thailand) on two occasions after the onset of the financial crisis, increasing its shareholding to around 20 percent. For the group as a whole, overseas commercial banking will continue to be an important source of business profits. The number of overlapping overseas offices will be reduced from fifty-nine at the end of March 2000 to thirty-six by March 2003.

Restructuring Actual operations of the holding company will be handled by six business units that will be established in April 2001. These include retail, corporate banking, global banking and trading, trust, asset management, and securities and investment banking. The group attempts to restructure the organization to increase operating profits substantially with the growth focus on retail and corporate banking. In international operations, the group aims to achieve its profit targets through the efficient utilization of risk assets and growth in noninterest income from trade finance and settlements and local currency business.

Daiwa Bank

Background Daiwa Bank is an Osaka-based city bank with retail banking with SMEs as its main activity. Although it is a regionally-based bank, it has a considerable operation in the Tokyo metropolitan areas and abroad. It is the smallest of all the city banks in asset size as of March 2000. In its restructuring program, it purports to become a "super-regional bank" based in the Osaka area, withdrawing entirely from overseas operations. In the sectoral restructuring scene, Daiwa is poised to go it alone among the Big Four. Daiwa will probably be the only bank standing alone in a sea of mergers and alliances, dwarfed by other banks; its asset size will be close to one-tenth of that of the largest of the four, Mizuho Financial Group (see Table 3.4).

Overseas Operations In the early 1990s, Daiwa was on an expansionary path, investing heavily in IT system development and acquiring a controlling share in a new spin-off securities company as the cross-sectoral operations between banking, trust banking, and securities trading were deregulated in 1993. The number of branches reached its peak in that year, both at home (211) and abroad (61), as did the number of personnel. Daiwa Bank was in the middle of the pack (of city banks) in terms of overseas exposure with 21 percent of total loans attributed to nonresident borrowers in 1993.

Daiwa's overseas exposure began to decline towards the mid-1990s by 8 percent per annum during 1993–1995, in accordance with sectorwide trends of retrenchment on overseas operations because of asset disinflation at home and the enforcement of the BIS capital adequacy guideline in 1993. Then, Daiwa's overseas exposure exhibited a precipitous decline in 1996 when the bank was barred from business in the United States in connection with a securities trading irregularity in its New York office operations the year before. Subsequently after the 1995 incident, Daiwa made a decision to withdraw from overseas operations with the exception of servicing domestic clients' needs overseas and information gathering. By 1998, outstanding overseas loans were down to 8 percent of total loans.

In East Asia, Daiwa Bank was heavily exposed to Indonesia and Hong Kong. Daiwa Bank has withdrawn from Indonesia and Hong Kong rapidly since the beginning of the regional financial crisis, and from other East Asian countries as well. The bank's Asian exposure declined by three-fourths in the last two years, now ranking the lowest in Asian exposure among the city banks, to less than one percent of total loans.

Restructuring Daiwa Bank's restructuring program began in 1997 in the aftermath of the New York incident with the express purposes of increasing transparency and retrenching from overseas operations. The restructuring program aims at a complete withdrawal from overseas operations and conversion into a superregional bank serving the Kansai area. It has as its specific agenda the following three items: (a) contribution to the financial stabilization and restructuring of the financial sector in the Kansai area, including the stable provision of credit to local firms and financing the recapitalization of regional banks in the area; (b) strengthening the trust banking department by creating a company-in-company dealing in trust banking and eventually creating a spin-off company; and (c) the reallocation of resources from overseas operations to help accomplish the above two agendas.

Daiwa Bank has not expressed any intention to merge or ally with any other city bank or group. Daiwa intends, however, to collaborate with Kinki Bank and Osaka Bank, regional banks in the area, first in sharing ATM facilities, and later expanding the areas of collaboration into ownership and operations.

VI. Conclusion

Faced with the dramatic changes in the market and nonmarket environments, Japanese banks are consolidating and restructuring their businesses and repositioning their core competency in a fierce battle for survival. The strategy common to most major city banks has consisted of (a) a merger, acquisition, or alliance in pursuit of economies of scale and new capacities in investment banking, asset management, pension schemes, and fee-based services; (b) the consolidation of their core business with traditional clients; and (c) a retrenchment on overseas operations, a tactical retreat for some banks. For all of them, the objective is now clearly to maximize the ROE in a departure from traditional quantitative targets such as expansion of market shares and transactions volume. These elements of the strategy are clearly indicative of their resolve for a rebirth in a new environment where they cannot expect any protection from the government beyond the provision of a stable macroeconomic climate and a regulatory and supervisory framework.

During the process of restructuring, the banks' strategic focus will be on the core business and clientele in the domestic markets where the stakes are high, while overseas operations are subordinated to the domestic agenda, at least for now. Thus, the main drama is played out in the domestic market while the banks' overseas operations are on retrenchment, as mandated by the Financial Supervisory Agency over the near term. The once-dominant position of Japanese banks in East Asia is now being threatened by leading U.S. and European banks even while Japanese banks still consider Asia their most important strategic overseas market.

The retrenchment of domestic and overseas operations and concentration on the Japanese and Japanese-affiliated borrowers is a general business direction mandated by the Financial Supervisory Agency in connection with the infusion of public funds for bank recapitalization. This mandate will be binding over the near term until the public funds are fully repaid. For some banks, however, this is a tactical retreat. At a minimum, Japanese banks will try to establish and maintain an international network of financial services in support of the overseas business activities of their clients at home, and will expand again in Asian markets when the market conditions are right. However, any serious reengagement in overseas operations will have to come only after order is reestablished in the domestic markets first, where the battle is for survival.

Notes

1. The authors thank Vinod Aggarwal and other conference participants at the first and second meetings for their comments on earlier versions of this chapter and David Bisbee for his editorial assistance. The findings, interpretations, and conclusions expressed in this paper are those of the authors and do not necessarily represent the views of the World Bank, its Executive Directors, the countries they represent, or the Bank of Japan. Our analysis is based on the theoretical framework developed in Chapter 1, by Vinod Aggarwal, in this volume.
2. Peek et al. (1997).
3. Portfolio investments and FDI were the major capital flow components that recorded net outflows. Those net outflows more than offset the net inflow in the banking sector, thereby financing the overall current account surplus.
4. Financial and capital liberalization in the region facilitated the expansion of FDI flows to East Asia, and was itself motivated by the East Asian governments' promotion of an export-oriented growth strategy that included the liberalization of inward FDI. See Kawai (1998). This process was followed by liberalization of bank loans and foreign bank operations that tended to support the businesses of foreign companies. See Urata's chapter in this volume for a more detailed discussion of Japanese investment in developing East Asia.
5. See Froot and Stein (1991), Kawai (1994), and Ito (1999).
6. The causes and consequences of the asset disinflation in the 1990s are well documented. See for instance Hoshi and Kashyap (1999) and Kanaya and Woo (2000).
7. Measured by commercial land prices in the six major cities (Noguchi, 1994).
8. This assertion, however, needs to be qualified, since some of the banks disclose their exposures to the region on a net basis that excludes the portion covered by prime collateral and guarantees. Japanese bank exposures to Japanese-affiliated clients in the region are understated to the extent that they are guaranteed by Japanese parent companies. The assertion can thus be interpreted that Japanese banks curtailed their risk exposure to non-Japanese affiliated borrowers to a greater extent than they did to Japanese affiliates.
9. According to the Financial Supervisory Agency, adversely classified assets of major Japanese banks accounted for 11.6 percent (¥41.6 trillion) of their total credit exposure as of the end of March 1999, as compared with 11.2 percent (¥44.1 trillion) at the end of March 1998.
10. Kanaya and Woo (2000).
11. However, it is possible that actual NPLs to South Korea are larger than nominal past-due loans; apparently current loans to South Korea possibly include evergreen loans and/or rate-reduced and other restructured loans.
12. As part of segment information related to consolidated financial statements, internationally active Japanese banks disclose segment profit/loss and segment assets by geographic area. Japanese banks geographically segment financial information by Japan, the Americas, Europe, and Asia.
13. It should be noted that Japanese and many other foreign banks' confidence in South Korea was improved significantly mainly because the government exercised stronger leadership and involved itself more closely in the financial and corporate restructuring from an early stage of the crisis. In August 1997, the South Korean government announced a guarantee on banks' external debt, and between the end of 1997 and early 1998 it worked with international creditor banks to restructure the banking system's short-term external debt by confirming the guarantees of the debt, which facilitated rescheduling of $24 billion short-term external debt of South Korean commercial banks. The government also provided 64 trillion won (about 15 percent of GDP) as fiscal support for bank restructuring and expects to spend another 40 trillion won to complete the second round of financial sector restructuring. In the corporate sector, under the out-of-court framework, the government took initiatives in restructuring *chaebols*, major clients of Japanese banks and other foreign creditors, including the reduction of debt-to-equity ratios of *chaebols* (*big deals*), the reduction of cross guarantees among corporations within each *chaebol*, the promotion of exchanging businesses among *chaebols*, and the shedding

of noncore businesses. These efforts helped reduce risks associated with debt restructuring, thereby enhancing confidence in Japanese and other foreign creditors.
14. In the view of Japanese creditors, an across-the-board debt reduction would have undermined ongoing restructuring efforts by inducing debtors' moral hazard and worsening the long-term confidence in the regional economies. Debt reduction should have been the last resort. But if it had been inevitable, a scheme should have been devised whereby the rate of reduction was differentiated according to viability and did not exceed the market discount rate. Moreover, availability of the scheme should have been tied to restructuring efforts. Debt rescheduling may have been a preferred course of action for Japanese creditors. To the extent that debt rescheduling with a concessionary discount rate was equivalent to debt reduction, the former should have been used, supported by an interest guarantee scheme and/or a backstop facility in support of the banks' term transformation.
15. It should be noted, however, that any exchange rate support would have a tradeoff in interest rates and would not reduce the burden on debtors. If the actual exchange rate had overshot the long-run equilibrium rate, it would revert to the latter in time.
16. However, because of risk considerations, Japanese banks' lending stance toward the East Asian region did not drastically change after the capital injection. Additionally, Japanese banks' capacity to raise dollar funds from U.S. and European banks would not be instantly enhanced by the capital injection alone until credit ratings of Japanese banks were upgraded and stabilized.
17. At home, competitive pressures are mounting from Japanese nonbanks as well as from foreign banks. Sony Corporation and Ito Yokado, both previously nonbank firms, have been licensed to enter into the banking business. The presence of foreign banks is increasingly felt both at home and in the East Asia region where Japanese banks have traditionally been major stakeholders. The number of foreign banks in Japan steadily rose in the 1990s, although the number declined slightly in the past year in the aftermath of its financial crisis. The trend in expansion of their presence reflected the effect of the "Financial Big Bang" since 1998, an expansion of overseas investments touched off by a low interest rate policy in Japan and a decline of investor confidence in Japanese banks. The expansion is most pronounced in the areas of corporate pension, asset management, derivatives, and other high-skill services.
18. The so-called Japanese "Financial Big Bang," adopted in 1996 and implemented in full by 2001, is considered "a bigger bang" than the original Big Bang in London in 1986. The latter basically involved deregulation of fees for stock transactions and opening up the London Stock Exchange to foreigners while the Japanese deregulation efforts brought down barriers between banking, securities, and insurance industries as well as the liberalization of foreign exchange transactions. That is, barriers to nonbank and nonfinancial institutions as well as barriers to foreign participation were dismantled, potentially leading, if successful, to greater competition and a more rapid reorganization of the financial industry than was experienced in the London Big Bang. It appears that foreign banks are poised to take advantage of opportunities in the country with the world's second largest domestic economy and abundant financial savings and that the Big Bang set the stage for their active participation in the Tokyo markets.
19. In the age of the IT revolution, banks will compete fiercely to provide high-quality and customized financial services at low costs. Individuals will demand services for asset management, pension schemes, and customized loans, while corporations will need services for liquidity management, cash management, risk management, and total portfolio management. This presents an opportunity and a challenge for banks in that winners will reap the lion's share of the markets while losers will perish. Also, the barriers between traditionally segmented sectors such as banking, security, insurance, and even commerce will diminish and the market participants will all strive to provide comprehensive financial services with the result that financial markets will become larger, more integrated, and competitive. Furthermore, there will be a need for infrastructure services for cyberspace finance such as electronic certification, identification, credit evaluation, payment settlement, and e-securities. Banks will, in partnership with IT-related corporations, develop and install the systems that will provide such infrastructure services.

20. Large corporations are increasingly relying on capital markets for fundraising in a fundamental shift away from bank borrowing. The overall demand for bank finance in the corporate sector is shrinking for that reason; in other words, the pie is getting smaller for the banking sector, forcing banks either to consolidate or to become major players in the capital markets. Thus, corporations' demands for bank services are changing from the loan business to investment banking and the development and provision of various services in wholesale banking (for example, services facilitating the liquidity of securities and project finance and technical services in developing and installing a new accounting framework for corporations designed to conform to international standards).
21. All city banks that received public fund infusions for recapitalization were ordered to submit in March 1999 a restructuring plan for sound management, "*Keiei no kenzenka no tameno keikaku,*" in which one finds references to core competency. Of all the city banks, Tokyo-Mitsubishi alone did not receive public funds and therefore did not submit such a plan.
22. One clear example of economies of scale has to do with pooling resources for IT-related investments. No single bank can afford a critical mass investment in IT development, although a number of them together could. Another has to do with streamlining and downsizing the managerial structure. The other form of reorganization under consideration relates to the staffing structure. Banks may strive to downsize the professional staff into a cadre of fewer highly specialized and highly paid professionals assisted by support staff whose salaries are relatively low, thereby increasing productivity and reducing the total wage bill.
23. Much of the information in this section has been gleaned from Takayasu (2001).

References

Froot, Kenneth A. and Jerome C. Stein (1991). "Exchange Rates and Foreign Direct Investment: An Imperfect Capital Markets Approach," *Quarterly Journal of Economics* 106, pp. 1191–1217.

Hoshi, Takeo (2000). "What Happened to Japanese Banks?" IMES Discussion Paper, No. 2000-E-7 (March), Institute for Monetary and Economic Studies, Bank of Japan.

Hoshi, Takeo and Anil Kashyap (1999). "The Japanese Banking Crisis: Where It Came From and How Will It End?" NBER Working Paper Series, No. 7250 (July).

Ito, Takatoshi (1999). "Capital Flows in Asia." NBER Working Paper Series, No. 7134 (May).

Kanaya, Akihiro and David Woo (2000). "The Japanese Banking Crisis of the 1990s: Sources and Lessons." IMF Working Paper, WP/00/7 (January), International Monetary Fund, Washington, D.C.

Kawai, Masahiro (1994). "Accumulation of Net External Assets in Japan." In *Japan, Europe and International Financial Markets: Analytical and Empirical Perspectives,* ed., by Ryuzo Sato, Richard M. Levich, and Rama V. Ramachandran (Cambridge: Cambridge University Press).

Kawai, Masahiro (1998). "Evolving Patterns of Capital Flows and the East Asia Crisis." EAP Working Paper Series, No. 98-04 (December). (Washington, D.C.: World Bank).

Kwan, C. H. (1997). "Deepening Asia–Japan Economic Interdependence—The Impact of the Yen's Appreciation." Discussion paper prepared for the World Bank (April).

Noguchi, Yokio (1994). "Land Prices and House Prices in Japan." In Yuko Noguchi and J.M. Poterba, eds., Housing Markets in the United States and Japan. (Chicago: University of Chicago Press).

Peek, Joe and Eric S. Rosengren (1997). "The International Transmission of Financial Shocks: The Case of Japan," *American Economic Review* 87 (September), pp. 495–505.

Pereira da Silva, Luiz A. and Masaaki Kuroyanagi (2000). "A Stylized Interpretation of the 1997–98 Asian Crisis, Based on Results of a Qualitative Questionnaire to Japanese City Banks," *JBIC Review* 2 (November), pp. 1–46.

Takayasu, Ken'ichi (2001). "Merger Plans and Asia Strategies of Japanese Banks," *RIM Pacific Business and Industries* Vol. II, No. 51 (March), Sakura Institute of Research, pp. 2–32.

World Bank (1999a). "Hong Kong: Financial Policies amid the Regional Crisis." Mimeographed (May), East Asia and the Pacific (Washington, D.C.: World Bank).

World Bank (1999b). "Singapore: The Financial Crisis: A Challenge and an Opportunity." Mimeographed (June), East Asia and the Pacific (Washington, D.C.: World Bank).

World Bank (1999c). "The Constraints on Japanese Creditors in Restructuring Private Debt in East Asia." AGRI Background Paper (April).

CHAPTER FOUR

Cartels, Competition, and Consolidation in the Japanese Chemical Industry

TAMETSUGU TAKETOMI[1]

I. Introduction

The Japanese chemical industry has stalled in its efforts to move from a domestic to an international focus. Although the Japanese chemical industry began using foreign direct investment (FDI) as a business strategy in the 1970s, especially in Asia, overseas revenue for the major chemical companies still comprises less than 20 percent of their total revenue. This figure is much less than the FDI revenue of Japanese firms in other sectors,[2] and revenue and profit margins of the leading Japanese chemical companies have consistently remained far below those of their global counterparts. Indeed, there has been much discussion among industry participants and industry watchers of the domestic orientation of Japanese chemical companies.[3]

This situation changed after the Japanese bubble economy burst in 1990.[4] The industrial structure that maintained regulated competition collapsed and the investment behavior of Japanese chemical companies changed in response. Since then, the market environment facing Japanese chemical companies has changed significantly. First, domestic market demand shrank as chemical producers shifted their operations overseas. Second, global competitors accelerated their rate of investment in the Asian market, forcing Japanese chemical companies to increase their own investments in the region in order to keep up. Third, regulations that protected the Japanese market from foreign competition were weakened and import tariffs reduced. Fourth, the Japanese financial industry underwent restructuring in a financial "Big Bang" that forced Japanese chemical companies supported by Japanese banks to restructure their own operations.

This chapter describes and analyzes the bases of the Japanese chemical industry's strategic adaptation to market and nonmarket pressures. By tracing the causes of these changes, I show that nonmarket factors such as government regulations and bank support have played a more important role than market factors in determining the strategy of Japanese chemical companies in Asia. Indeed, at certain times nonmarket factors were key in triggering strategic changes in the chemical industry. I then analyze the case of Mitsubishi Chemical as a representative example of Japanese chemical companies to illustrate the impact of nonmarket and market factors on the operations of a specific company.

II. Positional Analysis

Market Environment

Since 1990, the market environment facing Japanese chemical companies has changed dramatically. Prices in the domestic chemical market are increasingly linked to foreign market prices, subjecting Japanese chemical firms to global supply and demand (see Figure 4.1).[5]

As suggested in the forecast made by Japan's Ministry of Economy, Trade, and Industry (METI, formerly the Ministry of International Trade and Industry or MITI), supply in Southeast Asia will exceed demand in 2003 (Southeast Asia is represented as ASEAN in Figure 4.1). The market surplus in Southeast Asia is a result of aggressive investment by local companies that expected to maintain constant growth in the region. Additionally, the 1997 Asian economic crisis depressed demand and exacerbated the glut in the market, a situation that is expected to continue until 2002 or 2003. Downward pressure on prices is expected to continue—especially since forecasts made by METI tend to overestimate demand, reflecting the optimism of industry participants.

In regards to the Asian market in general, the glut in Southeast Asia is balanced by demand in the Chinese market, which is predicted to exceed 10 million tons in 2003. Suppose that actual demand is 10 percent greater than the forecasted level; a deviation of 1 million tons is almost equivalent to the *aggregate* demand of some Southeast Asian countries. This type of demand fluctuation has occurred in China in the past, which led to a tightening of supply that raised prices in the regional market. Because Japanese suppliers were positively affected by this previous fluctuation,

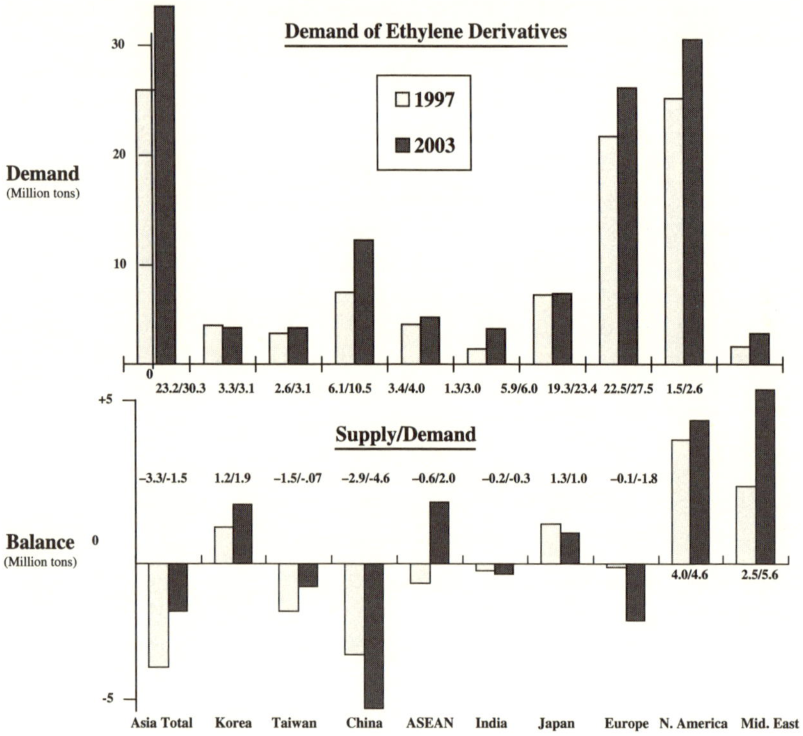

Figure 4.1 Global supply/demand trend of petrochemical products

Note: Ethylene derivatives: LDPE, HDPE, SM, PVC, EG.
Source: "Global supply/demand trend of pertrochemicals" Ministry of Trade and Industries (MITI) April, 1999.

some of them tend to overestimate Chinese demand and anticipate future opportunities for growth. However, most Japanese chemical companies also recognize the risks of investing in China, stemming from factors such as the unclear legal status of FDI, the threat of currency instability, and the hazards of economic transition. In light of the various sources of uncertainty in China, it is risky for Japanese chemical companies to depend on Chinese demand and FDI in China as the linchpin of their strategy in a globalizing market.

In addition to this uncertainty and risk in Asian countries, projected surpluses in the Middle East and North America will increase competition in the global market (see Figure 4.1). This oversupply is likely to result in depressed prices in the Asian market. Therefore, the predicted

Asian supply shortage in 2003 will not necessarily generate additional Japanese investment in the region.

Global Competitive Conditions (1990–1996) Foreign competitors undertook large-scale reorganizations during the 1990s. American firms reacting to recession in the early 1990s led the way in restructuring. For example, Imperial Chemical Industries (ICI) split off its pharmaceutical division into a separate company, Zeneca. ICI and DuPont also exchanged their acrylic and nylon businesses, allowing each to focus on its core operations.

Dow and DuPont trimmed their respective workforces by nearly a third between 1990 and 1996. After weathering a serious recession in 1992, U.S. chemical companies recovered rapidly by restructuring. As a result their return on sales (net income/sales) topped 9 percent in 1996. In Europe, and especially in Germany, firms also engaged in similar restructuring practices. The combined total of employees at Hoechst, Bayer, and BASF fell from approximately 480,000 in 1990 to 400,000 in 1996; average return on sales of these companies improved from 3.4 percent in 1990 to 5.1 percent in 1996. By restructuring, American and European chemical companies improved their business performance and financial condition while positioning themselves to take advantage of opportunities in Asia—the only region experiencing growth at the time.

Conventional wisdom dictates that this restructuring was mainly triggered by shareholder pressure for improvements in stock value. For example, ICI was motivated to spin off its pharmaceutical division because the average price of stock in the pharmaceutical industry was higher than in the chemical industry. ICI expected the stock price of the new pharmaceutical company to converge toward the average of the pharmaceutical industry, benefiting shareholders of both divisions. In contrast, although the Japanese chemical industry faced a similar economic environment and turned in a similar financial performance, it did not take aggressive action to restructure at the time because pressure to increase shareholder value was comparatively weak.

In terms of size, Japanese chemical companies are dwarfed by their European and American competitors. For example, companies that focus on the life sciences are represented by firms such as Aventis (a merger of Hoechst and Rhone Poulenc), Novartis, and Monsanto. Aventis's revenue in 1998 was $20 billion, making it the largest life science company in the world; its investment in research and development (R&D) alone was larger than the revenue of Takeda Pharmaceutical, the largest pharmaceutical company in Japan. Foreign companies that focus on high value-added chemical products include Bayer and DuPont; the largest Japanese competitor is Toray Industries, whose revenues are less than half of DuPont's. Companies focusing on petrochemicals include both subsidiaries of oil companies such as Shell Chemicals, Exxon Chemicals or BP Chemicals and chemical companies such as BASF, Dow, and Union Carbide. These U.S.- and European-based companies aggressively pursue economies of scale for their commodity products. For example, Exxon began operations of a 800,000 ton/year ethylene facility and a 480,000 ton/year polyethylene facility in Singapore in 2001. The combined capacities of these facilities are far larger than that of any Japanese company.

European and U.S. chemical companies continue to restructure and focus on their core businesses through mergers and acquisitions (M&A) and through alliances. These restructured companies have invested in Asia more aggressively in order to improve their competitive positions. A good example is Montell, which is the largest supplier of polypropylene in the world.[6] Montell established a 50/50 polypropylene joint venture (JV) with Japan Polyolefins (JPO) in 1996, named the Montell–JPO Company (MJC). Subsequently, Montell, JPO, and MJC established a JV with a local company in Thailand in 1997. The production capacity of Montell is larger than the aggregate production capacity of Japan's seven largest suppliers.[7] These examples imply that Japanese petrochemical companies are still in the process of adjustment and lag behind U.S. and European giants in the Asian market.

Change of Buyers' Bargaining Power A structural change in a client industry affects its buying behavior. For example, global competition has intensified in the automotive industry, one of the largest customers of the chemical industry. The number of players has fallen to five or six as a result of their efforts to reduce manufacturing costs by maximizing economies of scale. Internal sources have estimated that one of the leading automotive companies has reduced its suppliers from all industries by one-fifth and its components suppliers by one-third.

Plastics are a major input used in the automotive industry. The industry is trying to reduce the procurement cost of plastics through global sourcing. Auto firms ask suppliers to provide materials to their manufacturing sites throughout the world and technical support for new product development, while simultaneously requesting a volume discount. Montell, the largest polypropylene supplier for the automotive industry in the world, has recognized this change in the automotive industry's procurement strategy and reacted by expanding its supply sites around the globe. The lesson here is that chemical companies with a high percentage of clients in the automotive industry must globalize in order satisfy their clients' procurement needs.

Internal Rivalry   Internal rivalry in the Asian chemical market changed between the 1980s and the 1990s. The petrochemical market represents the typical market structure of the broader chemical industry in Asia. The petrochemical market can be divided into two market segments: the monomer and the polymer markets. In Asia during the 1980s, monomer production was very limited and supply was provided mainly by Japanese, American, and European companies. The polymer market was in a similar situation and required relatively moderate quality for its final products. Most polymers were imported from Japan, the United States, and Europe.

Japanese chemical companies did not develop the Asian market by themselves, but rather relied on Japanese trading companies to export materials to the region. Since East Asia was considered to be an emerging export market for excess supplies and unattractive for building local supply facilities, it was deemed more efficient to capture the market by using the network of trading companies.

In the 1990s, many Japanese manufacturers that were clients of Japanese chemical companies such as electronics, audio–visual, and component manufacturers, shifted their production facilities to Southeast Asian countries. Japanese chemical companies then began exporting materials to Japanese manufacturers in those countries.

In contrast to the Japanese recession, developing Asian economies boomed during the early 1990s. To maintain growth, Japanese, American, and European chemical companies shifted their strategic focus to the region, increasing the number of market players. South Korean, Taiwanese, and domestic suppliers also entered into competition with Japanese, American, and European firms, seeking to export petrochemicals, since their production capacity outstripped domestic demand.

During this period, the Asian polymers market separated into the industry-user market and the consumer-user market. The industrial market is comprised of automotive and electronic goods, while the consumer market is comprised of packaging and other miscellaneous goods. The market for industry-users requires high-quality inputs, while the market for consumer-users emphasizes low prices.

Initially, the market for industry users was occupied by mostly Japanese suppliers since industrial goods were designed by Japanese engineers using Japanese raw materials. In addition, there were high costs associated with switching component materials. Thus, the materials used did not change until new models were introduced that could use equivalent materials available on the local market.

As Japanese raw materials exports increased, Asia became a strategic market for Japanese suppliers. This state of affairs did not continue for long, however, as Japanese manufacturers in Asian countries moved to reduce production costs by finding alternative raw materials in local markets. Furthermore, the majority of necessary raw materials were available cheaply in each local market for consumer users. Although Japanese raw material suppliers were able to compete with them on the margin, they could not earn enough in the long run. As a result, Japanese chemical companies began to consider direct investment in the region.

Nonmarket Environment

Establishment of a Cartel Guided by MITI Historically, ethylene derivatives such as polyethylene or polyvinyl chloride were sold through cosales companies. After polyolefin companies struggled with overcapacity problems during the 1983 recession, MITI introduced the Specific Industry Structure Improvement Treatment Act (SISIT) to limit the intensity of competition within the industry. As the result, sixteen polyolefin producers formed four groups and established cosales companies for polyethylene. Four polyvinyl chloride (PVC) cosales companies were also established in 1983. All polyolefin commodity sales were shifted to the cosales companies, and salespeople were dispatched from each member company to its respective cosales company. In essence, cosales companies were organizations through which member companies could communicate with one another about pricing.

As the industry turned into a global business over time, however, the government-supported cartel was no longer competitive. Companies were forced to respond to the market more directly through mergers and acquisitions. Industry restructuring reached its high point with the mergers of Mitsubishi Kasei and Mitsubishi Petrochemical in 1994 and of Mitsui Toatsu and Mitsui Petrochemical in 1997. With the upsetting of the delicate balance of power that METI had constructed, the member firms of each organization were forced to look for new alliance partners in different organizations, and the cartel collapsed. The demise of the cartel structure illustrates the way in which global market pressures rendered METI's administrative guidance obsolete.

Import Tariff Trend Soon after Japan entered a deep recession in 1990, the Japanese government began to reduce barriers to foreign competition.

Table 4.1 Japanese import tariffs for petrochemical products

Era	Polyethylene	Polyvinyl Chloride	Polypropylene	Polystylene	ABS	Comments
Prior to 1961	20%	30%	—	—	—	—
1961–1968	¥54/kg	20%	—	—	—	Free Trade
1968–1972	¥35/kg	10%	—	—	—	GATT, Kennedy Round
1972–1979	¥28/kg	8%	—	—	—	GATT, Tokyo Round
1979–1986	¥28/kg	5.8%	—	—	—	—
1986–1993	¥22.4/kg	4.6%	—	—	—	Tariffs reduced 20%
After 1993	¥22.4/kg	3.9%	—	—	—	GATT, Uruguay Round
1998	¥16.76/kg	—	—	—	—	—
1999	¥15.35/kg	—	¥17.90/kg	8.9%	3.1%	—
2000	¥13.94/kg	—	¥16.36/kg	8.4%	—	—
2001	¥12.53/kg	—	¥14.82/kg	7.9%	—	—
2002	¥11.12/kg	—	¥13.28/kg	7.4%	—	—
2003	¥9.71/kg	—	¥11.74/kg	7.0%	—	—
2004	6.5%	3.9%	6.5%	6.5%	3.1%	—

Sources: Spectrum Chemical Industry, 25 February 1994, Decision Resources Inc, and Chemical Economy.

In 1993, it lowered import tariffs for petrochemical products (see Table 4.1), which followed their agreement at the Uruguay Round of global trade negotiations to reduce petrochemical tariffs to between 3.1 and 6.5 percent by 2004. In the early 1990s, a tariff of ¥22.4 per kilogram of polyethylene was approximately 20 percent of the product price, high enough to effectively insulate the Japanese market from foreign competition.

Kombinat Renaissance In 1998, METI introduced another plan called "Kombinat Renaissance" to restructure ethylene complexes in Japan. Two oil companies, Mitsubishi–Nippon Oil and Japan Energy, and two petrochemical companies, Mitsubishi Chemical and Asahi Kasei, announced the first agreement under these guidelines in 2000. Each company agreed to integrate its facilities via pipelines with the others located in Mizushima in the Okayama prefecture of western Japan. They generated savings in production costs by ensuring easy delivery of naphtha and other materials to one another. In all, the plan listed five regions to be integrated, with between two and eight firms involved in each. The total investment under this plan in the five regions is estimated to reach ¥20 billion by 2002, two-thirds of which is subsidized by the government.[8]

The Kombinat Renaissance plan demonstrates once again how non-market factors (in this case government guidance and subsidies) function to protect industry participants from foreign competition, to alleviate internal competition, and to strengthen the industry's competitive position. Regardless of whether the intervention actually strengthens the competitiveness of Japan's chemical industry or only postpones the retreat of weaker participants from the market, it is notable that METI still supports and controls the industry, and that industry participants continue to follow METI's guidance.[9]

Change of Business Custom   The typical barriers to entry that exist in the Japanese chemical market relate to distribution channels and pricing mechanisms, which are in turn based on Japanese business customs.

The chemical industry in Japan has two distinctive characteristics: (a) plastics molders are small and fragmented; and (b) wholesaler or trading companies act as agents between buyers and suppliers of chemicals. Because of the fragmented nature of the molding industry, trading companies have borne a high credit risk for payments. In the 1980s, plastic producers and trading companies developed exclusive supplier–buyer relationships in which the trading company makes interest-free loans to the molder with which to buy equipment. The molder in turn gives the trading company exclusive trading rights. For example, the Mitsubishi Corporation (a trading company) has created a group involving more than a hundred molders, each of which uses products of chemical companies belonging to the Mitsubishi group. This *keiretsu* (affiliation) coalition represents a formidable barrier to newcomers, and similar forms of *keiretsu* exist in almost all types of distribution channels (including other chemical channels) in Japan.

A second barrier to entry is the pricing mechanism. Prices for petrochemical products are settled between buyers and suppliers as much as a year after the actual transaction takes place. Each party has the right to negotiate a price that takes into account general economic conditions and the specific company's financial performance. This industry custom provides obvious benefits for both parties and fosters a "give and take" relationship. However, this arrangement does not hold in Asian export markets, where chemical companies trade with companies based in the target market rather than in the *keiretsu* group.

Furthermore, the persistent weakness of Japan's financial sector undermines *keiretsu* relationships. Major Japanese banks have begun restructuring through mergers and are moving toward aggregation into four groups.[10] One such merger triggered the announcement of a merger of

Mitsui Chemical and Sumitomo Chemical in 2002. This type of cross-*keiretsu* group merger has never happened in Japan, and bank restructuring will likely continue to encourage mergers of *keiretsu* companies.

Changes in the Accounting System   Beginning in 2000, the Japanese government began introducing reforms to the national accounting system. A consolidated accounting system was instituted in April 2000, and a market value-based accounting system is being introduced over the course of 2001 and 2002.

This system change will affect the management system and/or behavior of Japanese chemical companies in two areas in particular:

1. the preexisting single accounting system supported a lifelong employment system in which Japanese companies established subsidiaries where senior employees were dispatched to spend the rest of their business life until retirement.
2. each subsidiary was required to maintain break-even financial performance. The book value-based accounting system maintained a buffer for cash management. As long as a Japanese company possessed an unrealized asset such as land or securities, financial institutions were willing to lend it money.

After the change in the national accounting system, chemical companies began to review their strategies on a comprehensive basis and to make restructuring plans for their subsidiaries. They also started to alter their management systems and organization, considering changes such as creating a separation between board members and executives and introducing holding companies. These organizational changes are expected to support changes in the nature of managerial decision making.

Technological Impact of the Internet   It is well known that Internet sales in book retailing, online music delivery, stock brokerage, and ticketing have fundamentally changed the competitive structure of each product's market, reducing the revenue of existing distributors while increasing sales through Internet channels. Internet sales matter less in the chemical industry, since companies require a stable long-term supply. Even if buyers find a new supplier that offers a lower price, they do not switch to that supplier until they are able to secure a stable long-term supply. Instead, they use the lower prices of a competing supplier to negotiate prices with the existing supplier.

The Internet may erode some conventional barriers to entry. Internet sales often eliminate a trading company or a wholesaler by directly connecting manufacturers and buyers (i.e., "disintermediation"). The transaction fee paid to trading companies or wholesalers ranges from 3 to 10 percent of a transaction price. On many occasions, several wholesaler (including trading) companies mediate transactions. Transaction fees for a primary dealer are automatically paid to them without their actual participation in the deal and are therefore called "sleeping fees."[11] In the past, buyers and suppliers had no alternative channels aside from direct deals.

Recently established U.S.-based Internet chemical trading companies such as Chemconnect and Chematch have started trading on the Internet and they plan to launch an operations site in Japan. Prices may be expected to fall because: (a) Internet trading makes the lowest price on the market instantly available to every participant; and (b) Internet trading companies offer lower transaction fees than conventional trading companies. Although conventional trading companies retain advantages in credit risk and transportation management, Internet trading firms' propensity to lower market prices and reduce transaction fees will likely allow them to penetrate existing channels.

Thus, Internet trading companies have the potential to challenge existing *keiretsu* channels that posed conventional entry barriers and to establish new channels and business customs in the chemical industry. Japanese trading companies are investing in emerging Internet trading companies to avert head-to-head competition and to secure the position of their business channels and the existing fee system in Japan.

Market penetration by Internet trading companies is an example of how a nonmarket factor like changing technology can change *keiretsu* channels. If the market structure changes in the near future, it will be because of emerging nonmarket factors such as technology that render conventional nonmarket barriers (*keiretsu*) obsolete.

Firm Position

Whereas most American and European chemical companies are restructuring and focusing on specific areas to address global competition, their Japanese counterparts demonstrate a wider range of tactics in preparation for global competition. Asahi Glass and Toray Industries, for example, are leading global producers among Japanese chemical companies. Asahi Glass has already developed business sites around the world, while Toray industries shifted its operations overseas to Malaysia, Indonesia, and Thailand when the textile trade conflict took place between the United States and Japan in 1970s. Kao (segment 2), a leading consumer goods and cosmetic company, also developed its business internationally, focusing on the

United States and Europe, whose consumers can afford to buy Kao's products. These companies with long international operating experience have established their brand names in markets throughout the world, competing with other global players. Most companies described in this chapter, by contrast, are categorized in segments 4 and 5, and are representative of the Japanese chemical industry more generally. Their behavior has influenced other chemical companies and the Japanese government's industrial policy.[12]

In November 2000, Sumitomo Chemical and Mitsui Chemical agreed to merge into Sumitomo-Mitsui Chemical in October 2003. The merger will make the new company the fifth largest chemical company in the world. By announcing its intention to invest in an ethylene complex in Singapore that Sumitomo Chemical owns, Sumitomo–Mitsui showed its commitment to becoming a global player. The merger is also likely to stimulate further restructuring among other players in the industry.

III. Strategies and Tactics

Market Strategies and Tactics

In the past, the market strategy of Japanese chemical companies was simple: to take leading market shares in the domestic market and then reap the profits guaranteed by government intervention in the market to prevent "severe" (i.e., unprofitable) competition. This strategy functioned when constant market growth was secured and when the market was protected from foreign competition.

In this environment, Japanese chemical companies competed to expand their facilities, although it has been said that these investments were implicitly controlled by MITI. This competition sometimes caused an oversupply in the domestic market, which was often exported to maintain utilization of their facilities. Although export prices were significantly lower than domestic prices, making only marginal profits, the high utilization of facilities helped boost their total profits.

This general strategy was forced to undergo changes in 1992 when foreign products began to penetrate the Japanese market. Faced with this "domestic internationalization," the chemical industry began restructuring and increased direct investment in Asia, where high rates of growth were expected.

Japanese chemical companies recognized that the market environment surrounding them had completely changed and that they needed to invest directly in the region. The number of participants in the Asian market is twice that of North America or Europe, but the average capacity in Asia is far smaller than that of the other regions. Consequently, Japanese chemical companies, wary of potential oversupply and uncertain growth in the region in the early 2000s, are responding with strategic restructuring through M&As and alliances.

After the Plaza Agreement After the Plaza Agreement in 1985, which increased the value of the yen vis-à-vis the dollar, Japanese export-oriented companies came to see Asian countries as strategic markets and started to relocate their production facilities there.[13] For example, electronics industries shifted to Southeast Asia, where they built production facilities for exports to North America. This relocation accelerated rapid economic growth in the developing countries of Asia.

In the developing Asian chemical industry of the 1980s, no large chemical complex existed outside of South Korea and China. In order to supply raw materials to client companies that had shifted production from Japan to Asia, Japanese chemical companies exported products according to their requests. However, since the Japanese economy was still growing at the time, Japanese chemical companies focused on the Japanese market and expanded production capacities to increase their domestic market shares, leading them to vastly increase ethylene production facilities in Japan in the late 1980s and early 1990s. To maintain production utilization of chemical facilities, excess supply was exported, particularly to Asian markets. Because these exports were priced in dollars and the yen was appreciating against the dollar, total production costs exceeded export price. Thus, the chemical companies could only expect export price to exceed variable cost, basing their exports on marginal profit.

Domestic Internationalization In the early 1990s, most Asian countries expanded their petrochemical production capacities rapidly in accordance with their economic growth. Some of these countries, such as South Korea, expanded their production capacities in order to match demand in their domestic markets. These excess supplies went to export markets, gradually penetrating the Japanese market.

From 1986 to 1990, the revenue of Japanese petrochemical companies increased steadily, peaking at ¥4,331 billion in 1990. Although the bubble burst in 1990, the financial performance of these companies was still positive in 1991. Balance sheets became negative only in 1992, a symbolic year for Japanese petrochemical companies.

Comparing the performance of 1992 with that of 1986—the year after the Plaza Agreement—it is clear what happened in the Japanese petrochemical industry. Although ethylene production and domestic demand increased from 1986 to 1992,[14] utilization of ethylene facilities held steady at 91.4 percent. The import price of naphtha, which constitutes a major portion of ethylene production cost, also remained almost the same (¥17,890 in 1986 vs. ¥17,512 in 1992[15]).

The major difference between 1986 and 1992 is the market price of major petrochemical products in Japan. The market price dropped approximately 20 percent in 1992 and has not since returned to the price levels found in the years before 1991. Table 4.2 shows this trend. The export/import balance doubled from 1991 to 1992, while imports exceeded exports in 1986. This implies that Japanese petrochemical companies in 1992 maintained utilization of their production facilities by exporting excess supply when export prices were lower than domestic prices, making only marginal profit. This form of export dumping was called "starvation export." As a result, Japanese chemical companies saw a positive gross margin in 1986 turn to a negative gross margin by 1992. Since then, the domestic market price has been affected by the overseas market price (i.e., "domestic internationalization"), forcing Japanese chemical companies to develop a strategy for global competition.[16]

Japanese Chemical Companies' Investment in Developing East Asia In response to global competition, most Japanese chemical companies have accelerated their foreign investment. In the past Japanese chemical companies were domestically oriented and did not pursue aggressive strategies to invest in other countries. Large investments were represented by national projects usually led by a trading firm, which would typically bear the financial risks of a *keiretsu* group. Japanese chemical companies usually avoided investment risk and leveraged *keiretsu* power instead, especially by using the resources of a *keiretsu* trading firm and a *keiretsu* bank for FDI.[17] Once those projects were successfully completed and operations began, most of the trade to be generated by those projects would be controlled

Table 4.2 Prices of major petrochemical products in Japan (annual average) (yen/kg)

	1986	1987	1988	1989	1990	1991	1992	1993	1994	1995	1996	1997
LDPE	217	215	219	210	211	213	161	138	131	127	127	135
HDPE	207	206	211	205	206	210	158	130	113	107	108	117
PP	—	—	—	—	—	213	147	104	97	102	104	117
PS	223	228	245	240	239	213	149	109	100	111	119	119
SM	121	173	195	196	200	183	102	80	69	83	72	72
PVC	159	158	162	161	163	173	143	124	115	115	101	106
AN	162	143	160	156	154	132	96	88	91	113	104	90

Source: Average price of (major market) Japanese economic newspaper.

Table 4.3 Number of subsidiaries and overseas revenue ratio of major Japanese chemical companies

Firm	Number of subsidiaries in Asia	Ratio of revenue overseas (%)	Ratio of revenue in Asia (%)
Asahi Glass	34	43.6	12.0
Toray Industries	39	37.0	16.5
Kao Corporation	22	28.8	9.8
Asahi Chemical Industries	16	13.9	—
Sumitomo Chemical	16	20.0	13.5
Sekisui Chemical	6	—	—
Mitsubishi Chemical	14	19.1	9.7
Shin-Etsu Chemical	14	36.0	11.6
Mitsui Chemical	20	19.2	10.6
Teijin	16	27.7	15.8

Source: Annual reports.

by the trading firms that undertook the financial risks of investment. Whereas other foreign competitors had to bear such risks themselves, Japanese chemical companies leveraged *keiretsu* power to compete.

By the 1990s, however, international markets became the catalyst for Japanese chemical companies' FDI, particularly in developing Asia. When the yen-to-dollar exchange rate appreciated to less than 100 in 1995, the acceleration of investment started to catch up with Asian economic growth. This tended to integrate the Japanese and Asian markets, as management of Japanese chemical companies understood that the Japanese market would not be isolated from other Asian markets after the appreciation of the yen against the dollar and deregulation. This investment boom in the region by Japanese companies continued until 1997, when the Asian economic crisis hit the market.

Table 4.3 shows the number of overseas subsidiaries established by Japanese chemical companies in 1999. Such factors caused FDI in Asia by Japanese chemical companies to differ from FDI in other regions in the following ways:

- The number of subsidiaries in Asia is almost twice as large as that in North America or Europe.
- The number of subsidiaries established in North America and Europe decreased in the period, while the number in Asia is increasing. (Since the cumulative total before 1989 is four times as large as the years between 1990 to 1994, the number of subsidiaries established in Asia before 1989 is larger than the number between 1990 and 1994.)

CARTELS, COMPETITION, AND CONSOLIDATION

- Japanese chemical companies have almost 100 percent ownership of most subsidiaries in Europe and North America, while maintaining less than 50 percent ownership in one-third of joint ventures in Asia.
- The number of subsidiaries established in Asia increased rapidly after 1995. (Most of those subsidiaries were established between 1995 and 1997, before the Asian economic crisis.)

From the above points, it is clear that Japanese chemical companies focused on the Asian market and rapidly increased their FDI in Asia after 1995, recognizing that the Asian market had become a strategic market for all global players. Japanese chemical companies have concluded that they must secure their presence in the Asian market to compete with other global players.

Nonmarket Strategies and Tactics

The introduction of the Kombinat Renaissance in 1998 reinforced the tradition of strategic collaboration between the chemical industry and the government bureaucracy. In order to establish a strategy to strengthen the competitive position of each petrochemical company through industry restructuring, meetings were held periodically among governmental officers and chemical company executives. Through these meetings, a strategy to restructure each company was established. As such, METI has continued to lead strategy development and play an important role in industry restructuring. In this sense, Japanese chemical companies do not employ nonmarket strategies vis-à-vis the Japanese government per se but, rather, consult with MITI/METI as a strategic collaborator.

Organizational Strategies and Tactics

Domestic Restructuring After the international penetration of domestic markets, top management in each *keiretsu* group, including *keiretsu* banks and trading companies, recognized the need to restructure in the face of global competition. The first tangible action taken by industry participants was the merger of Mitsubishi Kasei and Mitsubishi Petrochemical in 1994 to create Mitsubishi Chemical, which became one of the top ten chemical companies in the world. Three years later, Mitsui Toatsu and Mitsui Petrochemical merged in 1997 to create Mitsui Chemical.

Companies that produce ethylene derivatives faced similar imperatives. After the Mitsubishi and Mitsui mergers, cosales companies ended their roles as cartel organizations.[18] Each cartel member began restructuring independently, recognizing that MITI's guidance was obsolete once it lost control of domestic prices. Some have separated these businesses from their core businesses and formed new joint ventures with others, reducing the total number of participants. The number of polypropylene and polystyrene producers was halved between 1993 and 1999, while the number of polyethylene and polyvinyl chloride producers fell by two-thirds over the same period. Meanwhile, Tokuyama and Idemitsu Petrochemical announced the establishment of a JV sales company for polypropylene in 2002, which should reduce the number of players in polypropylene to five by 2003.

During the late 1980s and early 1990s, many Japanese companies established strategic management companies in North America and Europe, which are expected to function as regional headquarters for all subsidiaries in each region. These organizations have been mainly employed by export-oriented companies that have overseas-to-domestic revenue ratios higher than 50 percent. Some Japanese chemical companies began to employ these organizational systems as well. This was a first step that Japanese chemical companies took toward reorganizing for globalization.

Japanese chemical companies also have responded to Japan's changing accounting system. As noted above, they have tended to take action on three fronts:

- creating holding companies;
- separating board members from operations officers;
- consolidating control of subsidiaries in Japan.

These strategic actions in association with organizational change are not limited to the Japanese chemical industry. Leading companies in other industries such as electronics or automobiles have taken the first strategic steps, followed by leading companies in the remaining industries. From this point of view, the Japanese chemical industry is a follower. Any strategic action associated with organizational change taken by a leading company in a leading industry in Japan is likely to be mimicked by Japanese chemical companies in the future.

IV. Case Study: Mitsubishi Chemical

Mitsubishi Chemical (formerly Mitsubishi Kasei and Mitsubishi Petrochemical) is one of the leading and oldest Japanese chemical companies, and is a core manufacturing company of the Mitsubishi group.

The company's strategy and its behavior have led the growth of the Japanese chemical industry. Its history parallels the history of the Japanese chemical industry as a whole and reflects the economic environment in Japan, including the effects of governmental guidance.

History

Mitsubishi Chemical started its operation as Japan Tar Industries in Kurosaki, Fukuoka Prefecture in 1934. After a few mergers and separations with other companies of the Mitsubishi group during and after the Second World War, it reemerged as Mitsubishi Kasei in 1952, just as heavy chemical industries began to take root in Japan. In the 1950s, while the petrochemical industry in Japan was still in an embryonic stage, Japanese chemical companies were not large enough to invest in petrochemical complexes by themselves. As a result, MITI formed a coinvesting risk group to start capital investment for petrochemical complexes. The Mitsubishi group including Mitsubishi Kasei, combined with the Shell group to establish Mitsubishi Petrochemical in 1956. Mitsubishi Petrochemical started its operation in Yokkaichi in Mie Prefecture as the first ethylene complex of the "Mitsubishi" group in 1959.

The Japanese petrochemical industry in general, and the Mitsubishi group in particular, grew in step with the Japanese economy. Mitsubishi Kasei established its ethylene complex in the city of Mizushima in Okayama Prefecture in 1964. Thenceforward, Mitsubishi Kasei and Mitsubishi Petrochemical developed their petrochemical businesses independently, competing with each other until they merged in 1994.

Like other Japanese chemical companies, Mitsubishi Kasei and Mitsubishi Petrochemical focused on the domestic market until the 1980s. In 1989, with the Japanese bubble economy still expanding, Mitsubishi Petrochemical planned a new ethylene complex in Kashima in Ibaraki Prefecture. The complex began operating in 1992, after the bubble had burst and prices of petrochemical products had started to fall. Although the complex had the largest ethylene capacity (600,000 tons per year) and featured the newest plant designs, it was not price competitive because of rapid depreciation of the complex's assets. Mitsubishi Petrochemical soon faced a cash shortage, as the Japanese chemical industry suffered a net loss in 1992 with the advent of foreign competition. The Mitsubishi group, led by Mitsubishi Bank (the main bank for both companies), coordinated the merger with Mitsubishi Kasei after the financial problems of Mitsubishi Petrochemical had become a serious issue for Mitsubishi Bank. The Mitsubishi group had previously recommended the merger, but the management of each company had wanted to maintain independent operations. Mitsubishi Petrochemical finally agreed to merge with Mitsubishi Kasei in 1994 after the sudden death of the president at the time, Masaki Yoshida, who was said to have insisted on operating independently. This merger triggered restructuring throughout the Japanese chemical industry.

Organizational Change

The profitability of Japanese chemical companies is very low compared with their U.S. competitors. The average U.S. return on sales in 1994–1998 was 3.0 percent.[19] Mitsubishi Chemical's return on sales in from 1991 to 2000 was 0.5 percent and between 1996 and 2000 was −0.5 percent.

In the past, low profitability was not necessarily as significant because the management of Japanese chemical companies believed sustainability was more important. Moreover, low profitability worked as an entry barrier to their foreign competitors. Since the same level of return on investment (ROI) for a project resulted in a comparatively high return for a Japanese chemical company and a low return for a foreign competitor, the Japanese chemical companies could justify the costs of investing in the project, but the foreign competitor could not.

After the merger, Mitsubishi Chemical became the largest chemical company in Japan in terms of revenues and began to react to global competition by seeking economies of scale. However, although its sales were large enough, it recognized that it was not ready for global competition because its financial position was weak, its foreign development (i.e., foreign sales or foreign investment) was still small, and its organization was still oriented toward the domestic market. To cope with global competition and to improve its financial position, it changed its organization to introduce an "inner-company" system, the first such reorganization attempted by a Japanese chemical company. Mitsubishi chemical established eight inner-companies: (1) basic petrochemicals and industrial chemicals; (2) polymer products; (3) raw materials for synthetic fibers; (4) carbon and agrochemicals; (5) information and electronics-related products; (6) pharmaceuticals and diagnostic systems; (7) specialty chemicals; and (8) functional materials.

By introducing this new organization system, Mitsubishi Chemical expected improvement on several fronts. Decision making for divisional strategy such as capital investment, profit management, human resource management, and the like would be delegated to each division. As a result, divisional management could make speedy decisions to cope with market requirements without having to steer through the central channels of corporate management. Profit responsibility (including asset responsibility) of each division would be clearly delineated to increase incentives for financial performance. To improve not only profitability but also efficient utilization of the assets of each inner-company, return on assets (ROA) was introduced as a measurement system. Such separation of individual businesses is expected to pave the way toward future holding company management in Japan's new consolidated tax accounting system.

This reorganization is expected to improve the firm's performance by redirecting resources toward areas of growth. By introducing the inner-company system and a new measurement system, Mitsubishi Chemical expected that resources would be shifted from old business areas such as petrochemicals and carbon and agrochemicals to new business areas such as functional and plastic-based products. Between 1991 and 2000, the functional and plastic-based products area increased its share, while the share of the carbon & agrochemicals area decreased. Because of the merger, the share of petrochemicals temporarily increased in 1994. Over the same period, carbon and agrochemicals have been the most profitable sectors, whereas petrochemical profits have fluctuated, making the former a more reliable source of stable growth and profits in the future.[20]

Mitsubishi's general global strategy was unclear for a couple of years after the organizational change. The president of each inner-company became narrowly focused and short-term oriented because they were evaluated by the annual performance of their own inner-company, and were officially discouraged from investing in foreign countries as a strategy for long-term sustainable growth. Instead, Mitsubishi Chemical started to select focus areas, mainly through alliances in Japan and M&A or termination of business overseas. Since lifetime employment is a major concern in Japan, alliances are taken as a "soft restructuring" of businesses.

Mitsubishi separated its polyolefin and ABS polymer businesses to establish joint ventures with Tonen Chemical and Japan Synthetic Rubber (JSR), creating Nippon Polyolefin and Technopolymer respectively in 1996. The polystyrene business was spun off to establish A&M Styrene with Asahi Chemical Industries in 1998. Meanwhile, floppy disk production facilities in the United States were shut down in 1998, and the polyester film venture with Hoechst was discontinued and restarted as its own business in 1998. Mitsubishi accelerated restructuring in 1999. The pharmaceutical business was separated and merged with Tokyo Tanabe to establish Tokyo-Mitsubishi Pharmaceuticals.[21] It sold its aluminum target business and high purity aluminum business, as well as its compounding business in the United States.

Table 4.4 History of foreign direct investment (FDI) of Mitsubishi Chemical

	1980		1990		2000
Asia	Dec 1972 * Mitsubishi Chemical Hong Kong (100%) — @ Asian Rare Earth (28%) (Ma) — Sep 1981 * Taiyo Kasei (100) (Taiwan) — Aug 1987 * Taiyo Deidok (100%) (Taiwan)	Jan 1988 @ San Nan Petrochemical (40%) (South Korea) — Mar 1989 * San Yang Kasei (50%) (South Korea)	* Mar 1991 PT Bakrie (57.4%) (Indonesia) — * Jul 1992 Mitsubishi Chemical Singapore (100%) — April 1994 * HMT Polystylene (67%) (Thai)	Feb 1996 * Taiyo Shingisha (100%) (Taiwan) — Dec 1995 * Mitsubishi Chemical Infonics (100%) (Singapore)	Feb 1997 @ MCC PTA India	April 1998 * Lithodun South Korea (70%) — Diachemical * (100%) (South Korea)
North America	Mar 1974 @ Ciquisine Conponhia Ptroquimica (27.9%) (Brazil) — April 1975 * Mitsubishi Chemical do Brazil (100%) — Dec 1980 * INTAC Automotive Products (50%) — June 1981 * USR Optonix (100%) — * Mitsubishi Chemical America (100%)	Dec 1986 * MYA Corp (100%) — Feb 1987 * Mytex Polymer (100%) — April 1987 * Western Litho Plate & Supply (100%)	* May 1990 Vebatim (100%) — * Mar 1991 Mimic (50%)	@ Jan 1996 Noltex (25%) — Sep 1995 * Pacific Western Ektruded Plastics (100%)	* April 1997 Texas Ultra Pure (100%) — * Dec 1997 M&C Sweetners (50%)	
Europe		July 1987 * Mitsubishi Chemical UK (100%) — * MKC Finance Amsterdam (100%)	Nov 1989 * Mitsubishi Chemical Europe (100%) (Germany) — Mar 1989 * Resindion SRL (100%) (Italy)		* Jan 1997 MC Infonics Ireland (100%)	

Source: Kaigai Shinshutsu Kigyou Ichiran, Tokyo Keizai.

Foreign Direct Investment

Table 4.4 shows the history of foreign direct investment in the chemical industry. Until 1980, the chemical industry invested abroad only in Brazil; in the early 1980s, it invested in North America and Taiwan. After 1985, when the yen began its long, steady appreciation, it began to invest in South Korea, Europe, and expanded operations in North America. In the early 1990s, it shifted its FDI target area to Southeast Asia, investing heavily, if somewhat episodically, in the region until the Asian economic crisis. To some extent, the focus on Southeast Asia was a response to U.S. and European competitors, who began investing significantly in the region in the mid-1990s. This competitive dynamic helps explain why Japanese companies remained in Southeast Asia despite the fact that cash flow on these investments turned negative in 1996.

To respond to competitors, Mitsubishi—as well as other leading Japanese chemical companies such as Toray Industries—made the decision to invest in Asia as a strategic region, regardless of its financial position. Although Japanese banks funded those investments, it is clear that Japanese chemical companies still have strong ties to Japanese banks. However, banks have been much more circumspect in lending since the Asian financial crises. By 2000, Mitsubishi Chemical and Toray Industries had established a beachhead in the Asian market for their strategic business areas, allowing them to increase investment in the region to compete with U.S. and European firms. Within a few years, Mitsubishi and Toray should be ready to compete successfully in the region.

In sum, the case of Mitsubishi Chemical is a good example to illustrate how Japanese chemical companies have developed their businesses in a competitive environment. By tracing the history of Mitsubishi Chemical, we can identify how nonmarket factors such as government guidance or bank support combine with market factors such as investment risk and a competitive international chemical market.

V. Conclusion

Japanese chemical companies have typically lagged behind their U.S. and European competitors, remaining domestically oriented and protected by high entry barriers and other nonmarket impediments. When faced with "domestic internationalization" in 1992, however, those barriers fell, forcing them to restructure their businesses by making alliances with outside companies or undertaking mergers in Japan, while simultaneously accelerating investment in Asian markets to keep pace with their foreign competitors. Although their relative financial performance was not good, Japanese chemical companies accelerated their investment to establish beachheads for their strategic businesses in the region to compete with their foreign competitors. The willingness of Japanese banks to underwrite these investments despite a negative cash flow has been essential to this investment strategy.

Although the economic and financial environment changed dramatically in Japan over the course of the 1990s, bank support still serves as an important factor in the investment decisions of selected Japanese chemical companies whose financial performance has suffered, by allowing them to continue to compete with their foreign counterparts.

There is no doubt that market factors, such as the advent of "domestic internationalization," which accelerated the restructuring of Japanese chemical industry, and the appreciation of the yen, which accelerated direct investment by Japanese chemical companies in Asian market, have played an important role in the transformation of the Japanese chemical industry. Still, organizational factors, such as bank support through *keiretsu* relationships and nonmarket factors such as governmental guidance, seem to have been more important in affecting the global competitive positions of the Japanese industry participants. Governmental guidance has functioned to support the overall industry, and *keiretsu* relationships with banks have functioned to support individual companies. Together, these multilayered factors have strengthened the competitive position of Japanese industry and individual companies. Although one could argue that governmental guidance does not in fact strengthen the competitive position of industry, it does not follow that this rule applies equally everywhere. The experience of Japanese chemical companies, both at home and in Asia, suggests the continuing relevance of nonmarket factors.

Notes

1. I would like to thank Vinod K. Aggarwal, Shujiro Urata, Ed Forgarty, and Elaine Kwei for comments on earlier versions of this article.
2. For example, overseas revenues account for roughly 50 percent of the total for Japanese automotive and electronics industries. For analysis of other sectors, see other chapters of this volume, all of which are based on the theoretical framework developed in Chapter 1 of this volume by Vinod Aggarwal.
3. Japanese chemical companies competed with each other in the domestic market under the regulated condition called the "Convoy Fleet" method by METI.
4. The Japanese stock price (Nikkei Average) increased from around 13,000 in 1986 to 39,000 at the end of 1989. However, it started to fall in 1990, reaching 24,000 in December 1990, and had fallen still further by the end of 1992. Land prices also collapsed, falling for the first time since World War II. Together these trends comprise the "bursting bubble" that began the decade-long descent of the Japanese economy.

5. This data is prepared by METI annually in collaboration with industry participants in Japan. Japanese petrochemical companies use this data for their medium term planning and capital budgeting for plant construction.
6. Montell, owned by the Royal Dutch/Shell Group, merged in 2000 with Targor, which was founded in 1997, as a 50/50 joint venture between BASF and Hoechst-and Elenac, which were owned by BASF and the Royal Dutch/Shell group. See http://www.montell.com/.
7. Petroleum Industry Association Montell Annual Report (1999).
8. *Nippon Keizai Shinbun,* February 5, 2001.
9. "Kombinat Renaissance" was named after the title of the book *Chemical Renaissance* published in 1998, which described the Japanese chemical industry and its strategic direction. Some industry participants argue that METI's guidance has become obsolete and does not function to strengthen the industry but, rather, weakens an industry facing global competition. However, because METI's subsidies are attractive to industry players, they follow their guidance. This shows a typical example of how the Japanese government controls the industry. Further arguments are made regarding the limitation of METI's guidance:

    (1) role of METI is limited to Japan, while competition of the industry is global; and
    (2) the role of METI is limited in a deregulated environment, pushing it to reestablish its role in ways that clash with corporate strategy.

    Since the main topics in this chapter do not involve the government role in the deregulated situation, I do not expand discussion on this issue further.
10. There were six major *keiretsu* groups in Japan: Mitsui, Mitsubishi, Sumitomo, Fuyo (Fuji), Dai-Ichi Kangyo, and Sanwa. The core members of a *keiretsu* are a leading bank, a leading trading company, and leading traditional manufacturers. For example, Mitsubishi Group includes Mitsubishi Bank, Mitsubishi Corporation, Mitsubishi Heavy Industries and others. *Keiretsu* manufacturers have an understanding to buy and sell each other's products and to be financially supported by a *keiretsu* bank. The banks merged into four groups in 2001. Those groups are: Tokyo-Mitsubishi Bank, Mitsui Sumitomo Bank, Sanwa-Tokai-Toyo Trust Bank, and Mizuho Financial Group (MHFG) (MHFG includes Dai-Ichi Kangyo Bank, Fuji Bank, and Industrial Bank of Japan).
11. "Sleeping fees" means that a trading firm obtains 3 to 5 percent fees for doing nothing but ordering and invoicing. The fees include credit risk management fees and/or sales development fees, and so on. Nissho Iwai and Nichimen, *keiretsu* trading firms of Sanwa Bank group, announced that they would merge their plastics division within a couple of years. For this purpose, a joint holding company was established in March 2001. Their revenues in the plastic business have been declining in the face of expanding e-commerce (*Nihon Keizai Shinbun* (Nikkei), March 9, 2001).
12. The market strategies and tactics analyzed in Section 3 are based on the behavior of these companies in Segment 4 and 5.
13. The Plaza Agreement was signed by the United States, the United Kingdom, France, West Germany, and Japan on September 22, 1985, at the Plaza Hotel in New York. The main aim of the agreement was to coordinate the economic policies of these countries, known as the Group of Five, or the G-5. All participants were to: devalue the dollar, agree on an exchange rate system/stabilize currencies, correct trade imbalances, and eliminate trade protection. After the agreement, the yen-to-dollar exchange rate appreciated from approximately 240 in 1985 to 170 in 1986, and then to 94 in 1995. The agreement, in retrospect, marked a turning point for Japanese export-oriented companies, and the Japanese economy as a whole.
14. MITI (Chemical Industry Statistics), Petrochemical Industry Association.
15. Statistics from Customs Clearance (MOF).
16. After 1990, because of the appreciation of the yen, Japanese buyers of petrochemical materials realized that they could purchase those materials at cheaper prices from Asian suppliers, which started production around that year. Japanese buyers negotiated with Japanese suppliers with samples from foreign suppliers whose materials were equivalent in quality and cheaper. As a

result, the prices of petrochemical materials in Japan dropped without an increase in the actual import of those materials. This event was called price import, and it dramatically changed the behavior of suppliers and buyers in Japan.
17. A good example is the Iran–Japan Petrochemical Company (IJPC) project led by Mitsui group in late 1970s. Mitsui Toatsu (now Mitsui Chemical) joined the project as a major player. When the Iran–Iraq war began in 1980, the project was terminated during the course of construction. Mitsui & Co., a trading firm of Mitsui group, suffered from the financial debt caused by this termination; Mitsui Toatsu did not.
18. Mitsui Nisseki Polymer (one of four cosales companies for Polyethylene)—established by Nippon Petrochemical, Mitsui Petrochemical, and Mitsui Toatsu—was dissolved after the merger of Mitsui Petrochemical and Mitsui Toatsu. After the merger, Nippon Petrochemical built a JV for Polyethylene with Showa Denko, which was a member of Ace Polymer (another cosales company). Tonen Petrochemical, which was a member of Ace Polymer, established a JV with Mitsubishi Chemical, which was a member of Dia Polymer (another cosales company). Each company looked to find an alliance partner across the cosales companies. Cosales companies thus collapsed and disappeared.
19. This figure is comprised of 168 chemical companies by "Analyst Guide" of Daiwa Institute of Research Ltd.
20. Mitsubishi Chemical Annual Report.
21. Tokyo–Mitsubishi Pharmaceutical announced a merger with Welfide Corporation in October 2001.

References

Annual Report (2000) of the following companies: Asahi Chemical Industries, Fujitsu, Hitachi, Honda Motor, Matsushita Electric Industrial, Mitsui Chemical, Nissan Motor, Sony, Sumitomo, Toshiba, Toyota Motor.
Annual Report (1999–2001), Mitsubishi Chemical.
AstraZeneca. *About Us,* http://www.astrazeneca.com/AboutUs/1990s.htm.
Aventis. *Introducing Aventis,* http://www.aventis.com/main/0,1003,EN-XX-19850-22400—,FF.html.
Chemical Section of Basic Industry Department, METI (1999). *Global Supply/Demand Trend of Petrochemical Products,* Attachment 1 & 2 (April).
Kagaku Keizai. [Chemical Economics] (November), pp. 12–21.
Petrochemical Industries in Asia (1997). *Juukagaku Kogyo Tsusinsha,* pp. 214–258.
Morikawa, Hidemasa (1992). *Sengo Keieishi Nyuumon Nikkei,* pp. 64–66.
Japan Petrochemical Industry Association (JPCA) (1999). *Production Capacity of Major Petrochemical Producers.*
Taketomi, Tametsugu (2000). "Differentiation in Net Era and Corporate Change," *Kagaku Keizai* [Chemical Economics] (April), pp. 47–54.
——— (1999). *Southeast Asian Chemical Market and Severe Competition.* Kagaku Kezai: Tokyo, Japan.
——— (1994). "Current Environment and Issues of Japanese Chemical Industry," *Chemical Renaissance,* ed. Kunio Yoshida. (Cambridge, Mass.: Spectrum Chemical Industry), pp. 11–15.
——— (1994). "Restructuring the Japanese Chemical Industry." *Spectrum Chemical Industry,* Decision Resources, Inc. (February 25).
Taketomi, Tametsugu and Hirabayashi, Takashi. (1996) "Restructuring the Petrochemical Industry and Issues," *Kagaku Keizai* [Chemical Economics] (January), pp. 58–66.
Toyo Keizai Shinposha (1999). *Kaigai Shinshutu Kigyo Souran* [List of Overseas Subsidiaries].

CHAPTER FIVE

On the Road to Asia: Japanese Automakers in ASEAN

GREGORY W. NOBLE[1]

I. Introduction

The automobile industry occupies a special place in Japan's remarkable economic development. The auto industry is the largest producer and exporter in Japan. Innovations in production technology and business organization pioneered at Toyota and other Japanese firms won universal recognition as pacesetters for the motorcar industry and manufacturing more generally. For many authors, the auto industry was emblematic of the economic superiority of Japanese production networks.[2]

The Japanese auto industry has been particularly dominant in the major markets of the Association of Southeast Asian Nations (ASEAN): Thailand, Malaysia, Indonesia, and the Philippines. Since Japanese companies uprooted Western auto firms in the 1960s and early 1970s, exports from Japan and local assembly of knocked-down kits[3] from Japan have accounted for 70 to 95 percent of all auto sales in the major ASEAN countries.[4]

Japanese auto producers in Southeast Asia faced strong tensions between economies of scale and scope that reward centralization of production, and marketing and political pressures pushing toward localization. At first, Japanese companies exported assembled cars or complete knocked-down kits from efficient plants at home. Then, starting in 1988, they reluctantly undertook cautious programs of localization to deal with market demands and political pressures in Southeast Asia. In the mid-1990s, they began a more serious effort at regionalization and globalization, including limited exports of parts and vehicles from Southeast Asia.

By the late 1990s, Japanese auto firms faced three major challenges to their dominant position in Southeast Asian markets. All were at least as much products of nonmarket forces as of changes in the immediate market environment.[5] The first challenge was to cope with the slump in auto demand caused by twin financial crises—lingering in Japan, and acute in Southeast Asia. Demand for autos in ASEAN began to recover in 1999, but the region was not expected to recover to precrisis levels until about 2004. A second challenge for Japanese automakers was to balance local, regional, and global production in an environment of slow and erratic trade liberalization. The final and most fundamental challenge was to counter the arrival of new rivals. In the early to mid-1990s, South Korean auto producers began to make inroads, particularly in low-end cars and in the least developed markets in Asia. In addition, Western automakers staged an unexpected competitive recovery and began to challenge Japan even in Southeast Asia. European and American auto firms benefited from strong economic growth and consumer preferences for pickup trucks, vans, and sport utility vehicles, which they excelled at producing. They also narrowed the quality gap with Japan and moved beyond Japan's famed "Toyota Production System" with rapid introduction of large modules, electronic commerce, and significant reorganization of the dealer system. In contrast, slumping domestic demand, uninspired models, and failure to revise traditional preferences for market share over profitability weakened many Japanese companies. By 2000, a wave of mergers and acquisitions had given Western automakers large stakes in the majority of Japan's auto assemblers.[6] Southeast Asia is shaping up as a key test case of whether the Japanese auto industry and the production model it pioneered are still dominant or increasingly outmoded.

II. Positional Analysis

Market Environment

Japanese firms established a leading position in the world auto industry in good measure because of the skill with which they handled the deep tensions in the industry between centralization of production in the home country and localization to meet the needs of households and governments in consuming countries (see Table 5.1). Pushing toward centralization are formidable economies of scale, learning, and agglomeration; shrinking product cycles; and stringent demands to improve

Table 5.1 Japanese automobile production

Year	Passenger cars	Trucks	Buses	Domestic total	Of which, exports	Overseas production and assembly		Knocked-down exports	Worldwide production
1982	6,881,586	3,783,218	66,990	10,731,794	5,590,513	NA		NA	NA
1983	7,151,888	3,903,823	55,948	11,111,659	5,669,510	NA		NA	NA
1984	7,073,173	4,319,538	72,709	11,464,920	6,109,184	NA		NA	NA
1985	7,646,816	4,544,688	79,591	12,271,095	6,730,472	1,332,000	(10.3%)	676,000	12,927,000
1986	7,809,809	4,407,666	42,342	12,259,817	6,604,923	1,617,000	(12.2%)	616,000	13,261,000
1987	7,891,087	4,308,600	49,987	12,249,174	6,304,918	1,968,000	(14.5%)	622,000	13,596,000
1988	8,198,400	4,433,994	57,413	12,699,807	6,104,152	2,422,000	(16.7%)	597,000	14,525,000
1989	9,052,406	3,931,255	42,074	13,025,735	5,883,903	3,083,000	(19.9%)	640,000	15,469,000
1990	9,947,972	3,498,639	40,185	13,486,796	5,831,212	3,755,000	(22.7%)	674,000	16,568,000
1991	9,753,069	3,447,914	44,449	13,245,432	5,753,379	4,040,000	(24.3%)	660,000	16,625,000
1992	9,378,694	3,068,585	52,005	12,499,284	5,667,646	4,354,000	(26.9%)	677,000	16,176,000
1993	8,493,943	2,685,528	48,074	11,227,545	5,017,656	5,069,000	(32.6%)	761,000	15,536,000
1994	7,802,037	2,702,970	49,112	10,554,119	4,460,292	5,784,000	(37.0%)	700,000	15,638,000
1995	7,610,533	2,537,737	47,266	10,195,536	3,790,809	6,346,000	(40.2%)	743,000	15,799,000
1996	7,864,676	2,428,897	53,126	10,346,699	3,711,718	6,710,000	(41.0%)	676,000	16,381,000
1997	8,491,480	2,421,373	62,234	10,975,087	4,553,202	6,742,000	(39.5%)	660,000	17,057,000
1998	8,055,763	1,937,076	56,953	10,049,792	4,528,875	6,100,000	(38.6%)	352,000	15,798,000
1999	8,100,169	1,746,912	48,395	9,895,476	4,408,943	NA		NA	NA

Source: Worldwide production = domestic production [including KD kits] + overseas production & assembly – KD exports. Nikkan Jidōsha Shinbunsha, Nihon Jidōsha Kaigisho, *Jidōsha Nenkan* [Automotive Yearbook] (Tokyo: Nikkan Jidōsha Shinbunsha, Nihon Jidōsha Kaigisho, 1999), pp. 60–61 and 2000, pp. 36–37; Overseas production & assembly and knocked down exports from Fourin and JAMA, reported in *Asian Automotive Business Review*, April 1999, p. 3.

quality and safety while reducing emissions. Estimates of minimum efficient scale in the assembly business average about 150,000 to 200,000 vehicles per year.[7] Scale economies can be even greater in parts, reaching 1.5 million units per year or more for alternators, starters, and spark plugs.[8] Recent developments in computer-aided design and manufacturing have increased economies of scope across models, as designers learn to base two or more distinctive models on a single chassis or platform.

Economies of learning and agglomeration also are significant. Autos are complex, expensive products that require the application of advanced techniques in materials, engineering and electronics to tens of thousands of parts. Shrinking product cycles, largely an outgrowth of increasing computerization of design, have increased the pressures to agglomerate so that parts suppliers and assemblers can learn from each other and coordinate their activities on successive models. Demands for quality, safety, and environmental responsiveness also have served to increase scale economies and raise major barriers to entry. Together these forces tend to create an oligopoly of producers and first-tier parts suppliers concentrated in a few major production regions around the world.

Counteracting these supply-side pressures to centralize are factors that tend to disperse production to new regions such as ASEAN. Even major global consumer brands such as McDonald's restaurants and Disney theme parks differ subtly from country to country, and tastes in autos can diverge substantially. Geography, demography, and government policies all affect consumer preferences. Geographically divergent demands for heating and air conditioning capabilities are an obvious example, but income levels, family size, petrol taxes and quality, width, and congestion of roads also vary significantly across countries, exerting diverse influences on choice of car models. For example, higher gasoline prices and narrower roads incline Europeans to prefer smaller cars and firmer suspensions than do Americans. Automakers are working feverishly to reduce the number of basic platforms they produce, but they are not reducing the variety of models they build upon those platforms.[9]

A second major task that follows from the size and complexity of the automobile is to devise an appropriate division of labor and responsibility. Auto firms must process a myriad of frequent and variable transactions, many of which involve highly specific assets such as giant presses, assembly plants, and computer-aided design systems. Once a party to a contract has dedicated specialized assets to a transaction, it is vulnerable to opportunistic behavior on the part of its business partners, such as demands for lower prices. The traditional American response to this dilemma was to vertically integrate crucial functions while acquiring less important parts through arms-length transactions in open markets.[10] The American strategy avoided bilateral monopolies and reduced opportunism, but paid a high price in bloated corporate size and reduced learning and information interchange between assemblers and their arms-length suppliers.

Japanese assemblers led by Toyota developed an alternative solution based on networks of independent but interlocked firms called *keiretsu* (more specifically, vertical or manufacturers' *keiretsu,* as opposed to the intermarket or horizontal *keiretsu,* which were clusters of trading companies, financial institutions, and manufacturers symbolized by the Mitsubishi or Sumitomo groups).[11] Japanese assemblers vertically integrated production of only the most crucial components. They purchased all other parts from suppliers with which they developed stable, long-term relations, often cemented by small holdings of stock, dispatch of executives from assemblers to suppliers, and regular group meetings. Assemblers provided financial and technological assistance to first-tier suppliers, who in turn helped second-tier suppliers, and so forth. The development of specific skills by suppliers freed assemblers to concentrate on core tasks: overall design conception, design of the chassis and engine, production of key components, and marketing. In order to prevent suppliers from taking advantage of this stable and supportive arrangement to become slothful or exploitative, assemblers reopened contracts for negotiation at model changeovers and double-sourced most important parts. Intimate knowledge of the operations of suppliers allowed assemblers to make accurate estimates of their production costs and demand periodic price reductions. In many Japanese industries such as retailing or construction, politically powerful small and medium-sized enterprises became cosseted and inefficient. By contrast, the export orientation and pyramidal character of the auto industry served to harmonize political and economic efficiency.

In addition to revolutionizing relations between assemblers and suppliers, Toyota and the other Japanese assemblers added conceptual and practical innovations to the mass production techniques first mastered by Henry Ford. Toyota's "lean production" system took advantage of Japan's stable, high-quality workforce and statistical techniques originally developed by the United States during World War II to increase quality and save time and materials by constantly reorganizing the production process to build quality in at the start, rather than fixing errors after the fact. Instead of building huge quantities of the same product at a steady pace and worrying about sales afterward, Toyota created a demand-pull system to link production to orders and to create slight variations on a product theme to satisfy various market niches. Toyota reduced inventories and increased pressures to organize the workflow correctly by creating a "just-in-time" production process. When Western governments imposed quantitative restrictions on auto exports, Japanese firms moved into the production of luxury models such as Toyota's Lexus line and Nissan's Infiniti series.

Southeast Asia For Japanese automakers, recreating the flexible and efficient production structure they had mastered at home in the diverse environments and limited markets of developing countries proved a difficult challenge. Southeast Asia has long been their most important market in the developing world.[12] By the middle of the 1990s, roughly twice as many small and medium-sized Japanese parts suppliers had established plants in Asia as in the much larger North American market.[13]

ASEAN markets were particularly suited to the competitive strengths of Japanese firms. Japanese corporate and governmental leaders had long regarded the populous nations of Southeast Asia as a source of raw materials and markets. By the 1980s and early 1990s, Southeast Asia, long one of the best performing developing regions, was enjoying the most rapid rates of growth in the world. Exports of manufactured products, particularly textiles and electronics, rapidly outpaced exports of agricultural products and natural resources. Income levels and demands for quality were initially modest, making them appropriate markets for the fledgling Japanese exporters of the 1950s and 1960s. In the 1970s and 1980s, Japanese firms learned to offer a bewildering variety of models and options without imposing excessive costs. Japanese strengths produced a winning formula in the ASEAN countries: high-quality small cars and pickups, attractively priced and produced relatively economically considering the small volumes (see Tables 5.2–5.5).

The acceleration of growth in the late 1980s convinced Japanese auto companies to respond aggressively to the emerging opportunities and looming challenges in the ASEAN region. Japanese assemblers made major investments in ASEAN, usually in the form of joint ventures with local firms in which the Japanese ownership share ranged from 25 to 50 percent, and strongly encouraged their parts suppliers to make complementary investments. Some of these expansion plans depended on regional interchange of parts, but many still were based on national markets. By the fall of 1995, the five leading Japanese assemblers announced plans to produce "Asia cars" and small commercial vehicles specially designed to be produced and marketed in the ASEAN region. All were designed to incorporate increased numbers of local parts, including such crucial components as engines and transmissions.[14]

Table 5.2 Economic environment in four large ASEAN countries

Country	Economic indicator	1989	1990	1991	1992	1993	1994	1995	1996	1997	1998
Malaysia	Population (million)	17.35	17.76	18.33	18.76	19.21	19.66	20.11	21.17	21.67	22.17
	Person per vehicle	9.40	7.32	7.49	7.14	6.66	6.94	6.71	5.60	5.13	—
	Per Capital GDP (USD)	$2,180	$2,408	$2,626	$3,092	$3,341	$3,688	$4,343	$4,690	$4,544	—
	GDP Growth rate	9.2%	9.7%	8.6%	7.8%	8.3%	9.2%	9.5%	8.6%	7.8%	−4.8%
	Exchange rate (RM per USD)	2.71	2.7	2.75	2.55	2.57	2.62	2.5	2.52	2.81	3.92
Thailand	Population (million)	55.21	55.84	56.57	57.29	58.01	58.71	59.40	60.00	61.12	—
	Person per vehicle	24.65	19.84	20.74	18.99	16.28	14.75	13.17	11.76	10.57	—
	Per Capital GDP (USD)	$1,303	$1,557	$1,740	$1,946	$2,156	$2,473	$2,805	$3,007	$1,959	—
	GDP Growth rate	12.2%	11.2%	8.6%	8.1%	8.4%	8.9%	8.8%	5.5%	−0.4%	−7.5%
	Exchange rate (Th B per USD)	25.8	25.1	25.5	25.4	25.4	25.0	25.1	25.5	40.7	41.1
Philippines	Population (million)	60.10	61.48	63.69	65.34	66.98	68.62	70.27	71.90	73.53	75.16
	Person per vehicle	109.61	101.81	50.33	47.54	43.11	40.54	38.41	35.59	33.28	—
	Per Capital GDP (USD)	$708	$721	$713	$811	$812	$934	$1,055	$1,165	$1,132	—
	GDP Growth rate	6.2%	3.0%	−0.5%	0.3%	2.1%	4.4%	4.8%	5.7%	5.1%	−0.5%
	Exchange rate (Ph P per USD)	21.7	24.3	27.5	25.5	27.1	26.4	25.7	26.2	29.5	40.9
Indonesia	Population (million)	179.14	179.83	181.39	184.49	187.59	190.68	194.75	196.81	199.87	202.93
	Person per vehicle	70.43	64.88	60.43	68.82	58.05	53.18	49.10	44.33	41.65	—
	Per Capital GDP (USD)	$566	$636	$707	$754	$842	$928	$1,038	$1,155	$1,074	—
	GDP Growth rate	7.5%	7.2%	7.0%	6.5%	6.5%	7.5%	8.2%	8.0%	4.6%	−15.0%
	Exchange rate (R per USD)	1,770.1	1,842.8	1,950.3	2,029.9	2,087.1	2,160.8	2,248.6	2,342.3	2,909.4	10,013.7

Source: Asian Automotive Business Review, July 1999, p. 15. Figures for 1998 are estimates.

Table 5.3 New auto sales in the ASEAN 5 before and after the financial crisis

Year	Thailand	Malaysia	Indonesia	Philippines	Singapore
1993	456,468	167,928	210,679	83,811	43,105
1994	485,678	200,435	321,760	103,471	37,599
1995	523,431	285,792	378,705	124,611	41,704
1996	540,629	364,788	337,671	156,721	36,915
1997	343,464	404,807	394,820	139,266	34,812
1998	137,471	163,851	58,857	77,762	37,493
1999	211,146	288,547	95,483	72,038	NA

Source: Fourin Kaigai Jidōsha Chōsa Geppō 175 (March 2000), p. 1; Asian Automotive Business Review, January 1999, p. 25.

Table 5.4 Automobile production in ASEAN 5 countries (including knock-down)

Year	Thailand	Indonesia	Malaysia	Philippines	ASEAN4	Japanese share (%)
1970	22,000	10,000	28,000	19,000	79,000	90–95
1980	72,000	174,000	101,000	93,000	444,000	90–95
1985	82,000	139,000	124,000	20,000	365,000	90–95
1990	305,000	272,000	205,000	40,000	822,000	79.2 [92.3]
1995	483,000	388,000	308,000	123,000	1,302,000	80.3 [95.3]
1996	559,000	325,000	396,000	137,000	1,417,000	74.0 [91.6]
1997	360,000	389,000	460,000	111,000	1,320,000	67.6 [91.0]

Source: Nikkan Jidōsha Shinbunsha; Fourin; reprinted in Jochen Legewie, "Driving Regional Integration: Japanese Firms and the Development of the ASEAN Automobile Industry," Philipp Franz von Siebold Stiftung Deutsches Institut fur Japanstudien, Working Paper 99/1 (Tokyo), p. 3. Figures in brackets indicate the share of Japanese manufacturers including the production of the Proton and Perodua in Malaysia in which Mitsubishi and Daihatsu are closely involved.

Table 5.5 Foreign investment in the ASEAN auto parts industry (January 1998)

Country	Total number of parts manufacturers	Japanese affiliates or subsidiaries	Share of Japanese affiliates or subsidiaries (%)	U.S. and European affiliates or subsidiaries	Share of western affiliates or subsidiaries (%)
Thailand	750–800	209	27.0	21	2.7
Indonesia	150–200	82	46.9	7	4.0
Malaysia	200–250	61	27.1	19	8.4
Philippines	150–250	54	30.9	5	2.9
Singapore	About 50	17	34.0	4	8.0
ASEAN5	1300–1500	423	30.2	56	4.0

Source: Fourin, reprinted in Jochen Legewie, "Driving Regional Integration: Japanese Firms and the Development of the ASEAN Automobile Industry," Philipp Franz von Siebold Stiftung Deutsches Institut fur Japanstudien, Working Paper 99/1 (Tokyo), p. 9.

To be sure, the significance of Southeast Asia must be placed in comparative perspective. Exports grew out of a large, firmly protected and intermittently promoted domestic market.[15] Moreover, through the late 1980s, North America and Europe each accounted for just under one-third of the Japanese auto industry's exports and the large bulk of its foreign direct investment. Still, the ASEAN market was strategically important in several ways. It was an early training ground for Japanese exporters. It was the most important market in the industrializing world—far larger than Latin America, the Middle East, and other more distant developing markets, where Japanese companies largely refrained from direct investments. Similar dynamics operated in areas adjacent to ASEAN, such as Australia and especially Taiwan, where local production of Japanese vehicles supplied the bulk of demand.

Five Market Forces in Southeast Asia Of the five strategic market forces analyzed by Michael Porter, two (substitutes and bargaining power of buyers) are of relatively minor importance for Japanese auto producers in Southeast Asia, two others (rivalry among producers and bargaining power of suppliers) have long been significant, and one—new entry—looms as a crucial issue.[16] Substitutes for autos are limited in Southeast Asia. Outside of densely populated and tightly regulated Singapore, mass transit systems in the region have been slow to develop and are limited in scale. Motorcycles provide some alternatives as transportation vehicles in the early stages of economic development, but demand shifts to autos as incomes rise. In the auto industry, the bargaining power of buyers is limited, because demand tends to be dispersed rather than concentrated. Even governments tend to be more important as regulators than as procurers of vehicles.

Traditionally, the bargaining power of suppliers also has been seen as strictly limited. For many years, most observers viewed the Japan as a "dual economy" in which large, modern firms such as vehicle assemblers exploited their many small suppliers. While that view has been supplanted in recent years by a perspective stressing that parent firms often become dependent on the specialized skills of their suppliers, few would argue that Japanese auto assemblers face much bargaining pressure from suppliers of parts and materials.[17] Local suppliers in Southeast Asian countries usually have been in an even weaker position unless they had the support of host governments willing and able to control access to the local markets. Within Japan, partial exceptions to this generalization have included steel, a relatively concentrated supplier industry, and regulated utilities such as electricity and telecommunications. Despite recent small efforts at deregulation, the strong bargaining position of these suppliers has provided some incentive for internationally competitive manufacturers, such as auto firms, to move offshore. However, the advantages of domestic production are still great, so the concentrated power of these high-priced supplier industries has had relatively little impact on the locational decisions of Japanese auto firms operating in Southeast Asia.

A more important change has been the growing power of first-tier suppliers such as Delphi, Visteon, TRW of the United States, and Robert Bosch of Germany. The combination of large economies of scale in the production of many parts, the amalgamation of the assembly industry, and the internationalization of production has pushed leading component manufacturers to acquire weaker firms and establish bases in all of the major production sites, including Japan. Many first-tier suppliers, particularly in Europe, are beginning to take responsibility for whole "modules" such as brake and steering systems or cockpits.[18] Some first-tier parts firms are beginning to assemble low-volume models. If this trend continues, some observers predict that first-tier suppliers could become more important than mass assemblers, as (according to some accounts) they were in the early years of this century. Opinion in Japan on the future of modules is sharply divided. Some agree that parts firms will continue to gain in importance, and that the power balance between suppliers and assemblers will shift. Others insist that the Japanese industry has already developed an efficient network relationship between parts makers and assemblers.[19]

Rivalry among Japanese assemblers is also important. Richard F. Doner argues that this rivalry has provided Southeast Asian countries with their greatest opportunity to obtain better terms from Japanese firms. Partly because Japanese firms proved particularly adept at operating with low volumes and multiple models, and partly because—until recently—Japan's rapid growth and permissive financial system encouraged manufacturers to compete for market share even at the cost of low profitability, all of Japan's assemblers established production bases in Southeast Asia.[20]

More recent is the threat of new entry by foreign auto assemblers. At the lower end, a challenge emerged from Korea, virtually the only auto producing country in the last half-century that has attained success by mimicking Japan's policies of protection and promotion.[21] Executives of Hyundai, Daewoo, and Kia promised to deliver a more appealing package to local consumers and governments: "We will provide everything more aggressively than the Japanese."[22] Daewoo and other low-cost South Korean producers moved aggressively into India, Vietnam, and Indonesia, as well as developing or transitional economies outside of the Asia-Pacific region, including Poland, Romania, and Uzbekistan. Investments in Thailand and Malaysia, ASEAN's most advanced and competitive auto markets, were smaller, later, and more tentative. Clearly, the South Koreans hoped to build up scale and experience in markets too small or difficult to attract a major Japanese presence, and then use those emerging markets as a base from which to mount an assault on the strongholds of the Japanese.

Before the final attack could be mounted, however, South Korean firms were overtaken by the financial crisis. Indeed, the inability of the South Korean government to deal with the failure of Kia (which was dragged down by its nonautomotive operations) was a major factor in the eruption of a full-scale crisis in Korea in 1997. Two years later, Daewoo fell into bankruptcy when it found itself unable to service the massive debt incurred in its aggressive expansion drives. Despite these grave difficulties, and long-standing structural weaknesses in the South Korean parts industry, most observers expect South Korean producers, especially Hyundai (now including Kia), to remain tough competitors in the lower end of the market, probably in conjunction with larger Western partners such as Daimler-Chrysler, which took a 10 percent stake in Hyundai.

Japanese firms faced inroads in the middle to high-end markets from Western firms, particularly Ford and GM.[23] Ford and its Japanese affiliate Mazda created Auto Alliance to produce one-metric-ton pickups in Thailand's Eastern Seaboard Industrial Park, about three hours southeast of Bangkok. The $750 million factory began production of basic Mazda B2500 Fighters and higher-end Ford Rangers in mid-1998, at the trough of the financial crisis. The companies originally planned to export 50 percent of the final capacity of 135,000 units, per year to Europe, Australia, and New Zealand, but because of the crisis, they raised exports to 85 percent.[24] Similarly, General Motors announced that it aimed to capture 10 percent of the Asian auto market, which it predicted would surpass in size those of North America and Europe by 2008. In June 1996, it won approval to assemble 80,000 to 100,000 units of the Opel Zafira, a one-box compact van based on the Astra, next door to Ford, Toyota, and a host of Japanese parts firms in the Eastern Seaboard Industrial Park. The outbreak of the financial crisis caused GM to scale back the investment from $750 million to $500 million, cutting initial capacity to 40,000 units per year. It delayed opening the plant until May 2000, thus escaping the worst effects of the crisis.[25] European firms such as BMW, Fiat, Volkswagen, and Renault also moved into Thailand with smaller investments or production consignment agreements. Western parts makers such as Visteon, formerly part of Ford, and Saint-Gobain, the French glass firm, also opened operations in Thailand, although they remained outnumbered by the Japanese.[26] Thus, once the level of market demand and production skill reached sufficient levels, Western firms moved in to capitalize on the considerable manufacturing base created by thirty years of patient investments by Japanese assemblers and parts firms. Their largest plants focused not just on the Thai or even ASEAN markets, but on global exports.

Nonmarket Environment

The environmental constraints facing Japanese carmakers include not only market size, but also government policies and other nonmarket factors. In most countries, governments devise policies to favor local production of automobiles and parts. The auto industry employs large numbers of workers and develops deep links with supply industries such as steel, glass, rubber, electronics, and machinery. Since the car is the most expensive durable good most consumers purchase, development of a local automobile industry becomes a potent symbol of industrialization, modernization, and autonomy. Differences in currency regimes also may persuade automakers to establish a local production presence so as to minimize fluctuations in earnings; for Japanese car firms, the tendency of ASEAN governments to align their currencies to the American dollar rather than the yen has been a major source of instability.

Local content requirements imposed by the four large ASEAN countries forced Japanese car companies to export semi-knocked-down kits, substituting local production for some of the simpler parts. Those policies increased costs by forcing car companies to produce parts in each country in small lots that fell far short of efficient scale. Local marketers and assemblers insisted on selling a full range of sizes and models and steadfastly resisted government efforts to rationalize. High production costs led to high sales prices that curbed demand and throttled the development of the local industry.

In response, Southeast Asian governments launched an "ASEAN Industrial Complementation Scheme" (AIC) in 1981. Regional governments agreed to grant reciprocal tariff reductions and credit toward fulfillment of local content requirements to parts and components produced in other ASEAN countries. In practice, the requirements for industrial reciprocity, balanced trade, and political consensus doomed the part-to-part complementation scheme to irrelevance as governments proved unwilling to grant concessions that might undermine production at home. Nor were Japanese assemblers enthusiastic about plans that threatened to increase their costs in the short run with little prospect of attaining significant economies of scale. Only seventeen items gained approval in 1981 and just five more in 1983. AIC items constituted less than 1 percent of intra-ASEAN trade.[27]

Faced with the failure of the AIC scheme and the steep appreciation of the yen after the Plaza Accord of 1985, ASEAN governments invited the Japanese assemblers to propose alternative arrangements. The Japanese, led by Mitsubishi, dusted off plans to encourage "brand-to-brand complementation" (BBC) by firms working in more than one ASEAN country. In return for maintaining a local content rate of at least 50 percent, the BBC scheme of October 1988 offered auto manufacturers a 50 percent tariff cut and credit toward local contents for parts exchanged among their production facilities within ASEAN. Like AIC, this arrangement conferred relative advantages on Japanese producers, who had production facilities throughout the region. However, ASEAN governments, determined to protect their own industries and reluctant to surrender tariff revenues, insisted that assemblers file new applications with each model change. Indonesia boycotted the scheme entirely until 1995, and even after that refused to give credit toward local content requirements. The volume of trade under the scheme remained tiny.[28]

Regional governments then devised yet another plan: ASEAN Industrial Cooperation (AICO). The new scheme, introduced in November 1996, widened coverage to include all manufacturers, including auto parts producers, reduced tariffs to 0 to 5 percent, decreased the local content requirement to 40 percent and (in principle, at least) eliminated the requirement of trade balance neutrality. However, to guard against the possibility that liberalization would sweep aside local auto parts producers, it introduced a requirement that all applicants must include at least 30 percent local equity. The companies most likely to be excluded by this requirement were precisely the Japanese auto parts companies that accounted for the bulk of local production. As a result, applications remained limited and approvals even more so. One analyst summarized the difficulties:

> Instead of achieving a fast approval of AICO applications, a prolonged bargaining process between single companies and ASEAN governments with few concrete results has dominated in 1997 and 1998. For example, the Malaysian government regards every privilege to be enjoyed by foreign car manufacturers as a threat to Proton and Perodua, its own national makers, [which] do not possess exclusive production networks within ASEAN. But even in countries with a more positive stance, as in countries without a national brand (Thailand, Philippines), the governments are only interested in AICO arrangements that promise a net increase of production and thus additional exports and jobs.[29]

At the Hanoi Summit in December 1998, ASEAN temporarily decided to exempt the 30 percent local equity requirement and to relax the application process to cope with the staggering recession brought about by the Asian financial crisis. As of the end of 1999, only thirty-three items had received eligibility (four of them provisional): one from the Ford–Mazda alliance in Thailand, three from Volvo (now a subsidiary of Ford), and the others Japanese. In 2000, however, applications suddenly jumped to ninety-six, with Thailand leading the way. Ninety percent came from Japanese firms, particularly Toyota and Honda.[30]

ASEAN governments also proclaimed their intention to expand the Common Effective Preferential Tariff Scheme (CEPT), which was scheduled to culminate by 2003 in an ASEAN Free Trade Area (AFTA) with tariffs of 5 percent or less. Most observers remained skeptical that this alphabet soup of schemes would actually fundamentally transform the domestic incentives for protection and promotion. By the end of 1999, all but Thailand had reneged on their commitment.[31] Malaysia insisted on a two-year delay, apparently largely to protect its national auto firms. Yet progress continued, and Japanese auto companies continued to invest in their Southeast Asian subsidiaries, increasingly with an eye to cross-shipments within ASEAN. Thus, while nonmarket pressures saddled auto assemblers with balkanized and redundant parts and assembly operations scattered throughout the ASEAN region, Japanese firms proved most adept at using local policy arrangements to ameliorate the effects of that balkanization.

Japanese firms have had to deal with varying nonmarket environments at the national level. Indonesia's auto industry has been a continual disappointment. Despite three decades of rapid growth, Indonesia remained poorer than its neighbors and suffered the greatest tension between the indigenous *pribumi* and ethnic Chinese. The Indonesian government persisted in an aggressive style of industrial policy promotion, but its measures intended to promote the local market effectively throttled it. In the 1990s, cronyism further complicated the picture, as President Suharto provided egregious preferences to protect a joint venture project between one of his sons and Korea's Kia to assemble a national car called the Timor. In July 1998, in response to protests from Japan, Europe, and the United States, the WTO issued a ruling that Indonesia's plan to exempt only the Timor car from import duties violated world trade rules. In June 1999, after the fall of Suharto, the government finally introduced a new auto policy that significantly reduced tariffs and local content requirements. The weakness of the market and volatility of the currency kept Indonesia in limbo, neither effective as an independent production center nor fully integrated into regional or global networks, though the country's huge population meant that it could not be ignored as a potential auto market.[32]

The Philippines also has disappointed expectations. For years, macroeconomic stability eluded the country while basic infrastructure such as roads and electricity languished. Policies toward the auto industry were inconsistent and irresolute.[33] Local production peaked in 1996 at only 137,000 units before falling to just 45,000 units in 1998. The next year the government reduced tariffs on imports of parts kits and reconfigured the structure of auto taxes, but then it delayed the elimination of local contents requirements, originally scheduled for January 2000, until the end of 2004.[34] The Philippines has emerged as a significant production site for transmissions and wire harnesses, but otherwise its prospects in the auto industry appear bleak.[35]

Malaysia implemented activist policies more consistently and successfully than either Indonesia or the Philippines, despite having a much smaller population. Dissatisfied with the failure of Japanese companies to transfer technology and at the lack of participation in the auto industry by the non-Chinese "bumiputra" (sons of the soil) who composed the heart of the ruling party's political constituency, industry minister Mahathir Mohamed secretly initiated a national car project in 1980. Two years later, as prime minister, he officially launched Proton as a joint venture with Mitsubishi Motors. Granted an exemption from 40 percent import tariffs, Proton quickly defeated three existing assembly operations (including one, ironically, that assembled Mitsubishi models) and moved close to minimum efficient scale. Proton insisted that exports to Australia and the United Kingdom were profitable, although most observers suspected that they were dumped.[36]

The company and its suppliers made only modest progress in parts production and less in engine and chassis design, however, and in the face of financial difficulties in the late 1980s, local managers gave way to executives dispatched from Mitsubishi. A disgruntled Mahathir engineered a series of moves to step up pressure on Mitsubishi and create alternative pathways to acquire skills and technology. Proton licensed technology from the French automaker Citroën (an affiliate of Peugeot), and in October 1996 purchased the renowned English racing and engineering group Lotus. The most important step came with the decision to create a second national brand, Perodua. The new company assembled small cars from Daihatsu, an affiliate and later subsidiary of Toyota. By 1997, the two companies accounted for two-thirds of the local auto market.

The national brands were somewhat cushioned from the Asian financial crisis by their position at the less expensive end of the market, but even they were deeply affected—the shrinkage of working time at Perodua, for example, caused about three-quarters of its 700 to 800 workers to resign.[37] The state oil company Petronas purchased a leading stake in Proton from the DRB/Hicom group, allowing Proton to continue investments in design and engineering. Proton and Perodua also made moves to abandon the protected and inefficient local parts industries, but the government, fearing the impact on local businesses, reacted by delaying the planned abolition of local parts requirements.[38] By 2000, Proton, in conjunction with Lotus, designed and produced its first engine and talked of building several variations of it. With this move, the company decreased its stiff license fees to Mitsubishi, but faced large increases in its R&D spending. Later that year, the government floated the possibility of selling up to 30 percent of Proton to leading foreign assemblers such as Ford, but its insistence on maintaining national control scuttled negotiations.[39] Despite the government's support and prodding, without new investments it is difficult to see how Proton and Perodua can avoid virtually complete dependence on Mitsubishi-Daimler-Chrysler and Toyota to keep up with the relentless pace of development of new models and environmental and safety technology demanded of today's auto producers.

Japanese auto firms have long played a dominant role in Southeast Asia's most successful auto assembly site, Thailand, particularly in the growing industrial district southeast of Bangkok. Where Malaysia and Indonesia insisted on creating national champion auto companies and the Philippines failed to provide coherent, stable policies, Thailand enticed foreign investors with sustained growth in demand, a cooperative pattern of government-business relations and restrained localization requirements.[40] Perhaps most important, the Thai government's tax policies deliberately or inadvertently favored production of one product—one-ton pickups—so that Japanese assemblers in Thailand were able to attain fair economies of scale. From the mid-1980s, foreign investors, including dozens of Japanese auto parts firms, poured into Thailand. Lacking demand from any one assembler sufficient to sustain economies of scale in production, and eager to try alternatives to existing arrangements in Japan, local subsidiaries and affiliates produced for the full range of Japanese and foreign assemblers rather than restrict themselves to supplying one or two assemblers along *keiretsu* lines. When the Thai government announced plans to increase local contents requirements for engines, archrivals Toyota and Nissan joined hands with GM subsidiary Isuzu to set standard specifications for local procurement for pickup trucks of five cast engine parts with large economies of scale (cylinder heads, cylinder blocks, connecting rods, camshafts, and crankshafts).[41]

When the financial crisis swept through Asia in 1997, new foreign direct investment declined drastically and Japanese banks and trading firms hastened to shrink overextended and unprofitable operations throughout the region.[42] Existing manufacturers, in contrast, mostly stepped up support to their local operations. Nowhere was this truer than in autos, particularly in Thailand. To encourage foreign investors, the Thai government eliminated bans on foreign majority ownership and extended tax-free treatment to new foreign investors. In reaction to the decline in the local market and the depreciation of the baht, Toyota, GM, and other major assemblers announced greatly expanded export targets. The Board of Investment actively encouraged American assemblers and parts suppliers to invest in Thailand to compete with the Japanese. Japan's aggressive response to the financial crisis demonstrated again the skill and persistence with which the government and auto firms have dealt with the complex and varying nonmarket environment of ASEAN and the major markets within it.

Firm Position

The large ASEAN countries have served as a small but important stronghold for the Japanese. Japanese firms retain a lead in productivity (although Western firms have closed the gap somewhat), in ever-shorter design cycles for new models, and in product quality.[43] In Southeast Asia, they have cultivated a swath of parts suppliers and shaped the nonmarket organizational environment in their favor. The durability of their dominant position seems in large measure attributable to the dense networks supporting their activities. Would-be new entrants can match any one factory with a sufficiently large investment, but inducing complementary investments by dozens or hundreds of suppliers, and then organizing them into a flexible and efficient network, is a much more complex task.

Over the longer run, virtually all strongholds are vulnerable to attack, and the position of the Japanese firms in Southeast Asia has come under increasing pressure. Costs of labor and land in Japan are high. The yen is a strong currency. Japanese banks are less willing to make loans just to maintain market share and increasingly insist that they and their clients achieve reasonable returns on investment. Many of the Japanese production facilities erected in Southeast Asia to overcome protectionism and feed small local markets are dispersed and lacking in economies of scale. For the next decade or more, Thailand's position as the premier assembly spot in Southeast Asia seems assured, although doubts remain about the levels of skill and education.[44] The problem from the Japanese perspective is that Western car manufacturers have been able to free ride on the special efforts the Japanese made to maintain an effective network of suppliers in Thailand.

III. Strategies and Tactics

The 1990s witnessed neither the unalloyed triumph of the Japanese production system nor its complete collapse in the face of economic stagnation and financial instability. Instead, the gap between the leaders, Toyota and Honda, and laggards, particularly Nissan and Mitsubishi, widened into a gulf. In many Japanese industries the now-repudiated "convoy" system of regulation deliberately restrained innovation by strong firms in order to protect weaker and slower firms. Traditionally, export-oriented manufacturing industries such as autos were less affected by domestic regulations and de facto cartels. Partly for that reason, from the early 1980s Japanese auto firms displayed marked differences in profitability and financial soundness. When domestic demand stagnated in the 1990s, overextended firms such as Nissan, Mitsubishi, and Mazda, and even relatively successful niche producers such as Suzuki, were forced to seek help from Western automakers and to consolidate their product lines. Leading Western assemblers and parts firms used their Japanese partners to launch a renewed attack on Asian markets (see Table 5.6).[45]

The differences between independent winners and newly subordinate losers affected almost every aspect of market strategy and corporate organization. With the partial exception of Nissan, however, it did not

Table 5.6 Leading global auto assemblers

Firm	Headquarters	Global market share (as of 12/98) (%)
General Motors (including Isuzu)	USA	14.9
Ford (including Volvo and Mazda)	USA	14.9
Toyota (including Daihatsu)	Japan	10.0
Renault-Nissan	France–Japan	9.1
Volkswagen Group	Germany	9.0
Daimler-Chrysler	Germany–USA	8.4
Fiat	Italy	5.0
Honda	Japan	4.3
Peugeot-Citroën	France	4.3
Mitsubishi	Japan	2.9

Source: *Jidōsha Nenkan* 1999 [Automotive Yearbook, 1999] (Tokyo: Nikkan Jidōsha Shinbunsha, Nihon Jidōsha Kaigisho, 1999), p. 187.

substantially lessen the long-term commitment of Japanese auto producers to Southeast Asia. Surveys conducted in late 1998 and early 1999 by MITI and its Japan External Trade Organization (JETRO) revealed that Japanese companies believed that existing operations in Asia were crucial to their long-term growth and that the ASEAN economies would soon recover. Fewer than 6 percent contemplated downsizing or withdrawing from the region. Indeed, with higher exports and some recovery, automakers began to rev up output by late 1999.[46] The real question was how to compete with the new Western players in the region or, in the case of the smaller or less successful firms, how to coordinate strategy with them.

Market Strategies and Tactics

In the face of weak demand and heightened competition, all Japanese automakers agreed on the renewed importance of cutting costs, but they adopted starkly divergent approaches to achieving that goal. Both the macroeconomic and demographic shifts noted above and excessive efforts in the 1980s to move upstream into more luxurious models and to fill all niches and provide all possible options drove up costs even for the better-organized Japanese producers. Toyota and Honda continued the relentless process of incremental rationalization that had proved so successful in the past, and strengthened their ties with leading suppliers. Under new foreign leadership, Nissan, Mitsubishi, and Mazda took drastic action to slash platforms, plants, and suppliers, and increase global sourcing, although they did not match the intensity of the cutbacks forced on Ford and Chrysler in the early 1980s, largely because Japanese law, politics, and social attitudes impeded the large-scale sacking of core male employees.

A second major option was to invest in research and development in the hope of making fundamental breakthroughs in automobile technology that could differentiate a firm from its competitors. Major foci of R&D in the auto industry are safety systems, emissions controls, and energy efficiency; cutting across these discrete systems are breakthroughs in materials, aerodynamics, and incorporation of advanced electronics. The central competitive challenge is in power plants. Most experts believe that in the next ten to twenty years traditional internal combustion engines will be supplanted by new engines or motors, possibly based on fuel cells. Of the Japanese automakers, only Toyota and Honda have made major commitments to next generation propulsion technologies such as fuel cells.[47] Honda has devoted the greatest share of resources to R&D, with particular emphasis on engines, its traditional area of strength. Toyota has invested even more in absolute terms, both independently and in conjunction with its leading suppliers, in a range of technologies to enhance safety, reduce emissions, and increase fuel efficiency. It has also moved into a few related areas of high technology, including mobile telecommunications. In contrast, Nissan sold off investments in mobile telecommunications, aerospace, and other noncore activities, and decreased its focus on automotive R&D. Mitsubishi, traditionally strong in engineering but weaker in quality control, focused on a narrower range of core automotive technologies, such as direct injection engines. Increasing global competition and the inroads of Western firms, directly and through their newly strengthened alliances with the smaller Japanese firms, rendered deep pockets and stronghold strategies largely moot. All Japanese auto firms concentrated on cost cutting, while the strongest invested heavily in next-generation technologies as well.

Nonmarket Strategies and Tactics

Traditionally, the Japanese auto industry has adopted a relatively low-profile approach toward governments (although small suppliers are involved in some of the usual political networks) and only in the mid-1990s did it take leading positions in Japan's premier business association, the Keidanren. Rather than engaging in overt lobbying, it has tended to rely on intimate links with regulatory agencies and sheer economic weight to convince governments to adopt congenial policies. The Toyota Foundation, established in the early 1970s, also emerged as one of the most important supporters of research on Southeast Asia, including studies of the auto industry. As Western firms bring a more aggressive attitude to the ASEAN region, however, Japanese companies may be forced to reconsider their relatively indirect approach.

The Japanese government has adopted many policies supporting the activities of Japanese auto and electronics manufacturers in Southeast Asia. The most obvious is "economic cooperation" (*keizai kyōryoku*)—the carefully coordinated combination of aid, trade, and investment. Aid projects have focused on infrastructure, such as roads and power grids, skill development and training programs, and support for dispatch of Japanese volunteers. Trade insurance, export–import funding, and market intelligence programs have also focused on Southeast Asia. In recent years, all such programs have devoted special attention to fostering the development of small and medium-sized manufacturers, not only because the Japanese believe that small firms were crucial to Japan's own economic development, but because while large conglomerates such as the *chaebol* of Korea often seek to compete directly with leading Japanese firms, small and medium-sized companies are valuable partners for the regional assembly operations of Japan's auto and electronics companies.[48]

Japan's aid and investment policies have sought not only to create a supportive physical environment in which Japanese firms can invest but also to encourage the development of regional, national, and local institutions that Japanese believe are conducive to the economic development with which they feel comfortable. At the regional level, Japan took the initiative in the creation of the Asian Development Bank and (with Australia) the Asia Pacific Economic Cooperation (APEC) forum. In the wake of the Asian financial crisis, the Japanese government provided guidance to Thailand and other Southeast Asian countries on developing a Japanese-style system of government-business consultation.[49]

A crucial component of Japanese-style industrial policy is strong industry associations. In 1995, the Japan Automobile Manufacturers Association (JAMA) established a committee on Southeast Asia. The committee issued a report suggesting ways to strengthen local supply industries and reorganize labor relations along more Japanese lines. In 1996, JAMA spurred the formation of the ASEAN Automotive Federation (AAF). The two associations soon established a joint technology committee that became a base to offer Japanese technology and know-how concerning harmonization of the standards and certification systems and the development of the vehicle inspection system. The first ASEAN10 Technical Harmonization Conference was held in Bangkok in April 1998 under the sponsorship of AAF. However, JAMA provided costs for the conference and travel and accommodation fee for participants from the government. JAMA also set up a representative office in Singapore in October 1996. A main objective of the establishment was to strengthen linkages with AAF.

MITI compiled a two-volume, 800–page report on supporting industries and sponsored regular meetings with representatives of the public and private sectors from Japan and Southeast Asia. MITI's trade promotion arm JETRO, JAMA, and the Japan Auto Parts Industries Association (JAPIA) also have sponsored conferences in Southeast Asia.[50]

Japan has also provided encouragement and direction for the creation and enlargement of industrial and engineering associations. For example:

> The Japanese mold-and-die association has, with JICA support, encouraged Thailand's Metal Industries Development Institute to foster associations of Thai small and medium-sized metalworking firms. JICA insisted that subsequent Japanese financial support for the Thai metalworking industry be channeled through associations

of mold and die firms ... Japan's Ministry of Finance has begun to organize training seminars in Tokyo explaining to developing country officials the virtues of public-private sector coordination and various sectoral interventions.[51]

These organizational links give Japanese firms a distinct advantage. A former GM executive in Indonesia claimed, "If I disclosed our confidential business plans to the ministry in the afternoon, the Japanese would know everything by dinner time."[52]

In addition to supporting institution building and regional trade liberalization, the Japanese government has taken some direct steps in recent years to strengthen the position of Japanese firms. After the advent of the Asian financial crisis, Japan pledged up to $35 billion for the "New Miyazawa Plan" to support recovery in ASEAN. Much of that money went directly and indirectly to support the local activities and affiliates of Japanese auto and electronics firms. In contrast, the Japanese government has encouraged, or at least acquiesced to, actions that would shore up Japan's competitive position in the region. For example, the exemption that the ASEAN nations have enjoyed from strictures against local content requirements under the WTO's Trade-Related Investment Measures (TRIMs) was scheduled to expire in 2000. To cope with the loss of protection for local supply industries, Thailand decided to increase tariffs on imports of completely knocked down kits to 33 percent from 20 percent in February 1999. Tokyo made no protests, even though Thailand's policy clearly contravened the spirit of trade liberalization enshrined in the WTO and ran counter to Japan's official espousal of liberalization.[53] According to a close observer,

> In contrast to their European and American competitors, such as Volkswagen, BMW, Ford and General Motors, which have concentrated production activities in Thailand, Japanese firms like Toyota and Honda will continue to use their various regional component-making and car-assembly sites to bargain for trade concessions in bilateral agreements. They stand to benefit the most from the slow pace of liberalization. In fact, they have as much at stake in slowing the process as the more protectionist of governments.[54]

With the exception of the WTO case, Japan has generally avoided direct challenges to the policies of Southeast Asian governments, preferring to rely on its soft organizational power. However, Japanese firms and government have been forced to take a more active approach to compete with the aggressive tactics of the new Western rivals. For example, when GM invested in its new Thai factory, it bargained with the Thai government to establish a jointly funded training center to ensure that its plant would have access to a well-trained workforce.[55] According to a director at Thailand's Ministry of Industry, "The Japanese come and ask what our laws are and then try to please us. The Europeans look at our laws, say they cannot abide by them entirely, but then try as much as possible. But the Americans come and say, 'This is all wrong, you have to change everything.'"[56] Although this account underplays the degree to which Japanese firms and government officials have participated in setting standards in the first place,[57] it does highlight their traditional reluctance to challenge Asian governments directly. After the economic crisis, Japanese firms reportedly articulated a tough line against relaxation of local content rules in the Philippines that would have hurt the suppliers to the Japanese while easing the way for new assembly operations by Western firms.[58] At the first meeting of the public-private ASEAN automotive dialog in July 1999, the Japanese side countered American pressures for rapid liberalization by stressing the prior need for "industrial cooperation" and domestic economic stabilization.[59]

Organizational Strategies

Increasingly challenged at both the global and regional level, Japanese auto firms confronted fundamental issues of organizational strategy, including where to draw the boundaries of the firm and how to balance trade and investment in rapidly changing overseas markets such as Southeast Asia. First and foremost was the choice of independence, dependence, or alliance. The most successful firms, Toyota and Honda, zealously protected their independence, although some analysts questioned whether Honda was large enough to keep pace with the expanding economies of scale and scope in the rapidly consolidating global auto industry. The three other traditional full-line producers, Mazda, Nissan, and Mitsubishi, initially sold large but not controlling stakes to foreign automakers, but as their troubles deepened, the foreign partners took over effective control and dispatched executive teams to implement thorough reorganizations. Three smaller, more specialized firms, Isuzu and Suzuki, both of which rapidly increased production capacity in ASEAN and other parts of Asia, and Fuji Heavy Industries (Subaru), sold significant shares to GM. Indebted Isuzu fell completely under GM's wing while the more successful Suzuki maintained a fairly high degree of independence. The world's largest auto producer hoped to use the

Japanese firms to increase its presence not only in Southeast Asia, but also in other parts of Asia. Isuzu, for example, shifted production of pickups from Japan to Thailand, with sales in Asia through GM's dealer network. GM also entrusted its Japanese affiliates with the design and production of diesel engines and small vehicles.[60]

A second major challenge for Japanese automakers has been reorganizing *keiretsu* networks. Strong and weak firms alike have begun to consolidate and exert more central control over their dealer networks. Toyota and Honda have strengthened relationships with parts suppliers, while Nissan and Mitsubishi, under orders from their new Western parents, have moved decisively toward loosening or even cutting loose from equity ties and long-term trading relationships with suppliers. In some cases, they have moved to create new relationships with the global suppliers of their parent companies.

Finally, Japanese auto companies have reconsidered their organizational approach to Southeast Asia. For companies defending existing market positions, a common response to entry by new rivals is to replace or supplement exports with FDI strategies designed to make models more attractive to local consumers and governments. In the case of autos in Southeast Asia, that has usually meant local production of a few key mainstream models, and perhaps key parts such as engines and transmissions. If volumes are sufficient, parts of the design process may also move from the mother company to local subsidiaries. Some investments are linked to cost cutting efforts, such as establishment of regional procurement offices to increase the share of inexpensive local components. The organizational strategies individual Japanese auto assemblers have adopted toward Southeast Asia since the financial crisis have been deeply affected by alliance patterns and the priorities of their dominant partners. Mitsubishi and especially Nissan have largely frozen operations in Southeast Asia while their new Western parents concentrate on reducing debt in Japan. Mazda has undergone restructuring under Ford, but also has (as noted above) invested in a joint venture to produce pickups in Thailand. Toyota extended massive support to its local affiliates even at the height of the financial crisis.

IV. Case Studies

A comparison of recent strategic shifts by Toyota and Nissan highlights the way in which diverging patterns of alliances have produced distinct approaches to the emerging challenges in Southeast Asia. All of the Japanese auto producers continue to view Southeast Asia as a crucial region in which they must continue to invest, but they have adopted significantly different strategies to those investments. Toyota, the largest Japanese auto producer and second largest assembler in the Asia Pacific region, represents the continuation of the traditional Japanese approach. Although its new models are a little less exciting than Honda's, Toyota is strong in engineering, research, and development. It has invested aggressively in next generation power plants, becoming one of the first auto companies to market a hybrid car with both a gasoline engine and an electric motor.[61] Relatively unburdened by excess capacity and corporate debt, Toyota has maintained employment levels and strengthened ties with its famously efficient network of suppliers. It has also strengthened its control of traditional affiliates such as truckmaker Hino and minicar manufacturer Daihatsu, an aggressive investor in Southeast Asia and China. Toyota accepts the move toward greater use of modules, but it wants those modules to be built by first-tier Japanese affiliates under its control rather than by independent global suppliers.[62] In recent years, Toyota has dispatched vice presidents to serve as vice chairmen of its three leading suppliers: Denso, Aisin Seiki, and Toyota Machine Works.[63]

Within the Asia-Pacific region, Toyota plans a major expansion of exports from Thailand and is making a belated but concerted effort to increase its investments in mainland China. Toyota has emphasized regional, rather than global, procurement and has made the most active use of schemes such as AICO.[64] During the Asian financial crisis, Toyota took heroic strides to support the financial and training operations of its parts affiliates, many of which had investments from Japan, even in the face of drastically reduced sales:

> Since the outbreak of the economic crisis, Toyota Motor Thailand Co. has managed to keep its family of 120 subcontractors afloat without a single bankruptcy, despite the fact that these suppliers are operating at just 20–30% of capacity because the automaker has slashed its vehicle output. The secret lies in advance payments and other forms of financial support Toyota Thailand continues to offer them. Such paternalism is shared by subcontractors in their own ways.[65]

After the crisis, Toyota moved to strengthen its control of local affiliates as the ASEAN region moved, however hesitantly, toward a more unified market. In February 2001, Toyota purchased 3 million new shares in Toyota Motor Thailand, raising Toyota's share from 69.6 percent to 85.3 percent. Toyota affiliate Daihatsu also swiftly expanded its Asia-Pacific production, from 88,000 units in 1989 to 239,000 units in 1997.

Daihatsu's main Asian production sites are China and Malaysia, with smaller operations in Indonesia.[66] Daihatsu and its marketing partner, Japan's Mutsui, took a 51 percent controlling majority in Perodua, Malaysia's number two national auto producer.[67]

Where Toyota has extended the Japanese model, Nissan exemplifies a radical shift in the Japanese auto industry. When domestic demand withered in the 1990s, Nissan fell behind Toyota and Honda. Without hit models, it lost market share and fell deeply into debt.[68] Eventually, France's Renault purchased 36.8 percent of its stock and launched an aggressive cost-cutting campaign that diverged sharply from that of Toyota. Executives dispatched from Renault took control of the company, shuttering outdated assembly plants factories, cutting employment, and developing a limited number of common platforms for mainstream models. Nissan shifted to a pattern of global sourcing, including vigorous efforts to cut loose from the very *keiretsu* network that observers had so long hailed, by shrinking its pool of parts suppliers, increasing single-source contracts, and divesting from all but a handful of key suppliers. Although domestic constraints against unemployment made it difficult to match the intensive restructuring undertaken by Ford or Chrysler in the 1980s, Carlos Ghosn of Brazil and other executives dispatched from Renault succeeded in engineering a dramatic turnaround from huge losses in 1999 to a record net profit in 2000–2001. Ghosn became a household name in Japan and was rewarded with the title of Chief Executive Officer.[69] With the entry of Renault, the nonmarket positions of the two companies reversed. Tokyo-based Nissan, a "new *zaibatsu*" sponsored by the government in the 1930s, had long been closer to government than the family-managed, Nagoya-based Toyota. However, when Nissan began cutting employment and squeezing contractors, officials from the government and ruling party expressed concerns about the impact on social stability and economic confidence. Joining them was Okuda Hiroshi, head of the Japan employers' association—as well as chairman of Toyota Motors.[70]

In the 1990s, Nissan's production capacity in Southeast Asia grew more slowly than those of its Japanese rivals. The company also resembled the Western carmakers in its concentration on Thailand. As of late 2000, Nissan procured even more engine parts in Thailand than did Toyota—eight to five, including cylinder blocks, heads, and connecting rods—but only one outside of Thailand (radiator hoses from Malaysia), compared to Toyota's reported total of 14.[71] After the Asian financial crisis, Nissan, like Toyota, worked to strengthen its local affiliates and increase its managerial control. In both Thailand and Indonesia, it worked to increase its ownership share in local joint ventures from a minority (25 percent in Thailand, 35 percent in Indonesia) to around three-quarters, succeeding in Indonesia but failing in Thailand.[72] It began to use its local subsidiaries to sell Renault vehicles, just as the home company began marketing Renaults in Japan; in return, Renault began selling Nissan vehicles in regions of Renault's strength, such as Europe and Argentina.[73] A revealing indication of Nissan's strained circumstances and newfound pragmatism was its decision in late 1999 to sell control of its Philippines subsidiary to Yulon Motors (Yulong), Nissan's long-time assembler in Taiwan. Nissan held 25 percent of Yulon's stock and had long resisted Yulon's efforts to develop an independent design capacity. Now Nissan planned to make more active use of Yulon to develop models and parts specifically for the Asian market.[74] Thus, while successful Toyota moved to expand its investments and its control over subsidiaries and affiliates both at home and in Southeast Asia, rationalization by financially strapped Nissan involved both enhanced control, as in Thailand, and pullback, as seen in the Philippines and in Japan itself. In both cases, Nissan's strategy was firmly subordinated to that of its new parent, Renault.

Other Japanese producers largely followed these two models. Profitable Honda resembled Toyota in its approach to new technology development, *keiretsu* organization, and sourcing. Its focus on passenger cars limited its presence in Southeast Asia, where pickups and commercial vehicles remained dominant. Mitsubishi more closely resembled Nissan. Overstretched and deeply indebted, Mitsubishi fell under the control of Daimler-Chrysler, which hoped to take advantage of its engine technology, strength in trucks and commercial vehicles, and position as the most active Japanese assembler in Southeast Asia. Almost all of the smaller Japanese producers also sought refuge in alliances with the leading Western firms. Many of these niche producers placed particular emphasis on Asia, although not always Southeast Asia. Mazda, as noted above, plays a junior role in a large new factory assembling pickup trucks in Thailand; it also has had a close relationship with the former Ford affiliate Kia in Korea. From 1989 to 1997, Suzuki ramped up its production in Asia more than sevenfold, from 60,000 to 450,000. In 1997, it assembled over 1 million units in its overseas facilities, becoming the first Japanese automaker to produce more units abroad than in Japan. Most of the increase came in India, where Suzuki secured a dominant position with production of 386,000 units in 1999, China, and Korea, but Suzuki assembled 68,000 vehicles in Indonesia as well. Despite Suzuki's success, it concluded that it could not keep up the pace of investment in new engine and environmental technologies by itself, and in late 2000 GM increased its holdings to 20 percent from 10 percent. The two companies then began to work out a detailed division of labor that included selling in Japan and Asia Chevrolet-badge vehicles designed and assembled by Suzuki. Isuzu, in which GM increased its stake to 49 percent from 37.5 percent, also increased its Asia-Pacific capacity rapidly, from 59,000 units in 1989 to 233,000 units in 1997. Thailand headed the list of production sites, followed by Indonesia, China, and Taiwan.[75]

V. Conclusion

Japanese auto assemblers and parts producers responded to the local markets and national localization policies of Southeast Asian countries with a carefully calibrated strategy of increasing local content in line with the gradual expansion of demand. Japanese industry associations and government agencies cooperated in efforts to build institutional capacities and regional production networks in Southeast Asia that would mimic and coordinate with their counterparts in Japan. Until the mid-1990s, these strategies seemed to be a solid success. Japanese firms held an overwhelmingly dominant position in a regional market that promised to grow as large as North America or Europe.

In the mid-1990s, three new trends emerged to threaten traditional Japanese strategies: financial crises, acute in Southeast Asia and endemic in Japan; continuing pressures to localize amid unstable national and regional policies and intensifying global economies of scale and scope; and the entry of new rivals—South Korean companies on the low-end, and Western producers at the middle-to-high end. The Japanese government and Japanese firms reacted quickly to counter the effects of the financial crisis in Southeast Asia. The crisis itself also put up major roadblocks to the progress of the South Koreans, although Hyundai in particular seems likely to reemerge as a major player in the global auto industry.[76] While Western, and particularly American, firms failed to make significant inroads under their own brands in Japan, they established a major presence through mergers, acquisitions and strengthening of relations with existing partners. Only Toyota and Honda remained "*hi no maru*" (all-Japanese) producers committed to the traditional production networks and regional strategy that had proved successful for so long.

The major remaining question is the ability of the Japanese auto producers, particularly Honda and Toyota, to revitalize their Southeast Asian networks to fend off the inroads of Western automakers, especially Ford and GM, which have free-ridden on the supplier base so carefully cultivated by Japanese firms. This competition is particularly interesting because the Western firms have concentrated their investments in one key country (Thailand) and have shown less inclination to invest in institution building than have the Japanese. Whether others can simply free ride on Japanese-initiated institutions—or indeed whether those institutions are actually indispensable—is a pressing question for the future of the Southeast Asian auto industry.[77] At home, Japanese assemblers face strong pressures to reconfigure their *keiretsu* networks and reorganize relations with their first-tier suppliers and dealers, yet the initial response has been limited and slow. Similarly, shrinking the existing "permanent employment" labor force and attracting new and more flexible employees in the future remain daunting tasks.

The implication is clear: despite the patient and (in recent years) heroic efforts of Japanese auto assemblers and major parts producers to build Southeast Asia into a major market and even an export base, a slow erosion of their dominant position is almost inevitable.

Notes

1. I would like to thank Vinod K. Aggarwal, Shujiro Urata, and Ed Fogarty for comments on earlier versions of this chapter.
2. Dyer (1998), pp. 233–254; Tate (1995); Cusumano (1985); Jones et al. (1990); Yoshinari et al. (2000).
3. A knocked-down kit is comprised of all the parts necessary to build a car in unassembled form.
4. Mukai (1997), pp. 223–230 (631); pp. 80–87 (632); Yuiko (1994), pp. 16–32; Takeuchi (1993), pp. 36–57.
5. See Chapter 1 by Vinod K. Aggarwal of this volume.
6. A comprehensive map and listing of mergers, acquisitions and alliances through early 2000 appears in *Fourin Kaigai Jidōsha Chōsa Geppo* 175 (March 2000), pp. 8–13. See also "The Global Six," *Business Week* (January 25, 1999) and "Global Pile-up," *The Economist* (May 10, 1997). Major announcements since then include Daimler-Chrysler's 34 percent (later 37 percent) share in Mitsubishi and 10 percent stake in Hyundai, and the increase of GM's share in Suzuki to 20 percent from 10 percent. Among the most useful industry news sites are http://www.autonews.com and http://www.auto-asia.com.
7. Ishizaki (1994), pp. 16–32.
8. Ishiro (1997), pp. 6–7.
9. *Automotive Engineering International* (June 1999), pp. 53–72 provides an excellent guide to differences across regions and countries. See also *Automotive Engineering International* (May 1999), pp. 74–90 on integration within the Americas.
10. Williamson (1991), pp. 269–296.
11. Dyer (1998); Gerlach 1992); Nishiguchi (1994); Ostrom (2000).
12. The leading student of this topic is Richard F. Doner. See Doner (1991a, 1991b, 1992). For a recent Japanese account covering the ASEAN countries as well as South Korea, China and Taiwan, see Yoshinari (1997). A good example of Japanese triumphalism shortly before the Asian financial crisis (and the inroads of GM and Ford) is Kiichi (1996), pp. 59–68.
13. According to one count, as of the mid-1990s, over 460 Japanese auto parts producers had invested in Asia (including China and India), compared to only 220 in North America. *Shūkan Tōyō Keizai,* December 21, 1996, p. 114.

14. *Nihon Keizai Shinbun,* October 10, 1995; *Nikkei Bijinesu,* March 20, 1995, pp. 16–17; *Nikkei Weekly,* August 2, 1995.
15. Restrictions on imports remained almost complete until 1980, by which time the industry was highly competitive. FDI was blocked until 1970 and limited from then until the late 1990s (Tate 1995; Mutoh 1988, especially pp. 316–319). Financial aid was crucial not only in the 1950s, as most analysts concede, but well into the 1960s. The government also played a major role in strengthening and consolidating the parts industry (Odano and Islam 1994, pp. 285–315). Nor has government completely disengaged from the auto industrial policy: for example, in the late 1990s MITI provided tax breaks to accelerate corporate restructuring at Toyota, Nissan, and other auto firms, struggled to uphold retail price maintenance, funded and coordinated research on new hybrid engine technologies, and developed standards for body recycling and fluorine recovery, not to mention its continuing involvement in international trade and investment issues affecting the auto industry. See the sections on "administration" in the *Jidōsha Nenkan* [Automotive Yearbook] published by Nikkan Jidōsha Shinbunsha, 1997 volume pp. 362–363 and 2000 volume pp. 326–327.
16. Porter (1980).
17. Smitka (1991).
18. Useful overviews include *Fourin Kaigai Jidōsha Chōsa Geppo* 171 (November 1999), pp. 8–13 and 176 (April 2000), pp. 8–13. For an interesting case study from Europe, see "Front-End Module Strategy," *Vehicle News* 243 (April 2000), pp. 50–53; for a comparison of the post-spin-off strategies of Delphi and Visteon, see *Business Week,* April 24, 2000.
19. "Mojūru kakumei ga susumeru buhin 'dai saihen'" [The Big Reorganization of the Parts Industry Driven by the Module Revolution] and "Mirai o kaketa Jidōsha Dai Kyōsō," [The Heated Competition in the Automobile Industry that is Betting on the Future] *Shūkan Tōyō Keizai,* October 16, 1999, pp. 26–41; *Nikkei Weekly,* July 12, 1999.
20. Doner (1991b), pp. 73–87.
21. For a positive review of the development of the South Korean auto industry stressing the aggressive shift to outward FDI, particularly in developing countries, see McDermott (1995), pp. 23–47; an account emphasizing the structural barriers facing late entrants is Woo (1993), pp. 335–357; on the imprudent and unsustainable expansion of Korea's Daewoo, see *Business Week,* August 30, 1999, pp. 24–25.
22. *Far Eastern Economic Review,* June 13, 1996, p. 54.
23. On global realignments, see *Fourin Kaigai Jidōsha Chōsa Geppo* 175 (March 2000), pp. 8–13; the position of global firms in Asia is examined in *Fourin Kaigai Jidōsha Chōsa Geppo* 177 (May 2000), pp. 20–25. On Ford's global activities, including acquisition of control of Mazda in 1996 and Volvo Cars in 1999, see *Fourin Kaigai Jidōsha Chōsa Geppo* 174 (February 2000), pp. 14–19; on GM's activities in Asia and its preference—questioned by many analysts—for forming alliances that respect the autonomy of its much-smaller Japanese partners Suzuki, Isuzu, and Fuji, see *Far Eastern Economic Review* (February 17), 2000, pp. 8–11.
24. *Fourin Jidōsha Chōsa Geppo* 159 (November 1998), pp. 36–37; *Fourin Kaigai Jidōsha Chōsa Geppo* 166 (June 1999), pp. 38–39; *Nikkei Weekly,* December 21, 1998; on export boom from Thailand, see *Nikkei Weekly,* October 11, 1999, p. 21.
25. Fourin, *Asian Automotive Business Review* (Nagoya) 10:1 (January 1999), pp. 2–8; *Far Eastern Economic Review,* November 14, 1996.
26. *Nikkei Weekly,* July 12, 1999 and October 11, 1999.
27. Doner (1991b); Legewie (1999), pp. 5–6.
28. Legewie (1999), pp. 8–12.
29. *Ibid.,* p. 15.
30. *Fourin Kaigai Jidōsha Chōsa Geppo* 174 (February 2000), pp. 40–41 and 185 (January 2001), p. 41.
31. *Asian Automotive Business Review* (January 1999), pp. 24–33; Legewie (1999), pp. 8–12.
32. *Asian Automotive Business Review* (October 1999), pp. 16–19; *Fourin Kaigai Jidōsha Chōsa Geppo* 174 (February 2000), p. 6.
33. *Fourin Kaigai Jidōsha Chōsa Geppo* 166 (June 1999), pp. 38–39.

34. *Asian Automotive Business Review* 10:4 (October 1999), pp. 22–23; *Fourin Kaigai Jidōsha Chōsa Geppo* 174 (February 2000), p. 7.
35. *Asian Automotive Business Review* (January 1999), p. 30.
36. Jayasankaran (1993), pp. 272–285.
37. *Asian Automotive Business Review* (January 1999), pp. 17–23; *Far Eastern Economic Review*, December 12, 1996; *Shūkan Tōyō Keizai*, October 16, 1999, pp. 44–46; *Business Week*, January 25, 1999.
38. *Asian Automotive Business Review* (October 1999), pp. 20–21; *Fourin Kaigai Jidōsha Chōsa Geppo* 174 (February 2000), pp. 4–5.
39. *AutoAsia*, May 4, 2001.
40. Doner (1991b, 1992).
41. Hatch and Yamamura (1996), p. 165.
42. *Far Eastern Economic Review*, July 29, 1999, pp. 52–54.
43. Dyer (1998); *FT Automotive World*, October 1999, pp. 24–25; *New York Times*, June 16, 2000.
44. Doner (1991b); *Fourin Kaigai Jidōsha Chōsa Geppo* 166 (June 1999), pp. 38–39. *Nikkei Weekly*, December 21, 1998; on the export boom from Thailand, see *Nikkei Weekly*, October 11, 1999, p. 21; Yoshimatsu (1999), pp. 495–515.
45. For variation among Japanese auto firms in strategy, structure, and relation to public policies, see Tate (1995).
46. *Nikkei Weekly*, March 15, July 26, and October 18, 1999.
47. *Nikkei Weekly*, March 27 and October 2, 2000; *Business Week* (Asian Edition), May 14, 2001. Tellingly, Nissan and Mitsubishi, unlike other Japanese auto producers, have declined to reveal recent figures on R&D spending. *Asian Automotive Business Review* 11:4 (October 2000), p. 6.
48. Yamazawa (1994), pp. 16–24.
49. Suehiro (2000), pp. 25–65.
50. Yoshimatsu (1999), p. 505.
51. Doner (1997), p. 227.
52. Quoted in Hatch and Yamamura (1997), fn. 44, p. 15.
53. *Fourin Kaigai Jidōsha Chōsa Geppo* 166 (June 1999), pp. 38–39.
54. Legewie (2000), p. 32.
55. *Asian Automotive Business Review* 10:1 (January 1999), pp. 2–8; *Far Eastern Economic Review*, November 14, 1996.
56. *The Economist*, June 24, 2000, p. 83.
57. Author interview, Taiwan Transportation Vehicle Manufacturers Association, August 1999.
58. *Asian Automotive Business Review* 10:4 (October 1999), p. 22.
59. *Jidōsha Nenkan* 2000 [Automotive Yearbook 2000], p. 214.
60. *Asian Automotive Business Review* (July 1998, April 1999).
61. *Shukan Toyo Keizai*, October 16, 1999, pp. 44–47.
62. *Nihon Keizai Shinbun*, September 9, 2000; see also *Nikkei Weekly*, March 13, 2000 and October 2, 2000.
63. *Shūkan Tōyō Keizai*, August 7, 1999, p. 28.
64. *Asian Automotive Business Review*, April 1999, p. 11 [pp. 3–39]; *Shūkan Tōyō Keizai*, October 16, 1999, pp. 44–46; *Business Week*, January 25, 1999, p. 71; *Asian Automotive Business Review*, July 1998, pp. 6–16; Legewie (1999), p. 12.
65. *Nikkei Weekly*, December 21, 1998.
66. *Asian Automotive Business Review* (July 1998, April 1999).
67. *AutoAsia* September 7, 2001; Daihatsu press release, December 5, 2001.
68. Maruyama et al. (2000), pp. 21, 149, 154.
69. *Japan Economic Institute*, JEI Report #41B, October 29, 1999, pp. 1–3; *Shūkan Tōyō Keizai*, October 16, 1999, pp. 48–50; *Fourin Kaigai Jidōsha Chōsa Geppo* 166 (June 1999), pp. 38–39; *AutoAsia*, May 20, 2001.
70. Japan Economic Institute, JEI Report #41B (October 29, 1999), p. 2

71. *Asian Automotive Business Review* (October 2000), pp. 24–25; this source is not categorical, however, so there may be some minor additional procurement.
72. *AutoAsia,* May 31, 2001 and Nissan Global Corporate Information, June 16, 2001 [in Japanese].
73. *AutoAsia,* June 15, 2001
74. *Nikkei Weekly,* November 15, 1999; Noble (1996), pp. 20–25.
75. *Asian Automotive Business Review* (April 1999), p. 11; *Business Week,* January 25, 1999, p. 70; *Nikkei Weekly,* May 5, 1997; *Nikkei Weekly,* September 11, 2000; Agence France-Press, June 29, 2001; Suzuki production data from *2000 Nen Shuyōkoku Jidōsha Tōkei* [Automotive Statistics for Major Countries, 2000] (Tokyo: Nihon Jidōsha Kōgyō Kai, 2000), pp. 44–45.
76. On the recovery of auto production and exports after the financial crisis, see *Fourin Kaigai Jidōsha Chōsa Geppo* 175 (March 2000), pp. 42–43.
77. There is limited evidence that some Western firms are investing in institutions and human capital in Southeast Asia, particularly in Thailand. As noted above, GM is engaging in joint training projects with the Thai government. GM also signed an agreement with APEC's "Partnership for Equitable Growth" to create an apprenticeship program for small automotive companies in APEC, presumably largely in ASEAN [*Asia-Pacific Automotive Report* 319 (April 5, 2000), p. 1]. On balance, though, the Western firms appear to have invested far less than their Japanese counterparts.

References

Aggarwal, Vinod K. (2001). "Analyzing European Firms' Market and Nonmarket Strategies in Asia." In *Winning in Asia, European Style,* ed. Vinod K. Aggarwal (New York: Palgrave).
Asanuma, Banri (1989). "Manufacturer–Supplier Relationships in Japan and the Concept of Relation-Specific Skill," *Journal of The Japanese and International Economies* 3(1), pp. 1–30.
Cusumano, Michael A. (1985). *The Japanese Automobile Industry: Technology and Management at Nissan and Toyota* (Cambridge, Mass.: Harvard University Press).
Doner, Richard F. (1991a). "Approaches to the Politics of Economic Growth in Southeast Asia." *The Journal of Asian Studies* 50(4), pp. 73–87.
——— (1991b). *Driving a Bargain: Automobile Industrialization and Japanese Firms in Southeast Asia.* (Berkeley: University of California Press).
——— (1992). "Limits of State Strength: Toward an Institutionalist View of Economic Development," *World Politics* 44(3), pp. 398–431.
——— (1997). "Japan in East Asia: Institutions and Regions." In *Network Power: Japan and Asia,* ed. Peter J. Katzenstein and Takashi Shiraishi (Ithaca, N.Y.: Cornell University Press).
Dyer, Jeffrey H. (1998). "To Sue or *Keiretsu*: A Comparison of Partnering in the United States and Japan." In *Networks, Markets and the Pacific Rim,* ed. W. Mark Fruin (New York: Oxford University Press).
Gerlach, Michael L. (1992). *Alliance Capitalism: The Social Organization of Japanese Business* (Berkeley: University of California Press).
Hatch, Walter and Kozo Yamamura (1996). *Asia in Japan's Embrace* (Cambridge: Cambridge University Press).
——— (1997). "A Looming Entry Barrier: Japanese Production Networks in Asia," The National Bureau of Asian Research, *NBR Analysis* 8(1).
Hidehiko, Mukoyama (1994). "Active Investment by Japanese Parts and Materials-process Industries in Asia: Exploring the Backgrounds of Their Moves in Thailand and China." *RIM: Pacific Business and Industries* 2, p. 24.
Ishiro Katsuji (1997). "Jiyūka no shinten ni yoru kyōsō no kōzō no henkaku to ajia ikinai seisan taisei e no ikō: ajia jidōsha sangyō to nihon chūshō kigyō no ajia senryaku no shiten kara" ["The effect of liberalization on the transformation of competitive structure and the movement to an

Asian regional production structure from the perspective of the automobile industry and the Asian strategies of Japan's small and medium-sized enterprises"], *Shōkō Kinyū* 47(2), pp. 3–15.

Ishizaki, Yukiko (1994). "The Automobile Industries of ASEAN Countries: Toward Greater Regional Cooperation and Competitiveness," *RIM: Pacific Business and Industries* 23(1) (March), pp.16–32.

Japan Economic Institute (1999). *JEI Report #41B* (October 29).

Jayasankaran, S. (1993). "Made-in-Malaysia: The Proton Project," *Industrializing Malaysia: Policy, Performance, Prospects*, ed. K. S. Jomo (London: Routledge).

Jones, Daniel T., Daniel Roos, and James P. Womack (1990). *The Machine that Changed the World* (New York: Rawson Associates).

Kageyama Kiichi (1996). "Ajia ni okeru jidōsha sangyō no hatten: toyota shisutemu o chūshin to suru kokusai teki sai hensei" ["The development of the Asian automobile industry: international reorganization centered on the Toyota system"], *Sekai Keizai Hyōron* 40(1), pp. 59–68.

Legewie, Jochen (1999). "Driving Regional Integration: Japanese Firms and the Development of the ASEAN Automobile Industry." Philipp Franz von Siebold Stiftung Deutsches Institut fur Japanstudien, Working Paper 99/1 (Tokyo).

——— (2000). "Cars get no Vroom from Afta," *Far Eastern Economic Review*, May 4, p. 32.

Maruyama Yoshinari, ed. (1997). *Ajia no Jidōsha Sangyō, shinpan* [The Automobile Industry of Asia, new edition] (Tokyo: Aki Shobo).

Maruyama Yoshinari, Kamo Mineko, and Ogura Takashi (2000). "*Jidōsha: 21 Seiki ni ikinokoreru meekaa wa doko ka*". *[Automobiles: Where are the Producers Who Will Survive in the 21st Century.]* (Tokyo: Ootsuki Shoten).

McDermott, Michael (1995). "The Development and Internationalization of the South Korean Motor Industry: the European Dimension," *Asia Pacific Business Review* 2(2).

Mukai Juichi (1997). "Dai Kyōsō Jidai no Shōsha wa Dare ka ["Who will be the winner in the Age of Mega-Competition"], *Sekai* 631 and 632, pp. 223–230, 80–87.

Mutoh, Hiromichi (1988). "The Automobile Industry." In *Industrial Policy of Japan*, ed. Ryutaro Komiya et al. (San Diego: Academic Press).

Nishiguchi, Toshiro (1994). *Strategic Industrial Sourcing: The Japanese Advantage* (New York: Oxford University Press).

Noble, Gregory W. (1996). "Trojan Horse or Boomerang: Two-Tiered Investment in the Asian Auto Complex." BRIE Working Paper 90 (Berkeley: BRIE).

Odano, Sumimaru and Saiful Islam (1994). "Industrial Development and the Guidance Policy Finance: the Case of the Japanese Automobile Industry," *Asian Economic Journal* 8(3), pp. 285–315.

Ostrom, Douglas (2000). "The Keiretsu System: Cracking or Crumbling?" Japan Economic Institute, *JEI Review*, 14A.

Porter, Michael E. (1980). *Competitive Strategy* (New York: Free Press).

Smitka, Michael J. (1991). *Competitive Ties: Subcontracting in the Japanese Auto Industry* (New York: Columbia University Press).

Suehiro Akira (2000). "Tai no keizai kaikaku: sangyō kōzō chōsei jigyō to chūshō kigyōshien." ["Economic Reform in Thailand: Industrial Restructuring Adjustment Enterprises and Support for Small and Medium Sized Businesses"], *Shakai Kagaku Kenkyū* 51(4), pp. 25–65.

Takeuchi, Junko (1993). "Foreign Direct Investment in ASEAN by Small-and Medium-Sized Japanese Companies and its Effects on Local Supporting Industries," *RIM: Pacific Business and Industries* 4(22) (December), pp. 36–57.

Tate, John Jay (1995). *Driving Production Innovation Home: Guardian State Capitalism and the Competitiveness of the Japanese Automobile Industry* (Berkeley: BRIE).

Williamson, Oliver E. (1991). "Comparative Economic Organization: The Analysis of Discrete Structural Alternatives," *Administrative Science Quarterly* 36, pp. 269–296.

Woo, Myung-oc (1993). "Export Promotion in the New Global Division of Labor: The Case of the South Korean Automobile Industry." *Sociological Perspectives* 36(4), pp. 335–357.

Yamazawa, Ippei (1994). "Promotion of SMEs for Industrial Upgrading in ASEAN," *ASEAN Economic Bulletin* 11(1), pp.16–24.

Yoshimatsu, Hidetaka (forthcoming). "The State, MNCs, and the Auto Industry in ASEAN," *Journal of Contemporary Asia*.

CHAPTER SIX

Ringing off the Hook! Japanese Telecommunications Responds to the Call of Asian Markets

YUMIKO OKAMOTO[1]

I. Introduction

The breakup of AT&T in the United States and the privatization of NTT in Japan and British Telecom in the United Kingdom profoundly affected the structure of the international telecommunications industry. Since early 1998, telecommunications markets have changed even more significantly, as a result of the European Union throwing open its markets to competition in the provision of infrastructure and services.[2]

The trend toward telecom reform is also sweeping across the developing world. Corporatization, privatization, and the introduction of competition are becoming increasingly widespread in Asian developing countries. The earliest example is Malaysia's privatization of its state telephone monopoly, Telekom Malaysia, in 1987.

There are two principal reasons for the recent popularity of these reforms.[3] First, many governments have come to realize that telecommunications play an increasingly important role in determining the competitiveness of nations. Second, even developed countries are now confronted with the problem of establishing a world-class telecommunications infrastructure without relying on private investment.

The development of privatization and competition in telecommunications has enhanced market growth and development. East Asia is among the fastest growing regions in telecommunications. Despite the setback in overall economic growth in 1997 and 1998, the information and telecommunication industries, particularly the Internet market, continue to grow.[4] In addition, East Asia, with the exception of Indonesia, has shown a strong recovery in GDP growth.

Beginning in the 1990s, emerging East Asian markets attracted a lot of attention from globally-minded telecommunications companies in the form of equity investment, the establishment of joint ventures, and build-transfer-operate (BTO) projects. The agreement made between the United States and China with respect to China's participation in the WTO will certainly increase the interest of multinational telecom companies.[5]

The Japanese penetration of East Asian markets was conditioned by several factors, the most important of which was the institutional non-market environment. Despite the early introduction of privatization policy, the segmentation in Japan between domestic and international telephone services continued well into 1997. The most common current strategy of global telecommunications firms in East Asia is horizontal and vertical integration across the country and the region.[6] The slow introduction of deregulation measures in Japan made it difficult for Japanese firms to think globally and strategize their entry into foreign markets.

In July 1999, NTT was finally divided into a holding company, two regional service companies, and a long distance and international service company (NTT Communications Corporation, or NTT Com). NTT Com expanded into international services while NTT DoCoMo, the mobile communications provider of the NTT Group, also sought to be a major player on the world stage. Further privatization, deregulation, and liberalization will be forthcoming in the East Asian region.[7] The extent to which Japanese firms succeed in penetrating international markets will invariably depend on their upcoming strategies.

II. Positional Analysis

Market Environment

Growth in the world telecommunications market has been remarkable in the 1990s. The industry's global revenue more than doubled between 1990 and 1999 from $508 billion to $1.1 trillion. Total revenues are estimated to reach around $1.3 trillion by 2002.[8]

The principal causes of this expansion of the world telecommunications market are the cellular mobile communications market and the Internet. Although fixed telephone lines remain the main component of

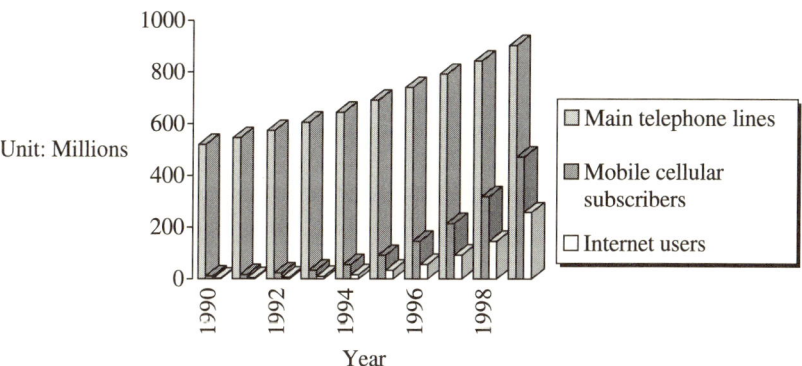

Figure 6.1 Key indicators of the world telecommunications sector
Source: *ITU News* (No. 9, 2000).

Table 6.1 Regional shares of worldwide fixed telephone lines and mobile-phone subscribers in percentage

Region	Fixed telephone		Mobile phone	
	1990	2000	1990	2000
Americas	35	31	53	27
Europe	40	34	34	36
Asia-Pacific	23	33	13	35
Africa	2	2	0	2

Source: *ITU News* (No. 1, 2001).

the information society, both mobile cellular subscribers and Internet users have increased rapidly.

The rapid increase in international traffic flow has had a profound impact on international telecommunications networks. The total volume of international telephone traffic more than tripled in the 1990s, from 33 billion telephone minutes in 1990 to one hundred billion at the end of the decade. Clearly, the flow of telecommunications traffic is increasingly international and borderless.[9]

The Asia-Pacific telecommunications markets have the highest growth rate in the world. Table 6.1 shows regional shares of global fixed telephone lines and mobile phone subscribers. During the 1990s, Asia-Pacific was among the world's fastest growing regions both in fixed and mobile telephony. The region's Internet market is also expanding at high rates. Five of the world's top ten Internet economies, ranked by number of Internet users, are in the Asia-Pacific region.[10]

Moreover, East Asia's share of global international telecommunications traffic is increasing rapidly as well. The region's share of outgoing international traffic doubled from less than 10 percent over the last two decades.[11] Fifteen years ago, Europe's share of worldwide traffic was almost 70 percent; it has since slipped to around 40 percent.[12] These trends reflect the fact that the region's economic activities are not only expanding but also becoming increasingly extraregional in nature.

Table 6.2 shows the growth rates of telecommunications main lines and mobile phone subscribers in East Asia, categorized by country. According to this table, during the 1990s the telecommunications market expanded

Table 6.2 Telecommunications access in APEC member economies, 1995–1999

Most developed	Main telephone lines per 100 inhabitants		Growth rates 1995–99	Cellular subscribers per 100 inhabitants		Growth rates 1995–99
	1995	1999	%	1995	1999	%
Australia	50.96	52.12	2.3	12.77	34.38	169.2
Canada	58.97	63.39	7.5	8.75	17.56	100.7
Japan	48.80	55.75	14.2	8.15	44.94	451.4
New Zealand	47.85	49.03	2.5	10.80	23.01	113.1
United States	62.57	66.13	5.7	12.84	25.60	99.4
Average	**53.83**	**57.28**	**6.4**	**10.66**	**29.1**	**172.9**
High-Income						
Brunei	23.99	24.68	2.9	12.63	15.60	23.5
Chile	13.20	20.55	55.7	1.38	6.50	371.0
Hong Kong	52.96	57.57	8.7	12.90	63.61	393.1
South Korea	41.47	44.14	6.4	3.66	50.44	1278.1
Mexico	9.58	10.36	8.1	0.70	3.50	400.0
Singapore	47.85	48.20	0.7	9.77	41.88	328.7
Taiwan	43.07	54.52	26.6	3.62	52.24	1343.1
Average	**33.16**	**37.15**	**15.6**	**6.38**	**33.40**	**591.1**
Developing						
China	3.35	8.58	156.1	0.30	3.42	1040.0
Indonesia	1.69	2.91	72.2	0.11	1.06	863.6
Malaysia	16.56	20.30	22.6	4.34	13.70	215.7
Philippines	2.09	3.95	89.0	0.73	3.66	401.4
Thailand	5.86	8.57	46.2	1.83	3.84	109.8
Average	**5.91**	**8.86**	**77.2**	**1.46**	**5.14**	**526.1**

Note: Data in italics refer to the year of 1998.
Source: APEC Economic Committee (1998, 2000). *ITU Telecommunication Indicators Update* (Oct.– Nov. – Dec. 2000).

faster in East Asian countries than in mature economies such as Japan, the U.S., or Canada. The same is true in the Internet market, although great disparities still remain among the region's high and low income countries in their numbers of Internet hosts and Internet users (see Table 6.3). This indicates that East Asian telecommunications markets possess tremendous growth potential in the coming decades. In fact, the International Telecommunications Union (ITU) forecasts that by 2010 the Asia-Pacific region will contain almost half of the world's fixed line and mobile phone subscribers.[13]

While supply factors such as the application of new technologies have transformed and expanded the telecommunications market, changes in demand have also been important. One of the most significant factors is the trend of changing needs of business enterprises, especially those of multinational corporations (MNCs).[14] As their transnational operations expand, MNCs are demanding the quick and reliable provision of

Table 6.3 Internet use in APEC member economies

Most developed	Number of Internet hosts (in thousands) 1996	Growth rates 1993–96 %	Internet users % of population 1999
Australia	514.8	79.1	29.6
Canada	603.3	91.2	42.3
Japan	734.4	158.0	21.4
New Zealand	84.5	144.6	18.3
United States	10112.9	89.9	39.0
Average	**2409.98**	**112.56**	**30.1**
High-Income			
Brunei	0.2	N.A.	7.8
Chile	15.9	126.2	N.A.
Hong Kong	49.2	104.8	36.2
South Korea	66.3	94.7	23.4
Mexico	29.8	103.0	0.6
Singapore	28.9	118.4	24.4
Taiwan	34.7	63.2	20.6
Average	**32.14**	**101.7**	**18.8**
Developing			
China	19.7	N.A.	0.7
Indonesia	9.6	N.A.	0.4
Malaysia	4.2	112.9	6.9
Philippines	3.6	N.A.	0.7
Thailand	9.2	222.4	1.3
Average	**9.26**	**167.7**	**2.0**

Source/Note: See Table 6.2.

seamless telecommunication services on a global scale. In addition to basic services, MNCs demand the provision of network management and maintenance. The desire to provide and market such services in one package to MNCs was a key motive for the formation of mega-telecom companies through global alliances.[15]

Nonmarket Environment

Although market factors undoubtedly played a significant role in changing and expanding telecommunication markets, many of these developments were possible only through regulatory reform. The benefits of the Internet, which users take for granted today, would not have been possible without the deregulation of telecommunications infrastructure and services. The emergence of cellular mobile communications and the Internet were the results of a decade of regulatory change.[16]

These regulatory changes consisted mainly of three aspects: privatization, introduction of competition (or removal of entry barriers), and deregulation with respect to foreign ownership. Each aspect is discussed below.

Privatization The inception dates of programs to privatize telecommunications monopolies in East Asian countries varied widely.[17] Japan was the first to privatize, followed by most of the region with the exceptions of India, China, and Vietnam, in which the role of the state is still much bigger than in the rest of Asia. Thailand planned to privatize both the Telephone Organization of Thailand (TOT) and the Communication Authority of Thailand (CAT) in 1999.[18] However, they had to postpone their plans mainly because of the reduction of economic activities caused by the currency and financial crises. Thailand re-announced its plans to privatize first CAT, then TOT, in 2000. The process is due to be completed by the year 2006.[19]

Taiwan was also relatively late in the privatization of its dominant public operator, Chunghwa Telecom Company, which holds a monopoly in providing all telecommunication services. Nevertheless, the Taiwanese government started the privatization process of the state public provider in 2000 so that the domestic industry could cope with the intensification of competition in 2001.

Introduction of Competition Across the region, privatizations in the 1990s were aimed at dissolving long-standing monopolies in telecommunications infrastructure and services. East Asian governments sought to end the monopolistic provision of telecommunications services and to introduce duopolies or competitive markets in the telecommunication industry. The adoption of competitive market structures was most apparent in the cellular mobile phone market.[20] Other markets were also liberalized through reforms in the 1990s, although the degree of open competition differed considerably across various countries and markets.

ASEAN countries (with the exception of Singapore) were much faster than the Asian Newly Industrialized Economies (ANIEs), such as Singapore and Taiwan, in adopting liberalization and deregulation policies. This is partly because the former's need for private capital and technology was greater than the latter's need for rapid development of good telecommunication infrastructures. Since 2000, however, the pace of liberalization and deregulation has accelerated both in Singapore and Taiwan.

Singapore introduced competition in the local and international telephony markets in April 2000, after having done the same in the cellular mobile phone market in 1997.[21] In the same year, Taiwan also issued a license to three new telephone company groups for the provision of local, long distance, and international telephone services.[22] These three groups began operations in 2001. One of the reasons for the sudden shift toward liberalization is that both Singapore and Taiwan harbor the ambition of becoming an Asian regional hub for the infocommunications sector.[23]

Although the privatization of dominant public telephone operators has yet to occur in India and China, both have made policy shifts toward liberalization. For instance, the government of India announced a New Telecom Policy in 1999, one that included the liberalization of long distance and international telephone markets in 2000.[24]

China's basic telecommunications market has become more open as a result of the establishment in 1994 of China Unicom, another major public telephone operator. China Unicom was established to compete with the incumbent dominant carrier, China Telecom. This 1994 reform failed mainly because the duopoly remained seriously unbalanced.[25] To resolve this continuing dilemma, China launched a new round of reforms in 1998. The idea was to form a more balanced market by simultaneously breaking up China Telecom and strengthening China Unicom through market restructuring.[26] In 1999, two more new companies, Jitong and China Net Communications (CNC), were established to enforce competition. These actions suggest that the government of China is serious in its reform of the telecommunications market.

Introduction of Foreign Direct Investment The need to introduce foreign capital and technology into local telecommunications markets was also an important motive behind regional regulatory reform. As Table 6.4

Table 6.4 Summary of APEC member economies' commitments under WTO agreement on basic telecommunications, 15 February 1997

Country	Foreign ownership limitation
Australia	None
Brunei Darussalam	Reserved for exclusive operator
Canada	46.7% direct and indirect investment in the voting capital
Chile	None
Hong Kong	None
Indonesia	35%; except personal communication services which only require a joint-venture with a local company
Japan	20% in KDD and NTT; 100% in all other supplier
South Korea	20% in South Korea Telecom, (33% from 2001); 33% in all other suppliers (49% from 2001)
Malaysia	30% in exiting licensed public telecommunication operator
Mexico	49%; higher limitations for cellular
New Zealand	None, except no single foreign share holder in TCNZ may hold more than 49.9%
Papua New Guinea	Reserved for exclusive operator
Philippines	40%
Singapore	49%
Thailand	20%
United States	None (indirect); Radio licenses 20% (direct)

(1) Foreign ownership limits of Taiwan, Vietnam, and India are as follows (Industrial of Japan 1998): Taiwan: 20% in Type I telecom carriers; Vietnam: Foreign direct investment in the telecommunications industry has not been allowed yet except the cellular mobile phone market. The entry of foreign capital is permitted only through the Business Cooperation Contract scheme. India: Local 49 percent; International 0 percent; Mobile 49 percent.

(2) The foreign ownership restriction to KDD in Japan was removed in 1998.

(3) According to *InfoCom Newsletter* (April 2000), the foreign ownership limit of Singapore was removed in April 2000 two years ahead of schedule.

Source: APEC (1998).

shows, in the 1990s many APEC member countries started to allow foreign ownership of domestic telecom companies, although full liberalization and deregulation remains to be seen in many East Asian countries.

The adoption of open policies toward foreign participation in the telecommunications market has accelerated since the late 1990s. Singapore, for instance, opened all segments of its telecommunications market to foreign investment in April 2000, alongside the introduction of competitive markets, two years ahead of schedule.[27]

China also agreed to open its telecommunication services sector to foreign investment in its WTO accession agreement with the United States in 1999. China's key telecommunication services markets in Beijing, Shanghai, and Guangzhou are being opened as a condition of its entry into the WTO. China offered to allow 49 percent foreign equity investment in all of the telecommunication services and 51 percent foreign share for value-added services and paging services in four years.[28]

Despite its having been so cautious in the past regarding foreign equity, South Korea has agreed to raise the foreign ownership limit of South Korea Telecom from 20 to 33 percent.[29] In 1998, Malaysia also increased the legal limit on foreign equity shares in existing basic telecommunications companies from 30 to 61 percent. However, this policy will only be effective until 2003.[30] Moreover, Thailand has announced that it will let 100 percent foreign-owned telecom companies into its domestic market in 2006. Thailand was the last among the ASEAN countries to engage in regulatory changes.

WTO Negotiations on Basic Telecommunications The processes of privatization and deregulation in Asia seem to have accelerated partly as a result of the involvement of multilateral negotiations, such as those of the WTO. The exact magnitude of this impact, however, is debatable.[31] On February 15, 1997, the WTO members finally concluded the negotiations on basic telecommunication services. Fifty-five WTO members representing sixty-nine governments made commitments to permit varying levels of market access and foreign investment in the telecommunications sector. These commitments became fully effective as of January 1, 1998.

According to J. P. Singh, WTO multilateral trade negotiations and bilateral negotiations with the United States were important factors in the opening of the South Korean telecommunication markets in the 1990s.[32] As part of the 1997 WTO commitments, the binding commitment made by the EU to extend its internal level of market access to non-EU service providers was matched by Japan, South Korea, Hong Kong, and Singapore in their agreements to liberalize their telecommunications sectors. Moreover, the "insurance policy" aspect of the WTO agreement cannot be neglected. The binding commitment to keep the telecommunications market open to foreign competition provides investors with the certainty and predictability that domestic liberalization alone cannot give.[33]

Firm Position

Domestic Restructuring in the Telecommunication Market

Regulatory changes, new technological innovations, and heavy demand from corporate customers have profoundly affected the Japanese telecommunications industry, forcing it to reorganize and globalize its operations (see Figure 6.2). After so many years of debates over divestiture, the NTT was restructured in 1999 under a holding company and

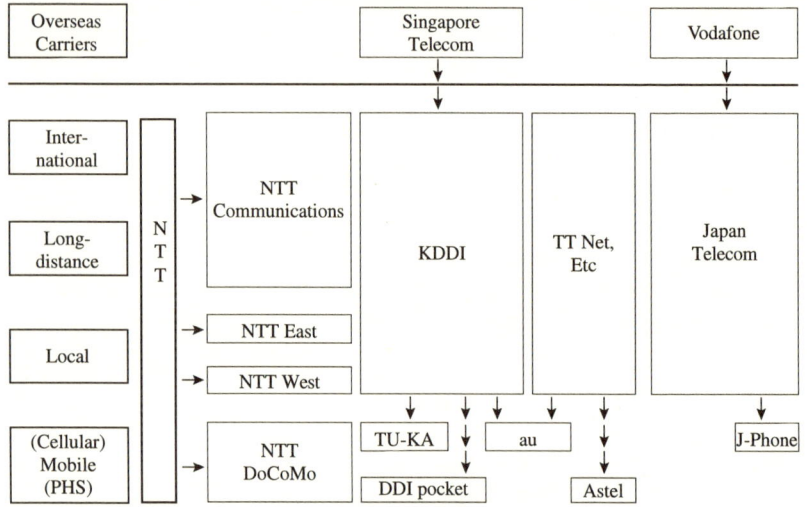

Figure 6.2 Restructuring of the telecommunications market in Japan

Notes:
(1) An arrow indicates equity participation.
(2) All of the shares of Japan Telecom used to be owned by AT&T and BT were sold out to Vodafone by May 2001.
Source: InfoCom research (2000b), p. 46.

divided into two wholly-owned local companies: NTT East and NTT West. In addition, NTT established NTT Communications or NTT Com (100 percent owned by the NTT holding company) in July 1999 to provide domestic long distance and international services.[34]

Several mergers and acquisitions followed as investors sought to take advantage of the more open competitive market. In 1998, KDD, the Type-I carrier in Japan, bought TeleWay Japan in order to enter the domestic long distance market. In 1999, KDD announced a merger with DDI and IDO, with DDI emerging as the surviving company that aimed at providing seamless mobile, domestic, and international services. The merger among the three companies was completed in October 2000.

Japanese domestic carriers have not escaped the pressures of globalization. Except for the case of NTT, restrictions on foreign capital have been removed and the Japanese domestic market is attracting foreign interest and investment. IDC, Japan's second-ranked international service provider, was acquired in June 1999 by Britain's Cable & Wireless and renamed C&W IDC. AT&T and BT bought 30 percent of Japan Telecom's shares, which then became the sole distributor of global services for multinationals within Japan. Most other new entrants, such as MCI WorldCom, are targeting the Internet Protocol (IP) network and wireless access markets.[35] Domestic restructuring severely affected the advancement of Japanese telecom companies into international markets. After being freed from both explicit and implicit restrictions in 1997, NTT paid increasing attention to global telecommunications markets through NTT Com, its new subsidiary. NTT Com expects to achieve global market share by providing seamless and value-added services through data communications and an IP-based network. Currently NTT DoCoMo, a mobile communication services provider in the NTT group since the early 1990s, is becoming more active.

In contrast, other Japanese companies such as DDI, KDD, and Japan Telecom are still in the process of consolidating their operations in Japan and trying to compete with the NTT group in the domestic market. Although the telecommunications market of broader East Asia has expanded rapidly since the early 1990s and possesses the highest growth potential in the world, the Japanese domestic market remains the most attractive in Asia. In fact, the Japanese telecommunications market is the second largest in the world. Despite the introduction of competition in the mid-1980s, NTT continued to dominate this market until the late 1990s. In 1998, NTT's share of total revenues from fixed domestic telephone services was 88.7 percent, and NTT DoCoMo's share of the cellular mobile phone market was 57.9 percent.[36]

Scarcity of Japanese Telecom Companies in the Global Market Despite the entry of so many companies and the mergers and acquisitions among them since the beginning of privatization in the mid-1980s, the presence of Japanese telecom companies in the world market has been negligible. Even NTT's international presence is limited, despite its size and massive revenue base.

Regardless of national origin, the internationalization of telecommunications companies is a relatively recent phenomenon. Among the top one hundred MNCs ranked by foreign assets in 1990, only two were telecommunications.[37] By 1996, there were five on the list: Cable and Wireless Plc (U.K.), BEC Inc. (Canada), AT&T (U.S.), Northern Telecom (Canada), and GTE Corporation (U.S.).[38] Although the number remains small, this increase indicates that telecommunication companies in Europe and in North America have responded strongly to the opportunities in international markets.

As early as 1991, AT&T was earning 24 percent of its revenue from international sources: 9 percent from operations located in other countries and 15 percent from U.S. operations that comprised international telecommunications services and export sales. The major customers of these expanding telecommunications services were large and medium-sized companies, the operations of which had become increasingly international.[39]

Globally minded Western firms responded strongly to changes in public policies of the Asian telecommunication market. For instance, Malaysia decided to privatize Telecom Malaysia, the state-owned, dominant public telephone operator, as early as 1987. In response, eight new telecom companies entered the market to compete with Telecom Malaysia.

At least four European (Deutsche Telecom, British Telecom, Swiss Telecom, and Telenor) and one U.S. (U.S. West) telecom companies have entered the Malaysian market since the mid-1990s. Deutsch Telecom established a joint venture called Celcom with a 21 percent equity share. Although Celcom began to offer a full range of services in 1994, it succeeded in capturing a high market share only in the provision of mobile phone services. U.S. West established a joint venture called Binariang with a 20 percent equity share whose operation began in 1996. The name of the company was changed into Maxis, and in 1998 BT acquired 33.3 percent of its total stock while U.S. West's percent of the equity share declined to 12.6 percent. Swiss Telecom established Mutiara with a 30 percent equity share and began the provision of domestic fixed phone services in 1997. However, all of Swiss Telecom's equity shares were purchased by Telenor in 1999.[40]

Unlike Malaysia, Taiwan was slow in reforming its telecommunications market. Since 1997, however, Taiwan has rapidly liberalized its services sector. The first reform that was passed introduced competition into the mobile phone market and allowed equity participation from foreign companies. Eight new companies entered the market. Although the market's foreign equity share is still small, foreign telecom companies were quick to take advantage of the new opportunities in Taiwan. GTE established a joint venture called Pacific Communications Services, in which it held a 20 percent equity share. Others followed: AT&T Wireless established Far East One with an 18 percent equity share; Bell Canada established KG Telecom with 20 percent; Deutsche Telecom established Mobitani with four percent; Southwestern Bell established TransAsia Telecom with 20 percent; and First Pacific (HK) established Smart Link with 16.6 percent.[41]

The introduction of competition into Taiwan's mobile phone market was followed by increased competitiveness in the local, long distance, and international telecom markets. The government of Taiwan issued three licenses to new telecom companies that provided complete telecommunications services. Three foreign firms showed high interest. Deutsche Telekom acquired 20 percent of the total shares of Eastern Broadband Telecom; Singapore Telecom acquired 18 percent of New Century Info Com; and GTE, now Verizon, acquired 15 percent of Taiwan Fixed Network Telecom.[42] Japanese firms did not participate.

Many of America's globally-minded firms such as AT&T, Bell South, Nynex, and GTE have shown willingness to cooperate technologically and financially with China in particular, despite the fact that mainland China has not yet permitted foreign ownership of its telecom companies.[43] With its size and rapid income growth, China possesses the region's most promising telecommunications market. U.S. giants such as AT&T have shown a strong interest in the Chinese market since the late 1980s, targeting their services to meet demands from various departments of the Chinese government, multinationals in China, and the Chinese consumer.[44]

Constraints on Globalization   Although NTT's global presence was relatively limited in the 1990s, the firm was nevertheless able to "globalize" in several important senses.[45] First, NTT offered telecommunications consulting and engineering services outside of Japan through subsidiaries like NTT International. Second, the firm offered its Japanese customers various alternatives for handling their international communications needs, which included leasing circuits from other international carriers for its customers' use. Third, NTT has involved itself directly in the overseas operations of Thai Telephone and Telecommunication company (TT&T) since 1992, the Philippine company Smart since 1995, and Sri Lanka's Telecom since 1997.[46] Beginning in 1995, NTT also participated in developing Indonesia's infrastructure through BOT projects, and since 1997 in the Vietnamese market through business cooperation contracts (BCC).[47]

All of this indicates that NTT has had a strong interest in international operations since the early 1990s. NTT has tried to meet the demands of its corporate customers for international telecommunication services abroad as well as in Japan.

Despite NTT's efforts to globalize in the 1990s, the firm's increased internationalization has faced certain constraints.[48] One of them was the slowness of regulatory change in Japan's telecommunication industry, especially the abolition of the provisions that had for a long time segmented domestic and international markets. The regulatory segmentation of markets put Japanese telecom companies at a great disadvantage in the global market.[49] Until these regulations were abolished, NTT was unable to engage in providing international services and KDD was unable to provide domestic services. New entrants (NCCs) were also subject to the same restriction.[50] That is, there was no opportunity for either incumbent or new carriers to provide a comprehensive package of local, long-distance, international, and mobile phone services. However, it is precisely this combination of services that is demanded by international customers. Until as late as 1997, Japan was the only country in the world, at least among developed economies, where the main domestic carrier was not allowed to operate internationally in an unimpeded manner.

Perhaps even more important than these legal limitations were the tacit regulatory constraints imposed by the Ministry of Posts and Transportation (MPT) on NTT's international activities. NTT was clearly aware that MPT, wary of NTT's rising revenues and influence, was reluctant to give it much freedom to operate internationally. NTT also confronted "a significant amount of uncertainty in deciding precisely where MPT draws the boundary between acceptable and unacceptable international activities."[51] As a result, NTT moved toward international markets with extreme caution.

III. Strategic and Tactical Analysis

Market Strategies and Tactics

The abolition of the MPT's regulatory segmentation of domestic and international activities, and more importantly changes in the MPT's position toward the globalization of Japanese telecom companies, strengthened the Japanese telecom companies' entry into international markets. The market strategies of telecom companies can be analyzed according to the users and the range of services provided. Table 6.5 summarizes the activities of subsidiaries or joint ventures of Japanese telecom companies in Asian markets. The table reveals part of the market strategy being pursued by Japanese telecom companies.

Table 6.5 shows that although NTT entered the global telecommunications market late, the firm was very quick in establishing subsidiaries or joint ventures in East Asian markets through NTT Com. NTT was clearly focused in its entry to the Asian markets.

To some extent KDD is similar to NTT in trying to establish a commercial presence in the East Asian market and to become a global carrier. Between 1997 and 1999 KDD established three new subsidiaries in South Korea, China, and Thailand. At the end of 1999, KDD also concluded a business contract with Singapore Telecom through equity

Table 6.5 Subsidiaries or joint ventures of Japanese telecom companies in Asia

	Year of establishment	Percentage of ownership	Paid capital	Number of employees	Content of service provided overseas
KDD					
South Korea	1999	49	3.325b won	NA	Provides telephone services.
China	1997	100	USD 0.7m	5	
Hong Kong	1989	100	HKD 51.43m	17	
Mongolia	1996	44.44	MNT 4.141b	57	Provides mobile and basic telephone services.
Thailand	1999	100	20.6m bhat	4	
Singapore	1989	100	SD 2.43m	16	
DDI					
Thailand	1998	24.5	175m bhat	200	Provides iridium satellite mobile phone services.
Japan Telecom					
Singapore	1998	100	SD 3m	NA	Provides corporate network services, system integration services.
NTT Com[1]					
South Korea	1999	100	3b won	11	Provides Arcstar-brand services,[2] system integration services and Internet Services.
China (Shanghai)	1997	51	USD 1m	26	
China (Beijing)	1998	49	USD 3m	21	
Hong Kong	1997	100	HKD 26m	20	Provides corporate global networking services.[3]
Taiwan	1998	100	NTD 100m	12	Provides Arcstar Frame Relay (FR), system integration services, etc.
Thailand	2000	NA	NA	NA	N.A. (replacing NTT Bangkok Representative Office)
Indonesia	2000	NA	NA	NA	N.A. (replacing PT Intechsys)
Singapore	1997	100	SD 3.27b	5	Provides Arcstar-brand services, Internet services, etc.
	1999	22	NA	NA	Provides Arcstar-brand services through StarHub.
Malaysia	1997	100	1.1b yen	100	
Philippines	1997	40	1m pesos	NA	Provides Arcstar-brand services
	1995	37.23	13.8b pesos	2,967	Provides local, toll, international and mobile telecom services with PLDT.
Sri Lanka	1999	15	USD 760m	NA	
	1997	35	NA	8,721	
NTT DoCoMo					
Singapore	1996	50	NA	NA	Provides cellular mobile phone services.

Notes:
(1) NTT Communication, Inc. also possesses a representative office in Beijing, Shanghai, and Hanoi, respectively.
(2) Arcstar's global services include basic network services, value-added network services, outsourcing services, and housing/hosting services.
(3) It includes the construction of a data tranmission network, the Internet Dedicated Access services, and new dial-up and housing/hosting services.

Source: Toyokeizai (2000), *Kaigai Shinshutsu Kigyosoran 2000. NTT Communications Digest*, several issues.

participation.[52] Compared to NTT, however, KDD's geographical reach in East Asia is limited. Moreover, Japan Telecom and DDI have almost no presence in the region. This indicates that Japanese NCCs intend to structure themselves as mini-NTTs offering a full spectrum of services from local and long-distance telephone calls to international phone service and the Internet. But before globalizing, they are first targeting the Japanese market (as mentioned in Section II).

The provision of telecommunications services on a global scale requires a huge amount of investment in R&D and basic facilities.[53] In 1998 the share of NTT's investment (including NTT DoCoMo) in fixed assets among Type-1 carriers was 68 percent.[54] NTT's share (including NTT DoCoMo) of total R&D expenditures of the entire Japanese telecommunication industry was even greater.[55] Certainly, domestic restructuring in the near future may lower NTT's dominance. The above figures indicate, however, that as of 2000 only NTT had enough resources and capabilities to compete against international foreign mega-carriers.

Second, the global market focus of Japanese telecommunications companies such as NTT and KDD has shifted away from the provision of basic telecommunications services toward that of more value-added services. As Table 6.5 shows, both NTT and KDD provide seamless global services through data communications and IP-based networks in Asia. The primary target customers are MNCs, especially Japanese corporate customers abroad. NTT in particular is aggressively seeking to retool its corporate strategy and culture in order to become a key player in the emerging multimedia field in Asia.[56]

The second market strategy of Japanese firms is exactly the one that the major global telecommunications carriers have implemented since the beginning of the 1990s. Large and medium-sized corporate customers, an important market segment, are increasingly involved in international activities. Major telecommunications companies therefore cater their services to meet the global telecommunications needs of these customers.[57] As described in other chapters of this book, Japanese companies, especially manufacturing companies, have globalized their operations since the mid-1980s, creating strong demand in Japan and abroad for international telecommunication services.

Nonmarket Strategy and Tactics

Political Bargaining Power

The trade dispute in 2000 between the United States and Japanese governments over interconnection charges that NCCs must pay to NTT for use of its network is a clear example of nonmarket strategy. This dispute included both domestic and foreign Japanese carriers. Making the most of foreign pressure (called *gaiatsu* in Japanese), NCCs pushed NTT for faster, cheaper interconnection. According to Japanese NCCs, these charges account for as much as 40 percent of their operating costs. If these interconnection charges were lowered, more NCCs could be competitive in the Japanese telecommunications market and, eventually, the global market as well.

However, NTT was reluctant to reduce interconnection charges unless two conditions were satisfied. First was the abolition of the provisions of NTT Law that mandate that only NTT may provide universal services. NTT had provided these services exclusively since the beginning of public telecommunication operation. Remote, rural areas were subsidized by urban areas, and un-economic services were subsidized by profitable ones. Second is the abolition of the provisions of the NTT Law that restrict the activities in which NTT East and NTT West may be involved.[58] Unless both NTTs can be exempted from this regulation, they do not have the means to make up for the losses that would be incurred from the reduction in interconnection charges.

This is the same strategy that NTT used in the debate over the divestiture process. After many years of debate with the Ministry of Posts and Transportation, NTT basically got what it wanted in return for its acceptance of divestiture: more international flexibility and an integrated company.[59] NTT has been trying to gain further freedom from government intervention in return for its acceptance of the U.S. government's proposal regarding interconnection charges.

Business Ties with the Japanese MNCs   NTT's entry into foreign markets in the late 1990s was welcome news to Japanese multinational companies. A possible reason why foreign carriers do not pose a serious threat to Japanese telecom companies in Japan is that it is difficult for foreign telecom companies to enter into business with Japanese companies.[60] On the other hand, despite its late entry into the global market, NTT was able to establish either subsidiaries or joint ventures in major Asian countries within a few years, partly because it had maintained a good long-term relationship with business customers in Asia (mainly Japanese) and was well-known among Japanese customers.

There is no guarantee that this kind of ownership advantage is sustainable over the long term. However, the close business relationship between Japanese MNCs and telecom companies is thought to give the latter an advantage over their foreign competitors, at least at the initial stage.

Organizational Strategy and Tactics

Telecom services are provided through networks installed in the country where the service is offered. Therefore, establishing a commercial presence in foreign countries is the preferred mode of delivery for most telecom services. This often requires the foreign establishment or foreign ownership of domestic telecom firms.

With respect to the choice between full foreign ownership and a joint venture, the former tends to be preferred over the latter in the field of telecommunications as long as there is no limit on foreign ownership. This is because the efficient and speedy provision of end-to-end network services can be ensured only under 100 percent foreign ownership.[61] It is important to note, however, that the matter of either majority or minority ownership is not equally applicable to every company. There are some differences among even Japanese companies, which will be discussed in Section IV.

Unlike Western mega-carriers, however, Japanese telecom companies have not yet entered into global alliances with foreign carriers. First of all, the presence of Japanese telecom companies in the global market remains relatively insignificant. Second, despite many attempts among foreign mega-carriers, there are few successful cases of global alliance. Third, Japanese firms prefer to form alliances on a case-by-case basis. For instance, NTT entered into an alliance with BT for equity participation in Star Hub of Singapore. Flexibility is perceived to be of greater advantage than even the improved access to services that an alliance provides.

IV. Case Studies of NTT Com and NTT DoCoMo

In July 1999, NTT, freed from government regulations, began business operations in the international information communication market through NTT Com. NTT DoCoMo, a provider of mobile communications services in the NTT group, also made a dramatic entrance into East Asian mobile telecommunications markets. This section highlights the strategies of these two Japanese telecom companies.

Market Strategy

Since it was established, NTT Com has followed a multipronged strategy.[62] First, NTT Com is aggressively shifting its focus from basic infrastructure services to more value-added services. Currently, NTT Com is expanding into IT-related businesses to provide global seamless network services through IP networks. NTT Com hopes that the provision of these global seamless network services through IP operations will become the firm's core competence and the key to its medium and long-term growth.

In this respect, NTT DoCoMo's strategy is similar to that of NTT Com. In addition to basic telecommunications services, NTT DoCoMo started to provide value-added services, such as the mobile Internet service *i-mode* in February 1999. *I-mode* proved successful, partly because HTML-based websites can be easily adapted and partly because it is priced according to information received and not usage time.[63]

NTT Com's second strategy has been to expand operations simultaneously in Asia, North America, and other regions in order to achieve full-scale global coverage. Although NTT Com continues to focus primarily on Asian markets, the firm's intention of becoming a global, not just regional, player is illustrated by its merger agreement with Verio Inc., a U.S. Internet services firm. Under the agreement signed on August 31, 2000, NTT Com purchased all of Verio Inc.'s stock, worth approximately $5.5 billion. This merger was expected to create a "Global One Network" with improved reliability, performance, and security based on the integration of NTT Com's IP backbone in Asia with Verio's IP backbone in the U.S. for seamless, end-to end IP network services.[64] Considering that Verio Inc. had also constructed a service infrastructure in Europe, the provision of high-quality global service is a short-term possibility.

In contrast, the geographical focus of NTT DoCoMo has been global from the beginning. Three factors account for this broader focus. First, unlike NTT Com, the main users of NTT DoCoMo's services are individuals, not large and medium-sized corporate customers. Therefore, there is no reason for NTT DoCoMo to focus on a particular region. Second, NTT DoCoMo has already established its core competence in mobile Internet services while NTT Com has not. NTT DoCoMo was the first worldwide to introduce *i-mode* service and was able to attract twenty million Japanese subscribers in just two years. NTT DoCoMo is now trying, through various means, to expand its *i-mode* system widely across a range of countries.[65] Moreover, with its introduction in 2001 of a third generation (3G) global mobile system, NTT DoCoMo's range of operations has clearly become global.

Nonmarket Strategy

In addition to these basic market strategies, other complementary tactics have played an important role in these firms' expansion. To enhance the quality of its Arcstar services abroad, NTT Com provides technical and operational cooperation. In 2000 NTT Com held a technical conference that gathered regional telecom operators, maintenance managers, and engineers. The objective was for Asian telecom's partners to use the knowledge they acquired at the conference to upgrade the quality of their services and to improve customer satisfaction. Given the limited extent to which NTT Com can participate in the operations of most major Asian telecom companies through equity partnership, NTT Com must seek other means of assuring the quality of its regional services.

NTT Com has also attempted to enter the market through contributions to human resource development in IT-related businesses in developing countries. As seen in Table 6.6, NTT Com has engaged in R&D activities and has sold network services, mainly to Japanese MNCs, through NTT MSC in Malaysia. The company's R&D center develops IP service applications for the Asian market, such as web-based machine translation and e-business applications, and works closely with local universities and technical institutions regarding IT-related R&D. NTT MSC is the first Japanese company in Malaysia to provide IP-based services under Arcnet, a locally-developed service launched by Prime Minister Mahathir in December 2000.[66] Although it is unlikely that these R&D activities in Malaysia will lead to immediate profits, NTT MSC is trying

Table 6.6 Capital and R&D expenditures by major telecom companies

	NTT	NTT DoCoMo	DDI	Japan telecom	TTNet	KDD
(a) Capital expenditure (100 million yen)						
1994	18517	3141	343	251	270	462
1995	19890	4215	313	292	348	373
1996	19911	7336	596	542	641	679
1997	18869	7293	934	846	840	952
1998	17279	8458	665	656	394	1182
(b) R&D expenditure (100 million yen)						
1994	2906	N.A.	N.A.	N.A.	N.A.	104
1995	2906	N.A.	N.A.	N.A.	N.A.	100
1996	2964	N.A.	N.A.	21	N.A.	129
1997	2466	N.A.	N.A.	29	N.A.	106
1998	2199	410	N.A.	39	N.A.	82
1999	2612	892	8.7	61	N.A.	105

Note: R&D figure for 1999 of NTT is the total amount of R&D expenditures spent by the NTT group as a whole excluding that of NTT DoCoMo.
Sources:
(a) InfoCom, Inc. (2000a).
(b) Various financial reports published by the Ministry of Finance.

to penetrate the Malaysian IT-related market through its contribution to human resource development and its active participation in the Malaysian government's ambitious projects, such as the Multimedia Super Corridor.

With respect to nonmarket strategies and tactics, NTT Com and NTT DoCoMo are similar in one important aspect, that which M. Fransman dubbed "the NTT Way," or a strong commitment to an innovation-driven approach.[67] As Table 6.6 shows, the NTT Group invests enormously in development and R&D. NTT DoCoMo's share in particular is increasing rapidly. As a result of these investments in R&D, around 3000 applications for patents are filed every year.[68] This has given NTT a strong technological advantage over its competitors.

In addition, NTT has participated actively in standardization activities as a result of its comprehensive range of research and development in information communications. Japan contributed 11 percent of the total standardization efforts submitted to ITU during the period of 1993–1996, and 6 out of that 11 percent were submitted by NTT.[69] This is another aspect of NTT's nonmarket strategy of spreading its own technology quickly and promoting both de facto and de jure standardization to cover the costs of R&D.[70] NTT DoCoMo in particular pursues this type of nonmarket strategy. In June 2000, NTT DoCoMo became the world's first operator of 3G technology. The initiation of services announced in May 2001 outpaced the European competition by several months.[71]

Organizational Strategy

To promote IT-related businesses, NTT Com has engaged in business alliances with other telecom and IT-related companies. There are two main types of alliance. The first is one that provides access to valuable assets that complement those of NTT Com and enhance its IT operations.[72] The alliance with Verio Inc. is a perfect example. NTT Com expects to acquire increased knowledge in IP network operations and e-business services and to utilize Verio's highly capable sales force.

Partnerships with HKNet and Cisco Systems fall into the same category as that with Verio Inc. In 2000, NTT Com purchased additional shares in HKNet from CCT Telecom Holdings Ltd., hoping to acquire knowledge in competitive Internet solutions. HKNet is expected to become a core IP company in the Asia-Pacific region as well as a gateway provider to the Chinese market.[73] The partnership with Cisco Systems, Inc. is expected to provide NTT Com with access to Cisco's cutting-edge IP technology. NTT Com is the first Japanese telecom carrier to partner with

Cisco Systems, Inc. with the intention of developing new IP business solution services.[74]

NTT Com is also working with major Asian telecom companies to expand the reach of its Arcstar brand data services in Asian markets. NTT Com prefers equity mergers with telecom companies, as indicated in the cases of the Philippines, Singapore, and Sri Lanka (see Table 6.5). In cases where foreign equity participation is not allowed, NTT has enhanced its regional presence through nonequity business partnerships with Asian telecom carriers including South Korea Telecom, Chunghwa Telecom (Taiwan), Telecom Malaysia, CAT (Thailand), and Indosat (Indonesia).[75] NTT Com has also expanded its Arcstar services into Vietnam and China through alliances with Vietnam Data Communication Company and China Telecom.[76]

Similarly, NTT DoCoMo has forged alliances with other major mobile communication companies through equity participation. Since 1998, NTT DoCoMo has developed business partnerships with some of the major mobile communications companies in the United States, Europe, and Asia. NTT DoCoMo's partnership with AOL Inc. through the establishment of AOL Japan is designed to provide seamlessly integrated Internet services across both fixed-line and wireless platforms in Japan and the United States.

The strategies of NTT Com and NTT DoCoMo are different in one important respect. While the former tries to participate fully or assume majority ownership in partner companies, the latter's equity share in the partner companies tends to be small. The true intention of DoCoMo's equity participation lies not so much in assuming management of partner companies as in disseminating its own developed *i-mode* system and global mobile communications standard (the world's first application of W-CDMA) worldwide through technical and market-based cooperation.[77]

Can NTT Com and NTT DoCoMo Become Global Carriers?

Beginning in Asia in the late 1990s, NTT Com has aggressively retooled its corporate strategy and culture in order to become a key player in the emerging multimedia field. Since then, NTT Com has become even more aggressive as a global player in the IT industry. Although there are important differences between the strategies of NTT Com and NTT DoCoMo, they have both sought to become global players in the rapidly expanding telecommunications sector.

However, as shown by the recent experiences of AT&T and British Telecom, overseas operations—with their high initial costs—do not necessarily guarantee high returns on investment. Moreover, the success of an alliance or merger is never automatic. As Fransman points out, although the chance for further globalization presents an important opportunity for Japanese Telecom companies, the difficulties involved should not be underestimated.[78]

Whether these NTT companies can really become global players depends on two questions. First, can they generate their own core competencies in the sales of their own services? In this regard, NTT DoCoMo succeeded with the *i-mode* system by establishing its competence in mobile Internet services. NTT DoCoMo sought to strengthen this core competence by introducing its own proprietary 3G mobile system, the first in the world, and making it a global standard. If it succeeds, this will give it a strong competitive advantage.

NTT Com's current principal objective is to establish its own core competence in multimedia services. As mentioned earlier, NTT Com's strategy is to combine its services with Verio Inc.'s IP network to provide global seamless network services. This global IP-network is expected to be the firm's core competence.[79]

The second question is whether NTT companies can increase the cost efficiency of their operations, including their expenditures on R&D? With the intensification of both global and domestic competition, profitability is likely to decrease. For instance, competition in Japan's domestic long-distance telecommunications market is expected to intensify. That will impose high pressure on companies like NTT Com to further reduce costs. This increased pressure may force the company to ensure that its R&D expenditures are adding value in terms of increased revenue. R&D, however, does not serve the interest of a particular company alone, but rather, the entire NTT group.

V. Conclusion

Currently, the telecommunication industry is a leading sector in the world economy. In addition to normal supply and demand factors, regulatory reforms at both the national and international levels have placed considerable constraints on the industry—particularly in Asia.

Japanese telecom companies were not significant players in any international market, even Asia, until recently. Since the early 1990s, NTT has tried to globalize its operations, but market and nonmarket barriers have limited its success. The position of the Japanese government, in its policies and otherwise, toward international activities seems to have put a major constraint on the international activities of telecom firms.

Since the late 1990s, NTT companies such as NTT Com and NTT DoCoMo have sought to become global players, not as traditional telephone companies, but as new, high value-added telecommunications service providers. Both of them have aggressively utilized market, nonmarket, and organizational strategies to achieve their objectives. However, their strategies and tactics differ in many important ways that include their geographical focus, the presence or absence of a clear core competence, and their degree of equity participation in established partners.

Other Japanese telecom companies such as Japan Telecom and KDDI do not seem to be ready to advance into the global market. Two reasons account for this delay. First is their lack of sufficient resources to begin costly and risky overseas operations. The second is their overriding focus on the Japanese telecommunications market.

The success of Japanese telecommunications companies such as NTT Com and NTT DoCoMo in competing as global players depends fundamentally on two factors: their ability to create solid core competencies and the cost efficiency of their services. Without either of these, no company will be able to survive global competition.

Notes

1. I would like to thank Vinod K. Aggarwal, Shujiro Urata, and the BASC staff for their comments.
2. OECD (1999), p. 25.
3. See Chowdary (1998), p. 259.
4. Bohlin et al. (1999), p. 214.
5. See *Nikkei Newspaper*, November 17, 1999.
6. Takahashi (1998), p. 31. See Chapter 1 by Vinod K. Aggarwal in this volume for the theoretical framework governing corporate strategy in market and nonmarket environments.
7. According to the recent trade agreement signed between the United States and China, the latter must allow for foreign equity participation of up to 50 percent in the telecommunications market. The foreign equity participation in the Internet market will be permitted as well in China (*Nikkei Newspaper*, November 17, 1999).
8. *ITU News*, No. 8 2000.
9. *ITU News*, No. 9 2000.
10. Taiwan–China, Australia, Rep. of South Korea, China and Japan are among the top ten Internet economies worldwide according to *ITU News*, January 2001.
11. *ITU News*, No. 9 1999.
12. *ITU News*, No. 8 1999.
13. *ITU News*, No. 1 2001.
14. Honma (1999), p. 4.
15. Fransman (1997), p. 189.
16. OECD (1999), p. 25.
17. Japan, 1985; Malaysia, 1987; Thailand, 2001–2006; Indonesia, 1994; Philippines, no state-owned major companies; Singapore, 1992; South Korea, 1991; Taiwan, 2000–2001; India, not yet;

Vietnam, not yet; China, not yet. Source: The Industrial Bank of Japan (1998); Singh (2000). *InfoCom Newsletter,* February 2001, October 2000.
18. TOT is engaged in the provision of local and long distance phone services. CAT is engaged in the provision of international phone services.
19. *InfoCom Newsletter,* October, 2000.
20. The Industrial Bank of Japan (1998), p. 12.
21. Singh (2000), p. 894.
22. *InfoCom Newsletter,* February 2001.
23. The Industrial Bank of Japan (1998), p. 2.
24. *InfoCom Newsletter,* August 2000.
25. Gao and Lyytinen (2000), p. 726.
26. Gao and Lyytinen (2000), p. 727.
27 *InfoCom Newsletter,* April 2000.
28. Mueller and Lovelock (2000), p. 739.
29. See Table 6.4.
30. *InfoCom Newsletter,* June 1998. It is important to note, however, that this does not apply to Telekom Malaysia. New foreign companies are also not allowed to enter.
31. The limited scope of liberalization created by the Agreement, the lack of precision of the regulatory principles of the Reference Paper, and the weakness of the sectoral approach are pointed out by three major shortcomings of the Agreement. See Blouin (2000), p. 135.
32. Singh (2000), p. 895.
33. Blouin (2000), p. 139.
34. NTT DoCoMo, a provider of mobile communications services in the NTT group, was already established in 1992 with NTT as its biggest share holder (67.1 percent).
35. InfoCom Research, Inc. (2000a), p. 12.
36. InfoCom Research, Inc. (2000a), pp. 40, 60.
37. Table 11.5 in UNCTAD (1998), p. 41.
38. Table 11.1 in UNCTAD (1998), pp. 36–38.
39. Fransman (1995), pp. 394–395.
40. The major sources of foreign equity participation in the new companies are The Industrial Bank of Japan (1998) and information provided at the NTT MSC.
41. Japan Development Bank (1998), p. 94.
42. *InfoCom Newsletter,* February 2001.
43. The Industrial Bank of Japan, (1998), pp. 84–85.
44. See Warwick (1994) to find out AT&T business history in China.
45. Fransman (1995), p. 395.
46. This is based on information provided by NTT Com.
47. The Industrial Bank of Japan (1998), pp. 44, 79.
48. Fransman (1995), p. 399.
49. Higashi (1999), p. 71.
50. Ozawa (1998), p. 32.
51. Fransman (1995), p. 400.
52. Based on information from the financial report published by Ministry of Finance, Japan.
53. Honma (1998), p. 11.
54. This is calculated from the table in page 35 of InfoCom Research, Inc. (2000a).
55. According to financial reports of various companies published by the Ministry of Japan, the total amount of 1998 R&D expenditures by NTT (excluding NTT DoCoMo), NTT DoCoMo, KDD, and Japan Telecom are ¥220 billion, ¥41.0 billion, ¥8.2 billion, and ¥3.9 billion, respectively.
56. Hayashi (1997), p. 101.
57. Fransman (1995), p. 395.
58. *Nikkei Newspaper,* June 30 and July 1, 2000.
59. Bohlin (1997), p. 83.

60. Ozawa (1999), p. 6.
61. This was pointed out at an interview with NTT Com, Inc.
62. NTT Communications *Digest*, February 2000.
63. See *ITU News*, No. 9, 2000.
64. See NTT Communications *Digest*, October 2000.
65. NTT DoCoMo, Inc. and DoCoMo AOL, Inc. began providing a service called AOLi, which gives *i-mode* users access to AOL e-mail on June 1, 2001. This was the first attempt by both NTT DoCoMo and AOL Inc. to provide seamlessly integrated Internet services across both fixed line and wireless platforms.
66. NTT Communications *Digest*, February 2001.
67. Fransman (1995), p. 354.
68. *NTT Research and Development: 1999 Review of Activities*, pp. 42–43.
69. *NTT Research and Development: 1999 Review of Activities*, p. 43.
70. Kawamata (1997), p. 156.
71. *ITU News*, No. 9 2000.
72. Process quality, capital base and R&D capability were stated as valuable assets for NTT (NTT Communications *Digest*, October 2000.
73. See NTT Communications *Digest*, December 2000.
74. NTT Communications *Digest*, June 2000.
75. NTT Communications *Digest*, December 2000.
76. NTT Communications *Digest*, December 2000, February 2001.
77. Kojima (2001), pp. 138–139.
78. Fransman (1995), p. 408.
79. NTT Communications *Digest*, February 2001.

References

APEC (1998). *Towards an Information Society: Developments in APEC* (Singapore: APEC Secretariat).
APEC (2000). *Towards Knowledge-based Economies in APEC* (Singapore: APEC Secretariat).
Blouin, C. (2000). "The WTO Agreement on Basic Telecommunications: A Reevaluation," *Telecommunications Policy* 24: 135–142
Bohlin, E. (1997). "Editorial-Restructuring Japan's Telecommunications," *Telecommunications Policy* 21 (No. 2): 79–84.
Bohlin, E. et al. (1999). "Editorial: Convergence and Development in East Asia," *Telecommunications Policy* 23: 213–216.
Chowdary, T. H. (1998). "Comment: Telecom Liberalization and Competition in Developing Countries," *Telecommunications Policy* 22 (No. 4/5), pp. 259–265.
Fransman, M. (1995). *Japan's Computer and Communications Industry: The Evolution of Industrial Giants and Global Competitiveness* (Oxford: Oxford University Press).
Fransman, M. (1997). "Towards a New Agenda for Japanese Telecommunications," *Telecommunications Policy* 21 (No. 2), pp. 185–194.
Gao, P. and Lyytinen, K. (2000). "Transformation of China's Telecommunications Sector: A Macro Perspective," *Telecommunications Policy* 24, pp. 719–730.
Hayashi, K. (1997). "NTT's Transformation: from Public Telephone Operator to Major Multimedia Enterprise," *Telecommunications Policy* 21 (No. 2), pp. 101–111.
Higashi, M. (1999). "Information and Telecommunication Era, and its Strategy" (Japanese) in *Globalization and Advances in Telecommunication and Information Industry*, ed. by I. Shirakawa (Tokyo: Tushosangyo Chosakai).
Honma, M. (1998). "World Telecommunications Market Facing Transition" (Japanese), *InfoCom REVIEW* 13, pp. 4–21.

Honma, M. (1999). "M&A Strategies of Global Telecommunication Carriers and Their Impacts" (Japanese), *InfoCom REVIEW* 19, pp. 3–18.

InfoCom Research, Inc. (2000a). *Information & Communications in Japan 2000* (Tokyo: InfoCom Research, Inc.).

InfoCom Research, Inc. (2000b). *Information & Communication Handbook 2001* (Japanese). (Tokyo: InfoCom Research, Inc.).

The Industrial Bank of Japan (1998). "Telecommunication Outlook in Asia," (Japanese), *Kogin Chosa* 285 (No. 3). (Tokyo: The Industrial Bank of Japan).

Kojima, I. (2001). *Why Is NTT DoCoMo Maing Doing So Well?* in Japanese (Tokyo: Subarusha).

Kawamata, T. (1997). "NTT's R&D: a Platform for Multimedia," *Telecommunications Policy* 21 (No. 2), pp. 143–163.

Mueller, M. and Lovelock, P. (2000). "The WTO and China's Ban on Foreign Investment in Telecommunication Services. a Game Theoretic Analysis," *Telecommunications Policy* 24, pp. 731–759.

OECD (1999). *OECD Communications Outlook*. (Paris: OECD).

Ozawa, T. (1998). "Japanese Telecommunication Trends," (in Japanese) *Nira Policy Research* 11 (No. 4), pp. 32–35.

Ozawa, T. (1999). "Deregulation and Promotion of Competition," *InfoCom REVIEW* 17, pp. 3–9.

Suzuki, T. (1998). *Prospects of Information and Telecommunication Industries in Korea,* (in Japanese). (Tokyo: Research Institute of Telecommunications and Economics).

Singh, J. P. (2000). "The Institutional Environment and Effects of Telecommunication Privatization and Market Liberalization in Asia," *Telecommunications Policy* 24, pp. 885–906.

Takahashi, K. (1998). "Restructuring of the Global Telecommunications Market in Japanese," in *Nira Policy Research* 11 (No. 4), pp. 30–31.

UNCTAD (1998). *World Investment Report 1998: Trends and Determinants* (New York and Geneva: United Nations).

Yoshida, D (2001). "Evolution of Business Models" (in Japanese), *Kogin Chosa* 300 (No. 2).

Warwick, W. (1994). "A Review of AT&T's Business History in China: The Memorandum of Understanding in Context," *Telecommunications Policy* 18(3), pp. 265–274.

CHAPTER SEVEN

Cracking the Code: Japanese Software Strategies in Asia

TREVOR H. NAKAGAWA[1]

I. Introduction

Although the absolute size of European and North American software markets dwarf those of developing Asia, that situation is rapidly changing (see Table 7.1 and Figure 7.1). Until the early 1990s, Asia has been no more than a peripheral part of the overall strategy of most software companies. Today, it forms a major strategic focus for many of the biggest players. With continuing economic growth, growing middle-classes, well-educated workforces, stable political systems, and expanding technological bases, East Asian computer hardware and software growth has been impressive throughout the past decade, reaching consistent annual growth rates of 30 percent in some countries (see Figure 7.1). Because the software industry is characterized by network externalities and high fixed costs, many believe that first-mover advantages are particularly strong in this industry.[2] Accordingly, firms compete vigorously for market share in the promising Asian region to establish a foothold for the upcoming Internet battles.

In addition, because many Asian countries consider the software industry critical to their economic prosperity, governments have made long-term commitments to information technology-related education and infrastructure while taking active roles in promoting the software industry by liberalizing trade policy and opening up to foreign direct investment (FDI). As enormous IT infrastructure plans are realized

Table 7.1 World traded software market size

Region	1987 market		1997 market		Software as % of GDP 1997	PCs/100 White-collar workers 1997
	Value	%	Value	%		
United States	23.61	52.3	145.47	42.4	1.87	104
Japan	3.99	8.84	52.76	15.37	1.08	24
Western Europe	9.63	21.34	105.09	30.62	1.14	88
Row	7.87	17.52	39.78	11.59	—	—
Total	45.12	100	343.10	100	—	—

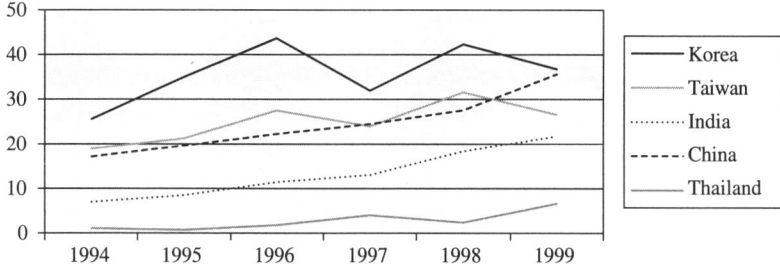

Figure 7.1 Software import market growth in developing Asia (selected Asian countries in US$ million)
Source: U.S. department of commerce, country software reports (1995–2000).

throughout the region in the coming decade, Internet demand for both business-to-business (B2B) and business-to-consumer (B2C) e-commerce is likely to offer even further opportunities for regional growth.

While U.S. firms have collaborated with host governments to capture the majority of the software market throughout developing Asia, their Japanese counterparts were slow to capitalize on regional advantages in these rapidly maturing computer hardware and software markets.[3] In a short period of time, the adoption of the powerful (and low-cost) personal computer (PC), client-server architecture, and the Internet has grown dramatically in Japan and developing Asia. Since 1990, Japanese companies that were able to take advantage of these new developments phased out their old commitments to mainframes and proprietary designs and positioned themselves well to compete in the newly "open" global market era.

Although Japanese software firms have not been successful in providing packaged products, they have produced quality customized solutions, skilled labor, and a solid IT infrastructure. Such attributes have allowed major Japanese software producers to adapt to the changing global dynamics of the industry and embrace the Internet in a relatively short period of time. Despite the late start, large enterprise software producers such as Fujitsu have become major players both globally and regionally by learning to collaborate with leading complementary technology partners (often from the United States) and to participate in emerging global software markets. Their willingness to recognize that competitors can be collaborators has led to global partnering strategies to expand markets, shorten developmental lead times, share service revenue strategy, and make larger investments in relationship building. As clients and partners, Asian governments also play key roles in lowering transaction costs, through easing regulatory burdens, offering positive tax and research and development (R&D) incentives, software use promotion, stronger enforcement of antipiracy laws, and relaxing restrictions on barriers to entry for software-related FDI. This chapter will outline the general positional analysis of the regional market and nonmarket environment with a focus on the enterprise software sector, where Japanese vendors have some demonstrated success. The case study section will highlight the market and nonmarket factors in Asia that has led to the success of one of Japan's most successful enterprise software vendors, Fujitsu.[4]

Communications software and components that permit efficient storage and transmitting of information are likely to continue to be a major growth industry on an increasingly global scale. As the Internet, network computing, and e-commerce continue to proliferate, the advantages of leveraging global software solutions to virtually any industry appear unlimited. In the most rapidly growing segments, and in the packaged computer software market in particular, U.S. companies have leveraged their IC, PC, and operating system advantages to enjoy dominant market shares across the board in East Asian countries, including Japan. Because Japanese core strengths lie in developing high-quality, customized software solutions coupled with proprietary mainframe platforms, they were not prepared for the rapid PC proliferation in Asia (including their own market) that continued at an unprecedented pace (see Table 7.2). As the dominant first movers, U.S. firms continue to consolidate their market shares throughout Asia.[5] Furthermore, with the high probability that the current e-commerce and Internet boom have only just begun in developing Asia, U.S. dominance of not only the Asian software market, but of the world as well, is likely to continue in the coming decade.

Mainframe software solutions based on proprietary machine specific standards were the norm in Japan as late as the early 1990s. This reflected the competition of early hardware producers to cater to specific industry

Table 7.2 Asian computer markets by country

Country	Total computer spending, 1995 ($ millions)	Growth in computer spending 1985–1995	Growth in computer spending 1995–2000*
Japan	96,590	9.5	13.9
South Korea	8,952	17.8	23.8
Taiwan	2,119	8.3	15.5
Hong Kong	1,887	17.1	29.4
Singapore	1,880	12.2	25.9
Malaysia	1,365	16.0	9.8
Indonesia	1,118	23.4	32.1
Philippines	573	27.0	23.5
Thailand	1,326	17.0	12.4
China	4,540	32.7	43.5
India	2,298	31.4	45.7

* These figures are projections based on data up to 1999 made by the IDC (2000), U.S. Department of Commerce (February 2000) and the Gartner Group (1999). This is not comparable data with the figures from 1985–1995.

Source: IDC, "Revenue Paid to Vendors for Systems, Software and Services, 1985–1995 (Framingham, Mass., IDC, 1997).

user needs. As Japanese computer manufacturers developed a line of products according to their own specifications for translating complex Kanji characters, each optimized their software applications for customized solutions for specific clients. In particular, Japanese customized solutions have been most successful for domestic manufacturing and wholesale and retail clients.[6] In addition, because intra-industry employment was relatively rare and demand for the home PC was nonexistent until only recently, there was little concern for making software user-friendly or for generic users.[7] Finally, the emphasis on the software industry as an input into the production process rather than as an output of independent development ensured that intra-industry software advances were favored over interindustry expansion.[8] Software factories that were closely linked with their hardware parents, rather than entrepreneurial and independent startups became the norm.[9]

But as connectivity via networks became possible with powerful workstations and PCs at an affordable price from the United States, loyalties to long-held relationships with the big Japanese computer companies were threatened. Moreover, with the increasing demand for PC and other computer networking in corporations throughout East Asia likely to continue in the future, it became imperative that Japanese manufacturers embrace the challenge of the Internet to provide packaged product solutions for multiple environments. Thus, while gradually fading out old legacy mainframe systems, networked PCs and the client-server architecture became the platform of choice for large companies by the early 1990s.

That is not to say that the Japanese software sector is a failure.[10] In fact, video game software represents a stunning global success story for independent Japanese software companies. Nintendo and Sony, for example, have clearly demonstrated their ability to create a packaged product for a global marketplace on an ongoing basis.[11] Furthermore, embedded software, such as that found in automobiles, electronic equipment, appliances, and machine tools, has always been a staple of Japanese innovative success.[12] But the producers of such software do not consider software to be a core part of their business and have not attempted to export the software independently from their product. Recognizing that they must adjust to the new globally competitive standards based on Sun and Microsoft software "layers," they have now devoted considerable resources to bear on this challenge.

In particular, the current shift away from operating system-specific standards to a more open system dependent on compatibility and information exchanges suggests that Japanese manufacturers will be able to leverage their competence in user needs of specific companies into more general ones related to packaged industrial solutions—so-called enterprise software. As the governments of developing Asian countries often play direct (e.g., procurement) and indirect (e.g., consortia and use promotion) roles in implementing enterprise software solutions for entire industrial sectors (such as banks, automobiles, education, and government services), Japanese solutions are finding multiple avenues to more effectively compete in the evolving Asian software markets. Since software is intrinsically related to inter- and intra-organizational transaction-cost efficiency, intimate knowledge of particular business models remains crucial to the lion's share of software revenue: B2B standardized enterprise solutions systems. As the single largest software subsector, B2B solutions will be the analytic focus of this chapter.[13]

There are also several practical and methodological concerns related to data collection that make the case-study approach of an enterprise software firm an excellent way to study software (see Appendix 1). First, because a great deal of software development is carried out within user firms, it is not surprising that internationally comparable data on sales of different types of software do not exist.[14] However, data for traded "packaged" and custom software, the dominant type of software produced by Japanese firms, do exist.[15]

Table 7.3 Traded, packaged software as a share of total software and service (percent)

Year	1987	1995	2000*
U.S.	31.85	36.93	39.8
Japan	18.34	23.66	27.6
Germany	28.03	39.55	43.7
France	22.07	31.75	35.6
UK	37.16	42.80	45.6
Italy	33.47	35.71	36.4

* Not comparable data to 1987 and 1995. See IDC (2000).

Source: OECD (1997). "Packaged" software consists of all software written for multiple customers and for all types of computer platforms. It is software that is not written to individual customer specifications ("custom software") but for distribution through a variety of channels. All figures in this report are quoted in current U.S. dollars.

Second, traded, "packaged" software is the fastest-growing software segment in the world (see Table 7.3). As increasingly sophisticated packaged products become available in line with rapidly growing PC and workstation environments, the market share of customized solutions is steadily declining. Thus, it is not surprising that the dominant global players of the industry are "packaged" software firms, primarily from the largest market, the United States (see Table 7.4). Although a few Japanese firms are large software producers, the majority of traded software revenue for both NEC and Fujitsu is not from the sale of packaged software (see footnote to Table 7.4). Rather, it is from complex contractual arrangements in which packages of hardware, specialized software telecommunications equipment, and support services are sold together.

To disaggregate the analysis to the level of traded software is much easier in enterprise software, the single largest software product category. This chapter will begin with an examination of market and nonmarket strategies relative to the respective market and nonmarket environments. Rather than attempt to make salient comparisons across segments (which is beyond the scope of this study), we will examine a case study of a single Japanese enterprise software firm that satisfies two conditions: (1) it has some degree of export-orientation toward Asia; and (2) it has established a niche in some type of traded software product. This focus provides us with an illustrative example of how the Japanese software sector evolved from customized to packaged producers in response to global trends. More specifically, we examine the experience of enterprise software producers because they are the first to be affected by changes in

Table 7.4 Leading firms in traded software (selected firms in US$100,000)

Firm	1984	Rank	1992	Rank	1996	Rank	1999	Rank	Country
IBM	3,197	1	11,366	1	12,911	1	13,158	1	U.S.
Microsoft	125	9	2,960	3	8,963	2	11,600	2	U.S.
Oracle	245	5	948	11	3,785	4	4,560	3	U.S.
CA/S	883	2	1,820	5	3,564	5	4,320	4	U.S.
SAP	84	13	545	19	2,459	6	4,310	5	Germany
Fujitsu★	200	6	3,535	2	4,754	3	5,765★	6	Japan
NEC★	300	4	1,840	4	2,263	7	3,318★	7	Japan
HP	n/a	—	n/a	—	1,187	11	2,190	8	U.S.
Hitachi	n/a	—	n/a	—	578	n/a	1,210	9	Japan
Adobe	n/a	—	189	n/a	544	n/a	760	10	U.S.
Olivetti	96	12	708	13	881	14	n/a	n/a	Italy
Siemens	39	14	1,058	6	1,010	12	680	15	Germany

★ Fujitsu and NEC data are *not* commensurate since services are included in this data. Rankings are based on IDC and McKinsey for 1999. According to the latter two sources, the revenues are Fujitsu 2,460 and NEC 2,201. Japanese companies offer packages that include services, which are very difficult to separate from product revenue. Data for software revenues were not separately kept for HP and Hitachi in earlier years.

Sources: Datamation, 1985, 1993, 1997; IDC (2000); McKinsey (2000).

the global dynamics of the industry. As large multinational enterprises are the first to adapt and take advantage of these new technological trends, enterprise software is one of the most important segments of this sector.

Because of the rapid diffusion of both cheaper workstations and PCs, widespread opportunities have emerged for creative software solutions in a broad range of highly specialized applications. To fill this gap, numerous groups of firms, including hardware producers, ISVs, services firms, consulting companies, and resellers, have entered the market. Furthermore, ongoing telecommunications deregulation, Internet expansion, wireless communications, and other technological developments have resulted in even tighter coupling between the computer software business and the "computer services/consulting" sector.[16] Although determining boundaries in the traded software sector does not escape these problems, the focus on firms that are primarily producers of traded software for sale in a global market allows us to track a specific commodity. Tracking the contribution of the packaged software component from services such as installation, systems integration, and maintenance is a more manageable task than disaggregating a customized solution. But to do this for a number of firms is daunting and beyond the scope of this study. As a result, this chapter seeks to balance macroeconomic analysis of the Japanese enterprise software sector with a crucial case study to disaggregate key components of a successfully integrated market-nonmarket corporate strategy.

Fujitsu was chosen for the focused case study because it is one of the few Japanese software firms that has a presence in the developing Asian market both as a producer and exporter. Not only is it the largest Japanese computer manufacturer, but it also has three growing independent software divisions in Japan (consolidated from six as of December 2000). In addition, Fujitsu is considered to be one of the top producers of high-quality software for the global market and was the first Japanese computer manufacturer to make the successful transition to a global software and services company. Accordingly, the next sections will provide a general context for the analysis of Fujitsu in relation to the software industry in developing Asia.

II. Positional Analysis

Market Environment

An increasingly rich, urbanized, and expanding population is predicted to generate one billion middle-income households in developing Asia by 2005. Consumer needs are becoming ever more sophisticated, providing the preconditions for a variety of emerging markets in the region. It has been estimated that developing Asia's subsequent demand for imports could generate close to a quarter of the West's economic growth over the next few years.[17] Because an increasing percentage of this total is composed of IT products (approximately 16.6 percent in 1999), the prospect for software trading opportunities in the region is tremendous (see Table 7.5). As Asian citizens begin to cross a number of so-called wealth effect thresholds, Internet and e-commerce related transactions are expected.[18] These consumption patterns are likely to spread throughout East Asia to a variety of different markets. In addition, the resilience of this market has been demonstrated in the wake of sluggish demand related to the currency crises that began in 1997.

However, computer hardware and software spending has dramatically risen in virtually all regional countries (except Thailand), exploding to near-record levels since the first quarter of 1998. Although Asia comprised only 5 percent of the total world IT import market from advanced industrialized countries, it is expected to triple that share in a decade.[19]

One of the most developed IT markets in Asia is Hong Kong, which had a total market size of over $1.8 billion in 1997.[20] Although much of this figure relates to the booming growth of software services and systems integration, packaged products alone accounted for $70 million. Of this total, the Internet boom, electronic data interchange (EDI), and

Table 7.5 Most promising IT markets (rankings), 1997

Countries	Growth rate (in %)	Consumption capacity	Commercial infrastructure	Market receptivity	Country risk	Market intensity	Overall potential
Singapore	1	10	2	1	1	9	1
Hong Kong	9	8	5	2	4	1	2
S. Korea	3	6	13	6	2	14	3
China	5	1	19	20	9	23	5
Malaysia	2	13	11	3	6	20	8
India	10	7	1	21	15	17	10
Thailand	4	19	21	7	8	19	13
Philippines	12	13	12	8	17	11	15
Indonesia	6	5	22	16	12	22	16

Note: This survey included all member OECD countries outside of G-7 and EU countries.

Source: MSU-CIBER, "Market Potential Indicators for Emerging Markets, October 17, 1997. Dimension definitions: market intensity: GNP per capita, private consumption/GDP; consumption capacity: percentage share of middle class in total consumption/income; commercial infrastructure: telephone lines, Internet hosts, TV sets, population/retail outlet and paved roads per capita; market receptivity: per capita imports, trade/GDP; and country risk: Euromoney, March 1997, IMF.

e-commerce solutions for small to medium-sized enterprises are driving the majority of demand and are expected to grow between 25–35 percent per annum over the next five years. Imported software products represent over half of total sales, with U.S. companies enjoying close to an 80 percent market share. Despite the increase in demand in packaged products, customized software systems continue to hold the majority of the software market with a sales value of over $700 million in 1997. Given Japan's core competence in turnkey customized software solutions, expected future growth in this segment provides many potential market opportunities. Yet, this is precisely the area where local producers have managed to maintain steadily growing market shares. It is also a market segment that is likely to undergo radical evolution as increasingly sophisticated packaged software products based on network computing gain significant market share in the near future.

With growth rates expected to maintain its 20 percent per year pace through 2002, continuing economic crises in Malaysia have affected the software industry the least. With government commitments to enhance IT use—especially the Multimedia Super Corridor and banking and finance—education and telecommunications software contributed close to 17 percent of total industry spending in each category. In addition, 16.7 percent of total IT sales in 1997 of $2.392 billion are spent on software.[21] With continuing PC and server growth forecasted, the expenditure on software will correspondingly increase in the near future with U.S. firms reaping the lion's share of revenue.

Similarly, the United States holds a 90 percent market share in the rapidly growing South Korean packaged software market, which broke the $1 billion threshold in 1996 with 32 percent growth from the previous year. Between 1993 and 1996, the packaged software market grew at an annual rate of 50 percent per year. Although the PC market has more than tripled in three short years from 1993 to 1996, from 800,000 to 1.8 million (39.2 percent of all households), local software firms have managed to maintain a dominant domestic position in word processing, MIS, and groupware for small businesses. As a result, the value of imports was valued at $437 million in 1996, accounting for 41 percent of the total traded packaged market. This is primarily a reflection of language localization, the unique paperwork environment of South Korean firms, and rampant piracy of U.S. software by local vendors. While the growth of packaged software has slowed to 22 percent in 1998 to 2000, it has picked up again in the second half of 2000. Given record-level PC sales and servers in 2000, steady demand for enterprise-software solutions for specific large-scale industrial end users is likely to continue with the significant decline in average sale prices.

Although the software industry in Taiwan is still in its infancy, the packaged software market alone was valued at $717.3 million in 1997. Representing approximately 60 percent of the total software product market, this leaves a stagnant but healthy 40 percent of the market for customized software solutions. As customized producers, Taiwan is one of the countries where Japanese companies have maintained a visible market share since the late 1980s, peaking at 11 percent for their hardware and operating systems software (NEC, Hitachi, Fujitsu, Toshiba, Omron). However, with strong demand for PCs, "open" client-server architecture, and Internet-related software, visible U.S. market dominance in packaged software is expected to increase steadily every year.

The Chinese market offers a different kind of challenge for software companies. Although the IT industry doubled every two years during the 1990s, low household incomes, poor and unevenly developed infrastructure, unstable political and legal environments, and unchecked piracy make China a tantalizing but difficult market. Nevertheless, Chinese government reports indicate that foreign and domestic software producers generated $1.4 billion in sales revenue as early as 1995 and had two hundred local development enterprises employing over three hundred thousand people.[22] With 30 to 40 percent average annual PC sales increases throughout the 1990s, sales were estimated to reach five million units by

2000.[23] In addition to the fact that software localization is mandated by law to be done by Chinese computer professionals on the Chinese mainland (an often cheaper option most leading software companies would have taken anyway), software is often pirated at reported levels as high as 98 percent.[24]

Although networking capabilities are not yet economical throughout China, the market for foreign database software and systems integration has enjoyed the biggest profit margins of any segment. This is not surprising, because multinational enterprises have a long history of investment in this region. Primarily because of the absence of local competition, enterprise system providers like Oracle and SAP have made steady inroads. While the systems integration segment grew 36 percent per year from 1995 to 1998 to reach a total of $81 million, applications development for database technology alone was estimated at $30 million as early as 1996.[25]

For those who are patient, have a leading edge product (to scare off local competitors), and deep pockets, China is an attractive market. In particular, large complex systems are attractive for a large end user, because they are nearly impossible to replicate, much less to maintain, by would-be IPR violators. For now, the best prospects for software importers are to take advantage of the local talent located in the numerous government-funded software industrial bases. It is not surprising that joint ventures make up the majority of foreign investment in the Chinese software sector. Thus far, only U.S. companies have been able to make significant inroads in selected Chinese software niches where piracy is a nonissue.

Nonmarket Environment

Recognizing the long-term strategic importance of the IT industry to economic growth, developing Asian governments have made long-term commitments to various IT promotion programs and policies. Science parks, the easing of FDI restrictions, export promotion and relocation incentives, computer science training, controlling piracy, and IT infrastructure development in general now form a fundamental part of the economic policy agenda of all developing Asian countries as well as Japan.

In fact, developing Asia's investment in infrastructure will accelerate in the upcoming years, owing to pressure to provide more extensive and modern networks to support business expansion. Much of the existing infrastructure is outdated and requires massive capital infusion to revitalize. Mirroring the Malaysian Multimedia Super Corridor, the Taiwanese government has already begun to implement an ambitious $300 billion infrastructure investment plan to tackle the accumulation of market pressures outlined above. South Korea has made similar commitments, including the creation and expansion of so-called "Software Parks" that will encourage global software players to locally produce alongside other world-class IT players.

This has become the consensus strategy for policy in developing Asia. On the whole, average East Asian government capital expenditure could well rise to 10 percent of total GNP within the coming decade, which would quadruple the present rate in the EU and the United States.[26] Japanese companies have not hesitated to establish partnerships with best of breed companies in various complementary technologies to drive a record number of strategic alliances in the software, hardware, and telecommunications sectors.

The central objective for the firm is to be the builder of the IT infrastructure, of which software has become a major component. In order to attract such FDI, all developing Asian countries realize they must use nonmarket means to help build the IT infrastructure necessary to promote economic growth for the next millennium. Accordingly, the policies of Asian countries are designed not only to train skilled workers and promote its use among their local businesses and consumers but also to liberalize and deregulate the business environment to encourage global players to locate there.

Taiwan is the consummate regional example of a country with policies designed to encourage local industrial development at the expense of local multinational corporation penetration. Concerned with building a thriving software industry, however, the Taiwanese government has committed vast resources to becoming an "intelligent island" that is open to the challenge of globalization and the Internet. The core of this plan is exemplified by the $10 billion commitment to creating the National Information Infrastructure that promises to provide the environment necessary to take advantage of the Internet. In fact, from 1997 to the end of 2000, Taiwan spent over $552.8 million on Internet applications software, services, and educational programs alone.

South Korea has made similar efforts to promote its software industry. To facilitate the development of the still-infant domestic software industry, the South Korean government implemented a five-year plan beginning in December 1996 to develop the packaged software, multimedia content, and system integration/database segments. The government alone plans to spend $112 million to provide the capital, training, and education necessary to realize this goal. In line with their concerns, South Korea has been a relatively business-friendly place for leading software companies to invest and the government has recently cracked down on piracy.

China and India are playing a different role in the strategies of leading software companies. Rather than serving as primary markets for export (such as Singapore), their vast government commitments to computer science and related IT training has resulted in a large pool of skilled programmers located in well-developed areas with the latest technologies and modern infrastructures. In short, they are providing the labor for the industry both at home and abroad. While China has generally focused on providing skilled labor for computer hardware and related complementary technologies, India has provided skilled software professionals for well over a decade to the biggest companies in the world. A recent government survey even found that the Indian software market had become a $4 billion industry in 2000, providing software production and services to 185 of the Fortune 500 companies in 2000.[27] Between 1995 and 2000, the compound annual growth rate (CAGR) of the Indian software and services industry has averaged 50 percent. Software companies with a presence in India had a market capitalization of $55 billion as of June 2000. Clearly, favorable policies that allow 100 percent FDI in e-commerce, software, and other IT-related industries as well as participation in the WTO's Information Technology Agreements play large roles in enabling such developments. Although China is gradually relaxing its FDI policies for software and e-commerce related industries, it still does not allow foreign software companies to localize products for the Chinese market without using Chinese workers. Both the Indian and Chinese governments' broad measures to ensure that their respective populations will be trained to meet the global challenge of the Internet is being increasingly emulated by other countries in developing Asia, as well as in Japan.

In this phase of regional development, however, it may be too optimistic to predict that developing Asian players will become global independent software vendors (ISVs). Rather, the concern for the present and immediate future is to train the people necessary to participate in these technological developments. In infant markets, it is clear that the greatest demand throughout developing Asia is for traded packaged software that has a proven track record in advanced industrial markets. Accordingly, localization costs related to language and diverse business environments are substantial and account for the majority of investment in all developing Asia countries. To some degree, this detracts from the natural scale advantages of packaged products. But perhaps the biggest nonmarket industry concern is the rampant piracy rates throughout East Asia. Although they have significantly improved from the 90 percent

Table 7.6 World software piracy rates and losses, 1994–1998

	Piracy rates (%)					Retail revenues ($ million)		
	1994	1995	1996	1997	1998	1994	1996	1998
TOTAL Asia-Pacific*	68	64	55	52	49	3,144.5	3,739.3	2,954.8
China	97	96	96	96	95	364.0	703.8	1,193.4
Hong Kong	62	62	64	67	59	64.5	129.1	88.6
India	79	78	79	69	65	103.1	255.3	197.3
Indonesia	97	98	97	93	92	104.5	197.3	58.8
Japan	66	55	41	32	31	1,399.8	1,190.3	596.9
South Korea	75	76	70	67	64	510.6	515.5	197.5
Malaysia	82	77	80	70	73	66.7	121.5	79.3
Philippines	94	91	92	83	77	40.6	70.7	31.1
Singapore	61	53	59	56	52	37.3	56.6	58.3
Taiwan	72	70	66	63	59	112.0	117.0	141.3
Thailand	87	82	80	84	82	67.8	137.1	48.6
Vietnam	100	99	99	98	97	3.9	15.2	10.3
Total W. Europe	52	49	43	39	36	2,783.0	2,574.9	2,760.3
Total N. America	32	27	28	28	26	3,931.1	2,718.3	3,195.8
U.S.	31	26	27	27	25	3,589.5	2,360.9	2,875.2
Total World	49	46	43	40	38	12,346.5	11,306.3	10,976.5

* The Asia-Pacific also includes Australia, New Zealand, and Pakistan.

Source: International Planning and Research Corporation, 1999 Global Piracy Report (Business Software Alliance and Software and Information Industry, 2000).

estimates of five years ago to 75 percent levels in 1998, high piracy rates continue to severely cut into profit margins (see Table 7.6).

Thus, although rapid PC expansion continues, the trend toward more open networked systems promises to expand midrange and mainframe computing within East Asian markets. With continuing infrastructure improvements, Japanese companies may find niche opportunities to serve large-scale end users in manufacturing, wholesale, and retail businesses. There is anecdotal evidence that such inroads are gradually being made on these fronts. In addition, the increasingly large role of East Asian governments in direct purchasing to enhance administrative capabilities has already resulted in a bigger Japanese market share in Taiwan. However, as dominant U.S. market shares reflect, it will take several years before more significant inroads can be made.

Organizational Environment: The Evolution of the Japanese Software Industry

As the beneficiary of the third-largest software market in the world, the explicit focus of generations of industrial policy, and one of the world's leading computer hardware producers, it may seem odd that few Japanese enterprise software products have come to dominate global markets. As discussed earlier, rather than attempt to explain why Japan has failed to produce globally competitive software solutions until very recently, this section will attempt to provide a sectoral overview to provide a context for the focused case study.[28]

The Japanese software industry has three general characteristics. First, it has been dominated by the production of customized software solutions with high dependence on mainframe computer manufactures. Second, the existence of a scaled, hierarchical division of labor in the industry has resulted in the organization of the industry into a routine coding business that does not require skilled and creative labor. Third, the strong user preference for customized software over packaged products has resulted in an industry structure that reflects the administration of major industrial clients rather than developments in computer technology. Accordingly, many Japanese manufacturers have spent the majority of their unit labor costs developing highly customized software systems that reflect company-specific rules, routines, and functions rather than general industry needs. Because software has been traditionally viewed as an input into the production process, software sales are merely one component of a finished product. It is not surprising then that revenue in packaged software in Japan from 1985 to 1991 was only 9.4 to 16 percent of the market, while the comparable figure in the United States was 47.6 to 76.2 percent (and roughly 60 percent throughout the other G-7 countries).[29]

There are four primary factors that explain this situation. First, the range of variability in business procedures, customs, rules, and terminology is considerable among Japanese firms.[30] Standardized packages were inadequate to the task, resulting in firm-specific customized software. Second, early IBM competition led Japanese mainframe manufacturers to promote their own custom solutions to their clients. Consistent with industrial trends of the time, software was considered a by-product to induce customers to purchase hardware. Because software contracts were bundled with hardware sales, market proximity and local relationship advantages could be maximized.[31] Even after the six major computer manufacturers agreed to unbundle their software and services in 1977, this situation remained relatively unchanged. Third, computer science professionals were rare, making it difficult to develop packaged applications software at home. Finally, the corporate *keiretsu* structure reinforced the tendency to stick with long-term producer–supplier relationships even in the face of the introduction of cheaper, higher quality products and services from abroad.[32]

This is the context for a Japanese software industry that was almost entirely based on the mainframe since its inception. From the early 1980s through 1991 (the so-called bubble period), an enormous number of mainframe computers were introduced as labor-saving devices and infrastructure improvements designed to enhance capacity and efficiency. Personal computers were primarily utilized as terminals for these mainframe machines, coupled with large numbers of dedicated word processors in the workplace. But just as mainframe sales peaked in Japan in the late 1980s, the PC was taking off in the U.S. and Europe (see Figure 7.2). Furthermore, as U.S. firms started to downsize, the Japanese bubble finally burst in 1991. Under these conditions, it is no wonder that promising technological breakthroughs in CPUs, ICs, and software were slow to result in foreign PC expansion into the Japanese market.

The slow introduction of these new PCs in Japan, which were based primarily on packaged products, was also due in no small part to the technical difficulties in Japanese language processing. Because PCs evolved from scientific calculation of numerical values to information processing emphasizing data that includes characters, it was initially impossible for small computers to handle Kanji characters. This led to the large-scale introduction of machines dedicated to word processing to the detriment of PC growth, whereby Japanese manufacturers had to modify hardware through the production of specially designed chips.

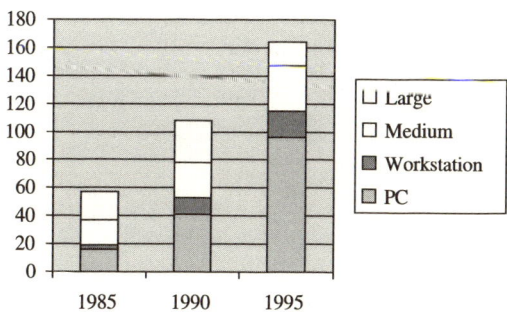

Figure 7.2 Global computer hardware sales by processor type (based on value of total sales revenue)
Source: McKinsey & Company (1996).

As discussed earlier, another reason for slow PC growth is related to domestic competition, which led to hardware differentiation related to the processing of kanji. Thus, even after the IBM compatibles paved the way for "wintel" standardization (i.e., Intel CPUs and Microsoft operating systems (OSs), Japanese PCs remained fundamentally incompatible with one another.[33] It is easy to see why packaged software vendors seeking to maximize economies of scale would have a hard time reaping profits in such a fragmented environment that involved four major kanji standards. Thus, while high volume marketing led to cheaper PCs and market expansion in the U.S. and European markets, Japan's market remained fragmented not only among PC makers but with alternative stand-alone devices.

However, technological breakthroughs in ICs by the end of the 1980s made it possible to process kanji with commonly available software (stored on hard drives) that did not require special chips dedicated to language processing.[34] Because it became possible to process kanji with standardized software, the market finally began to expand, particularly with the introduction of low-priced PCs adapted to the Japanese language (DOS-V). Although the software industry began posting double-digit sales growth rates in the 1980s, when the asset-inflated economy was swelling, they were blindsided by the bubble economy demand for software based on mainframe computing. Mainframe sales and usage persisted much longer in Japan than in the domestic markets of their leading competitors in the United States and Western Europe (see Table 7.7).

By the end of the 1980s, however, the PC was becoming increasingly affordable with each passing year, leading to the importation of the cheaper foreign alternatives. In 1992, the computer hardware and software industry, including data-processing services, enjoyed record sales of ¥7.12 trillion ($69.7 billion)—twelve times the figure of thirteen years before. The same year, the number of employees reached 480,000.

Table 7.7 Mainframes as a share of total hardware (percent)

Year	1987	1995
U.S.	46.82	21.57
Japan	72.33	42.85
Germany	55.82	30.16
France	53.19	32.39
UK	53.41	27.74
Italy	66.11	44.64

Sources: OECD (1997); Torrisi (1998), p. 49.

Yet, because much of this growth still relied on proprietary bundled hardware–software products, it wasn't until 1995 that the more open standard PC growth started to take off. Coupled with the move by Fujitsu, Toshiba, Hitachi, and others to commit to the production of PCs based on international standard specifications, the enormous popularity of Windows 95 led to 70 percent PC growth in 1995 alone. Although this dropped off a bit from its peak in 1996 and remained sluggish through the end of the Asian Crisis in 1998, the strong growth of 1999 has continued through the first quarter of 2001, reaching 14.13 million units throughout 2000 (30.4 percent year-on-year growth) with home use reaching an unprecedented 47.8 percent.

PC growth has also led to the dramatic influx of U.S. software products, especially system software. Since OSs define the parameters for application software development, U.S. firms like Sun, Oracle, IBM, Microsoft and their developer partners have a tremendous advantage. In addition, increasing complexity closely related to changing graphical user interfaces (GUI) make application software increasingly difficult to develop over time. Having spent most of their time honing skills to meet specific user needs through customized solutions based on mainframe environments, Japanese workers were not accustomed to providing general packaged software products intended for multiple groups of unspecified users. Finally, OS dependence makes it difficult to time product releases to make them profitable in an increasingly global market that demands continuous upgrading of product versions amid intensified competition, in a timely fashion to meet industrial end users' needs.

As a market follower in a burgeoning market at home and in Asia, Japanese computer firms were forced to localize imported software products to boost sales. From an organizational standpoint, many Japanese computer and electronics firms that produced complementary products were forced to keep pace with developments abroad. This led to increasing R&D budgets for software products and solutions that led to the start of wide experimentation with new horizontal organizational forms. Following the lead of cutting-edge U.S. firms that collaborated with local firms to localize their products and capture the majority of the early emerging software market in developing Asia, licensing agreements and other strategic alliances became commonplace.

By keeping abreast of global market demands at home and in developing Asia, many Japanese firms were able to take advantage of the rapid adoption of the powerful PC client-server architecture and the Internet within a few short years. Japanese firms that were able to take advantage of these new developments by phasing out their earlier commitments to proprietary hardware designs and utilizing their core competencies in open systems positioned themselves well to compete in this new global marketplace. Unlike the old software factory organization that divided software development along functional lines, new organizational changes were made to outsource products and technical solutions from industry leading firms. Through complex strategic alliances with numerous partners, they could offer more comprehensive enterprise solutions in collaboration with potential competitors. As illustrated later in this chapter, such thin organizational strategies helped major Japanese software producers quickly adapt to the changing global dynamics of the industry and embrace the Internet. Fujitsu's success owes much to its ability to recognize and take advantage of changes in the marketplace by learning to collaborate with leading complementary technology partners and by embracing the Internet.

III. Strategy and Tactics

Market Strategies: The Global Market Context

The dominant packaged enterprise software firms are IBM, SAP, Oracle, Microsoft, Computer Associates/Sterling, and a host of late entrants ranging from Fujitsu to Hewlett Packard. Although they originally targeted specific industrial users, their programs were scalable and adaptable to a multitude of different clients. They also tended to specialize in specific niches so that they did not always directly compete with each other. But as demand intensified for total enterprise solutions (as opposed to a collection of best-of-breed industrial and/or functionally-specific software products), opportunities for comprehensive enterprise solutions flourished. This is primarily because software development plays an increasingly crucial role in the overall growth of many industries. For example, as early as 1985, the OECD reported that software costs accounted for over 80 percent of total costs (including hardware) related to new information technology applications.[35] A survey conducted in the Netherlands found that 23 percent of total business R&D expenditure was accounted for by software in 1994.[36] Furthermore, five of the world's ten largest IT firms ranked by R&D intensity were software producers.[37]

Regardless of the difficulty of accounting for such estimates given the increasing network alliance structure emerging in this sector, it is clear that software has become the core technological lever that drives the field. At a minimum, the case study of this chapter complements an examination of the aggregate statistical trends to help us better understand the competitive dynamics of the industry. This focus creates a generalizable framework with which to orient the case study of one of the major Japanese firm strategies along market and nonmarket parameters. As a latecomer to the industry, Japanese software firms have focused on disrupting the status quo by creating a series of temporary advantages.[38] A disruption can involve creating strategically placed niche products as well as lobbying the government to block the entrance of superior foreign products. As we will see, Fujitsu's success owes much to its effectiveness at implementing an integrated strategy on multiple levels to leverage generalizable industrial software solutions for an expanding global market.

The availability of software for specialized industrial end-users increasingly drives the production of hardware products in computers and microelectronics. Growth continues to flow from widespread software adoption in diverse industrial application settings. As microprocessors continue to improve, rapid reductions in hardware costs fuel the widespread global diffusion of multiple computer platforms, especially workstations and microcomputers. The recent eclipse of Moore's Law with the advancement of chip technology highlights the likely continuation of the decades-long trend of a "software solution explosion" that has led to the rapid expansion of market niches with a virtually endless array of applications and application tools. The firms that establish first-mover advantages in the maturing industrial markets in developing Asia found themselves well-positioned to benefit from this rapid market expansion. As the global de facto standards-setters, it is not surprising to see U.S. companies such as IBM, Oracle, and Microsoft continuing to take market share throughout the region.

Japanese software producers' late entrance also allowed them to take advantage of new market demands associated with increasingly complex heterogeneous computing environments along with Internet utilization. As a group of relatively new markets, Asia became the new battleground for newly improved software products that were scaled to take advantage of new technological developments. As large corporations increasingly desired to centralize their regional operations in Asia from central headquarters location, increasingly sophisticated software that could handle back- and front-office functions in an integrated way were at a premium. With FDI in Asia increasing within regional and global production networks, the region was prime for IT investment as well. Since no single vendor could provide total enterprise solutions to meet all the needs of diverse industrial clients, strategic alliances and partnering became crucial to maximize market shares in a timely manner. In addition, because enterprise software is complex and sophisticated, they often require extensive training, upgrading, and maintenance schedules to ensure future revenue flows.

In short, Japanese firms found themselves well-positioned to maintain their relations with old clientele by partnering with leading global software and hardware vendors to offer the best comprehensive solution available on the market with a customized, localized, and user-friendly interface.

Nonmarket Strategies

Given the fragmented "craft" nature and high fixed developmental costs associated with this producer market, it is no wonder that both home and potential host governments have become actively involved in the promotion of the software sector. While developed countries focus on standards/process coordination of the private sector, developing countries pursued FDI and export promotion strategies. Both have also launched long-term educational policies as well as programs designed to encourage business, citizen, and consumer use, as well as interfirm production collaboration.[39] Furthermore, virtually all Asian countries under discussion here are closely involved with liberalizing international agreements for software, such as the recent expansion of the Information Technology Agreement (ITA and ITA II) under the direction of the WTO. It is imperative that any software firm looking to do business in Asia take a long-term view by first familiarizing oneself with the dense nonmarket environment characterized by heavy government involvement.

Although U.S. first-mover advantages in hardware led to the emergence of the first domestic packaged market, the links between hardware and software development are complex and the "correct" direction for policy remains unclear. This ambiguity has resulted in public policies in the region that are aimed less at creating national champions than at providing the conditions necessary for IT development. Thus, even though all Asian countries have targeted the software industry, few have been able to produce successful local competitors. With weak local competition, foreign firms can focus on partnering with companies for the sole purpose of product localization. As discussed earlier, long-term IT infrastructure commitments in hardware, telecommunications, and training ensure that skilled personnel throughout Asia will increase over time.

Because the software divisions of large companies like Fujitsu, Hitachi, and NEC primarily served large-scale enterprises, their first step was to "package" their customized solutions for specific clients to a more general market abroad. Since U.S. products dominated the United States and EU already, they chose to scale their products to Japanese "legacy"[40] clientele investing in developing Asia. Big MNCs in banking, automobiles, materials processing, and other large-scale industries became the first targets for their enterprise software products. As the largest provider of ODA for several years running and with primary investments in developing Asia, this target market was readily apparent. In addition, given the ties that have been established between the linkages of such aid to Japanese corporate interests in the region, it is a strategy that could often result in direct benefits if aid money matched by local government funds were deployed for investment in improving software.

In addition, Asian governments are often active in software promotion, seeking foreign companies to locate their production facilities within their boundaries. Along with the promise of training, localizing production would ensure the further dissemination of their efficiency-increasing potential. Not only would the government take an active role in the promotion of new software products for businesses, but it would also become a major user of such systems and products. In short, while relaxing rules and regulations to streamline the process for foreign companies to enter, trade, and produce software, governments would also set up agencies to assist in such business development as they incorporated the latest software developments in their own organization.

Finally, setting up and funding IT and software training facilities as well as industry consortia for ISPs (Internet service providers) and domain name management involves close host-government relations. More often than not, host governments offer land, reduced rent, and tax breaks for companies that agree to create, maintain, and run such facilities. Establishing cooperative business-government relations early on allows the follower firm to take advantage of government initiatives in the initial business development process.

In short, participating in trade fairs, exhibitions, and forums, as well as the traditional market strategies of heavy advertising and service support, are not the only sufficient conditions for success in Asia. Directly partnering with governments provides not only a host of nonmarket benefits and a large customer but also leads to further local partnering as well. Establishing an early foothold in these countries will ensure that people will learn how to use a firm's products early and often. Although this may involve cutting profit margins in the beginning, especially in the face of heavy competition, it promises a long stream of steady profits in the long run.

Organizational Strategies and Tactics

While U.S. software companies who enjoy competitive advantage in tools and operating systems development have capitalized on their advantages in developing regions, their dominance is by no means guaranteed in the future.[41] In fact, local competition and complex global strategic alliance structures in the industry continually change the dynamics of the industry. In particular, the ability to create sophisticated software for small to medium-sized enterprises has been a market that has come into its own in the past five to ten years. It is likely that this lucrative enterprise-software niche will continue to provide ample opportunities around which the major Japanese software players will reorganize.

In the immediate future, Japanese firms will manage to remain dominant in their own domestic applications solutions market, extending them to the foreign affiliates of their clients with operations in Asia. Primarily because of local market needs for both "user friendliness" and adaptation to local operating conditions such as non-English language and character considerations, Japanese firms have maintained an edge in supplying custom software to local firms in their home market. But, as discussed earlier, this continued success is dated. Embracing the open standard PC and client-server architecture to take advantage of the Internet has become the norm. Realizing this, Fujitsu, NEC, and Hitachi have found a way to partake of the emerging IT value chain in both global and developing Asian markets. By devoting large resources to R&D in leading markets to keep abreast of new developments in the United States and other key markets, they have been able to reorganize internally to focus more explicitly on software and the Internet. Because the newly installed base of cheap PCs in Asia is for small-scale purposes preinstalled with primarily U.S. software, there was no apparent need to create local substitutes for cutting-edge products. More in line with their core competencies associated with their customized software solutions and intimate, long-term relations with corporate clients, the higher-end enterprise solutions segment is a much more promising arena for growth. Thus, the best prospects for Japanese companies reside in creating the servers and enterprise application software for the SME market in various industries.

The second part of their strategy is to ally with the best technology partners in the world to offer "one-stop-shop"-type software solutions, whether on their hardware or not. Target markets for these product offerings were generally large MNCs in advanced countries like the United States and the EU. However, given the international scope of

Japanese MNC operations, such products could often be scaled to their Asian affiliates or local competitors in the region.

Although Japanese companies have been slower to utilize the emerging software labor pools in India (and to some degree China), they were quick to join their U.S. counterparts in the region through strategic alliances to make joint product offerings throughout the region. By taking advantage of consolidated "suite" offerings bundled with hardware, they could establish a world-class reputation in enterprise niche segments for specialized industrial processes and machines.

As the market follower, large Japanese firms that produced software generally followed three primary organizational strategies. First, they initially sought to maintain their customized software solutions for existing clients by strengthening their existing corporate value chain. But once they found themselves losing market share in hardware and other industrial machines requiring specialized software, Japanese producers often relied on a strategy of anchoring by diversifying into supporting upstream and/or downstream industrial businesses. This strategy is aimed at capturing more of the surplus value and improving functional linkages to enhance efficiency and lowering transaction costs. Toshiba and Hitachi excelled in the deployment of this strategy in their offerings of workstations and networked PCs for the corporate environment while localizing software products through the creation of unique interfaces for specific industries. The third way to strengthen the existing corporate value chain is to diversify into related complementary businesses. Potential benefits are expected to ensue from complex interactions between the focal and related industrial activities. For a firm with a strong competitive position in servers or switches (i.e., Fujitsu) for example, there is high potential to increase growth rates and profitability by applying existing competencies to more attractive new markets. This is the strategy most closely followed by Fujitsu in its desire to shed old businesses with decreasing returns and to enter new ones with increasing returns, like enterprise-software solutions. The last section of this chapter shows how Fujitsu underwent radical reorganization and relied on new software and Internet divisions that leveraged existing core competencies to return to profitability.

IV. Case Study: Fujitsu

When Fuji Electric incorporated its telephone equipment division in 1935, the company Fujitsu was established. The firm began with the commercialization of Japan's first digital calculator, later expanding into switching systems and other electric and electromechanical equipment. By 1954, Fujitsu unveiled Japan's first nonprogrammable computer, later expanding into a broad range of communications and office equipment, including data processing services, computers, and computer peripherals. Fujitsu has long been the largest IT vendor in Japan and ranked as high as second to IBM in the world in 1995. Fujitsu's revenues peaked in 1992 to profits of $94 million from revenues of $21 billion. In the wake of the crisis of 1997, however, it experienced a loss of $125.5 million in FY 1998. But primarily as a result of its "Everything on the Internet" strategy (and shedding unprofitable businesses), Fujitsu realized $397 million profit on over $43.3 billion in net sales for FY 1999. For the first half of FY 2000 alone, Fujitsu reaped a $160 million profit on over $23 billion in total revenue.

Although revenues used to come primarily from communication systems and semiconductors, Fujitsu's profits increasingly came from computer hardware and systems software, large-scale custom applications, and specialized custom application packages. Fujitsu develops and sells multiple platforms, including mainframes, minicomputers, work stations, and PCs. Since 1990, although a significant amount of sales came from the information processing division (44.9 percent), the software and services divisions (28.7 percent) surpassed the other two core businesses (telecommunications and electronic devices) combined (see Table 7.8). In fact, because of higher profit margins, the software and services business is considered the most profitable group of the corporation. In short, Fujitsu has become primarily a producer of software and servers for the Internet in a relatively short period of time.

Fujitsu used to be organized into several operation groups divided by hardware, sales, and data processing services. The Systems Engineering and Computer Systems were responsible for the core of software development. While the former were involved with data processing services, the latter were involved with systems software and factory automation software for their hardware. Because of their stated commitment to be an integrated computer and telecommunications company, software has played an important strategic role in the overall development of the company. As a result, Fujitsu has always made commitments to hire the best talent (not just engineers) coupled with careful study of the leading U.S. technologies to maintain broad and deep competence on the frontier. Their software-development approach at their main facility in Numazu has been described as a "software factory," considered typical of Japanese firms in this industrial sector in the 1980s. It focuses on centralized programming operations in decentralized domains within a single facility, while applying

Table 7.8 Fujitsu limited core businesses

Group (business segment)	Main products and services	Percentage of sales
Software and services	Operating systems, middleware, application software, system integration services, professional services (including consulting, introductory support, operational support, help desk, educational and training services), network services, outsourcing services, maintenance and construction	28.7
Information processing	High-performance computers, global servers, UNIX servers, IA servers, workstations, PCs, LAN, financial terminal equipment, smart card, POS systems, handheld terminals, medical systems, magnetic and magneto-optical drives, magnetic tape units, printers, word processors	44.9
Telecommunications	Digital switching systems, ATM switching systems, optical transmission systems, optimal submarine cable transmission systems, radio systems, satellite communication systems, corporate information network systems, communications application systems, mobile communication systems, cellular telephones	17.6
Electronic devices	Memory ICs (DRAM, flash memory devices), logic ICs (ASICs, microcontrollers, system LSI chips), liquid crystal displays.	8.8

Source: Fujitsu Limited Interim Report on First-half FY 2000 Financial Results, September 30, 2000.

rigorous zero-defect standards on a comprehensive design to maintenance basis. But Fujitsu is considered to have risen above its competitors because of its willingness to be an independent industry leader in all computer systems.[42] Although Hitachi, NEC, and Toshiba have similar corporate cultures, Fujitsu invests more heavily in bottom up and ongoing training for programmers and system engineers and procedures and tools that evolve to become the industry standard at any particular time.

Because the core of Fujitsu's business has long been in the M-Series mainframe computers, it is from this platform that it has made inroads in Asian, European, and U.S. markets for their software solutions. For Japanese end users, the Numazu software group offers a full complement of system processors in conjunction with the versatile and diverse hardware line. These include a line compatible and comparable to IBM's full complement, including a relational database system and extensive communications software support and services. Because their M-series processors are targeted for both medium- and large-sized organizations in either commercial or governmental settings, banking, and finance became the primary export target markets. To date, Fujitsu has an installed base in these industries in Taiwan, South Korea, Singapore, Indonesia, Malaysia, the Philippines, and Thailand.

Through marketing IBM-like mainframes that have higher capacities but cheaper selling prices than their competitors, the firm has done solid business in Japanese-owned companies in the United States, Europe, and Asia, as well as at home. While becoming a large shareholder of its chief U.S. competitor, Amdahl, Fujitsu has not focused primarily on the U.S. market. Instead, the firm has opted to sell customized solutions for Japanese multinationals abroad. But, since banking and finance clients have a larger market presence in advanced industrialized economies, Fujitsu has not sought a major market presence in developing Asia through sectoral specialization in finance.

Instead, Fujitsu has committed itself to a broad global strategy that leverages its proprietary hardware advantages and customized software solutions modules and methods to transform itself into a global IT software and services company. Facing hard times in the early 1990s and taking a big hit in 1998 from a severe setback from both semiconductor and telecommunications equipment losses (close to $2 billion in fiscal year ending March 1999), it was the software and services business that has enabled Fujitsu to consistently post positive earnings, reaching $43.3 billion in fiscal year ending in March 1999. Through the creation of the Fujitsu Software Corporation (FSC) in 1991 and the Global Software Technology Division of the new Fujitsu Network Communications (FNC) division, Fujitsu was well on its way to becoming a leading provider of comprehensive IT and network software solutions for the global marketplace and the telecom industry.

The strategy of FSC has been to create a worldwide technology team in every significant market around the globe to become a fully integrated, cutting-edge comprehensive IT software and services provider. This meant that Fujitsu would have to enter the developing Asian markets indirectly. Rather than compete head-on with leading U.S. competitors, why not join them? For example, by purchasing the British company ICL (which is now a wholly owned subsidiary), Fujitsu has greatly expanded its mainframe presence in Europe. In addition, by selling its hardware and software solutions through Siemens-Nixdorf, it has assured itself a quality control partner to ensure localization is done on a consistent and reliable basis. Similar moves were made by coupling their software and services with Amdahl mainframes and the DMR Consulting Group (also Fujitsu affiliates).

Today, Fujitsu is comprised of over five hundred group companies and affiliates with world-class hardware and software technology in computers, telecommunications and microelectronics, employing a corps of over 55,000 systems and services experts around the world. Altogether, the Fujitsu Group employs over 188,000 employees with operation in over one hundred countries, including Hong Kong, Indonesia, Malaysia, Singapore, Thailand, the Philippines, and China. It is primarily through the localization and implementation of their software solutions projects done in conjunction with their Western partners that Fujitsu has established a presence in developing Asia.

Because Fujitsu had specialized in creating customized solutions for a variety of large-scale clients, it was able to turn its core competencies of software modules and programs designed to create, monitor, test, and troubleshoot software application solutions in industries as diverse as finance, telecom, utilities, retail, Internet content, and government. In addition, it was able to embrace the business of connectivity and compatibility by creating application servers like Fujitsu Interstage that were capable of connecting diverse platforms in various older languages (like COBOL) with newer object-oriented database management systems and leading edge message exchange services. This particular project involved many partners, of which Sun Microsystems was the most visible. Similar tie-ups with IBM's Tivoli, Cisco, and other cutting-edge U.S. competitors have allowed Fujitsu to do quite well in the global market for information exchange and data transfer.

It is in the area of telecommunications software and services that Fujitsu has been able to gain significant market share in developing Asian counties. For example, by leveraging its expertise in telecommunications switches with the development of asynchronous transfer mode (ATM) for high-speed multimedia transmission, it has remained a major international telecom player and standards setter. Although it is difficult to determine the value of software and services sans switches and ATM transmission products, major Fujitsu clients include Samsung, Chunghwa Telecom, Malaysia Telecom, South Korea Telecom, Singapore Telecom, and Hong Kong Telecom. Because telecommunications technology upgrading often closely involves host governments throughout developing Asia, having the best technological software solutions is critical to market success in the region. Often the ability to work with local companies in the localization and implementation of the project is also instrumental, especially in China. Finally, taking an active role in the provision of specialized software training is a way that a firm can show commitment to the successful implementation and maintenance of a large-scale software project as well as host country prosperity. To this end, Fujitsu has signed on with Qinghua University and other software research institutes to focus on research and development to create compatible search engines, e-mail technology, and other application software. It has set up or contributed to the creation of training facilities and promotional use centers throughout the Asian region.

Thus, Fujitsu's strategy in developing Asia is intricately intertwined with its general business philosophy. Entitled "Everything on the Internet," Fujitsu reorganized after its dismal FY1998 to bring an Internet focus to all of its activities. This applies not only to its products and services but also to its internal operations and sales activities as well as communication with customers and vendors. The four main components of this strategy are:

1. Enhancing Internet-based solutions: The idea here is to become a total solutions provider of high-quality products and to make the fullest possible use of the constantly expanding Internet infrastructure to provide a wide range of solutions that meet the diverse needs of a broad range of clients around the world.
2. Providing multiple platforms and key devices for the Internet age: Believing in its wide range of technologies developed in-house, Fujitsu aims to remain a comprehensive provider of multiple platforms and Internet devices. R&D focuses even more on network-related technologies to produce products such as high-speed fiber optic transmission systems, servers, and PCs that are central to e-commerce and the Internet.
3. Creating a virtual city of expanding "Netizens": To consolidate Fujitsu's brand recognition as Japan's leading ISP, @Nifty was made a wholly owned subsidiary, merging with other big name companies in various countries, including Yahoo! Japan and AOL Japan. With a subscriber base of over thirteen million, Nifty aims to become a leading online service for secure online shopping and banking, as well as educational and entertainment use.
4. Become a leading Internet user: By applying optimal Internet-based organizational strategies to Fujitsu itself, it hopes to not only closer link its global operations through extensive use of intranets and extranets but also learn how to implement new management styles.

In fact, such technological implementations have allowed Fujitsu to streamline its own software operations from six to three units beginning in December 2000. First, the Nagoya software engineering factory and the Matsumoto operations system research facility have been consolidated into the Fujitsu Prime Software Technology Ltd. Second, the Kobe software technology research center and the Niigata Software Translation facility will now be combined and called the Fujitsu Hyper Software Factory. Third, the Shizuoka software engineering factory was renamed the Fujitsu Info Software Technology Ltd. The Numazu facility will remain relatively unchanged, acting as the central software factory site. These changes mirror the emphasis on leveraging new and existing Fujitsu hardware, devices, and equipment with the best software user interfaces to offer a total solution.

With computing costs continuing to decline, the dot-com craze in the United States crashing, and IT spending slowing down, more and more companies look to developing Asia as the next battleground. With relatively undeveloped and heterogeneous computing markets, Fujitsu has realized that the best way to maintain its strong brand recognition is to partner with skilled partners in the region to build new customer relationships in Asia. The 2000 strategy slogan of "The Possibilities Are Infinite" captures the emphasis on the global nature of its Internet branding strategy. Only by having the best technology and support service—or linking with the best foreign technology partners and service professionals—will Fujitsu be able to constantly build new partner relationships. With IT infrastructures rapidly emerging throughout developing Asia and total hardware and software enterprise solutions' ASPs in decline, the time appears to be ripe for Asian companies to become the next consumers of existing software solutions. With market growth in developing Asia three to ten times greater than that in the United States and the EU, the scramble for Asian market share has only begun for enterprise applications and e-commerce.

V. Conclusion

Although Fujitsu and other Japanese computer manufacturers such as NEC, Hitachi, and Toshiba focused on developing customized software solutions for the end user based solely on the mainframe, it seems clear that it is premature to call the Japanese software industry a failure.[43] Because of the close connections between hardware developments, ICs, and other chip technologies, as well as a whole host of related inventions, software development will likely remain a complex task requiring sophisticated localization and customization skills. As conglomerates with experienced personnel in a variety of disciplines, it is not unlikely to see other Japanese companies like NEC and Hitachi make similar global inroads on the path to recovery—and indeed they may already be well on their way in areas where they remain at the technological frontier, such as ATM switches. Needless to say, Fujitsu's experience further suggests that fully embracing the Internet is paramount to survival.

As we noted at the outset, software is intimately connected to hardware. As a result, we can expect that Japanese manufacturers will compete in increasingly heterogeneous computing environments for multiple opportunities to leverage their previous core competencies, no matter how specialized they seem. Indeed, we have seen how the Japanese software factory has created the basis for the creation of modules that are intricately involved in the process of creating software itself. However, because Japanese software firms like Fujitsu do not necessarily have "killer apps" software capable of generating market demand as stand-alone products, they are forced to learn to compete by integrating into the global value chain of the emerging international "information superhighway" via the Internet. Accordingly, outside of areas like telecommunications—where they enjoy some proprietary hardware technological advantages—it is difficult to enter less mature markets like those in developing Asia without partners. For now, it seems that Fujitsu is best-served through a broad range of strategic alliances and partnering strategies aimed at increasing value for clients seeking to do business in developing Asia. Given its track record since 1999, it is a lesson that similarly positioned Japanese software companies would do well to heed.

Appendix 1: Methodology

Software is everywhere. As the set of operating instructions in any electrical device, software programs are embedded in an increasingly wide array and variety of products. In fact, virtually every corporation today produces software and utilizes it to enhance productivity somewhere along the value chain. In order to talk at all about the "software industry," the literature focuses on the companies whose major product is *traded* software that performs the functions of data processing, information retrieval, and other information-related capabilities.[44] In general, there are primarily two types of software, which have already been alluded to: (1) packaged software products, which offer generalizable solutions; and (2) customized software designed and implemented for a specific user on a contract basis.

Although there are no internationally established rules of classification, the two basic categories used to keep statistics are applications software and systems software. The former refers to business applications such as spreadsheets, word processing, scientific computation, machine operation controls, and image processing. The latter refers to operating systems, language processors, utility programs, databases, and data communications. Of course, both of these categories of software can be produced on either a custom or packaged basis. While customized solutions are highly user-oriented applications that require a good understanding of user needs, packaged software is designed for the general needs of the customer.

For practical and methodological concerns related to data collection, the focus of this chapter is on software firms in the "traded" software sector with secondary emphasis on the "packaged" industry segment. "Traded" software refers to software that is produced by one firm for sale to another.[45] "Packaged" refers to standardized software that offers general application solutions that are not "customized" for a particular end user, industry or business. While all packaged software is traded, customized software may also be traded. Unlike packaged software, custom software is normally sold in conjunction with broader "computer services."[46] Focusing on traded software intended for sale is practical since it establishes boundaries for the unit of analysis. Because a great deal of software development is carried out within user firms, it is not surprising that internationally comparable data on sales of different types of software do not exist.[47] However, data for traded packaged and custom software, the dominant type of software produced by Japanese firms, does exist.[48]

Emphasis is given to "packaged" software because it is the fastest growing software segment in the world (see Table 7.3). Furthermore, as increasingly sophisticated packaged products (including development tools) become available in line with rapidly growing PC and workstation environments, the market share of customized solutions is steadily declining. Thus, it is not surprising that the dominant global players of the industry are "packaged" software firms, primarily from the largest market, the United States (see Table 7.4). Although a few Japanese firms are large software producers (as Table 7.4 illustrates), it should be noted that the majority of traded software revenue for both NEC and Fujitsu is not from the sale of packaged software (see footnote to Table 7.4). Rather, it is from complex contractual arrangements where packages of hardware, specialized software telecommunications equipment, support and services are sold together. In order to disaggregate the analysis to the level of traded software, this analysis will focus on the single largest software product category, enterprise software.

Accordingly, the focus on traded software also makes sense for methodological reasons as well. First, the rapid diffusion of both cheaper workstations and microcomputers has generated widespread opportunities for creative software solutions in a broad range of highly specialized applications. As a result, at least four groups of firms are active in the traded software sector: (1) computer hardware producers; (2) independent software vendors; (3) independent computer services firms, including value-added resellers; and (4) IT consulting firms. Furthermore, telecommunications deregulation, the advent of the Internet, wireless communications and other technological developments has resulted in even tighter coupling between the computer software business and the "computer services/consulting" sector.[49] Although determining boundaries in the traded software sector does not escape these problems, the focus on firms that are primarily producers of traded software for sale to a global market allows us to track a specific commodity. Disaggregating the software creation value of a consulting or computer services firm that has a general IT contract for a large organization would be difficult to discern as well as compare. However, tracking the contribution of the packaged software component from services such as installation, systems integration and maintenance is a more manageable task than disaggregating a customized solution. In addition, only firms that have a packaged software product are likely to penetrate the Asian software market to any significant degree. In fact, declining PC and client-server costs as well as Internet demand are the primary drivers behind the rapidly growing installed base of computers in developing Asia.

Notes

1. I would like to thank Vinod K. Aggarwal and Ed Fogarty for their comments.
2. Varian and Shapiro (1999); and Evans and Wurster (2000).
3. Indeed, some research indicates that tapping into local talent to create international production networks was the key to the success of the rebounding U.S. electronics industry; see Borrus (1997) and Ernst (1997).
4. I use "enterprise software" in the broadest sense, that is, software that is primarily intended for use by corporations. A more narrow definition would refer to specific software subcategories, such as ERP software, SCM software, and so on. See Chapter 1 by Aggarwal in this volume for a discussion of the theoretical framework for analyzing market and nonmarket strategies.
5. See Arthur (1989) and David (1993) for a discussion on network externalities.
6. Sato (1996).
7. Fransman (1990, 1995); Sato (1996); Cusumano (1991); Nakahara (1993); Baba et al. (1995).
8. Cusumano (1991, 1994).

9. Cusumano (1991).
10. Anchordouguy (2000).
11. But like their industrial giant peers, they have their own proprietary hardware with competing standards as well.
12. Fransman (1995); Kenney and Florida (1991); and Fruin (1993).
13. Furthermore, there are several methodological problems related to discerning general characteristics of the "software" industry. Today, virtually every corporation produces software and utilizes it to enhance productivity somewhere along the value chain. In order to talk at all about the "software industry," this chapter focuses on the companies whose major product is *traded* software for end-users with an emphasis on enterprise software for corporate use. In contrast to customized software designed and implemented for a specific user, traded software provides generalizable solutions (e.g., spreadsheets) for multiple types of end users. See Appendix 1.
14. Steinmueller (1996).
15. "Packaged software" generally refers to software sold in a shrink-wrapped box that offers general solutions to multiple end users. It is a subset of traded software, which includes complex enterprise products. However, "traded" is often used synonymously with the term "packaged." The OECD, the International Data Corporation (IDC), the U.S. Department of Commerce, the National Trade Development Bank, the European Commission, and many private consulting companies that specialize in IT collect data in both packaged and customized software. This does not imply that their categories are either identical or comparable without qualification.
16. Even the OECD and IDC are not in agreement as to what constitutes services, for example, systems integration.
17. The Economist Survey (1997).
18. The Economist Survey (1996, 1997).
19. Salomon Smith Barney (1999).
20. Dataquest (1997).
21. IDC (1998).
22. IDC (1997).
23. Globus and NTDB (1996).
24. Business Software Alliance (1995–2000).
25. Ibid.
26. Ibid.
27. Asia Pulse (2001).
28. See Anchordouguy (2000) for a nonmarket analysis of Japan's software industry development.
29. OPEC (1989); MITI (1991).
30. Aoki (1988); Gerlach (1987, 1992).
31. Cusumano (1991).
32. Gerlach (1992).
33. Flamm (1987); Borrus and Zysman (1998).
34. Flamm (1987, 1988).
35. OECD (1985).
36. Torrisi (1998), p. 91.
37. OECD (1997).
38. See Aggarwal, Chapter 1 in this volume for more detail.
39. Steinmueller et al. (1993) and Steinmueller (1996).
40. Legacy systems refer to obsolete systems still in use because of high replacement costs or prohibitive budgets.
41. Flamm (1987, 1988); Mowery (1996); Siwek and Fuchtgott-Roth (1993).
42. Cusumano (1991), Fransman (1995).
43. Anchordouguy (2000).
44. Mowery (1996) for an overview.
45. Mowery (1996).

46. However, given the increasing complexity of some packaged solutions intended for large firms or organizations, the need for related computer services is growing at a rate that by some estimates, exceeds that of the packaged market itself. See USDOC (1998).
47. Steinmuller (1996).
48. See footnote 14.
49. See footnote 15.

References

Aggarwal, Vinod K. (2001). "Integrated Market and Nonmarket Corporate Strategies in Asia." In *Winning in Asia, European Style,* ed. by Vinod K. Aggarwal (New York: Palgrave).

Anchordoguy, Marie (2000). "Japan's Software Industry: A Failure of Institutions?" *Research Policy,* March 29(3), pp. 391–408.

Anderson, Erin and Hubert Gatignon (1986). *The Multinational Corporation's Degree of Control Over Foreign Subsidiaries: An Empirical Test of a Transaction Cost Explanation.* (Cambridge, Mass.: Marketing Science Institute).

Aoki, Masahiko (1988). *Information, incentives, and bargaining in the Japanese Economy,* (New York: Cambridge University Press).

Arthur, W. Brian (1989). "Competing Technologies, Increasing Returns and Lock-in by Historical Events," *Economic Journal,* pp. 116-131.

Asia Pulse (2001). "Indian Economic Software Survey," Nationwide Financial News, 26 February, 2001.

Baba, Yasunori, Takai, Shinji and Mizuta, Yuji (1995). "The Japanese Software Industry: The "Hub Structure" Approach." *Research Policy* (May), 24(3), pp. 473–486.

Bandinelli, Salvatore, A. Fuggera, L. Lavazza, M. Loi, and G. Picco (1995). "Modeling and Improving an Industrial Software Process," IEEE Translation, *Software Engineering* 21(5), pp. 440–454.

Baron, David P. (2000). *Business and its Environment,* 3rd Edition. NJ: Prentice Hall.

Borrus, Michael (1997). *Left for Dead: Asian Production Networks and the revival of U.S. Electronics.* BRIE Working Paper No. 100.

Borrus, Michael and John Zysman (1998). *Globalization with Borders: The Rise of Wintelism as the Future of Industrial Competition.* BRIE Working Paper No. 96B.

Bresnahan, Timothy F. and Manuel Trajtenberg (1995). "General Purpose Technologies: Engines of Growth?" *Journal of Econometrics,* pp. 83–108.

Business Software Alliance (1995–2000). *World Software Piracy Report* (Washington, D.C.: BSA).

Cusumano, Michael A. and David B. Yoffie (1998). *Competing on Internet Time: Lessons From Netscape and its Battle with Microsoft* (New York: The Free Press).

Cusumano, Michael A. (1991). *Japan's Software Factories* (New York: Oxford University Press).

D'Aveni, Richard (1994). *Hypercompetition: Managing the Dynamics of Strategic Management* (New York: The Free Press).

Dataquest (1997). *Asia IT.*

David, Paul A. (1993). "Path-dependence and Predictability in Dynamic Systems with Local Network Externalities: A Paradigm for Historical Economics." In *Technology and the Wealth of Nations,* ed. by D. Foray and C. Freeman (London: Pinter Publishers).

Dedrick, Jason and Kenneth Kramer (1998). *Asia's Computer Challenge* (Oxford: Oxford University Press).

Economist, The (1996). "The Software Industry Survey." May 25, 1996.

Economist, The (1997). "Telecommunications Survey." September 13, 1997.

Ernst, Dieter (1997). *From Partial to Systemic Globalization: International Production Networks in the Electronics Industry.* BRIE Working Paper No. 98.

ESPRIT (1997). "Software Best Practices (ESSI)." at http://www.cordis.lu/espirit/src/essi.htm.
Evans, Philip and Thomas S. Wurster (2000). *Blown to Bits: How the New Economics of Information Transforms Strategy* (Boston, Mass.: Harvard Business School Press).
Flamm, Kenneth (1988). *Creating the Computer* (Washington, D.C.: The Brookings Institution).
Flamm, Kenneth (1987). *Targeting the Computer: Government Support and International Competition* (Washington, D.C.: Brookings Institution).
Fransman, Martin (1995). *Japan's Computer and Communications Industry: The Evolution of Industrial Giants and Global Competitiveness* (New York: Oxford University Press).
Fransman, Martin (1990). *The Market and Beyond: Cooperation and Competition in Information Technology Development in the Japanese System* (New York: Cambridge University Press).
Fruin, W. Mark (1992). *The Japanese Enterprise System: Competitive Strategies and Cooperative Structures* (Oxford University Press).
Gerlach, Michael (1992). *Alliance Capitalism: The Social Organization of Japanese Business.* (Berkeley: University of California Press).
Gerlach, Michael (1987). "Business alliances and the strategy of the Japanese firm," *California Management Review* 30(1) (Fall), pp. 126–142.
Gibbs, W. W. (1997) "Software's Chronic Crisis," *Scientific American (Int. Ed.)* 271(3), pp. 72–81.
GLOBUS and NTDB (1996). *China's Software Market.* ISA, 1 January 1996.
Gomes-Casseres, B. (1992). "International Trade, Competition, and Alliances in the Computer Industry." Working paper 92-044 (Boston: Division of Research, Harvard Business School Press).
Hoch, Detlev J. et al. (2000). *Secrets of Software Success* (Boston: Harvard Business School Press).
International Data Corporation (IDC) (1994). *Packaged Software 1993.* February 1, 1994.
IDC (2000). *Packaged Software 1999.* January 25, 2000.
IDC (1998). *IT Software/Services in Asia.* March 1, 1998.
IDC (1997). *China.* November 15, 1997.
International Planning and Research Corporation (2000). *1999 Global Piracy Report.* (Washington, D.C.: Business Software Alliance and Software and Information Industry).
Joly, Herbert, Jurgen Kluge, and Lothar Stein (1994). "Europe's Structural Weakness." *The McKinsey Quarterly* 1, pp. 33–38.
Kenney, Martin and Richard Florida (1993). *Beyond Mass production: The Japanese System and Its Transfer to the U.S.* (New York: Oxford University Press).
Malerba, Franco and Salvatore Torrisi (1996). "The Dynamics of Market Structure and Innovation in the Western European Software Industry." In *The International Computer Software Industry: A Comparative Study of Industry Evolution and Structure,* ed. David Mowery (Oxford: Oxford University Press).
Maxwell, Katrina, Van Wassenhove Luk, and Soumitra Dutta (1998). "Performance Evaluation of General and Company Specific Models in Software Development Effort Estimation." *Management Science,* 45(6), pp. 787–803.
Maeissner, Gerd (1997). *SAP—Die Hemiliche Software-Macht (SAP—The Secret Software Power)* (Hamburg, Germany: Hoffman and Campe).
McKinsey and Company (1996). *The 1996 Report on the Computer Industry* (New York: McKinsey and Company).
Miles, Raymond and Charles Snow (1986). "Organizations: New Concepts for New Forms." *California Management Review* 28(3) (Spring), pp. 62–73.
Moschella, David C. (1997). *Waves of Power.* (New York: Amacom).
Mowery, David (1996). *The International Computer Software Industry: A Comparative Study of Industry Evolution and Structure* (Oxford: Oxford University Press).
MSU-CIBER (1997). "Market Potential Indicators for Emerging Markets." October 17, 1997.

Nakahara, Tetsushi (1993). *The Industrial Organization and Information Structure of the Software Industry: A U.S.–Japan Comparison.* CEPR Publication No. 346 (Stanford, CA.: Center for Economic Policy Research, Stanford University).

National Research Council (1992). *Keeping the U.S. Computer Industry Competitive* (Washington, D.C.: National Academy Press).

OECD (1985). *The Software Industry* (Paris: OECD).

OECD (1997). *Information Technology* (Paris: OECD).

OECD (2000). *Information Technology Outlook 2000* (Paris: OECD).

Ovum Consultancy. *IT in the EU* (1997–1998).

Sato, Jun (1996). *A Breakthrough for the Japanese Software Industry?: Responsiveness to Users' Need is the Key.* JDB Research Report No. 61 (Tokyo, Japan: Japan Development Bank).

Saxenian, Annalee (1994). *Regional Advantage: Culture and Competition in Silicon Valley and Route 128* (Cambridge, Mass.: Harvard University Press).

Siwek, Stephen E. and Furchtgott-Roth, Harold W. (1993). *International Trade in Computer Software* (Westport, Conn.: Quorum Books).

Smith Solomon Barney (1999). "Forecasts 2000."

Snow, Charles, Jessica Lipnack, and Jeffrey Stamps (1999). "The Virtual Organization: Promises and Payoffs, Large and Small," *Journal of Organizational Behavior,* pp. 615–630.

Steinmueller, W. Edmund (1996). "The U.S. Software Industry: An Analysis and Interpretive History" In *The International Computer Software Industry: A Comparable Study of Industry Evolution and Structure,* ed. David Mowery (Oxford: Oxford University Press).

Steinmueller, W. Edward and Kang, Soong Moon (1993). *Applications of Modern Industrial Technology in Developing Nations: Government Policy and Its Consequences in Brazil* (Stanford, CA: Center for Economic Policy Research, Stanford University).

Teece, David (1986). "Capturing Value from Technological Innovation: integration, strategic partnering and licensing decisions." *International Business Working Paper* No. 1B-6 (Berkeley: University of California, Berkeley Business School).

Torrisi, Salvatore (1998). *Industrial Organization and Innovation: An International Study of the Software Industry* (Cheltenham, U.K.: Edward Elgar).

United States Department of Commerce (1998). *World Computer/IT Software/Services Best Markets Report,* November 13 (Washington, D.C.: Department of Commerce).

Varian, Hal R. and Carl Shapiro (1999). *Information Rules: A Strategic Guide to the Network Economy* (Boston: Harvard Business School Press).

Vernon, Raymond (1985). *Exploring the Global Economy: Emerging Issues in Trade and Investment* (Lanham, MD: University Press of America).

CHAPTER EIGHT

Short Circuiting Keiretsu: Japanese Electronic Firms in Asia

HIDETAKA YOSHIMATSU[1]

I. Introduction

Asia has become a major production base of electrical and electronic products. Not only has the electronics industry been a main engine of economic growth, but it has also served as the most important export sector in most East Asian countries. The growth of the electronics industry in the region has been sustained by the massive inflow of foreign direct investment (FDI). In the late 1960s and 1970s, most East Asian countries changed their basic industrialization policies from import-substitution to export-expansion, setting up export processing zones in which preferential measures were granted to export-oriented foreign multinational corporations (MNCs). Japanese electronics firms have been major investors and sustained the development of the electronics industry in East Asia by establishing meshed production networks and by systematically linking manufacturing plants in the region as a means of seeking an optimal international division of labor.

In the 1990s, the electronics industry in Asia has experienced crucial changes in technological development, industrial structure, and business forms, and Japanese electronics firms have been forced to reconsider their strategies responding to these changes. They have also faced challenges from other East Asian and western rival firms in the Asian markets. Several policy-induced market integration trends have also urged Japanese electronics firms to reconsider their manufacturing operations in East Asia. The Association of Southeast Asian Nations (ASEAN) countries have strengthened their commitments to market integration and liberalization in the 1990s by launching the ASEAN Free Trade Area (AFTA) and ASEAN Industrial Cooperation (AICO) programs, which has intensified intercorporate rivalry and induced the reorganization of production networks of Japanese electronics firms.

In this chapter, I will examine the strategies of the Japanese electronics industry in rapidly evolving Asian markets.[2] The second section considers locational environments of Japanese electronics firms in Asia from market and nonmarket perspectives. It identifies the major characteristics of the Japanese electronics industry, the advancement of Japanese electronics firms into Asia, and recent policy-oriented conditions. The third section investigates what corporate strategies Japanese electronics firms have adopted in order to secure their presence in Asia and respond to changing environments for their business operations. It examines Japanese electronics firms' market strategies to raise the efficiency of their operations in Asia. At the same time, it highlights their nonmarket strategies designed to strengthen their position in Asia by utilizing linkages with the Japanese government.

II. Positional Analysis

Market Environment and Firm Position

The electronics industry, in general, incorporates a wide variety of products: consumer electronic equipment, which covers audio–visual products and household electrical appliances; industrial electronic equipment, which includes radio communication systems, broadcasting equipment and applied electronic equipment; and electronic components, which includes electronic tubes, integrated circuits, and liquid crystal devices. The Japanese electronics industry has three prominent features. First, major Japanese electronics firms are vertically integrated, comprehensive producers engaging in various subsector businesses. While most electronic parts are manufactured by a number of firms, the assembly of major electronics products and the production of core electronic parts such as semiconductors and crystal devices are conducted by a few large firms. Major electronics firms have manufactured various products ranging from electrical appliances such as air conditioners and refrigerators to industrial electronic equipment including facsimiles, computers, and semiconductors. This corporate structure blurred the core business of firms and reduced the need for division of labor with other firms to some extent because they manufactured a wide range of core components for internal use.

Second, Japanese electronics firms have set up close relationships with subcontracting parts suppliers. Manufacturing of electronic products is divided into a number of stages using a multilayered subcontracting system.[3] Electronics producers, which manufacture a large portion of parts in-house, are less dependent on parts suppliers than auto producers. However, electronics assembly makers have set up a tight relationship with parts suppliers by encouraging them to organize supplier associations through which the assembly makers negotiate over various trade conditions and provide cooperative assistance. Moreover, the assembly makers and parts suppliers jointly undertake activities for quality improvement and cost reduction.

Third, Japanese electronics firms have had a tendency to follow similar corporate strategies, with a strong habit of following the crowd in the industry. They have tended to imitate successful products or manufacturing methods developed by competitors. These strategies have led to the production of similar items without distinctive sales points and a resultant pursuit for market share-enabling mass production. For instance, all major semiconductor producers in Japan, by and large, manufactured a wide range of products with an emphasis on dynamic random access memories (DRAMs).

The electronics industry spearheaded multinational production in Japanese industry. In the late 1960s and the 1970s, electronics producers made inroads into East Asian countries, especially in the newly industrialized economies (NIEs) (see Table 8.1). The aim of the relocation was to capture local markets protected by import barriers, but this was later superseded by an objective to establish export platforms for the markets

Table 8.1 Number of production bases of Japanese electronics firms in Asia

Period	NIEs	ASEAN4	China	Asia total	Europe	North America	World total
–1970	33	13	0	46	7	11	72
1971–75	51	12	0	66	10	12	97
1976–80	38	12	0	50	7	19	79
1981–85	8	12	7	30	19	22	74
1986–90	52	142	17	215	58	71	347
1991–95	24	94	201	329	24	33	389
1995–00	11	60	48	135	18	50	205
Total	217	345	273	871	143	218	1,263

Note: The ASEAN4 includes Thailand, Indonesia, Malaysia and the Philippines.
Source: EIAJ (2000, p. iv).

of developed countries. In the early 1980s, then, Japanese electronics producers increased their investments in North America and Europe. The aim of investment was to circumvent restraints of exports by antidumping and import quotas in these regions.

A sharp appreciation of the yen after the Plaza Agreement in September 1985 reduced the price competitiveness of Japanese electronic products. In addition, Japanese electronics firms faced other constraints in Japan such as increased wage costs and shortages of labor and land for plants. These factors encouraged Japanese manufacturing industries including electronics to expand foreign operations. The value of FDI in electrical machinery increased greatly from roughly $2.2 million in 1981–1985 to $16.6 million in 1986–1990. In the second half of the 1980s, Southeast Asia became the main location for FDI. The number of newly established production facilities in the ASEAN 4 increased from twelve in 1981–1985 to 142 in 1986–1990. Japanese electronics firms aimed to exploit cheap labor costs there for parts production and assembly processes that were rather labor-intensive.[4] In the 1990s, Japanese electronics firms focused on China as a manufacturing base with the number of newly established production bases in China increasing dramatically from seventeen in 1986–1990 to 201 in 1991–1995. In addition to China's allure as a potentially huge market for consumer electronic products, further market opening policies adopted after Deng Xiaoping's tour of the south in 1992 stimulated the advancement for Japanese electronics firms into China.

In 1997, the overseas production ratio of Japanese electronic machinery was 21.6 percent. Although this figure was below 26.0 percent of the United States' and 28.3 percent of Germany's in 1996, it was far higher than the 12.4 percent average of Japanese manufacturers as a whole.[5] Some Japanese electronics firms have been deeply involved in the local economies. For instance, in 1999, the Matsushita group had nineteen local subsidiaries, including fourteen production plants and two research and development (R&D) facilities in Malaysia. These companies, with twenty-nine thousand workers, exported some 70 percent of total products, creating 3 percent of total exports of the country.[6]

Importantly, relocations of assembly manufacturers have often been accompanied by those of subcontracting small and medium-scale enterprises (SMEs). Based on close linkages in domestic production, the subcontracting suppliers followed core firms in overseas operations. When assembly manufacturers faced a need to increase local supply for reducing production costs or to respond to the local government's demand for higher localization, they often encouraged relevant subcontracting SMEs to begin local production. According to survey data from Japan's Ministry of International Trade and Industry (MITI, which, in 2001 became the Ministry of Economy, Trade, and Industry, METI), the number of overseas subsidiaries of Japanese electronics firms was 12.3 for large-scale firms and 2.0 for SMEs in 1995 (MITI, 1998: 75, 104). By contrast, SMEs have compensated for their size-related disadvantages by allocating a higher proportion of their investment to Asia.[7] Although the number of FDI cases by SMEs in electronics alone is not available, total number of FDI cases in machinery sectors was 403 in 1991–1995, the 295 or 73.2 percent of which were directed toward Asia.[8] In FDI cases in three machinery sectors (general, electric, and transport machinery), Asia accounted for 60.3 percent (1,319 out of 2,187) out of the total in 1991–1995.[9]

Enhanced offshore operations also increased reverse imports of consumer electric products. According to MITI's survey data, the share of exports to Japan by subsidiaries of Japanese electronics firms in Asia in total sales increased steadily from 22.2 percent in fiscal year 1986 to 27.2 percent in FY 1992 and to 33.0 percent in FY 1998 (see Table 8.2).[10] In particular, a rise in exports by subsidiaries in the ASEAN4 is salient: from 7.4 percent to 27.7 percent to 41.9 percent during the same period. This propensity stemmed from the strength of the ASEAN4 as major production bases of consumer electronic products. A sharp rise in reverse imports can be confirmed in each product. According to data by the Electric Industries Association of Japan (EIAJ), imports of consumer electronic products increased by 3.6 times from ¥113 billion in 1990 to ¥404 billion yen in 1997. In particular, imports of color TVs and VCR's increased from ¥23 billion to ¥148 billion and ¥7.5 billion to ¥71 billion respectively in the same period.[11] The Japanese electronics industry has imported more color TVs and VCRs than it exported since 1990 and 1993, respectively.

Table 8.2 Sales destination of subsidiaries of Japanese electronics firms in Asia, 1986–1998 (percent)

	NIEs			ASEAN4			Asia	
	1992	1998	1986	1992	1998	1986	1992	1998
Local	52.2	44.2	43.0	38.4	17.2	42.5	45.7	32.3
Asia	16.3	18.4	33.6	20.6	28.3	15.2	17.7	24.8
Japan	24.7	28.9	7.4	27.7	41.9	22.2	27.2	33.0
Others	6.8	8.5	16.0	13.3	12.6	20.1	13.5	9.9

Note: The ASEAN4 includes Thailand, Indonesia, Malaysia and the Philippines.
Source: MITI (1989, 1994, 2001).

In the 1990s, there were three critical changes surrounding Japanese electronics firms in Asia. The first was increased competitive pressure against Japanese electronics firms. While Japanese firms still dominate the consumer electronic product markets in Asia, South Korean firms have gradually caught up with their Japanese rivals. While South Korean firms were manufacturers of low value-added, niche products until the early 1990s, they enhanced their competitiveness, entering relatively high-value added markets by the late 1990s. For instance, South Korean firms raised their presence in the semiconductor industry: between 1991 and 1998, the South Korean semiconductor production grew from near 0 to 11 percent of the world total, while that of Japan declined from 39 percent to 22 percent in the same period.[12]

The second change is the increasing importance of information technology (IT) in the electronics industry. The worldwide expansion of computer-based information exchanges has created increasing demand for IT equipment and parts. For instance, worldwide personal computer shipments increased from 21.9 million units in 1989 to 114.1 million units in 1999.[13] This expansion has had a crucial impact on the Asian electronics industry, a major supply base of electronics and electrical products and parts. Local firms in NIEs have developed as the major producers of IT related products. Taiwan has emerged as the world's primary production base of major information hardware. In 1998, Taiwan producers accounted for a substantial share of PCs and their peripherals: 40 percent of notebook PCs, 58 percent of monitors, 61 percent of motherboards, and 84 percent of scanners.[14] Computer producers in developed countries have expanded their procurement from Taiwanese firms under original equipment manufacturing (OEM) contracts. IT equipment has accounted for a growing share of the output of the electronics industry even in the ASEAN countries, decreasing the importance of consumer electronic products. Moreover, IT equipment has come to account for nearly 30 percent of total production in the electronics industry in the Philippines and more than 50 percent in Thailand.[15]

The third change is a rising influence of electronics manufacturing services (EMS) firms. The EMS firms that developed from the OEM manufacturers engage in design and logistic management as well as manufacturing. Under growing trends toward outsourcing of electronic manufacturing services, the EMS industry has attained 28 percent and 30 percent of annual growth in 1998 and 1999 respectively, and is expected to maintain this high growth trend.[16] Financially strong EMS firms such as U.S.-based Solectron and Canada-based Celestica have aggressively advanced into East Asia, where they can obtain relatively cheap labor and low manufacturing overhead. In 2000, Solectron purchased Singapore-based NatSteel Electronics, the world's six largest EMS firms, and two Sony plants based in Japan and Taiwan. The effective utilization of EMS firms becomes crucial for existing electronics firms to reduce the risk of investment. At the same time, the growing importance of EMS companies has forced Japanese electronics firms to reconsider their core competence; Japanese firms are forced to shift their business focus from the traditionally strong manufacturing area to other areas such as design, product development, and marketing.

Nonmarket Environment

While advances by Japanese electronics firms in North America and Europe were encouraged by political factors (trade frictions), market factors were the major reasons why Japanese electronics firms advanced into and shifted their operations in East Asia. At the same time, some political concerns qualified operations of Japanese electronics firms in Asia. In the early 1960s, East Asian countries adopted import-substitution policies and imposed high tariffs on imported products. Japanese electronics producers shifted their strategies from exports to local production in order to secure the local markets that they exploited through exports. Then, the local governments implemented export-oriented policies. In 1965, Taiwan set up the first export-processing zone. Singapore and South Korea adopted a similar policy in 1970, followed by Malaysia and the Philippines. In these zones, foreign MNCs were allowed to enjoy higher ownership shares and were exempted from duties on imported intermediate inputs and materials. These policies at first encouraged U.S. semiconductor producers to make inroads into Taiwan, Malaysia, and the Philippines, and then Japanese electronics firms established production plants responding to these policy changes. Products manufactured in these export-processing zones were exported to world markets.

In the 1990s, the Southeast Asian governments intensified market liberalization policies. In January 1992, the ASEAN states declared at the Fourth Summit in Singapore that they would establish AFTA by the year 2008. Under the Common Effective Preferential Tariff (CEPT) scheme, the main mechanism for reaching AFTA, existing tariff rates would be 0 to 5 percent and quantitative restrictions and other nontariff barriers would be eliminated. This initiative derived from various factors including the search for a new rationale for ASEAN, the growth of regionalism in the world, and fear of investment diversion to China.[17]

The ASEAN members also envisioned the promotion of industrial complementation in the region. In October 1988, the ASEAN governments adopted the Brand-to-Brand Complementation (BBC) agreement.[18] While the scheme had problems (such as the nonparticipation of Indonesia), it worked relatively well, especially compared with the ASEAN Industrial Complementation (AIC) plan adopted in 1981. Nevertheless, its narrow focus on the automobile industry invited criticism. While some manufacturing industries asked why the automobile industry alone should enjoy preferential benefits, some local officials considered the scheme to help privilege Japanese auto MNCs while giving few or no benefits to local companies.

The introduction of a new industrial cooperation scheme was agreed in September 1995, and the Basic Agreement on the ASEAN Industrial Cooperation (AICO) plan was signed in April 1996. The scheme is open to any ASEAN-brand company that has a minimum 30 percent ASEAN national equity and is willing to undertake resource pooling, industrial complementation, or other industrial cooperation activities. The AICO-approved products obtain a preferential tariff rate in the range of 0 to 5 percent, local content accreditation, and other nontariff incentives.

The AICO scheme had an aspect of the advanced implementation of the CEPT agreement. The AICO was expected to provide significant benefits for electronics firms because they could enjoy immediate tariff reductions that would be granted in the CEPT. When AICO was introduced, most ASEAN governments maintained relatively high import tariffs in major consumer electronic products: Malaysia and the Philippines imposed 30 percent tariffs on imports of air conditioners and parts; Thailand imposed 45 percent duties on imports of washing machines, air conditioners and their parts (see Table 8.3). Electronics producers would immediately enjoy 0 to 5 percent tariffs instead of these high tariffs when

Table 8.3 Import tariffs of major electronic products in Southeast Asia (percent)

Production item	Category	Indonesia	Malaysia	Philippines	Thailand	Singapore
Color TVs	final product	25	40	30	30	0
	part	0–15	25	20	20–30	0
Refrigerators	final product	20	25	30	45	0
	part	0–15	25	10	25	0
Washing machines	final product	20	25	30	45	0
	part	0–15	25	10	45	0
Air-conditioners	final product	5	30	30	45	0
	part	5	30	30	45	0

Note: The rates are as of December 1996.
Source: Noda (1999, p. 125).

they could get an AICO approval. As explained below, Japanese electronics firms could not utilize the scheme effectively because of strict restraints on its application and the diverse stance of the ASEAN governments.

III. Strategic and Tactical Analysis

Market and Organizational Strategies and Tactics

Japanese electronics firms have developed their overseas strategies in Asia by responding to market conditions and policies adopted by the local governments. In the 1960s, Japanese electronics firms began local production, responding to import-substitution policies in major East Asian countries. In advancing into these countries, they selected joint ventures with local partners both because local governments imposed regulations on foreign ownership and because they needed to secure sales channels in the local markets. In the 1980s, Japanese electronics firms established manufacturing plants in East Asia mainly designed to export products to third markets, and held 100 percent ownership in most cases.

As the case of FDI shows, overseas operations of Japanese manufacturing firms (including electronics) were responses to external factors such as import-substitution policies and trade friction. In particular, the sharp appreciation of the yen after 1985 forced Japanese electronics firms to accelerate overseas operations rather quickly. They went multinational passively, without envisioning global management, in which they could have discovered business opportunities from a global perspective and utilized local management resources more effectively.[19] As a consequence, Japanese electronics firms adopted closed production strategies with low-level localization in terms of procurement, technology transfer, management, and personnel.

Japanese electronics firms relied on imports of capital goods and intermediate inputs from Japan. As a consequence, trade imbalances between Japan and East Asia increased substantially as local manufacturing of final products expanded. Between 1985 and 1995, the aggregate trade deficits of the NIEs with Japan grew from $5.5 billion to $25.9 billion in all electronic products and from $1.3 billion to $13.8 billion in electronic parts (see Table 8.4). A similar tendency is seen in the ASEAN4. Furthermore, because subcontracting parts suppliers followed their core firms, procurement from local markets was heavily dependent on Japanese-affiliated suppliers.

Japanese electronics firms were also reluctant to transfer high value-added activities to their subsidiaries in Asia. According to MITI's survey data, the ratio of R&D in total sales in subsidiaries of Japanese electronics

Table 8.4 Asia's trade balances with Japan in electronic products ($million)

Asia	Category	1985		1995		Trade balances	
		Exports	Imports	Exports	Imports		
NIEs	Electronics total	1,051	6,537	16,692	42,544	−5,486	−25,852
	Electric parts	350	1,601	5,685	19,453	−1,251	−13,768
ASEAN4	Electronics total	197	1,326	6,587	14,195	−1,129	−7,608
	Electric parts	174	256	1,688	6,256	−82	−4,568

Source: Takayasu, Toyama and Mori (1997, p. 27).

firms was 0.4 percent in Asia compared with 2.0 percent in North America and 2.3 percent in Europe in 1996. The expenditure for R&D per firm was ¥25 million in Asia compared with ¥196 million in North America and ¥332 million in Europe.[20] Furthermore, Japanese firms had low-level representation of local staff in managerial positions.[21] This propensity stemmed from various factors including language barriers and the replication of Japanese business practices such as lifetime employment and seniority-based promotion.

Japanese electronics firms gradually changed the closed production and procurement system after the mid-1990s in major areas. They have pursued more efficient and systematic procurement strategies, increasing procurement from Asian firms. As rival companies from Asia emerged as the major manufacturers of consumer electronic products, price competition became intense. For instance, prices of VCRs and air conditioners dropped by roughly 50 percent and 40 percent respectively between 1990 and 1998 in terms of the domestic wholesale price index in Japan.[22] Japanese electronics firms were forced to abandon the pursuit of perfection in products and to utilize Asian intermediate products with a certain quality level.

In order to expand procurement from local and Asian companies, major electronics firms have established international procurement offices (IPOs) in Singapore, Hong Kong, and Taiwan.[23] Some firms have strengthened the function of these IPOs and introduced new systems and institutions to achieve the central control of procurement information and expand procurement volume in each office. For instance, Matsushita established Asian procurement information networks in order to control information about parts and materials used in manufacturing plants in Asia.[24] The integrated control of this information led to the standardization of common parts used for different products and significant cost reductions. In June 1998, Sharp set up an inspection center for parts procured in the ASEAN region in Malaysia to increase efficiency in local procurement.[25]

Table 8.5 Procurement of subsidiaries of Japanese electronics firm in Asia, 1986–1998 (percent)

	NIES		ASEAN4			Asia		
	1992	1998	1986	1992	1998	1986	1992	1998
Local	34.3	37.2	31.1	39.7	35.8	36.4	36.6	35.7
Asia	15.9	20.5	13.4	15.9	29.2	8.2	15.2	26.4
Japan	48.7	41.8	55.3	42.1	33.8	54.6	46.7	37.0
Others	1.1	0.5	0.2	2.2	1.2	0.8	1.5	0.9

Note: The ASEAN4 includes Thailand, Indonesia, Malaysia, and the Philippines.
Source: MITI (1989, 1994, 2001).

Less dependence on imports from Japan and more reliance on sourcing from Asia are shown by MITI's survey data. According to data on procurement sources of Japanese subsidiaries in Asia in electrical machinery, procurement from Japan declined from 54.6 percent in FY 1986 to 46.7 percent in FY 1992 and to 37.0 percent in FY 1998 (see Table 8.5). Although MITI's data did not show a rise in local procurement, another survey by the Japan Bank for International Cooperation does show this trend. According to this data, local procurement of electrical and electronics assembly manufacturers in ASEAN countries rose from 31.0 percent in 1990 to 42.9 percent in 1994 to 58.7 percent in 1998.[26]

Some Japanese electronics firms have increased outsourcing from producers in the NIEs in the semiconductor and computer fields. Given the increasing need to maintain the optimal production scale in response to fluctuations in market demand, and to concentrate management resources on their core business by compensating product lines, it has become increasingly important to divide manufacturing operations and allocate some processes or products to newly emerging East Asian firms. For instance, major Japanese electronics firms transferred the production technology of liquid crystal displays (LCDs). In 1999, Sharp set up a joint venture with Quanta Computer to produce LCDs used for flat PCs and procured them from this company. This strategy aimed at reducing investment burdens and concentrating capital and human resources on the development of next-generation LCDs. Other Japanese electronics firms also forged alliances with Taiwanese firms and transferred the technology of LCDs.

Increased linkages with Asian firms led to the expansion of imports of IT-related products. Imports of integrated circuits, data processing devices, memory devices, and input/output devices increased dramatically between 1995 and 2000 (see Table 8.6). In 2000, more than half of these imports came from Asia. Table 8.5 shows that subsidiaries of Japanese

Table 8.6 Imports of major electrical/electronic products in Japan (100 million yen)

Ranking in 2000	Imported items	Import value 2000	Import value 1995	Increase rate (percent)
1	Integrated circuits	19,296	10,215	89
2	Line electrical apparatuses	5,127	1,609	219
3	Electrical machines	3,086	1,583	95
4	Transformers/converters	2,611	1,339	95
5	Insulated electric conductors	2,227	987	126
6	Television receivers	1,947	1,306	49
7	Switching apparatuses	1,821	992	84
8	Parts for reception apparatuses	1,767	948	86
9	Diodes, transistors, etc.	1,745	904	93
10	Radio reception apparatuses	1,395	1,028	36

Source: The author compiled data from Japan Tariff Association, *Japan Exports and Imports: Commodity by Country*.

electronics firms in Asia increased procurement from other Asian countries: from 8.2 percent in FY 1986 to 15.2 percent in FY 1992 and to 25.1 percent in FY 1997. This trend means that the subsidiaries also increased procurement from Asian firms.

Increased commitments to local production are seen in R&D activities. Reliance on parent firms in Japan for R&D activities put Asian subsidiaries in a defensive position in competition. While the main categories of consumer electronic goods gradually shifted from conventional products such as color TVs and VCRs to more high value-added DVD players and digital TVs, competitive pressure from South Korean producers intensified even in the category of high valued-added products. Japanese electronics firms had to transfer production of even newly developed products to Southeast Asia in order to respond to these changes. Yet, reliance on Japan for R&D impeded the development of locally oriented products with price competitiveness and the reduction of lead-time for development.

Japanese electronics firms have gradually given more emphasis to high value-added activities in local markets, establishing R&D facilities in Asia. According to EIAJ data, in 1994, the number of R&D facilities of Japanese electronics firms was thirty-three in Asia compared with twenty-four in Europe and fifty in the United States, although the number of production bases was 626, 120, and 158, respectively. Yet, the number of R&D facilities in Asia increased to fifty-four by 2000 (see Table 8.7). In 1998, Matsushita and Mitsubishi Electric established an R&D center for air conditioners in Malaysia and Thailand, respectively. JVC, Sanyo Electric,

Table 8.7 The number of R & D facilities of Japanese electronics firms by region

	Asia	Europe	North America
1994	33	24	50
	(626)	(120)	(158)
2000	54	37	79

Note: The figures in parentheses are the number of production bases.
Source: EIAJ (2000, p. iv, xii).

and Sharp also transferred or strengthened design capabilities for audio-visual equipment in local subsidiaries in Southeast Asia.[27] The strength of design capabilities has contributed to a higher localization and cost reduction by increasing the use of parts locally available. The production of relatively high valued-added products also became salient. In late 1996, Sony transferred the production of minidisk (MD) component players to Malaysia. This strategy was peculiar because MD component players were one of a few production items in which Japanese electronics firms could retain competitiveness even in domestic production. However, Sony pursued a localization strategy of high value-added products.[28]

Thus, Japanese electronics firms have intensified strategies to promote locally/regionally-oriented production and procurement, becoming more like U.S. firms. However, a crucial factor in the direction of change is the speed of change. Japanese electronics firms may be altering their strategies too slowly given rapidly changing environments in the regional electronics industry. Major U.S. electronics firms actively concentrated on core competence, and forged linkages with OEM and EMS firms in Asia. But, their Japanese counterparts seem to find difficulty in breaking with the mindset of comprehensive producers.

This is particularly true in semiconductor production. For the past decade, U.S., South Korean, and Taiwanese semiconductor companies intensified specialization in production items or production processes. The major U.S. producers concentrated their resources on specific product categories: Micron specializing in DRAMs; Texas Instruments in digital signal processors (DSPs); and Intel in microprocessor units (MPUs).[29] While South Korean producers concentrated on DRAM production, Taiwanese producers were engaged in foundry operations. In contrast, Japanese semiconductor producers have undertaken the whole process of the semiconductor business from design, production, and inspection of a wide range of products. It was not until the late 1990s that major semiconductor producers, including Toshiba, Fujitsu, and Mitsubishi Electric, looked to the selection and concentration strategy by intensifying the outsourcing of standardized DRAMs from Taiwanese foundry companies.

The formation of AFTA means drastic reductions of tariffs and resultant competition even within the same corporate group. Some Japanese electronics producers were forced to restructure operations in Southeast Asia, responding to market liberalization and integration. The restructuring efforts were particularly serious for firms that advanced into Asia at the earlier time. A typical example is Matsushita, which spearheaded overseas operations among Japanese electronics firms by establishing a TV plant in Thailand in 1961. Matsushita began to reorganize its operations in Southeast Asia in the mid-1990s. This consumer electronic giant established mini-Matsushita in major Southeast Asian countries and Taiwan in the 1960s and 1970s in order to secure local markets that were protected with high tariffs. The mini-Matsushita manufactured a wide range of products such as radios, electric fans, rice cookers, TV sets, and so on, with extremely little production volume. For instance, its Malaysian subsidiary manufactured 1.8 billion units of air conditioners annually, while production volume at A. P. National in Thailand, one of the mini-Matsushitas, was only ten thousand units.[30] Despite small production lots, mini-Matsushita could make profits in the local markets protected with high import tariffs.

However, given a likely intensified competition as a result of market liberalization, Matsushita was forced to revitalize operations of mini-Matsushita by selecting production items and consolidating production. Matsushita began the Business Process Reengineering project in order to investigate the restructuring of mini-Matsushita in the headquarters in Osaka and local subsidiaries collaboratively.[31] Matsushita implemented a series of restructuring: in 1995, Matsushita Electric Philippines (MEPCO) transferred production of electronic parts to imports from Malaysia and China; in September 1996, A. P. National in Thailand transferred the production of air conditioners to imports from Malaysia; and in 1997, Taiwan Matsushita suspended the production of compressors for air conditioners, transferring imports from Malaysia. At the same time, some mini-Matsushitas were divided into independent companies manufacturing particular products. Between 1996 and 1998, National Thai spun off eight of its corporate divisions into independent companies. These companies were integrated into the overseas strategies of relevant divisions and group companies in Japan. This spinoff strategy aimed to enable each company to benefit from economies of scale and from ASEAN's commitments to tariff cuts.[32]

Some Japanese electronics firms sought to utilize AICO as a means to promote restructuring programs in Asia. Matsushita began to investigate the possibility of using the AICO scheme for transactions of electric fan parts in ASEAN in June 1996. Matsushita became one of the first applicants of the scheme in December 1996, submitting a proposal in which MEPCO would exchange fan parts with its sister companies in Indonesia, Malaysia, and Thailand. In November 1996, Toshiba also set up a project team to investigate the possibility of utilizing AICO for transactions of color TVs and refrigerators in the ASEAN region. However, the AICO plan was ineffective for them. Matsushita had to wait for more than two years to get an AICO approval because of the diverse stances of the national governments. While the Thai and Indonesian governments issued an approval within half a year, the Malaysian and Philippine governments did not accept the applications for more than one year.[33] Toshiba did not proceed with the AICO procedure because it failed to meet the 30 percent national equity condition. Eight out of fourteen manufacturing plants operated in the five ASEAN countries did not meet this criterion.[34]

Nonmarket Strategies

Which nonmarket strategies did Japanese electronics firms adopt when advancing into Asia? Some Japanese electronics firms were forced to adopt nonmarket strategies designed to secure market integration policies favorable to them. Matsushita's commitments to the AICO scheme present an example. As already explained, Matsushita became one of the first applicants to the AICO scheme, but it faced great difficulty in obtaining approval. When Matsushita submitted a proposal, five local firms in the Philippines strongly opposed it. The Philippine Board of Investment (BOI) denied Matsushita's proposal at first on the grounds that its project would jeopardize the interest of domestic manufacturers. The BOI was also anxious about trade deficits because MEPCO, a Matsushita subsidiary in the Philippines, would import $715,000 from the three countries while exporting $374,000.[35] In order to mitigate this opposition, Matsushita held public hearings several times and eventually won over the Philippine Electronic Fan Association. Matsushita proposed fostering local parts suppliers and rectifying trade imbalances within the Matsushita group. Although the benefits of tariff reduction applied to transactions of fan parts were ¥30 million annually, Matsushita was serious in this because it intended to expand the scope of AICO to more important products.[36]

In the 1990s, Japanese electronics firms have pursued the formation of institutional linkages with relevant industries in Asia as a main nonmarket strategy. The Japan Electrical Manufacturers' Association (JEMA) and EIAJ, the two main industrial associations of Japanese electronics firms, have strengthened consultation networks with their ASEAN counterparts. In July 1997, JEMA and EIAJ began the "Business Dialogue" and held five meetings through 2000. At these meetings, representatives from the Japanese and Southeast Asian associations have exchanged information about demand forecasts of consumer electronic goods, human resources development, and supporting industries. The dialogue was expected to combine the interest of the companies concerned and help to resolve common industrial problems in Southeast Asia.

The dialogue aimed at helping the electronics industries in Southeast Asia form the *gyokai* system.[37] In Japan, the *gyokai* system has functioned as a liaison body to coordinate interests and resolve common problems among companies in the industry. The system has also worked as a counterbody in the private sector to the bureaus and sections of administrative agencies concerned, and contributed to efficient policy by reducing asymmetry in information sharing between the public and private sectors.[38]

The initiation and development of the Business Dialogue have been sustained by commitments of the Japanese government. In November 1991, the ASEAN Economic Ministers and the Ministry of International Trade and Industry decided to institutionalize dialogue, and the first ASEAN Economic Ministers and the Ministry of International Trade and Industry of Japan (AEM–MITI) meeting was held in Manila in October 1992. While AEM had functioned as a forum to discuss tariff rates and trade issues, AEM–MITI highlighted broader issues including investment, industrial development, and the integration of Southeast Asia.[39] For instance, AEM–MITI issued a report in 1993 entitled *Prospects and Challenges for the Upgrading of Industries in the ASEAN Region*.

In September 1994, AEM–MITI established the Working Group on Economic Cooperation in Cambodia, Laos, and Myanmar (CLM-WG) to sustain industrial development in Indochina and Myanmar.[40] In August 1995, the CLM–WG issued a report on industrial cooperation in seven areas, including the promotion of transition to market economies, policy review on trade and investment, and the development of mineral resources. The report also recommended the establishment of expert groups in seven sectors, including consumer electronics. In the consumer electronics sector, the ASEAN10 Consumer Electronics Expert Group was organized. The group, comprised of government officials and private representatives from the electronics industry held its first meeting in January 1996 in Bangkok and has organized a meeting twice a year. The group provided opportunities to discuss common problems in Southeast

Asia and possible measures to promote industrial cooperation between the old and new ASEAN members. At the same time, the group has functioned as a place in which the Japanese government and industry communicated their interests in and demands on ASEAN policies. For instance, the Japanese side stressed the importance of transparent administration of the AICO at the several group meetings.[41]

Importantly, the expert group encouraged private representatives from the electronics industry to establish the Business Dialogue. The operations of the dialogue and group were highly coordinated. The dialogue meetings have been organized when the group meetings were held. The costs for inviting private representatives to the dialogue meetings were paid by the Japanese government.

Another public commitment that has sustained the Business Dialogue was provided by JETRO, a MITI-affiliated organization for overseas activities. In 1996, JETRO began the Asian Industrial Network Program. This program has supported the promotion of industrial linkages between Japan and other East Asian countries through the dispatch of industrial specialists, the holding of seminars, and the development of databases regarding parts provision and procurement. Significantly, one of the main objectives of the program was to help local industries to formulate *gyokai* and vitalize *gyokai* activities. For this objective, JETRO invited key *gyokai* participants to seminars and conferences, and sent Japanese experts who had know-how and experience on *gyokai* activities to Asia. Between 1996 and 2000, JETRO organized the industrial exchange conference targeting the electronics industry six times, inviting a total of sixty-four representatives from the electronics industry in Southeast Asia to these conferences.[42] EIAJ and JEMA have been involved in the industrial exchange conference as the cosponsors, and interindustry meetings between Japanese and ASEAN electronics industry have been organized during the conference.

There are two distinctive features in the ASEAN Consumer Electronics Expert Group and the Business Dialogue. First, they reflect particular institutional settings developed in Japan. As already explained, the Japanese government and industry have formulated the *gyokai* system as a private-sector counterpart of administration in each industry. The government and the industry have also utilized sector-specific advisory councils as a means of formulating basic guidelines for policies and authorizing them. They seek to duplicate these systems in East Asia by developing the Business Dialogue (the *gyokai* system) and the ASEAN10 Consumer Electronics Expert Group (the advisory council system).

Second, the group and dialogue reflected the evolving character of the Japanese commitment to industrial development in East Asia. Previously, the Japanese government and firms provided assistance and cooperation on a by country or by company basis. However, this kind of commitment became less effective in promoting the regional integration and helping the regionwide restructuring of Japanese firms. Accordingly, the new commitment aimed to upgrade the overall industrial bases in the ASEAN region through the formation of the *gyokai* system and the coordination of the interests of the regionwide industries. This direction of activities was consonant with the strategies of Japanese electronics firms to promote regional integration and restructuring.

IV. Conclusion

In this study, I have examined market and nonmarket environments where Japanese electronics firms are located in Asia and their strategies to respond to changes in them. Japanese electronics firms have established a solid status in East Asia as a consequence of massive outflows of investment after the mid-1980s. Factors such as the exploitation of low-cost production sites in Asia and tight relationships with Japanese subcontracting suppliers led Japanese electronics firms to set up the closed production system with low-level localization in terms of procurement, R&D, and management.

In the late 1990s, the development and challenges of other Asian firms forced Japanese firms to promote more locally and regionally oriented market strategies. They increased sourcing from Asian firms in order to promote a more efficient division of labor. They also strengthened R&D capabilities at local subsidiaries in order to produce more locally oriented competitive products. Thus, Japanese electronics firms surely departed from the conventional Japan-centered production system, although whether the speed of change was swift enough to respond to rapidly changing business environments remains unclear.

Significantly, changes in nonmarket environments urged Japanese electronics firms to restructure their production networks in Asia. Responding to the likely formation of the AFTA, some Japanese electronics firms implemented the restructuring of existing production units to raise production efficiency. They sought to utilize the AICO scheme in order to facilitate their restructuring efforts.

In nonmarket strategies, Japanese electronics firms strove to strengthen institutional networks with the Asian electronics industries. Their industrial associations began the Business Dialogue with their counterparts in Southeast Asia in 1997 to discuss issues and problems regarding the electronics industry in Southeast Asia. This private initiative has been sustained by public activities such as the ASEAN 10 Consumer Electronics Expert Group and JETRO's Asian Industrial Network Program. Japanese electronics firms adopted U.S.-style corporate strategies, intensifying the integration of Asian capabilities with their production at the individual firm level. At the same time, they sought to transplant key features in the Japanese-style institution-building represented by the *gyokai* system and close linkages between the public and private sectors.

Notes

1. I would like to thank Professor Aggarwal, Professor Urata, and the entire BASC staff for comments on previous versions of this chapter.
2. For analysis of other sectors, see other chapters of this volume, all of which are based on the theoretical framework developed in Chapter 1, by Vinod Aggarwal, in this volume.
3. Ito and Shibata (1995), pp. 190–193.
4. Even in 1993, the labor costs of Thailand and the Philippines were less than one twentieth of those of Japan. The labor cost per hour in the manufacturing sector was $16.91 in Japan compared to $0.71 in Thailand and $0.68 in the Philippines. See Milelli (1997), p. 199.
5. MITI (2000), p. 42.
6. Denshi, October 1999, p. 31.
7. Ernst (2000), p. 91.
8. Urata and Kawai (2000), pp. 86–87.
9. MITI (1998), pp. 703, 706.
10. These data, collected by MITI, are not necessarily suitable for comparison between years because the number of companies surveyed is different from year to year. Nonetheless, it is useful to know the general trend.
11. EIAJ (1998), p. 137.
12. Amano (1999), p. 24.
13. Daiwa Institute of Research (2000), p. 99.
14. Koryu Kyokai (2000), p. 13.
15. Takeuchi (2001), p. 40.
16. Daiwa Institute of Research (2000), p. 51.
17. Ravenhill (1995).
18. The BBC scheme allowed an approved auto part to enjoy a minimum of 50 percent margin of tariff preference and local content accreditation if it was a component for the manufacture of any product in the participating countries.
19. Yoshihara (1997), p. 270.
20. MITI (1998), p. 365.
21. Ravenhill (1999), pp. 265–266.
22. Noda (2000), p. 125.
23. JMTCI (2000: 85)
24. Nikkei Sangyo Shimbun, 27 March 1998.
25. Uchihori (1999), p. 16.
26. Noda (2000), p. 135.
27. Noda (2000), pp. 128–129.
28. Nihon Keizai Shimbun, 14 Feb 1997.
29. Amano (1999), p. 10.
30. Ikemoto (1999), p. 107.
31. Denshi, October 1999, p. 33.

32. Nation, 8 August 1998.
33. Sudo (1999), p. 111.
34. Noda (1999), p. 127.
35. News Net Asia, 14 November 1997.
36. JETRO (1998), pp. 33, 53.
37. *Gyokai* normally means a formal industrial association that represents the interests of a specific industrial sector. However, the definition of *gyokai* as aggregate entities that fall in the particular sector including firms, industrial association, and leading business leaders captures real functions of *gyokai*. See Sone (1993), p. 300.
38. Yonekura (1993).
39. Otsuji (2000), p. 335.
40. The CLM—WG began under the leadership of Japan and Thailand, countries with strong interests in Indochina and Myanmar. In December 1997, the CLM—WG was transformed into the AEM—MITI Economic and Industrial Cooperation Committee in order to extend Japan's industrial cooperation to the developed ASEAN members.
41. Denki, May 1997, p. 16.
42. These were held in Singapore in October 1996, Kuala Lumpur in August 1997, Tokyo and Osaka in April 1998, Singapore in October 1998, Shanghai in November 1999, and Singapore in September 2000.

References

Amano, Kyoko (1999). "Corporate Strategies in the Japanese Semiconductor Industry," *Nihon Kaihatsu Ginko Chosa* 259, pp. 2–72.

Daiwa Institute of Research (2000). *Asian Electronic Systems Manufacturers* (Singapore: Daiwa Institute of Research).

EIAJ (1998). *EIAJ Half-Centennial* (Tokyo: EIAJ).

EIAJ (2000). *The List of Overseas Subsidiaries, 2000* (Tokyo: EIAJ).

Ernst, Dieter (2000). "Evolutionary Aspects: The Asian Production Networks of Japanese Electronics Firms." In *International Production Networks in Asia: Rivalry or Riches?*, ed. Michael Borrus, Dieter Ernst and Stephan Haggard (London: Routledge).

Ikemoto, Yukio (1999). "Real aspects of the economic crisis in Southeast Asia: A case of the consumer electronics industry in Thailand," *Kaigai Jijo* 47(4), pp. 96–113.

Itoh, Motoshige and Jun Shibata (1995). "A study of the operations of Japanese firms in Asia: the electrical machinery industry." In *Corporate Links and Foreign Direct Investment in Asia and the Pacific* ed. E. K. Y. Chen and Peter Drysdale (Pymble, N.S.W.: Harper Educational).

Japan Machinery Center for Trade and Investment (JMCTI) (2000). *The Development of Industrial Clusters in Asia and Symbiotic Relationship with Japan* (Tokyo: JMCTI).

JETRO (1998). *The Influence of the Asian Currency and Economic Crisis on the Electronics Industry in ASEAN* (Tokyo: JETRO [mineo]).

Koryu Kyokai (2000). *The Current State of OEM in Taiwan* (Tokyo: Koryu Kyokai).

Milelli, Christian (1997). "Asian economic integration and the role of the Japanese corporate networks: The case of the electronics industry" In *Perspectives on Economic Integration and Business Strategy in the Asia-Pacific Region,* eds. Sam Dzever and Jacques Jaussaud (New York: St. Martin's Press).

MITI (1989). *The 3rd Statistical Report on Foreign Investment* (Tokyo: Keibun Shuppan).

MITI (1994). *The 5th Statistical Report on Foreign Investment.* (Tokyo: Okurasho Insatsukyoku).

MITI (1998). *The 6th Statistical Report on Foreign Investment.* (Tokyo: Okurasho Insatsukyoku).

MITI (2001). *The 29th Survey on Overseas Activities of Japanese Firms* (Tokyo: Okurasho Insatsukyoku).

Noda, Hidehiko (2000). "The future business direction of the Japanese consumer electronics industry in ASEAN," *Kaihatsu Kinyu Kenkyu Shoho* 2, pp. 119–142.

Noda, Shigenao (1999). "Toshiba." In *Industrial Cooperation Scheme,* ed. by Kosei Boeki Senta (Tokyo: Kosei Boeki Senta).

Otsuji, Yoshihiro (2000). "The deepening of commercial strategies toward Asia" In *The Political Economy of Asia,* ed. by Suehiro Akira and Yamakage Susumu (Tokyo: NTT Shuppan).

Ravenhill, John (1995). "Economic cooperation in Southeast Asia: Changing Incentives," *Asian Survey* 35(9), pp. 850–866.

Ravenhill, John (1999). "Japanese and U.S. Subsidiaries in East Asia: Host-Economy Effects." In *Japanese Multinationals in Asia: Regional Operations in Comparative Perspective,* ed. Dennis J. Encarnation (New York: Oxford University Press).

Sone, Yasunori (1993). "Conclusion: Structuring Political Bargains: Government, Gyokai, and Markets." In *Political Dynamics in Contemporary Japan,* ed. Gary D. Allinson and Yasunori Sone (Ithaca, N.Y.: Cornell University Press).

Sudo, Makoto (1999). "Matsushita Electric Industrial." In *Survey on the ASEAN Industrial Cooperation Scheme,* ed. Kosei Boeki Senta (Tokyo: Kosei Boeki Senta).

Takayasu, Kenichi, Junko Toyama, and Minako Mori (1997). "Industrial structure of ASEAN," *Kan taiheiyo bijinesu joho RIM* 4(39), pp. 12–39.

Takeuchi, Junko (2001). "The role of clustering in the development of electrical and electronic industries in Asia," *RIM Pacific Business and Industries* 1(50), pp. 38–53.

Uchihori, Takanori (1999). "Differences in responses of Japanese, American and European Firms in Asia after the Currency Crisis," *Fuji Research Institute Kenkyu Repoto.*

Urata, Shujiro and Kawai, Hiroki (2000). "The Determinants of the Location of Foreign Direct Investment by Japanese Small- and Medium-Sized Enterprises." *Small Business Economics* 15, pp. 79–103.

Yonekura, Seiichiro (1993). "The function of industrial associations." In *The Origin of Contemporary Economic System in Japan,* ed. T. Okazaki and M. Okuno (Tokyo: Nihon Keizai Shimbunsha).

Yoshihara, Hideki (1997). *International Management* (Tokyo: Uhikaku).

PART THREE

Conclusion

CHAPTER NINE

Lessons from Japanese Firms' Strategies in Asia

VINOD K. AGGARWAL[1]

I. Introduction

The regional Asian currency crises of 1997–1998 complicated but failed to diminish foreign firms' ardor for the region. Asia includes many of the world's fastest growing markets, and promises to be a dynamic and fiercely competitive arena for decades to come. Both before and after the crises, firms have attempted to devise trade and investment strategies that would give them a competitive advantage over their rivals.

The purpose of this volume and its two companion volumes has been to present a novel framework to understand the market, nonmarket, and organizational strategies that have enabled many Japanese firms to win in Asia.[2] An economic overview of the performance of Japanese firms, both with respect to trade and investment, sets the stage for specific sector analyses. The case studies in this book—including the banking, auto, telecommunication, chemical, software, and electronics industries—allow us to compare and contrast how firms in these sectors have attempted to enhance their competitive positions. In many cases, the authors have provided valuable comparisons of Japanese firm strategies with American or European firms, thus providing insight into the impact of national origin on competitive performance. These sectoral analyses also show how firms have attempted to build effective relations with governments in the region, in Japan, and with regional institutions. In doing so, our objective has been to identify the most successful strategies for meeting the unique challenges of Asian markets.

This chapter is organized as follows. Section II begins with a focus on the context within which Japanese firms have operated, concentrating on the economic characteristics of the Asian market and the relative performance of Japanese firms. Section III provides a positional analysis for the six industrial sectors covered in this volume. Section IV reviews the theoretical and empirical aspects of the strategies and tactics pursued by Japanese firms in Asia. The fifth section concludes with a discussion of lessons that emerge from the book's analysis and offers directions for future research.

II. The Overall Economic Context: Competing in Asia

What is the nature of the strategic challenges and opportunities in Asia? In Chapter 2, Shujiro Urata examines Japanese trade and investment patterns in developing Asia. With respect to investment, Urata documents the importance of foreign direct investment (FDI) to both the recovery and development of Asian economies. Japanese firms in particular have occupied a prominent position in among investors in Asia. Geographical proximity, expansion of local sales, promising returns on investment, and a cheap, well-disciplined labor force have encouraged Japanese firms to invest in this region.

Before the 1997 Asian financial crisis, Japanese FDI to Asia—fueled by the appreciation of the yen and liberalization efforts of East Asian governments—rose steadily. China's position relative to other Asian FDI recipients was relatively weak, with four members of ASEAN or (Association of Southeast Asian Nations), Thailand, Malaysia, Indonesia, and the Philippines (referred to here as ASEAN4), collectively receiving a much larger portion of Japan's FDI. The 1997 crisis had both an encouraging as well as a discouraging effect on FDI in Asia. On the positive side, devaluation of the Asian currencies increased the attractiveness of these countries as FDI hosts. Moreover, coupled with the collapse in local stock prices, sharp currency devaluation allowed foreign firms to invest in extant Asian firms at bargain prices. On the negative side, the significant decline in local economic activities, combined with heightened uncertainty in the macroeconomic performance of many Asian countries, tended to discourage Japanese investment into Asia. The effect on Japanese FDI levels during and after the crisis, however, was not uniform across countries: investment in Hong Kong, Taiwan, Indonesia, the Philippines and China decreased sharply, while in South Korea and Malaysia it *increased* significantly.

The impact of the crisis on firms' sales has varied with location and sector. The ASEAN4 group was less affected by the crisis than the NIE4

(Newly Industrializing Economies) group, which consists of South Korea, Hong Kong, Taiwan, and Singapore. Meanwhile, the transport machinery and metal products sectors suffered most seriously. In general, firms in sectors with high export-sales ratios performed better than firms in sectors with lower ones. Faced with depressed demand and currency depreciation, firms failed to shift their sales from the domestic to the export market as expected. Instead, Asian firms held export–sales ratios at a relatively constant level during and after the crisis.

With respect to likely Japanese FDI, a recent survey from the Export–Import Bank of Japan shows a negative trend. This reduction in FDI can be attributed to the current Japanese recession as well as uncertainty in exchange rates for Asian currencies. A recent Japan External Trade Organization (JETRO) survey, however, presents a more encouraging picture of Japanese FDI in Asia. It shows a strong Japanese trend to expand operations in the ASEAN4, Vietnam, Singapore, South Korea, and China. Although the results of the two surveys are mixed, both do predict a recovery to precrisis level at least within ten years.

Asian affiliates of Japanese firms have pursued similar strategies in the wake of the financial crisis. First, firms have developed plans to increase their export orientation, both with respect to their sales and local procurement of parts and components. Second, these firms have engaged in substantial intrafirm, interprocess division of labor. Finally, Asian firms have aimed to reduce the cost of production and to improve the quality of their products while diversifying product lines.

Urata demonstrates that FDI and trade strategies can be complementary rather than simply substitutes for one another. Throughout the last decade, Japanese exports to Asia have been more significant than FDI in the region. This is primarily because geographical proximity is more important for exports than it is for investment. This phenomenon is also accounted for by restrictions on FDI in host Asian countries as well a heightened risk for investing in developing countries as compared to simply exporting products there. Urata concludes his analysis by noting that despite grim speculation about dwindling FDI in Asia, increases can be expected if host economies make efforts to provide a suitable environment for investment.

III. Positional Analysis

Before firms can formulate a successful strategy, they must consider not only the broader economic context discussed in Section II but also the contours of the specific markets in which they operate, the nonmarket factors that affect their business, and their specific core competencies. With respect to each of these three elements, firms must take into account the nature of their activities at the national, regional, or global levels. On this latter score, I suggest in Chapter 1 that firms must make decisions about locating their trade or investment operations at the national, regional, and/or global level and also decide on the target market for sales.

Review of the Theory

To examine the opportunities and threats firms face at these three levels, I suggest in Chapter 1 that a good approach to the examination of the nature of markets is Michael Porter's "five forces model."[3] Using this model, the case studies consider the barriers to entry presented by firm rivalry, the potential of new competitors entering the market, threats presented by possible market substitutes, the bargaining power of suppliers, and the bargaining power of buyers. With respect to nonmarket analysis, I build on David Baron's recent work that provides insight into the nonmarket environment of firms.[4] Baron argues that firms must be attentive to possible threats and opportunities arising from the nonmarket environment. Specifically, they must understand the issues involved, the interests of major groups, the institutional setting for policy resolution, and the information available to actors. Finally, in terms of firm positioning, considerable debate continues over how one might best examine a firm's capabilities. While this question is somewhat less central to the interests of this volume, Gary Hamel and C. K. Prahalad's focus on "core competencies," which entail both tangible and nontangible capabilities, provides a useful entrée into understanding the abilities of firms.[5] In sum, because these three sets of factors interact, firms attempting to succeed in Asia must analyze systematically their market structure, nonmarket environment, and core competencies in formulating and implementing strategy. The case studies provide an insightful positional analysis of several key sectors.

Banking

In their examination of Japanese banks, Masahiro Kawai, Yuzuru Ozeki, and Hiroshi Tokumaru focus on the context of lending in East Asia. From the perspective of market dynamics, they argue that the tremendous success of Japanese banks in East Asian markets in the 1980s and 1990s was driven by a buoyant stock market, abundant liquidity, and low interest rates. In addition, a key factor in their expansion was the banks' support of the activities of Japanese firms in East Asia, which themselves were driven to invest by the strong yen. This combination of factors enabled Japanese banks to secure a dominant market position in Asia and elsewhere in the 1980s, with the world's ten largest banks in assets being Japanese. In the early 1990s, collapsing asset and property markets in Japan damaged their capital base and the quality of their portfolio, subsequently leading to an equally dramatic reversal in their fortunes.

The Japanese nonmarket environment was marked by relatively weak regulation of lending. The deregulation of capital markets, changes in interest rate controls, and removal of restrictions on nonbank lending led to much stiffer competition among Japanese firms. These changes were paralleled in part by financial liberalization (not necessarily simultaneously) in several Asian countries—including, to varying degrees, South Korea, Thailand, Indonesia, Malaysia, and the Philippines—leading to strong competition to lend in these countries. Other nonmarket changes proved to be of great significance, particularly the change in the Bank for International Settlements (BIS) Basel capital adequacy ratios in 1992. International Monetary Fund (IMF) and World Trade Organization (WTO)-driven financial service liberalization, especially after the crisis, also has had a significant effect on competition in Asia.

With respect to their core focus, Japanese banks successfully used the protected domestic market to engage in traditional deposit taking and lending activities, which they then expanded in East Asian markets as they followed Japanese firms into the region. While the primary focus of Japanese banks at the peak of their regional activity in the mid-1990s was on Japanese-affiliated firms, they also engaged in local lending in selected countries, driven in large part by nonmarket changes in the host countries. With the Asian crisis, however, Japanese banks were forced to retrench and shift their focus back to the Japanese domestic market.

Chemicals

Tametsugu Taketomi shows how Japanese chemical companies have operated in an industry marked by a high degree of government intervention. Until the Japanese financial bubble burst in the early 1990s, Japanese companies had focused primarily on their domestic market. This domestic focus was driven by the advantages provided by high barriers to entry (a result of government regulations in the Japanese market discussed below). In sharp contrast to their Japanese counterparts, U.S.

and European firms, which did not receive such benefits and undertook dramatic restructuring in the 1990s, were highly competitive and made inroads into Asian markets. In addition to this growing rivalry among existing producers, new entry by South Korean, Taiwanese, and other suppliers—in a market already faced with significant oversupply—created stiff competition among firms for market share. Japanese firms shifted away from their domestic focus with the appreciation of the Japanese yen against the U.S. dollar in the mid-1990s, leading them to follow in the footsteps of other Japanese multinationals by relocating to Southeast Asia. In terms of the bargaining power of buyers, the intensification of competition and subsequent consolidation among the chemical industry's major industrial customers—the automotive industry—also has put pressure on Japanese chemical companies. Specifically, as auto firms have pursued global sourcing, they have demanded discounts in exchange for their large purchases. With respect to substitutes, in the chemical industry's consumer users market of packaging, Japanese chemical producers faced local producers who could displace much of their demand in Asian countries, and thus began to lose market share.

With respect to the nonmarket environment, the Japanese chemical industry has been marked by significant intervention, including government-sponsored cartels and mergers, subsidies, and trade restraints. The industry was actively cartelized through the Ministry of Trade and Industry's (MITI) actions in the 1980s. This cartel, however, proved unstable over time, as the industry faced the need to compete globally, and firms began to engage in mergers in the 1990s. The Japanese chemicals market also was protected by high tariffs, which are being progressively reduced as a result of the Uruguay Round agreement. For example, a tariff of about 20 percent in the early 1990s for polyethylene is to be reduced to 6.5 percent by 2004.

In terms of positioning, Japanese firms have traditionally been much smaller than European and American competitors. This holds for life-science product companies, high value-added chemical firms, and petrochemical firms. Many of the chemical companies, however, have been organized into *keiretsu* relationships, with exclusive supplier–buyer relationships and financial support from *keiretsu* banks in the group. These arrangements have begun to erode, however, as a result of financial problems for Japanese banks in these groups, the need to compete in multiple Asian markets, and the advent of Internet-based purchasing of chemicals. In response, chemical companies are once again undergoing merger activity, leading to the creation of much larger global players.

Autos

Gregory Noble's chapter provides a systematic positional analysis of the Japanese auto industry with a focus on its activities in Southeast Asia. At the broadest level, as Japan's largest manufacturer and exporter, the automotive industry has been critical to Japanese economic growth. With respect to market forces in the Southeast Asian auto industry, Noble argues that substitutes have been of relatively minor importance, because mass-transit systems in the region have been late to develop and are limited in scale. The bargaining power of buyers has been limited, as demand tends to be dispersed rather than concentrated. By contrast, suppliers have increased their bargaining power, although Japanese auto assemblers still face little bargaining pressure from their suppliers of parts and materials and local suppliers have generally been in an even weaker position. Instead, the major challenge comes from the growing power of major international suppliers such as Delphi, Visteon, and TRW of the United States and Robert Bosch of Germany. More generally, two major considerations continue to affect the position of Japanese firms. First, Japanese auto firms continue to compete intensively against each other in Southeast Asian countries, giving those countries significant leverage in their negotiations. Second, foreign auto assemblers now pose a looming threat, with South Korean manufacturers competing at the low end and Western automakers competing at the higher end.

The nonmarket environment in autos is particularly complex, with a host of political issues at both the regional and national levels that affect firm strategies. At the regional level, in view of the many backward and forward linkages in the auto industry, governments in Southeast Asia have attempted to work together to boost regional content through a variety of organizational mechanisms. These accords call for various types of tariff reductions, credit toward fulfillment of local content requirements for parts and components produced in other ASEAN countries, and other regional cooperation efforts. After the Asian crisis, the ASEAN Industrial Cooperation Agreement has reduced local content requirements. This shifting political environment has posed a challenge to all auto producers in Southeast Asia, but to this point Japanese firms have been most successful at dealing with the intricacies of these arrangements. At the national level, auto firms face many different types of problems, necessitating a multi-domestic strategy tailored to individual markets. For example, in Indonesia, cronyism, ethnic tensions, and efforts to favor local producers have led to protests by foreign auto manufacturers in the WTO. Malaysia, for its part, has been active in promoting a local auto industry in cooperation with chosen foreign allies. In Thailand, by contrast, the government has attracted investment because of its political and policy stability and growth in demand, making it an attractive production location (and one where the Japanese have achieved a dominant position). In response to the financial crisis, Thailand has further encouraged investment and American firms have been quick to respond to enter and benefit from the supplier network that has been developed by the Japanese over the years.

From an organizational standpoint, auto firms face several competing pressures. With significant economies of scale, shrinking product cycles, and pressures to adapt to environmental, safety, and quality concerns, the outcome has been the development of a few large, complex, and global companies. At the same time, pressures to disperse production come from geographical constraints and government policies to increase local content and production. In Southeast Asia, the ability of Japanese firms to create organizational structures (*keiretsu*) to cope with these demands and meet the needs of different market and nonmarket environments has given them a competitive edge. Together with approaches such as "lean production" and an ability to link production to orders and to create slight variations on a product theme to satisfy various market niches, companies such as Toyota have reduced inventories and organized the workflow efficiently by creating a "just-in-time" production process. The result has been a dominant Japanese position in Southeast Asia based on high-quality small cars and pickups that are priced attractively and produced relatively economically. This outcome has been qualified, however, by the pressure on *keiretsu* networks to improve their flexibility, the moves away from *keiretsu* organizations by some firms, and the demonstrated ability of Western firms to free ride on the supplier base Japanese firms have developed in Southeast Asia.

Telecommunications

Yumiko Okamoto's chapter provides an integrated analysis of the market and nonmarket factors that have affected the position and organizational dynamics of the Japanese telecom industry. With respect to market forces, she argues that the advent of new technologies, which led to the creation of cellular communications and the proliferation of Internet-based operations, dramatically changed the competitive market dynamics in this industry. Together with the booming demand from the entry of multinational corporations (MNCs) in the region, the result has been that the Asia-Pacific is the fastest-growing telecom region in the world, marked by intense rivalry. U.S. and European global mega-carriers, which are considerably more dynamic because of early privatization and deregulation in their home countries, have achieved early entry and significant presence in this market and Japanese firms are only now beginning to catch up.

The most significant force affecting the market position of telecom companies has been critical changes in the nonmarket environment such as privatization, the removal of barriers to entry, and deregulation with respect to foreign ownership. The international telecom market underwent a dramatic change in the 1980s and 1990s as a result of shifting government policies that led to the breakup of AT&T and the privatization of NTT in Japan and British Telecom in the United Kingdom. In East Asia, privatization began as early as 1987 and accelerated across East Asia in the late 1990s. More recently, countries throughout East Asia are increasing their openness to foreign investment. The latter changes have been driven in part by the WTO Global Agreement on Basic Telecommunications, which was negotiated in the mid-1990s and took effect in 1998.

With respect to firm position and organization, Japanese telecom firms NTT and KDD suffered through much of the 1990s under state regulation of their operations and range of products. Significant deregulation in 1998 and 1999 and concurrent corporate restructuring allowed these firms to integrate various service and product divisions—especially domestic and international divisions previously divided by law—and thereby to offer more comprehensive and competitive packages of domestic and international service (including global IP-based and data communications networks). Deregulation also significantly increased foreign investment in Japanese Telecom; together, British Telecom and AT&T own 30 percent of the conglomerate's shares. Since these reforms, Japanese firms have competed more effectively in Asian markets. Even as they compete internationally, however, NTT, KDD, and DDI have sought to improve their services and operations at home because of increased competition in the Japanese market from foreign competitors. Still, the intercorporate and state-business ties that Japanese telecom firms enjoy with Japanese MNCs and other actors in local East Asian markets have helped them to establish successful subsidiaries and local alliances quickly, reducing the dominance of U.S. and European carriers.

Software

Trevor Nakagawa's chapter on Japanese software analyzes the position of the Japanese software industry in East Asia and provides a case study of Fujitsu, arguably Japan's most successful software company today.

Although developing Asia has historically been no more than a peripheral part of the overall strategy of most software companies, it is an increasingly fundamental target market for many of the biggest players. With continuing economic growth, growing middle classes, well-educated workforces, stable political systems, and expanding technological bases, East Asian countries have seen impressive growth in demand for software throughout the past decade. Because the software industry is characterized by network externalities and high fixed costs, first-mover advantages are particularly strong. Accordingly, U.S. firms remain dominant through their alliances with hardware firms with respect to preinstalled software and package deals. Unable to compete in the rapidly growing PC consumer market and with the Windows operating system in particular, larger Japanese firms such as Fujitsu, NEC, and Hitachi decided to focus on the enterprise software market to leverage their expertise of the Japanese corporate environment. With the rapid evolution of increasingly powerful PCs, servers, and workstations, substitutes have not been feasible to maintain as local suppliers found themselves with declining market share relative to their U.S. competitors at home and within Asia. Even with their entrenched corporate position in proprietary mainframe and other hardware systems, cheaper and more powerful hardware and software systems that utilize Internet connectivity experienced increasingly heavy demand. Accordingly, Nakagawa's analysis illustrates how Japanese software firms had little choice but to conform to U.S. global standards. While smaller firms opted to become value-added resellers to localize foreign products, larger suppliers such as Fujitsu chose to collaborate with their potential competitors to provide total enterprise solutions. With the relative infancy of the Internet in developing Asia, firms compete vigorously for market share to establish a foothold for the coming Internet battles.

The nonmarket environment for Asian software is complex, but generally receptive on both regional and national levels to aggressive firm strategies. Because many Asian countries consider the software industry critical to economic prosperity, governments have made long-term commitments to IT-related education and infrastructure while taking active roles in the promotion of the software industry through fostering government procurement and use, liberalizing trade, and opening up to foreign investment. As enormous IT infrastructure plans are realized throughout the region in the coming decade, Internet demand for both B2B (business-to-business) and B2C (business-to-consumer) e-commerce is likely to offer further opportunities for regional growth. Accordingly, foreign firms are also enticed by advanced infrastructure provisions in "software parks" that offer them close proximity to other leading firms, as well as R&D credits and other incentives. Furthermore, protection of intellectual property rights is not as relevant for complex enterprise software as it is for simpler applications; and finally, governments have made gestures toward controlling rampant piracy rates that are reflective of the generally friendly FDI environment. In summary, despite varying national contexts, there are many similarities in the nonmarket contexts in which Japanese software firms operate.

From an organizational and firm position standpoint, Japanese enterprise software companies have had to experiment with many horizontal forms to deal with a wide array of competing pressures. While industry-leading U.S. firms collaborated with their hosts to capture the majority of the early emerging software market throughout developing Asia, their Japanese counterparts were initially slow to capitalize on regional advantages in these rapidly maturing computer hardware and software markets. By following the leader and the dictates of the global market both at home and within developing Asia, however, many Japanese firms were able to take advantage of the rapid adoption of the powerful (and low-cost) PC, client-server architecture, and the Internet in a relatively short period of time. Since 1990, those Japanese companies that were able to take advantage of these new developments by phasing out their old commitments to proprietary mainframes designs have positioned themselves well to compete in this new global "open" market era. To keep up with rapid developments in both hardware and software abroad, Japanese firms saw little choice but to enter partnerships with leading software vendors and systems integration consultants from leading global companies and local labor pools. Through complex strategic alliances with numerous partners, they could offer more comprehensive enterprise solutions to firms in a timelier manner. Such thin organizational strategies have allowed major Japanese software producers to adapt to the changing global dynamics of the industry. Thus, even though they have gotten a relatively late start, large enterprise software producers such as Fujitsu have become major players both globally and regionally by embracing the Internet and by learning to collaborate with leading complementary technology partners (often from the United States).

Consumer Electronics

Hidetaka Yoshimatsu's chapter analyzes the position of the Japanese electronics industry in developing Asia. First, on the supply side, he notes that while electronics producers come in a variety of sizes, the major

Japanese electronics firms are vertically integrated, comprehensive producers that engage in a variety of sub sector businesses. Major firms also supply key core electronic parts such as semiconductors and crystal devices to other firms. Second, with respect to the power of buyers, while large electronics producers manufacture their parts in-house, assemblers have nourished close relationships with subcontracting parts suppliers. By fostering the creation of supplier associations, the major assemblers and smaller parts suppliers have cooperated to improve quality and reduce costs. Third, relatively low barriers to entry have allowed products and manufacturing methods developed by one firm to be quickly imitated by competing firms, resulting in a market with firms making similar products and competing to mass-produce to capture greater market share. Firms also have sought to cope with increasing wage costs and land shortages in Japan by expanding operations into North America, Europe, and Southeast Asia in the late 1980s. Fourth, particularly in the 1990s, new entrants, especially South Korean firms, have challenged the dominant position of Japanese firms in the Asian electronics market. Fifth, substitutes have posed a challenge to firms in this market in two ways. Technological innovation in the late 1990s created a pronounced spike in demand for information technology (IT) and a concurrent reduction in the importance of consumer electronic goods. Meanwhile, electronics manufacturing services firms have become major players in the electronics industry as they branched out from original equipment manufacturer (OEM) production.

Several nonmarket factors have also had a significant impact on trends in the electronics industry. East Asian import-substitution policies and high tariffs on imported products initially prevented Japanese firms from establishing a pronounced presence in the region through exports. As a consequence, Japanese firms began to engage in local production. By the later 1960s and early 1970s, this environment began to change as Taiwan, Malaysia, and the Philippines began to encourage a greater foreign presence in their electronics market and shifted to export-oriented policies. Another significant change in the nonmarket environment came with the ASEAN countries' commitments to market integration and liberalization in the 1990s. From an institutional context, the ASEAN Free Trade Area (AFTA) and ASEAN Industrial Cooperation (AICO) programs, the latter of which provided preferential tariffs to regional firms, have encouraged resource pooling, industrial complementation, and other industrial cooperation activities among ASEAN firms.

From the perspective of firm positioning and organization, Japanese multinational electronics firms have established a solid presence in

Northeast Asia since the 1960s and in Southeast Asia since the mid-1980s, particularly after the Plaza Accord of 1985. The Japanese production networks in electronics have been characterized by their exclusive nature with low levels of localization in terms of procurement, technology transfer, R&D, and management. This orientation stemmed from various factors including language barriers and the replication of unique Japanese business practices. However, the Japan-centered production system has revealed several shortcomings since the mid-1990s. First, reliance on parent firms in Japan for R&D impeded the development of locally oriented, price-competitive products and the reduction of lead-time for development. Second, the closed production system has impeded Japanese electronics firms' utilization of expertise and technological capability in the emerging Asian supply base. Finally, the devaluation of local currencies after the Asian financial crisis increased the import price of intermediate goods from Japan.

IV. Strategic and Tactical Analysis

The positional analysis of markets, firm competencies, and the nonmarket environment in different geographical contexts, provides the context for firms to undertake strategies and implement them in the Asian market. Because strategic and tactical analyses are deeply interrelated and frequently overlap in the case studies, we can examine these two aspects together in discussing our findings.

Review of the Theory

Strategic analysis refers to how firms respond to and attempt to manipulate market forces. Efforts to develop market strategies have been analyzed from many perspectives. Particularly helpful is the work of Richard D'Aveni, who argues that firms compete in four different *arenas:* cost and quality, timing and know-how, strongholds, and deep pockets.[6] In the cost and quality arena, firms begin with a homogenous product and compete for market share through price differentiation. As price wars escalate, they must shift their focus to quality and service to gain market share. Timing and know-how refer to the ability of firms to seize control of the market, based on such classic concepts as first-mover advantages (or disadvantages) and the innovative character of their products. Strongholds are crucial because they may provide firms with the ability to exclude competitors from particular regional, industrial, or product segments. But in a dynamically changing market, such barriers are likely to erode quickly and firms must seek new strongholds. Finally, the deep pockets arena focuses on the ability of some firms to utilize superior financial resources to discourage weaker competitors.

At the level of nonmarket strategy, firms must engage in calculations about their possible supporters and opponents on issues of critical importance for success. These include questions about the demand side (what benefits will different actors receive if they are successful in securing their objectives on a particular issue?) and on the supply side (who will be able to generate political action?).

Organizational strategy considers how firms restructure to compete in light of their positional analysis and choice of market and nonmarket strategy. While this is not a central focus of the volume, key issues include how to organize to compete in trade and investment, based on transaction cost considerations. For example, with respect to investment, should firms attempt to create wholly owned subsidiaries or would a minority owned operation suffice? Market forces and strategies will clearly affect this decision. Might a minority owned operation use the home firm's technology to become a competitor down the line? Often, however, a more critical question concerns the nonmarket environment in which firms are operating, including political hazards.

Turning to tactics, firms must assess their abilities to execute market and nonmarket strategies and to build competencies in this area as needed. Market tactics refer to firms' decisions regarding R&D, production, and marketing as they strive to compete in various market arenas. Nonmarket tactics concern policies that might be pursued to advance both market and nonmarket strategies. These include lobbying, grassroots activity, coalition building, testimony, political entrepreneurship, electoral support, communication and public advocacy, and judicial strategies.[7] Finally, organizational tactics involve the internal restructuring of their management and organizational structure.

We next turn to an examination of how these market, nonmarket, and organizational strategies, along with tactics to implement these strategies have played out in various industries.

Banking

In the wake of the Asian crisis, Kawai, Ozeki, and Tokumaru note that Japanese banks have dramatically shifted their strategies. While they were heavily engaged in and targeted foreign Asian markets in the 1980s, the Japanese slowdown combined with the Asian crisis to encourage

Japanese banks to return to their home market. Several large banks ceased foreign operations altogether, while others began to reduce their foreign involvement by closing branches and cutting personnel, all with an eye to improving their financial position. With respect to foreign market positioning, banks have shifted to servicing the operations of Japanese firms and their affiliates. As competition has increased as a result of deregulation activities, Japanese banks have also been forced to seek new sources of revenue. To meet this objective, banks are now increasingly focused on investment banking, cash management services, and various types of e-businesses.

At the level of nonmarket strategies, following the Asian crisis, Japanese banks have aggressively pushed for intervention, both by international financial institutions and by governments. Their objective has been to secure some type of financial commitment on the part of these actors to guarantee debt servicing—including such ideas as exchange rate guarantees and yen-based loan conversions—but in the end these nonmarket strategic efforts failed to yield results. Rather than helping banks, international financial institutions and governments aided debtor countries, but without an overall scheme to guarantee debt repayment. Japanese banks also rejected calls by debtor countries for debt forgiveness, but as Kawai, Ozeki, and Tokumaru show, the market value of debt has declined dramatically, thus leaving banks with a de facto outcome that they sought to prevent.

Organizationally, to implement their market and nonmarket strategies, banks also have been actively engaging in alliances or mergers to achieve economies of scale, reduce operational costs, and strengthen their position in various market niches. The result of this tremendous burst of merger activity has been to create four major financial groups. These policies have been undertaken under the guidance of the Banking Sector Revitalization Commission and the Financial Supervisory Agency.

Chemicals

As Tametsugu Taketomi notes, the Japanese chemical industry has been forced to take dramatic action to shore up its position. Previous market strategies that relied on the protected domestic market quickly became unviable as liberalization allowed foreign competitors to enter the Japanese market. Japanese firms responded to this increased competition by undertaking foreign investment in growing Asian markets and beginning a process of restructuring that would only accelerate in the latter part of the 1990s. With respect to foreign investment, the appreciation of the yen, particularly after 1995, combined with dynamic Asia markets, led to a boom in investment by Japanese firms through the establishment of subsidiaries. This strategy became less viable after the Asian crisis.

In the nonmarket realm, although the government no longer provides the same degree of protection to the domestic market through tariffs and cartel management as in the 1980s, it still continues to work closely with the industry. The most dramatic development has been the recent significant change in the organizational structure of the industry. In 1998, for example, MITI introduced the "Kombinat Renaissance" plan to restructure ethylene complexes. Two oil companies—Mitsubishi-Nippon Oil and Japan Energy—and two petrochemical companies—Mitsubishi Chemical and Asahi Kasei—agreed in 2000 to integrate their facilities.

The organizational structure of the industry has thus been going through a dramatic transformation, both because of management and MITI-led initiatives. For example, the merger of Mitsubishi Kasei and Mitsubishi Petrochemical in 1994 into Mitsubishi Chemical created one of the top ten chemical companies in the world; in 1997, Mitsui Toatsu and Mitsui Petrochemical were merged into Mitsui Chemical. Changes in management structure also are underway. Companies have sought to develop regional headquarters for their activities in Europe and North America, and have responded to changes in Japanese accounting methods by creating holding companies and independent boards of directors. Leading companies such as Mitsubishi Chemical have also created a more systematic division structure, giving core segments within the company greater management autonomy. By introducing new measures for profitability, this new approach has also encouraged the shift of resources to newer business areas.

Autos

Noble shows how Japanese automakers pursued a variety of market strategies to cope with the Asian financial crisis. Foremost among these was cost-cutting, but different auto firms chose different approaches to this end. While Toyota and Honda continued to implement standard cost cutting measures, Nissan, Mitsubishi, and Mazda began to slash their product offerings, the number of plants, and turned to global sourcing in an effort to reduced costs. In addition to such efforts, firms made new investments in research and development. For example, Honda pursued new propulsion technologies and improvements in engines, while Toyota made major investments in safety, emission, and fuel efficiency technology. Other firms such as Nissan have focused on their core competencies and shed interests in mobile telecommunications, aerospace, and other non-core activities. Finally, Mitsubishi has attempted to gain competitive advantage in a narrow segment, direct injection engines.

To complement its market strategies, Japanese auto firms have been under increasing pressure since the Asian crisis to lobby governments more aggressively in Southeast Asia. In the past, their primary focus had been on ties to regulatory agencies, but as Western auto manufacturers have made both a strong market and nonmarket push, these Japanese firms have been forced to move toward a more direct approach. For its part, the Japanese government has used aid, trade, and investment-promotion policies to create a favorable climate for its firms. These efforts include the promotion of regional, national and local institutions that the government believes will be conducive to its firms, such as the Asian Development Bank and the Asia Pacific Economic Cooperation (APEC) forum. It also encompasses more technically oriented associations in the auto sector and the creation of the ASEAN Automotive Federation. Financial support from the Japanese government after the Asian crisis also has indirectly helped affiliates of Japanese auto firms. Furthermore, the government has not been averse to standing aside when national governments have taken trade actions that might contravene the WTO but that would benefit Japanese firms, as in the recent case of Thai auto tariffs. More narrowly, the government has worked with firms on discussion of bilateral agreements that may prove beneficial.

With respect to organizational strategies, the crisis in Asia and problems in Japan have forced automakers to choose whether to pursue independence, dependence, or alliance. Although firms such as Toyota and Honda have maintained their independence in view of their stronger financial position, Mazda, Nissan, and Mitsubishi initially sold large stakes to foreign automakers, but after the crisis, effectively ceded control to their foreign partners. Other smaller firms such as Isuzu, Suzuki, and Subaru have sold significant equity to General Motors. With respect to their *keiretsu* networks, while Toyota and Honda have strengthened their ties to parts suppliers, Nissan and Mitsubishi have moved toward greater global sourcing and loosening ties with existing suppliers. These choices have, of course, been affected by ownership and alliance patterns. Independent Toyota, for example, lent tremendous financial support to its affiliates, while Mitsubishi and Nissan have largely frozen operations in Southeast Asia. Meanwhile, Mazda has restructured under Ford's leadership but also invested in a joint venture in Thailand.

Telecommunications

As Okamoto notes, although Japanese telecom firms remain committed to maintaining their domestic market dominance, NTT and KDD have rapidly expanded operations in other East Asian markets, especially through the formation of local subsidiaries. This has required tremendous investment in R&D and training. In terms of positioning, their market focus has shifted away from the provision of basic telecommunications services toward meeting the complex needs of medium and large-sized businesses, and MNCs in particular. NTTcom (NTT's international division) and KDD have developed partnerships and alliances with foreign firms, both local Asian firms and international data and communications specialists like Verio Inc. and Cisco Systems, to offer more value-added services. These services include the development of seamless global connections services through data communications and IP-based networks in Asia and international connections through subsidiaries. NTT Com and NTT DoCoMo have expanded simultaneously into North American and European markets, along with the East Asian market, with the long-term goal of becoming global instead of regional players. Their first primary targeted customers are MNCs, especially Japanese corporate customers abroad.

With respect to nonmarket strategies and tactics, the Japanese government has faced steady international pressure for deregulation of its telecom industry. NTT has agreed to changes in its operations, but in exchange has pushed the government to reduce restrictions on its operations. With their massive investments in R&D, NTT Com and NTT DoCoMo also have courted the favor of the governments of developing East Asian countries such as Malaysia by cooperating with local training and infrastructural development programs. These firms also enjoy an international advantage over their foreign competition in servicing long-standing Japanese MNC partners and in exploiting Japanese networks in regional markets. To create barriers to entry and increase return on R&D, NTT—and Japanese firms more generally—have actively participated in the International Telecommunication Union's (ITU) standardization efforts.

Organizationally, NTT in particular has embraced Internet technology to make all of its operations and services IP-based and network friendly. Instead of forming global mega-alliances, NTT Com and NTT DoCoMo prefer case-by-case alliances or subsidiaries either for more effective operations and delivery in local Asian markets, or to tap into specialized expertise (as with Cisco Systems and Verio Inc.). These firms prefer flexibility and the pursuit of specific ends over broader leverage, and have thus far shunned the global mega-alliances that U.S. and European telecom companies have pursued.

Software

As a latecomer to the industry, Japanese software firms have focused on a market strategy of disrupting the status quo through the creation of a series of temporary advantages. They have strategically placed niche products or lobbied the government to block the entrance of superior foreign products. As Nakagawa's analysis illustrates, Fujitsu has been successful primarily because it has effectively implemented an integrated strategy at multiple platform levels to leverage unique software solutions to an increasingly global market. While all major Japanese enterprise software providers generally adopted an open standards approach, they varied on their commitment to the Internet in the initial stage of booming PC demand in the early 1990s. But all shared attention to R&D and technological developments abroad. Establishing a presence among leading suppliers in various complementary technologies was a linchpin of this strategy. By adopting an "Everything on the Internet" business strategy, Fujitsu sought to leverage its other core businesses by focusing on becoming a leading software solution provider for multiple platforms and networks as well as a leading Internet service provider and user. With software and services carrying the load of growth to profitability, Fujitsu's global Internet strategy has resulted in overseas sales that account for over half of its total revenues since 1999. With more advanced IT infrastructures emerging, declining computing and software costs mean that Asia will continue to play a key role in this continuing growth.

To complement these market strategies, Fujitsu sought to establish closer ties with local or national government authorities to promote their large-scale enterprise solutions throughout the economy and amongst the governments themselves. While seeking cooperation with local host governments to set up local training centers and seminars, they worked with commerce agencies to promote their use among industrial clients as well. Simultaneously, they also promoted software and Internet use in cooperation with local vendors and leading foreign suppliers through exhibitions, trade fairs, and local business associations. Furthermore, they took advantage of a wide array of favorable trade, tax, and R&D policies to use Asian countries as both an export base to third-party markets and as localization centers.

With the rapid diffusion of both cheaper workstations and PCs, opportunities have emerged for creative software solutions in a broad range of highly specialized applications. Since no single supplier could offer a total enterprise solution, Fujitsu opted to take a broad alliance strategy to cooperate, rather than directly compete with leading-edge firms. While other Japanese firms sought to create stand-alone in-house solutions, Fujitsu openly created horizontal alliances to sell its products and services. As a result, numerous groups of firms, including hardware producers, independent software vendors, services firms, consulting companies and resellers were put together on a project-to-project basis. Fujitsu's success has led other leading Japanese firms to follow suit in a move toward greater global sourcing and loosening ties with existing suppliers. Fujitsu's home organizational strategy was affected as well, as it consolidated its six more functionally divided software divisions into three independent ones with more focused market niches.

Consumer Electronics

Hidetaka Yoshimatsu shows how the East Asian import-substitution policies of the 1960s caused Japanese electronics firms to focus on a strategy of local production, rather than exports. The sharp appreciation of the yen after 1985 quickly forced Japanese firms to accelerate overseas operations. They also began to face increasing competition and were forced to compete on price with local companies in Asia. Even in high-value goods such as DVDs and digital TVs, Japanese firms face sharp price competition and have been forced to reduce costs by sourcing locally. Still, compared to their American counterparts, Japanese firms have been relatively slower to respond in terms of undertaking local sourcing and other cost-cutting measures. Japanese firms also remain reluctant to shift from their position as comprehensive producers. In semiconductors, for example while American, South Korean, and Taiwanese firms have focused on particular product niches, Japanese firms continued their focus on the full range of design and production, and only began to outsource in the late 1990s. The rise of electronic manufacturing services companies in the 1990s also has forced Japanese firms to increasingly reposition themselves away from their core competency in manufacturing and toward design, product development, and marketing.

From a nonmarket perspective, some Japanese electronics firms have sought to utilize the AICO as a means of enhancing their competitiveness in Asia. The Matsushita group, for example, became one of the first applicants to the AICO scheme, but it faced great difficulty in obtaining an approval. In order to appease local opposition, Matsushita held public hearings and persuaded local producers only after proposing to foster local parts suppliers and to rectify trade imbalances within the Matsushita group. Japanese electronics firms also have sought to strengthen institutional networks with other Asian electronics industries. Their industrial associations began the Business Dialogue in 1997 as a liaison meeting, and the Japanese government has encouraged such a move. Japanese firms also have sought to utilize these networks to aggregate the interests of electronics industries in Asia. Previously, the Japanese government and firms provided assistance and cooperation on a country or company basis. However, this kind of commitment became less effective in promoting the regional integration and helping the region-wide restructuring of Japanese firms. Accordingly, the new commitment aims to upgrade the overall industrial bases in the ASEAN region through the formation of the *gyokai* system and the coordination of the interests of the region-wide industries.

From an organizational perspective, Japanese firms responded to East Asian import-substitution policies by undertaking joint ventures with local firms. This strategy allowed them to cope with local Asian government regulations on foreign ownership and secure sales channels. After the liberalization of East Asian markets in the 1980s and 1990s, Japanese firms established manufacturing plants in East Asia that were designed to take advantage of the new export-oriented policies and began to export their products to third-party markets. Japanese ownership in these plants rose to nearly 100 percent in most cases, as East Asian governments began to nurture foreign ownership to encourage growth. At the same time, intercorporate rivalry intensified and induced the reorganization of production networks of Japanese electronics firms. Their push into the North American and European markets was also driven in part by nonmarket changes. In particular, Japanese firms responded to pressures for trade restraints in such products as VCRs and televisions by engaging in local investment. In the mid-1990s, as local companies in Asia emerged as major rivals in consumer electronic manufactures, heightened price competition led Japanese firms to pursue more efficient procurement strategies and to transfer more management positions and R&D to East Asian branches. They also have increased procurement from East Asian firms and concluded strategic alliances. For example, imports of integrated circuits, data-processing devices, memory devices, and input/output devices from other Asian firms increased dramatically between 1994 and 1999.

264   Vinod K. Aggarwal

V. Strategic Lessons

Firms attempting to penetrate Asian markets, either through trade or foreign direct investment, have faced significant market and nonmarket obstacles. In the sectors that we have examined, firms responded by using a variety of market, nonmarket, and organizational strategies. In many cases, similar strategies were applied successfully in various sectors; in others, their effectiveness has been limited by specific sector characteristics. In this section, I discuss general lessons from the case studies and suggest directions for future research.

To get a sense of the types of generic strategies that appear to be successful in Asia, I consider both market and nonmarket challenges faced by firms. We can categorize market challenges based on four of Porter's five forces that we examined for our focus on positional analysis.[8] For nonmarket challenges, I consider the role of governments in production, trade, and foreign direct investment. As we have seen, firms respond to each by undertaking market, nonmarket, and organizational strategies. Figures 9.1 and 9.2 combine these two categories of problems and three types of responses to categorize strategies that seem effective.

Responding to Market Challenges

Figure 9.1 reviews the market, nonmarket, and organizational strategies that have proven successful in responding to market conditions across various sectors.

Rivalry Among Firms Product and technological innovation have been key responses to growing competition in Asia. New types of services are now being offered by banks; auto makers have developed new technologies for engines, fuel emission, and safety; telecom firms are adding value-added services; software firms such as Fujitsu have sought to provide solutions for multiple platforms; and consumer electronics firms have created new, higher value-added goods such as DVDs and digital TVs. Cost cutting also has been an important strategy, with Japanese banks extracting themselves from developing Asia after the financial crisis, auto firms pursuing a variety of methods including reducing their offerings and plants, chemical companies significantly restructuring, and consumer electronics firms engaging in local sourcing and other measures.

Nonmarket strategies to respond to rivalry have focused on involving the Japanese government in a variety of aid policies to enhance firms' competitive positions. Related tactics have included unsuccessful calls by

		Strategic Responses		
		Market	Nonmarket	Organizational
MARKET CHALLENGES (in italics)	*Rivalry among firms*	• Product, service, and technological innovation; • Cost cutting through local sourcing and changing product offerings.	• Pressure for financial aid • Cartel formation • Lobby home government to provide financial aid to host markets	• Mergers • Strategic alliances • Sales of equity to foreign investors • Improve management structure
	Changing barriers to entry	• Seek new markets • New investment strategies • Seek Japanese firms in Asia as clients	• Push home government for concessions as barriers drop • Strategic investments to curry favor with Asian governments • Work with standardization organizations • Cartels	• Home government aid in restructuring and mergers • Partnerships with local and international firms
	Power of buyers	• Use Japanese relationships to work with Japanese buyers in East Asia	• Lobby to pressure buyers (borrowers) • Link to government buyers and use them to promote products	• Government promotion of vertical integration • Corporate driven vertical integration
	Power of sellers	• Close links to sellers through keiretsu relationships • Financial assistance to suppliers	• Push home government assistance to suppliers	• Move to global sourcing • Local sourcing to cope with local competition

Figure 9.1 Market challenges and Japanese firms' strategic responses

banks for government aid for Japanese affiliates and earlier cartel promotion efforts in the chemical industry. From an organizational standpoint, to improve their competitive abilities firms have actively undertaken mergers and alliances. Japanese banks continue to be involved in significant consolidation, auto firms have sold equity stakes and strengthened ties to parts suppliers, and telecom firms are engaging in selected strategic alliances. Chemical companies have also been merging and rationalizing their management structure, while software firms have developed horizontal alliances and consumer electronics firms are engaging in local alliances.

Changing Barriers to Entry In many sectors, the protected Japanese market has served to keep out non-Japanese firms, although deregulation is now lowering these barriers to entry. For example, in the aftermath of deregulation in the banking, telecom, and chemical sectors, affected firms have sought to cope with new competition in their home markets by seeking new outlets for trade and investment in developing Asia. At the same time, Japanese firms have faced significant regulatory and cost barriers in their own efforts to enter developing Asian markets. In some cases, as in the banking and telecom sectors, ready-made clients in the form of multinational Japanese firms have allowed them to overcome the difficulties in setting up lending operations.

The most significant response to changing barriers to entry has been in the realm of nonmarket and organizational strategies. As pressure has grown on Japan to deregulate its telecom industry, NTT has successfully bargained with the Japanese government to give it freer reign in the Japanese market. At the same time, it has engaged in massive investments in R&D and cooperated with programs to develop infrastructure in developing Asia, thus currying favor with governments and creating barriers to entry for prospective competitors. Most significantly, by actively participating in ITU standardization efforts, Japanese telecom firms have sought to create barriers to entry. In the chemicals sector, the promotion of cartels by the government clearly served to create barriers to foreign firms. As pressure to remove protection in the Japanese market has increased, chemical firms have been able to substitute government promotion of cartels with government encouraged restructuring and mergers, creating large, powerful firms that pose a challenge to new entrants. Similar structural impediments have been created by the creation of *keiretsu* networks of suppliers in the auto sector. Partnerships with local and international firms, as in the telecom industry, have often helped to ease entry.

Power of Buyers Japanese firms have benefited from their relationships to closely linked buyers in several different sectors. For example, Japanese banks' ties to multinational Japanese firms in their home market have carried over to the East Asia markets as these multinationals have invested in these countries. This has allowed Japanese banks to benefit from their preexisting relationships with "buyers" (borrowers). After the onset of the Asian crisis, Japanese banks were able to retreat into their relatively protected relationship with existing Japanese customers in their home market. Similarly, telecom firms also have sought to service Japanese MNCs operating in foreign markets, and have successfully used their preexisting links to find ready customers.

From a nonmarket perspective, Japanese banks have attempted to influence their relationship with borrowers by calling on the Japanese government and international financial institutions to create repayment guarantees. In software, Fujitsu has developed ties to local governments who can serve both as buyers and as promoters of their software solutions. From a nonmarket and organizational standpoint, government-led restructuring of the oil and petrochemical sector has led to greater vertical integration, both on the buyer and supplier side. Similarly, in software Fujitsu has reorganized to emphasize the provision of a full range of services, up and down the value chain.

Power of Sellers Developing and maintaining close ties to sellers has been a key strategy for Japanese firms. Still, growing competition is changing this close relationship in several sectors. In autos, East Asian production networks that build on Japanese *keiretsu* relationships has ensured that Japanese firms have a steady and reliable source of supply as they enter new markets. In the wake of the Asian crisis, however, strategies toward suppliers have diverged. Toyota, for example, has provided financial assistance to its affiliated suppliers in an effort to ensure a reliable source of supply. Others, such as Nissan and Mitsubishi, have sought to increase their competitiveness by moving toward global sourcing. But while this organizational strategy has reduced costs, it has also pitted Japanese firms against considerably more powerful suppliers such as Delphi, Visteon, and TRW in the United States and Robert Bosch in Germany, rather than on their relatively compliant *keiretsu* network of suppliers. Similarly, software firms have moved to greater global sourcing, which has reduced costs at the expense of their close ties to existing suppliers. In the consumer electronics area, sharply increased local competition in developing Asian markets has led Japanese firms to source locally.

Responding to Nonmarket Challenges

Figure 9.2 reviews the market, nonmarket, and organizational strategies that have proven successful in responding to the nonmarket environment in production, trade, and direct foreign investment.

Production Asian markets have been marked by extensive government intervention. More recently, the move toward significant liberalization in East Asian markets also has created new challenges for firms, and they have pursued a variety of strategies to respond. From a market perspective, both banks and telecom firms have faced an increasingly deregulated market. Banks have responded to regulatory liberalization by promoting new services and focusing on Internet-related businesses. NTT, a key Japanese telecom firm, developed a nonmarket strategy of actively lobbying the Japanese government to allow it to enter new markets and remove restrictions on its activities to cope with deregulation. For their part, auto firms have actively moved from seeking ties to regulatory agencies to direct lobbying as well. From an organizational standpoint, firms have responded to deregulation in two ways: by undertaking restructuring under MITI guidance in the case of chemicals; and by forming new industry associations to promote their interests in the case of electronics and autos.

Intervention in Trade Historically, many Asian countries have imposed a variety of trade restraints, both formal and informal, in a number of sectors. Firms often are not able to export directly to these countries, or even secure needed parts. A common market and organizational strategy has been for firms to enter these markets through the use of local suppliers and distributors and the development of strategic alliances. In addition, firms have jumped trade barriers by investing directly in protected markets through joint ventures or wholly owned plants. From a nonmarket perspective, firms have worked with existing trade agreements or sought the negotiation of new ones that might be favorable to their activities. Japanese software firms were active in the negotiation of the Informational Technology Agreement (ITA), an agreement that liberalized information technology products. And Japanese auto firms have been particularly active in pressing for bilateral agreements, working through APEC to promote their industry, and lobbying the Japanese government on WTO issues. In the latter case, the Japanese government favored its firms by *not* pushing for enforcement of WTO violations in Thailand.

Foreign Direct Investment Policies Many countries have imposed local content requirements on firms, forcing them to source locally for a portion of their production. Japanese electronics firms, for example have engaged

		Strategic Responses		
		Market	Nonmarket	Organizational
NONMARKET CHALLENGES (in italics)	*Production regulation*	• New services and products in response to deregulation	• Lobby actively for decreased restrictions on activities • Shift from working with regulatory agencies to direct lobbying	• Corporate restructuring • New industry associations
	Trade intervention	• Use local suppliers to enter protected markets	• Promote new multilateral and minilateral trade regimes • Promote bilateral trade agreements • Lobby to use existing trade regimes selectively	• Strategic alliances and joint ventures to jump trade barriers
	FDI intervention	• Invest with local partners to avoid FDI barriers	• Lobby on regional investment schemes • Secure aid and trade policies from home government to foster investment	• Local parts sourcing • Create associations with other firms to aid lobbying efforts • Use associations to promote corporate restructuring

Figure 9.2 Nonmarket challenges and Japanese firms' strategic responses

in joint ventures in response to import-substitution policies in developing Asia. This strategy of investment also allowed them to use low-cost labor in these countries to set up plants that would supply third-country markets. When these countries then subsequently liberalized, including changes in regulations on foreign ownership, Japanese electronics firms moved to 100 percent ownership.

From a nonmarket perspective, firms also can lobby governments or engage in other tactics to enhance their position. For example, Matsushita held public hearings to decrease opposition in connection with the AICO program of brand complementation that grants tariff and local content preference. More generally, the Japanese government has been responsive to auto firms' interests by engaging in favorable aid and investment policies with Southeast Asian countries as well as working with ASEAN governments on investment and industrial development issues. With respect to organizational strategies, local parts sourcing and joint ventures have addressed restrictive investment policies. Associations of various kinds, such as the ASEAN10 Consumer Electronics Expert Group that link Japanese and Southeast Asian firms, have also been used to address investment and industrial policy issues. These associations also have been active in aiding region-wide corporate restructuring efforts.

Future Avenues for Research

This book has provided a framework for examining how firms can succeed in Asian markets. Positional analysis has highlighted the diversity of different sectoral environments, and a focus on strategic responses to market and nonmarket challenges has provided insight into winning strategies for Asia. The broad set of sectors covered by the case studies unveils a spectrum of experiences from which we can draw in generalizing about optimal market, nonmarket, and organizational strategies.

What types of research and further investigation will allow us to better understand the development of firm strategies for Asian markets? First, while the case studies promote comparative analysis, the focus of this book has been the experiences of Japanese firms. Together with an understanding of the strategies employed by European and American firms in penetrating Asian markets, this work should help us to advance our understanding of the role played by different home governments as well as the unique characteristics of firms of different nationalities.

Second, firm strategies may change over time in response to the evolving market environments (especially as a result of the Asian crisis) and to bilateral, regional, and international arrangements. Will progressive liberalization in Asia as a response to the recent financial crises and pressures from international financial institutions, create a significantly different regional environment? These questions have been important to our analysis, because we have been able to examine firm strategies before and after the Asian crises.

Although firms will have to continue to anticipate changes in Asian markets, I hope that the analytical framework presented in this book, together with knowledge of how firms have attempted to compete in Asia in the past, will give firms the foundation for creating a winning edge. For scholars, the complexity of business–government interaction in Asia should ensure that this topic will remain a growth industry for years to come.

Notes

1. For comments, I would like to thank Ed Fogarty and Shujiro Urata.
2. *Winning in Asia, European Style: Market and Nonmarket Strategies for Success, Winning in Asia, American Style: Market and Nonmarket Strategies for Success,* both edited by Vinod K. Aggarwal. All three books are published by Palgrave (New York).
3. Porter (1980).
4. Baron (1999, 2000).
5. Hamel and Prahalad (1994).
6. D'Aveni (1994).
7. See Baron (1999, 2000) for discussion of these nonmarket tactics.
8. As the positional analysis indicates, the importance of substitutes has been relatively minor in these sectors, and thus we do not include it for purposes of strategic analysis.

References

Aggarwal, Vinod K. and Charles Morrison, eds. (1998). *Asia-Pacific Crossroads: Regime Creation and the Future of APEC* (New York: St. Martin's Press).

Baron, David (1999). "Integrated Market and Nonmarket Strategies in Client and Interest Group Politics," *Business and Politics* 1(1) (April), pp. 7–34.

Baron, David (2000). *Business and Its Environment,* 3rd edition (Upper Saddle River, N.J.: Prentice Hall).

D'Aveni, R. (1994). *Hypercompetition: Managing the Dynamics of Strategic Maneuvering* (New York: The Free Press).

Hamel, Gary and C. K. Prahalad (1994). *Competing for the Future* (Boston: Harvard University Press).

Porter, Michael E. (1980). *Competitive Strategy* (New York: The Free Press).

INDEX

Bold represents tables/figures

3G wireless, 175, 177, 178, 179
@Nifty, 212

AAF, 143
ABS, 105, 117
Aerospace industry, 8, 259
Aggarwal, Vinod, 3–26, 243–275
Agriculture industry, 8, 31, 32, **38**, 40–42, **44**
AIC, 135
AICO, 135, 227–228, 234, 236–237, 254, 262–263, 270
Aisin Seiki, 147
A&M Styrene, 117
Amdahl, 210
AOL, 53, 91, 123–124, 126, 128, 130–134, 136, 139, 141–145, 147, 163, 165, 178, 212, 221–225, 227–230, 234–237, 244, 249, 254, 263, 270
    Automotive Federation, 143, 259
    Consumer Electronics Expert Group, 235, 237, 270
    Free Trade Area, 136, 221, 226, 233, 237, 254
    Technical Harmonization Conference, 143
A.P. National, 233
Arcstar, 176, 178
Argentina, 149
Asahi Bank, 71, **82**, 84, 90

Asahi Chemical Industries, **112**, 117
Asahi Glass, 108, **112**
Asahi Kasei, 105, 258
Asia Pacific Economic Cooperation, 4, 7, 8, 9, 53, 143, 259, 268
Asian Currency Crisis
    see Asian Financial Crisis
Asian Development Bank, 62, 143, 259
Asian Financial Crisis, 3, 13, 22, 27–28, 34, 41, 49, 50, 53, 61, 63, 65, 68, 72, 74–75, 77–81, 124, 133, 139, 148, 150, 162, 192, 201, 243, 244, 256–259, 270–271
Asian Industrial Network Program, 236
Asian Rare Earth, 118
Association of South East Asian Nations, 7–8, 30, 30, 34–35, 41–44, 46–47, 59, 52
AT&T, 157, 167–169, 178, 251
Australia, 131, 133, 137, 143, 160–161, **164**
Automotive industry, 20, 22, 41, 46, 49–50, 102–103, 123–125, **130**, 140–141, 205, 243, 249, 258

BASF, 101–102
Baht, 73, 139
Bank of Japan, 75, 79
Bank of Tokyo, 89–90
Bank of Tokyo-Mitsubishi, 71, **82**, 84, 89, 90

Index

Bangkok International Banking Facility, 73
Baron, David, 11, 16, 246
Bayer, 101–102
BEC, 167
Bell Canada, 168
Bell South, 169
BIS, 64, 67–68, **70**, 92, 247
BMW, 133, 144
Bosch, Robert, 132, 249, 267
BP Chemicals, 102
Braun, 50
Brazil, 48, 119, 148
British Telecom, 157, 168, 174, 178, 251
Brunei Darussalam, 160, **164**

Cable & Wireless, 166–167
Canada, 4, 46–47, 160–161, **164**, 167, 225
CCT Telecom Holdings, Ltd., 177
Celcom, 168
Celestica, 225
Ceramics industry, 41–42, **44**
chaebol, 75, 142
Chase Manhattan Bank, 85–86
Chematch, 108
Chemconnect, 108
Chemical Bank, 85–86
Chemical industry, 9, 22, 31–33, 37–38, 40, **42**–44, 46, **49**, 98–101, 106–107, 109, **111**, 113, 115, 119, 243, 247–248, 257, 266
Chile, 160–161, **164**
China, 3, 9, 29–30, 34–35, 41–51, 53, 65, **76**, 86, 88–100, 110, 147–150, 158, **160**, 162–164, 169–171, 178, **185**, **187**, 192–194, 196, **197**, 207, 211, **222**, 223, 226, 233, 244, 245
China Net Communications (CNC), 163
China Telecom, 163, 178
China Unicom, 163
Chrysler, 141, 148
Chunghwa Telecom, 162, 178, 211
Ciquisine Conpohia Ptroquimica, **118**
Cisco Systems, 177, 211, 260
Citroen, 137
CMS, 90–91
COBOL, 211

Common Effective Preferential Tariff (CEPT), 226
Communication Authority of Thailand (CAT), 162
Computer Associates/Sterling, 202
Construction industry, 31–32
Core competency, 6, 12, 62, 80, 81, 93, **209**, 259, 262

D'Aveni, Richard, 14–15, 255
Daewoo, 132–133
Dai-Ichi Kangyo Bank, 71, 82–86
Daihatsu, 137, 147, 148
Daimler-Chrysler, 133, **140**, 149
Daiwa Bank, 82, **84**, 91–92
DDI, 166–167, **171**–172, 251
Deepening, 8
Delphi, 132, 249, 267
Denso, 147
Deregulation, 23, 157–158, 162
Deutsche Telecom, 168
Diachemical, 118
Disney, 126
DMR Consulting Group, 210
Dollar, 66, **70**, 78, 110, **112**, 248
Doner, Richard F., 132
DRAM, 222, 232–233
DRB/Hicom, 138
DuPont, 101–102

ebusiness, 62, 80, 107, 185–186, 190, 192, 196, 213, 252, 257
e-commerce
  see ebusiness
East Asian Crisis
  see Asian Financial Crisis, 81
Eastern Broadband Telecom, 169
Electric Industries Association of Japan, 24, 231, 235–236
Electric machinery industry, 31–33, 35, **38**, 40–44
Electronics, industry, 8, 22, 49–51, 103, 110, 208–209, 220–221, 243, 253, 262
EMS, 225–226
Ethylene, 100, 104, 109–111, 113, 258
Europe, 28, 63–64, 68, **70**, 72, **76**, 101, 109, 118–119, 132–133, 149, 168, **222**, **232**
European Commission, 8

INDEX

European Union, 4, 7, 46–47, 52–53, 195, 205–206
Export and Import Bank of Japan, 41, 45–47, **49**, 51
Exchange rate, 13, 62, 65–66, 78, 112
Export-sales ratio, 43–45, **49**, 50
Exports, 22, 29, 34, 41, 43, **52**, **229**
Exxon Chemicals, 102

Far East One, 168
FDI, 21–22, 27–28, 30–34, 36–39, 41, 45–46, 50–54, 63, 65, 67–69, 72–74, 98, **100**, 111, 112, 118–119, 146, 163, 184, 186, 194–196, 203–204, 220, 223–224, 228, 244–245, 253, 268–269
Fiat, 133, **140**
Financial services, 8, 22, 31–33, 35, 61, 192, 205, 243, 246, 256
Firm position
  see positional analysis
Firm strategy
  see strategic analysis
Firm tactics
  see tactical analysis
First Pacific, 168
Fisheries, 9, 31–32
Five Forces Model
  see Porter, Michael - Five Forces Model,
Ford, 133, 133, 136, 140–141, 144, 146, 148, 150, 259
Ford, Henry, 127
Foreign portfolio investment, 69, 74
France, 133, **140**, 148, 189, 200
Fransman, M., 177, 179
Fuji Bank, 71, 76, 82–**86**
Fuji Electric, 207
Fuji Heavy Industries, 145
Fujitsu, 23, 186, 189–190, 193, 201–204, 206–207, 209, 210–212, 214, 233, 251–253, 262, 264
Fujitsu Network Communications, 210
Fujitsu Prime Software Technology Ltd., 212
Fujitsu Software Corporation, 210

gaiatsu, 173
GDP, 68–69

Germany, 101, 132, **140**, 189–190, 200, 223, 249, 267
General Agreement on Tariffs and Trade, 8, 21, 104
General machinery industry, 31–32, **38**, 39, 40, **42**–44, 46
General Motors, 133, 137, 139–140, 144–146, 150, 259
Ghosn, Carlos, 148
GTE, 167–169
gyokai, 235–237, 263

Hamel, Gary, 12, 246
Henisz, Witold, 18
Hewlett Packard, 202
Hino, 147
Hiroshi, Okuda, 148
Hitachi, 23, 193, 201, 204, 206–207, 209, 213, 252
Hoechst, 101, 117
Hokkaido Takushoku Bank, 72
Honda, 140–141, 144–148, 150, 258
Hong Kong, 29, 30, 34–35, **52**, 65, **76**, 86, 92, **118**, 160–161, 164–165, 168, **171**, **187**, 190, 192, **197**, 211, **229**, 244–245
Hong Kong Telecom, 211
Hypercompetition, 14–15
Hyundai, 132–133

i-mode, 175, 178–179
IBM, 198, 200–203, 208–209, 211
Idemitsu Petrochemical, 114
Imperial Chemical Industries (ICI), 101
Imports, **52**, **229**, **231**
India, 48, **118**, 132, 149, 162–163, **185**, **187**, 192, 196–197, 207
  New Telecom Policy (1999), 163
Indonesia, 27, 29–30, 34–35, **44**, **49**, **52**, **64**, 67–69, 72, 74–76, 78, 92, 108, **118**, 123, **130**, 132, 136–138, 144, 148–150, 158, **160**, 164, 169, **171**, 178, **187**, 192, **197**, 210–211, **222**, **227**, 234, 244, 247
  Debt Restructuring Agency (INDRA), 78
Indosat, 178
Industrial Bank of Japan, 83–86

Industrial Sectors
  aerospace, 8, 259
  agriculture, 8, 31, 32, **38**, 40–42, **44**
  automotive, 20, 22, 41, 46, 49–50, 102–103, 123–125, **130**, 140–141, 205, 243, 249, 258
  ceramics, 41–42, **44**
  chemical industry, 9, 22, 31–33, 37–38, 40, **42**–44, 46, **49**, 98–101, 106–107, 109, **111**, 113, 115, 119, 243, 247–248, 257, 266
  construction, 31–32
  electronics, 8, 22, 49–51, 103, 110, 208–209, 220–221, 243, 253, 262
  financial services, 8, 22, 31–33, 35, 61, 192, 205, 243, 246, 256
  iron and steel, 8, 10, 37–38, 40–41
  manufacturing, 31–33, 35, **38**–41, 53, 65
  metal products, 31–33, 37, 41–44
  microprocessors, 199, 203, **209**, 232
  petrochemical, 34, 38, 40, 100, 110–111, 115, 117, 267
  real estate, 31–33
  telecommunications, 9, 22–23, **164**, **171**, 192, 208, **209**, 243, 250
Information technology, 8, 80, **83**, 90–91, 174, 176–178, 184–185, **190**, 192, 196, 203, 205, 208, 210, 213, 225, 230, 254, 261
Information Technology Agreement, 4, 9, 196, 204, 268
INTAC Automotive products, 118
Intel, 200, 232
Intellectual Property, 8, 178, 194, 253
Interconnection charges, 172–173
International Monetary Fund, 4, 13, 62, 66, **69**, 247
International Telecommunications Union, 19, 161, 177, 266
Internet, 107–108, 161–162, 185–186, **190**, 195, 208, 212, 214, 253, 261
Internet Protocol, 167, 175, 177, 179, 260
Ireland, 118
Iron and steel, 8, 10, 37–38, 40–41
Isuzu, 138, 145–146, 150, 259
Italy, 140, 189–190, 200

Japan, 3, 4, 21–22, 28–32, **38**, 45–46, 49, **70**, **76**, 103, 108, 131, **140**, 146, 149–150, 157–158, 160–161, 164–165, 172, 178, **185**, **187**, **189**, **190**, **197**, 200, **224**, 226, 228, 230, 251, 268
  Banking Sector Revitalization Commission, 79, 257
  Big Bang, 80, 99
  Bubble Economy, 22, 66, 98, 110, 115, 124, 199, 247, 256
  Convoy Scheme, 62, 80, **140**
  FDI in Asia, 33–36, **42**, 47, **49**, 53
  Financial Revitalization Committee, 81, 83
  Financial Supervisory Agency, 79, 83, 93, 257
  Japan External Trade Organization, 45, 47, **49**, **52**, 141, 143, 236, 245
  Kombinat Renaissance, 105–106, 113, 258
  Law Concerning Emergency Measures for Early Consolidation of the Financial Sector, 83
  Ministry of International Trade and Industry, 22, **38**, 40, **42**, **44**, 99, 104, 109, 113–114, 141, 143, 224, 228, 230, 235–236, 248, 258, 268
    Specific Industry Structure Improvement Treatment Act (SISIT), 104
  Ministry of Economy, Trade and Industry, 36, **42**, **44**, 99, 104, 106, 113, 224
  Ministry of Finance, 31–32, **35**, 144
  Ministry of Posts and Transportation, 170, 173
  New Miyazawa Plan, 144
  Prompt Corrective Action (1997), 75
Japan Auto Parts Industries Association, 143
Japan Bank for International Cooperation, 48, 230
Japan Electrical Manufacturers' Association, 235
Japan Energy, 105, 258
Japan Telecom, 166–167, **171**–172, 180
Jitong, 163
Joint ventures, 18, 20, 102, 114, 174, 194

INDEX 277

JPO, 102
Jusen, 74
JVC, 231

Kanji, 187, 199, 200
Kao, 108, 109, 112
Kawai, Masahiro, 22, 61–97, 246, 256
Keidanren, 142
keiretsu, 22, 87–89, 106–108, 111–113, 119, 127, 138, 146, 148–149, 151, 199, 248, 250, 259, 265–267
keizai kyoryoku, 142
kenzenku keikaku, 83
Kia, 132–133, 136, 149
Kinki Bank, 92
Korea, 27, 29, **35**, **42**, **44**, 47, 49, **52**, **76**, 103, **118**, 149, 150, 160–161, **164**, 170–171, **185**, 195, 210, 231
Korea Telecom, 165, 178, 211

Landline telecommunications, 158–159, 160–161, 167, 178
Latin America, 47
Lithodun Korea, 118
Lobbying, 20, 23, **265**, **269**
London Rules, 78
Lotus, 137

M&C Sweetners, 118
Malaysia, 27, 29, 30, 34–35, **42**, **44**, 47–49, 51–52, 64–65, **67**, **69**, 72–74, **76**, 108, 123, **129**, **130**, 132, 135, 137–138, 148, 157, **160**, 164–165, 168, 176–177, **187**, **192**, **197**, 210–211, **222**–223, **227**, **229**, 231–234, 244, 247, 249, 254
    Multimedia Super Corridor, 177, 192, 194
Malaysia Telecom, 211
Manufacturers and Hanover Bank, 85, 86
Market Forces
    see positional analysis; strategic analysis; tactical analysis
Market position
    see positional analysis
Market strategy
    see strategic analysis
Market tactics
    see tactical analysis

Matsushita, 223, 229, 231, 233, 234, 263, 270
Matsushita Electric Philippines (MEPCO), 233
Matsushita group, 262
Maxis, 168
Mazda, 133, 136, 140–141, 145, 149, 258–259
McDonald's, 126
MCI-WorldCom, 166
MEPCO, 234, 234
Mergers, 36, 63, 85–86, 88, 93, 101–102, 106, 107, 109–110, 113, 117, 136, **265**
Metal products, 31–33, 37, 41–44
METI
    see Japan – Ministry of Economy, Trade and Industry
Mexico, 160, **164**
Microprocessors, 199, 203, **209**, 232
Microsoft, 188, 200–203
Mimic, 118
Ministry of International Trade and Industry
    see Japan – Ministry of International Trade and Industry
MITI
    see Japan – Ministry of International Trade and Industry
Mitsubishi, 119, 127, 138, 140–142, 145–146, 149, 258–259, 267
Mitsubishi Bank, 89, 115
Mitsubishi Chemical, 99, 112–118, 258
Mitsubishi Chemical Europe, 118
Mitsubishi Chemical UK, 118
Mitsubishi Chemical do Brazil, 118
Mitsubishi Corporation, 106
Mitsubishi Electric, 231, 233
Mitsubishi Kasei, 104, 113–116, 258
Mitsubishi Motors, 137
Mitsubishi Petrochemical, 104, 113–114, 116, 258
Mitsubishi Tokyo Financial Group, 83–84, 89
Mitsubishi Trust and Banking Corporation, 89–90
Mitsubishi-Daimler-Chrysler, 138
Mitsubishi-Nippon Oil, 105, 258
Mitsui Bank, 87

Mitsui Chemical, 107, 109, 112–113, 258
Mitsui Petrochemical, 104, 113
Mitsui Toatsu, 104, 113
Mizuho, 85, 87
Mizuho Financial Group, 83–87, 91
Mizuho Holdings, 85
MKC Finance Amsterdam, 118
Multinational corporations, 23, 161–162, 172, **176**, 205–206, 220, 226–227, 250–251, 260, 267
Mobile telecommunications
see wireless telecommunications; 3G wireless
Mohamed, Mahathir, 137, 176
Mongolia, 171
Monsanto, 101
Montell, 102
Moral hazard, 62, 74, 78, 80
Multifiber Arrangement, 8
Mutiara, 168
MYA Corp, 118
Mytex Polymer, 118

Nakagawa, Trevor, 23, 184–219, 251–252, 261
Naphtha, 105, 111
NatSteel Electronics, 226
National Thai, 233
Neault-Nissan, 140
NEC, 23, 189, 193, 204, 206, 209, 213, 252
New Century Info Com, 169
New Zealand, 133, 160–161, **164**
Newly industrializing economies, 34–35, 41–42, **44**–45, 47, 52–53, **222**, **224**–225, 228–230, 244–245
Nintendo, 188
Nippon Polyolefin, 117
Nippon Trust Bank, 84, 89–90
Nissan, 128, 138, 140–142, 145–146, 148–149, 258–259, 267
Noble, Gregory, 22, 123–156, 249
Noltex, 118
Nonmarket position
see positional analysis
Nonmarket strategy
see strategic analysis
Nonmarket tactics
see tactical analysis

North American Free Trade Agreement, 21, 53
Novartis, 101
NPL, 66, 74–75, 79, 81–82, 85–86
NPL ratio, 75, 85, 87, 89–90, 157–158, 165–167, 169–180, 251, 260, 268
NTT DoCoMo, 158, 166–167, **171**–172, 174–175, 177–180, 260
NTT East, 166, 173
NTT Law, 173
NTT MSC, 176
NTT West, 166, 173
Nynex, 169

OECD, 73, **189**, 202
Oil
see petrochemical
Okamoto, Yumiko, 23, 157–183, 250, 260
Omron, 193
Oracle, 194, 201–203
Organizational Analysis
see Positional Analysis; Strategic Analysis; Tactical Analysis
Organizational strategy
see strategic analysis
Organizational tactics
see tactical analysis
Osaka Bank, 92
Ozeki, Yuzuru, 22, 61–97, 246, 256

Pacific Communications Services, 168
Packaged software, 188–189, **190**, 192, 195, 198, **209**
Papua New Guinea, 164
Personal computers, 185–187, 189, 193, 197, 201, 206–207, 225, 230, 252, 262
Petrochemical, 34, 38, 40, 100, 110–111, 115, 117, 267
Peugeot-Citroen, 140
Pharmaceutical industry, 8, 101
Philippine Electronic Fan Association, 234
Philippines, 27, 29–30, 34–35, **42**, **44**, **48**–49, 51–52, **64**, 67–69, 72, 74, 86, 123, 129–130, 135, 137–138, 149, 160–161, **164**, **171**, 178, **187**, 192, **197**, 210–211, **222**, 226–227, 234, 244, 247, 254
Board of Investment, 234

INDEX 279

Piracy, 193–197, 253
Plaza Accord, 135, 255
Plaza Agreement, 110, 223
Poland, 132
Porter, Michael, 7, 9, 12, 15, 131, 246, 264
   Five Forces Model, 7, 10, 12, 15, 131, 246, 264
Portfolio investment, 27, 63
Positional analysis, **5**, 6–13, 66–76, 99–109, 124–140, 158–170, 191–202, 221–228, 245
   Case Study: Banking in East Asia, 63–76
      Firm Position, 74–76
      Market Position, 63–72
      Nonmarket Position, 72–74
   Case Study: Japanese Chemical Industry, 99–109
      Firm Position, 108–109
      Market Position, 99–104
      Nonmarket Position, 104–108
   Case Study: Automakers in ASEAN, 124–140
      Firm Position, 139–140
      Market Position, 124–134
      Nonmarket Position, 134–139
   Case Study: Japanese Telecommunications Industry, 158–170
      Firm Position, 165–170
      Market Position, 158–162
      Nonmarket Position, 162–165
   Case Study: Japanese Software Industry, 191–202
      Firm Position, 198–202
      Market Position, 191–164
      Nonmarket Position, 194–197
   Case Study: Japanese Electronics Industry, 221–228
      Firm Position, 221–226
      Market Position, 221–226
      Nonmarket Position, 226–228
Precision machinery, 38, **42**, 43, **44**
Prahalad, C. K., 12, 246
Protectionism, 19, 74
Proton, 138

Qinghua University, 212

Research and Development, 19, 20, 23–24, 51, 101, 138, 141–142, 172, **176**, 179, 186, 201–202, 206, 212, 223, 228–229, 231, 237, 253, 255–256, 260–261, 263, 266
Renault, 133, 148
Rhone Poulenc, 101
Romania, 132

Saint-Gobain, 133
Sakura Bank, 71, **82**, 84, 87, 88
Samsung, 211
San Nan Petrochemical, 118
San Yang Kasei, 118
Sanwa Asia Bankers Forum, 91
Sanwa Bank, 71, 76, **82**, 84, 90, 91
Sanyo Electric, 231
SAP, 194, 202
Sears, 21
Sekisui Chemical, 112
Semiconductors, 50, 208, 210, 221–222, 225–226
Sharp, 229–230, 232
Shell, 115
Shell Chemicals, 102
Siam Commercial Bank, 91
Siemens-Nixdorf, 210
Sin-Etsu Chemical, 112
Singapore, 4, 29–30, **35**, 41–42, **44**, 47–49, **52**, 65, 72, **76**, 86, 102, 109, **118**, 130–131, 160–161, 163–165, **171**, 174, 178, **187**, 191–192, **197**, 210–211, 226–227, **229**, 245
Singapore Telecom, 166, 169–170, 211
Singh, J. P., 165
Small and Medium Enterprises, 66, 86, 88, 91, 206, 223, 224
Smart Link, 168
Software, 22, 184, 243, 251, 261
Solectron, 225–226
Sony, 188, 226, 232
South Korea, 30, 34, 36, 41, 47, 64–65, 67–69, 72–75, 110, 119, 136, **164**, **187**, 192–193, 195, **197**, 225–26, 232, 244–245, 247–249, 262
Southwestern Bell, 168
Sri Lanka, 171, 178
Sri Lanka Telecom, 169
Star Hub, 174

Steel
  see iron and steel
Strategic analysis, **5**, 13–19, 62–63, 77–85,
  109–114, 140–151, 170–174, 177,
  202–207, 228–237, 255
  Case Study: Banking in East Asia,
    77–85
    Market Strategy, 80–85
    Nonmarket Strategy, 77–80
    Organizational Strategy, 80–85
  Case Study: Japanese Chemical
    Industry, 109–114
    Market Strategy, 109–113
    Nonmarket Strategy, 113
    Organizational Strategy, 113–114
  Case Study: Automakers in ASEAN,
    140–151
    Market Strategy, 141–142
    Nonmarket Strategy, 142–145
    Organizational Strategy, 145–146
  Case Study: Japanese
    Telecommunications Industry,
    170–174, 177
    Market Strategy, 170–172
    Nonmarket Strategy, 172–173
    Organizational Strategy, 174
  Case Study: Japanese Software Industry,
    202–207
    Firm Strategy, 207–213
    Market Strategy, 202–204
    Nonmarket Strategy, 204–206
    Organizational Strategy, 206–207
  Case Study: Japanese Electronics
    Industry, 228–237
    Market Strateg, 228–234
    Nonmarket Strategy, 234–237
    Organizational Strategy, 228–234
Subaru, 145, 259
Suharto, 136
Sumitomo Bank, 71, **76**, **82**, 84, 87–88,
  127
Sumitomo Chemical, 107, 109, 112
Sumitomo Mitsui Banking Corporation,
  83–84, 87–88
Sumitomo-Mitsui, 109
Sumitomo-Mitsui Chemical, 109
Sun Microsystems, 188, 201, 211
Suzuki, 140, 145, 149–150, 259
Swiss Telecom, 168

Tactical analysis, **5**, 19–21, 77–80,
  109–114, 140–151, 170–174,
  202–207, 228–237, 255
  Case Study: Banking in East Asia,
    77–80
    Market Tactics, 80–85
    Nonmarket Tactics, 77–80
    Organizational Tactics, 80–85
  Case Study: Japanese Chemical
    Industry, 109–114
    Market Tactics, 109–113
    Nonmarket Tactics, 113
    Organizational Tactics, 113–114
  Case Study: Automakers in ASEAN,
    140–151
    Market Tactics, 141–142
    Nonmarket Tactics, 142–145
    Organizational Tactics, 145–146
  Case Study: Japanese
    Telecommunications Industry,
    170–174
    Market Tactics, 170–172
    Nonmarket Tactics, 172–173
    Organizational Tactics, 174
  Case Study: Japanese Software Industry,
    202–207
    Firm Tactics, 207–213
    Market Tactics, 202–204
    Nonmarket Tactics, 204–206
    Organizational Tactics, 206–207
  Case Study: Japanese Electronics
    Industry, 228–237
    Market Tactics, 228–234
    Organizational Tactics, 228–234
Taiwan, 29–30, 34–35, 41–42, **44**, **48**, 50,
  52, **76**, 86, 103, 118–119, 131, 150,
  160–161, 163, 168, 178, **185**, **187**,
  193, 195, **197**, 210, 225–226,
  229–230, 232–233, 244–245, 248,
  262
  National Information Infrastructure,
    195
Taiyo Deidok, 118
Taiyo Kasei, 118
Taiyo Shingisha, 118
Taiyo-Kobe Bank, 87
Takeda Pharmaceutical, 101
Taketomi, Tametsugu, 22, 98–122, 247,
  257

INDEX

Technology transfer, 4, 7, 29, 54
Telecom Malaysia, 178
Telekom Malaysia, 157, 168
Telenor, 168
Teleway Japan, 166
Texas Instruments, 232
Textiles industry, 8, 31–32, 37–38, 40–41, 43–44, 46
Thai Telephone and Telecommunications Company (TT&T), 169
Thailand, 27, 29–30, 35–36, **42**, **44**, 48–52, 64–65, 67–69, 72–74, **76**, 86, 91, 102, 108, **118**, 123, 129–130, 132–136, 138, 143–146, 148–151, 160–162, 164–165, 170–171, 178, **185**, **187**, 192, **197**, 210–211, **222**, 225, **227**, 231, 233–234, 244, 247, 250, 259, 268
    Bangkok International Banking Facility, 73
    Eastern Seaboard Industrial Park, 133
    Metal Industries Development Institute, 143
    Ministry of Industry, 145
    Provincial International Banking Facility, 73
    Telephone Organization of Thailand, 162
Tiananmen Square Incident, 30
Tokai Bank, 71, **82**, 84, 90
Tokumaru, Hiroshi, 22, 61–97, 246, 256
Tokyo Tanabe, 117
Tokyo-Mitsubishi, 76
Tokyo-Mitsubishi Pharmaceuticals, 117
Tonen Chemical, 117
Toray Industries, 102, 108, **112**, 119
Toshiba, 193, 201, 207, **209**, 213, 233, 234
Toyo Trust Bank, 84
Toyota, 123, 127–128, 133, 137–141, 144–147, 150, 250, 258, 267
    Demand Pull Production System, 127
    Just in Time Production System, 128, 250
    Lean Production System, 127
Toyota Foundation, 142
Toyota Machine Works, 147
Toyota Motor Thailand, 147

Toyota Thailand, 147
Trade Related Investment Measures, 8, 144
TransAsia Telecom, 168
Transport machinery, 31–33, **38**, 40–44
Transport services, 31–32, 54

U.S. West, 168
UFJ Group, 84, 90–91
USR Optonix, 118
Union Carbide, 102
United Kingdom, 48, **118**, 137, 157, 167, **189**, 200, 251
United States, 4, 8, 20, 23, 28–29, 46–48, 52–53, 63–64, 68, **70**, 72, 92, 102–103, 108–109, 117, 127, 132, **140**, 157–158, 160–161, **164**, 167–169, 172, 175, 178, **185**–187, 189–190, 192–193, 195, 197–198, 200, 205–207, 213, 223, 225–226, 231–232, 247, 249, 252–253, 262, 267
Urata, Shujiro, 22, 27–27–57, 244, 245
Uruguay Round, 8, 21, **105**, 248
Uzbekistan, 132

Vebatim, 118
VER, 8
Verio, 175, 177, 260
Verizon, 169
Vietnam, 29, 47, 49, 86, 132, 162, 178, **197**, 245
Vietnam Data Communication Company, 178
Visteon, 132, 249, 267
Vodafone, 166
Volkswagen, 133, 140, 144

W-CDMA, 178
Widening, 8
Williamson, Oliver, 17
Windows (Microsoft), 201, 252
Wireless telecommunications, 158–159, 160–161, 167–168, 175, 177–178, 190, **209**, 259
World Bank, 62
World War II, 127
WTO, 4, 8, 53, 72, 144, 158, 164–165, 196, 204, 247, 249, 259, 268

WTO Global Agreement on Basic Telecommunications, 251

Xiaoping, Deng, 223

Yahoo! Japan, 212
Yamaichi Securities, 72
Yasuda Trust Bank, 84

Yen, 41, 65–66, 78, **82**, 110, **112**, 119, 139, 244, 248, 257–258, 262
Yoshida, Masaki, 116
Yoshimatsu, Hidetaka, 23–24, 220–240, 253, 262
Yulon Motors, 149

zaibatsu, 148
Zeneca, 101